9

7.50

vc

COLOMBIA

COLOMBIA

A Contemporary Political Survey

by

JOHN D. MARTZ

Chapel Hill

THE UNIVERSITY OF NORTH CAROLINA PRESS

PRINTED BY THE SEEMAN PRINTERY, DURHAM, N. C.

To my parents—in belated appreciation of their more than ample encouragement and understanding.

Preface

A SERIES OF RECENT developments have shaken the United States' complacent attitude toward Latin America, resulting in renewed concern with hemispheric affairs. This awareness of Latin America has been compounded by the recent election of a North American administration which has promised high priority to Latin American affairs. At the same time, the complexities of the Cuban situation have tended to obscure important events in less turbulent republics. As a consequence, North America remains comparatively ignorant of the extraordinary political experiment initiated in Colombia following the 1957 overthrow of an oppressive dictatorship.

At this writing, in the spring of 1961, Colombia is operating under an arrangement whereby the two traditional parties have agreed upon absolute parity of representation from national to local level. The presidency itself is to be occupied alternatively by Liberal and Conservative nominees until 1974. The outcome of the experiment remains in doubt, yet one must note the unique attempt to adapt Colombian institutions to the realities and necessities of twentieth-century life.

Responsible Latin American leadership, confronted with urgent social and economic problems which have deeply stirred the masses, is searching for approaches less extreme than those urged by demagogues of the far Left. In Colombia the present effort is hopeful of breaking the shackles of oligarchical elitist rule. Despite unique aspects of the situation, there are many possible lessons to be learned. Thus a study of contemporary Colombia may erect signposts pointing toward political developments far beyond the confines of national borders.

In this examination of contemporary Colombia, greatest emphasis is placed upon the political sphere. What will follow is discussed primarily in terms of politics and of comparative government. For Colombia in recent years affords the political scientist an exceptional opportunity to observe a wide variety of governmental approaches attempting by different means to meet the needs of the people. Within the past two decades, Colombian political institutions have operated under several basically different philosophies of government. Each of these will be discussed in turn.

The introductory comments of Part I will present a brief framework within which recent political events have occurred. On the advice of several readers of the first draft, I have substantially reduced what was originally a lengthy section dealing with geographic, social, and economic circumstances. Pertinent comments have largely been incorporated into the text later. Thus major emphasis will be upon a broad look at the essence and dynamics of Colombian politics, measured against the some-times quite different constitutional principles.

New political developments began to take shape in the late 1940's. Part II discusses an early attempt at a coalition "National Union" government under Conservative direction, with the opposing Liberals sharing responsibility. The breakdown of this effort led to a situation in which widespread social and political tensions increased, culminating in the 1948 Bogotá riots that virtually razed the entire business district.

Events led, as seen in Part III, to a reactionary authoritarianism with overtones suggestive of the corporative Italian system of Mussolini. At the time, the ideological orientation grew reminiscent of Franco's Spain. Prominent Colombian politicians were attracted to the concept of *hispanidad*. Only a military *coup d'état* prevented the establishment of a corporative state in constitutional form. The resulting military dictatorship, following the breakdown of democratic party politics, is treated in Part IV. The early Messianic fervor of the military, welcomed by the populace, gradually wasted away under an unenlightened attempt to imitate the Argentine regime of Juan Perón.

After nearly four years, the nation rose in protest. Students, the church, the business community, and the political leaders banded forces to oust the military. Following a temporary provisional *junta,* political power was restored to civilian hands and led to the present unique bipartisan system. This experiment in controlled democracy, dedicated to the education of the masses and the traditional parties in the realities of responsible self-government, is outlined in the concluding section.

In preparing this work, I have been aided substantially by the staffs of the Library of Congress, the Columbus Memorial Library of the Pan American Union, and the University Library in Chapel Hill. My personal debt to a large number of individuals forbids separate acknowledgment here. To those who are not mentioned, my hope must be that they are already aware of my gratitude. Several must be singled out for having contributed in a variety of ways to this undertaking. William C. Davis and George Wythe of The George Washington University were helpful on numerous occasions. At the University of North Carolina I am particularly indebted in several ways to Federico G. Gil and Harold A. Bierck. Charles B. Robson, although not a Latin Americanist, has given many insights into a wide variety of political problems, for which I am most appreciative. I am also under obligation to Frederic N. Cleaveland, Chairman of the Political Science Department, who kindly permitted a revision of my academic obligations that I might have time to complete work on the manuscript.

I wish to acknowledge my indebtedness to the Ford Foundation for generous aid in the publication of this book by a grant under its program for assisting American university presses in the publication of works in the humanities and the social sciences.

Many errors of fact and judgment have been avoided through the suggestions of others. Had I further heeded their advice, the pages to follow would no doubt be improved. But the ultimate judgment was necessarily my own; thus the errors or misstatements are wholly mine.

John D. Martz
Chapel Hill, North Carolina

CONTENTS

CONTENTS

Part V

BIPARTY EXPERIMENT IN CONTROLLED DEMOCRACY

Part I
ELEMENTS OF NATIONAL LIFE

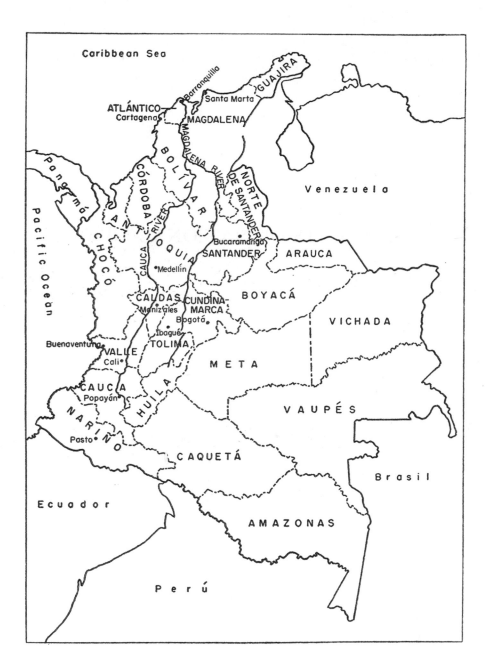

Chapter One

ENVIRONMENT AND SOCIETY

THE FOURTH MOST populous republic of Latin America, Colombia is the only one to the south of Panama fronting extensively on both the Pacific and Caribbean. Lying to the extreme northwest of the southern continent, the "Gateway of South America" with its 439,519 square miles[1] equals the combined areas of France and the Iberian Peninsula.[2] A land of geographic contrast, Colombia is perhaps the most Andean of the mountain republics. It is divided basically into two major regions, the mountainous western highland and the Llanos Orientales to the east. Roughly one-third of the nation lies in the highland, where some 90 per cent of the population lives.

There are several important geographic features. The Magdalena River, the "Life Stream of Colombia," has been virtually the sole means of communication with the interior since colonial days. Even the advent of modern transportation has caused but slight diminution of its importance to national trade and commerce. Littoral lands are set apart from the highland center of activity. While the Pacific coast is poor in natural ports, the northern coast has valuable facilities at the ports of Barranquilla and Cartagena, which have loomed large in importance for five centuries. The major non-mountainous region is the Llanos, home of descendants of the untamed *llaneros* who numbered among Bolívar's most effective forces. This Colombian "Wild West" today remains largely outside national life. To the south lies the jungle, a matted, tangled, hellish verdure which gives little promise of future development.

Fortuitous geographic conditions include the two shorelines, variation of elevation and climate, rivers of some size and importance, and considerable potential in hydroelectric power. At the same time, the ruggedly divisive mountainous barriers and over-all proximity to the equator with its accompanying debilitating conditions have created problems which can be surmounted only with difficulty. Throughout its history Colombia has been harassed by the stern realities of geography. This has become increasingly evident through present efforts to achieve an economically viable, politically stable, and socially enlightened life in consonance with the world of the mid-twentieth century.

Geographic problems notwithstanding, the national economy has prospered in many sectors since the close of World War II. In 1957 the rate of growth was 3.4 per cent,[3] second only to Venezuela in all of Latin America. Gross production per capita and national income per capita increased annually, the former at a rate of 4 per cent, the latter at 6.[4] Improved terms of trade brought a noticeable increase in income, owing primarily to the continued dominance of coffee, which accounts for over 80 per cent of the value of exports. And although coffee has been of greatest importance to an essentially agricultural economy, there have been other positive factors. Petroleum, foreign investment, and industrial development have contributed significantly. With coffee exports operating as a mainspring to economic expansion, a new spirit of entrepreneurial activity has taken hold, adding an element of dynamism to the economy.

Both positive and negative aspects have been outlined by the rapid population growth. By 1962 the population will approach 14 million. Between the census years of 1938 and 1951 the annual growth rate was 2.2 per cent,[5] and there are indications that it is slightly higher today. Decreasing mortality rates and rising births have been perceptible. From 1951 to 1954 the average birth rate was 32.7 per thousand, with deaths registered at 13.2 per thousand.[6]

Ethnically the Colombians are not an "Indian" people; changes brought by the Spanish Conquest included that of racial composition. Within a century the primitive tribes were decimated by disease or had withdrawn to the trackless jungle, while others united with Spaniards in contributing toward today's *mestizo* complex. Upon arrival the conquerors had found most of the tribes to be either migratory hunters and fishers or "shifting cultivators."[7] Only the Chibchas of the east were sedentary farmers. Thus the Spaniards undertook the importation of Negro slaves, who in time outnumbered the whites in certain regions, notably the Pacific lowlands.

Intermarriage of Spaniard and Indian contributed to the disappearance of the true Indian, and the number of pure whites was also reduced, although the latter retained political control. Assumption by the white aristocracy of an elitist role was spurred by continuing miscegenation. Upper-class whites tended to marry into their own group, thus maintaining a position of social elevation. Some observers today would go so far as to claim that a "tri-ethnic Colombian seems slowly to be evolving."[8] It is too early to determine how far this may go. Certainly the exact composition of today's population is unknown. A comparison of existing estimates suggests that perhaps 60 per cent are *mestizo*; pure Negroes comprise no more than 5 per cent, and pure Indians a bit less. There is a small, slowly-increasing number of mulattoes, and from 20 to 25 per cent are considered pure white.[9]

The Colombian people have historically been rural, and more than half of the population still works and lives on the land. However, the urban sector has virtually doubled in the past forty years, while the rural group is no more than 60 per cent. Today both urban and rural sectors are undergoing disruptive pressures. The magnetism of the city has proved a strong urbanizing force, with tens of thousands leaving the countryside to seek government or industrial employment. The burgeoning industrial expansion in particular has placed new strains on the social fabric, strains which have yet to be adjusted to economic reality.

Growing technological demands for labor have drawn needy or dissatisfied rural folk in search of a better existence. The dream of accumulated "riches" and an improved standard of living is universal, and the peasant arrives in the city hoping to become an industrial worker with fixed wages. Beyond this, an increasing awareness of the benefits of modern life has created in the people a greater self-consciousness. The flow of workers to the city has been further impelled by general dissatisfaction over subsistence conditions of rural society and the dis-

astrous civil war that has raged for more than a decade. Rapid urbanization has also brought a shift in occupational distribution. There was,
for example, a reduction of 5 per cent in those engaged in agricultural
pursuits in the first eight years after the close of World War II.[10]

The swollen, often jobless, urban proletariat is amorphous and disorganized, but conditions have grown increasingly serious. Housing
has become more than simply a nagging annoyance. The multiplication
of city slums has been appalling, as housing projects have failed to keep
up with the influx from the countryside. Furthermore, public funds
have most often been channeled into the construction of soccer fields,
office buildings, and impressive skyscrapers that contribute little to the
lot of the urban worker. Traditional Latin materialism remains of the
"tangible" variety.[11]

As a consequence, the worker has been left in a pugnacious mood that
can detonate into an explosion of frightening proportions. The riots of
April, 1948, shocked the nation's leaders as had nothing else. Yet that
outbreak was symptomatic of the plight of the worker. Strength of
numbers and slow progress toward organizational unity have given
the dissatisfied a more purposeful power to disrupt the nation both
politically and economically. Hunger, want, and poverty are not un-
common. Social consequences have been predictable—resort to pros-
titution, alcoholism, and psychological degeneration.

In the days of early industrial expansion, management looked to
rural areas in supplementing the inadequate urban labor force. The
rural exodus to the cities was encouraged, as the subsistence-level agricultural worker was uprooted and transplanted. Only recently have
political leaders come to the realization that the situation is fundamentally
unsound. As the urban problem remains unsolved, there is scant consolation in recalling that "the conflict between the Colombian city and
province would not have had reality if the latter had opposed a high
grade of organization to the impetuous advance of the former."[12] Only
since the inauguration of bipartisan government in 1958 has there been
a positive effort to ameliorate social conditions. Even so, it is late in the
day.

The rural problem is scarcely less serious. Agriculturally Colombia is
a nation of small farms, despite notable exceptions in the Cauca coffee
plantations and the Santa Marta banana complex along the Caribbean.

The rural sector is based upon a landed aristocracy under which the *campesino* works his land inefficiently, utilizing primitive methods. The typical unit averages but five acres, and there are at least 700,000 such farms.[13] Agricultural production is low, irrigation inadequate, and mechanization rudimentary at best. Credit is inadequate despite the availability of limited funds through the Banco de Crédito Agrario and the Instituto de Crédito Territorial. One expert observer has expressed surprise that productivity is not even lower.[14]

Uneconomic land utility is characteristic. Small farmers turn loose their few head of cattle to graze freely on level terrain, while crops are cultivated on the precipitous slopes. The soil there is less fertile, and erosion is common. The over-all problem has not been helped by traditional attitudes of large landowners. "Many . . . are less interested in the income they derive from their holdings than in the value of . . . holdings as a source of security and as a hedge against inflation."[15] There is reluctance to relinquish title to idle fields. Land taxes on the large landowner have been negligible, while prices have followed inflationary trends. Indeed, over the years "it cannot be denied that such holdings have proved excellent investments from the standpoint of security and increase of principle."[16]

Political manifestations of the rural question are seen in widespread banditry and countryside terrorism. Although small farmers have been a positive force for democracy in certain Latin republics, this has not been true of Colombia. The *minifundio* of five acres or less is economically unable to provide adequate production for national consumption. Byproducts include recurrent inflation and a high cost of living. Fluharty has put it simply and accurately: the land simply does not produce for the people and "is failing because the small tract is not capable of giving back more than a mere subsistence to those who till it."[17] Under such circumstances the *campesino* cannot be brought into the main stream of national life. Dissatisfied, frustrated, choked by the lack of adequate low-interest credit, faced by official reluctance to ease his difficulties, he is fair game for demagogic appeals to the baser political passions. He will continue a divisionistic factor until his lot is improved through removal of virtual economic serfdom as imposed by the environment and the interests of the landholding oligarchy.

Colombian geography has also contributed to traditional regionalism and a spirit of localism. The rugged Andean topography, ideally suited for the heritage of Spanish particularism, even today is working against the integration required at all levels of national life. From colonial days, regional loyalties and personal traits have been molded into distinctive personal characteristics which today are striking. Each region has its own social and economic characteristics. Politically, Colombia has reflected "centrifugal tendencies of the several regions . . . so powerful that only an exceptionally strong central government could keep them from flying apart."[18]

While Colombian leaders have long been blind to the demands of social needs, they have also exhibited complacency over the education of the masses. Paradoxically Colombia enjoys a tradition of culture despite an estimated illiteracy rate of 44 per cent.[19] Colombians have often been called the most cultured of the Latins, and citizens refer to their capital city as the "Athens of the Americas." From the early days of independence, Colombia has basked in a hemispheric reputation of political and social culture.[20] The upper class devotes leisure time to literature, art, and music. Political leaders have often come from the intelligentsia. One of its poets—Rafael Núñez—became president in 1879. Another, Guillermo Valencia, was a prominent if unsuccessful presidential candidate in the early twentieth century. Certainly there is respect for culture and erudition.

This interest in things intellectual has unhappily been less than a mass movement. One of the reasons for political immaturity has been widespread illiteracy that has never been attacked with necessary vigor and determination. Public education is free and, since 1927, compulsory. But the shortage of teachers, lack of school buildings, and general deterioration of facilities have retarded the advance of education. The national budget has customarily provided twice the sum for military as for educational appropriations. The more enlightened attitude of present leaders permits but a glimmer of guarded optimism.

National social and economic demands have become almost staggering. The slow but perceptible emergence of what might be termed a "middle sector" has exerted increasing presure. If not heeded, it threatens to seize control of governmental organs to achieve its ends. To understand the events of recent years, attention must first be directed at the informal, extra-constitutional forces characteristic of Colombian politics.

Chapter Two

THE ESSENCE OF COLOMBIAN POLITICS

The Place of Values

Public attitudes are of fundamental importance to any political process. Few would deny that the "raw material of which effective representative government is made is a society present with the awareness of political activity and the freedom to act in accordance with information freely acquired. . . ."[1] Political awareness in Colombia is based upon a concept of democracy foreign to that of the United States. It implies a minimum of responsibility and maximum freedom of action, which in its extreme form leads to anarchy.

Colombians are vocal in their advocacy of democratic principles. Intellectuals are often well-read in the great political philosophers of revolutionary France and the United States. However, there is a delusion that the declaration of democratic beliefs will transmit ideals into reality. For the Colombian shares the underlying Hispanic emphasis on the inherent uniqueness of each person, of one's own inner worth. Individualism differs in connotation from the common Anglo-Saxon usage.

This is reflected in the attitude toward a national constitution. To Colombians it is not immutable, sacrosanct; there is little reluctance to change it drastically rather than labor to improve conditions without revising the document. Thus, the Colombian does not view constitutional revision as a breaking of faith with the past. "Therefore he is not disturbed when his representatives in Congress adopt an amendment to this constitution. To him this is a normal and proper congressional function. . . . Congress not only has the power to amend the constitution, but . . . when doing so, it does not labor under the shadow of popular antipathy to such action."[2]

As a way of life, *personalismo* calls up great self-reliance in terms of individual pride and sensitivity. This is fundamental on both a personal and institutional level. *Personalismo* is egoistic and frankly self-centered. The impact of public policy upon society is less important than its effect upon the individual. Such a philosophy is personal and deeply introspective, rather than broadly social. Personalistic values are magnified by translation into the political process.[3]

The preservation of traditional values of Hispanic culture, with this striking individualistic creed, is manifested politically in almost unlimited personal freedom. Politics are shaped by a philosophy embracing the individual as the irreducible and ultimate unit.[4] In this connection, Stokes has pointed out perceptively that Latin intellectuals have realized that "individualism, democracy, and liberalism . . . apparently resulted in values in United States culture which were contrary to their [Hispanic] idealistic expectations."[5] While affection for democracy is sincere, there is too little understanding that democracy demands an acceptance of compromise and an accommodation of rights and duties, of privileges and responsibilities.

In political organizations as well as governmental institutions, democracy is a system in which majorities are basic. In its simplest form, practical democracy is rule by a head-counting process in which the magical formula is 50 per cent plus one. Refinements of the system include the delegation of authority and the exercise of representation. Responsible leadership requires a willingness to hear opposing views, accepting the existence of disagreement without imposing a tyranny of the majority. The system rests upon sovereignty as an expression of all members of the state, not upon the majority, however overwhelming.

Hispanic particularism has survived to the present. The essentially antisocial nature of limitless individualism has, in the eyes of some observers, acquired a permanent status. Such pessimism is extreme. To be sure, the Iberian heritage can work at cross purposes to representative government. However, "nothing in the pattern precludes the establishment of a stable government reflecting the conventions of the society."[6]

There are indications that the fires of experience have taught that a viable democratic system demands a dedication to more than mere verbal expression.

Despite environmental and intellectual changes, Colombia has been reluctant to subordinate its singular individualistic philosophy to an acceptance of compromise and negotiation. The ruling political parties mirror the one-sided view of democracy. By-products have included an unwillingness to cooperate with one another, as well as internecine disputes within each party. Conservatives and Liberals alike have in large part abdicated their responsibility to the citizenry. This fact cannot be ignored, for the very heart of the Colombian political process is its two-party arrangement.

The Party System

Multi-party systems are as characteristic of Latin America as the two-party arrangement in the United States.[7] Only through certain peculiarities of its historical development has Colombia maintained a dualism of parties. Most of the Latin republics began their independent existence with two parties. "The two great issues which determined party alignment during the first half of the century of independence were the separation of Church and state and centralization. These controversies of deep social and political significance divided the ruling and nonruling groups into embittered and hostile factions. All other issues were purely personal and factional."[8] The power structure was far simpler than it is today. Under the classic Conservative-Liberal division, both parties drew from the ranks of the aristocracy in becoming custodians of the political power structure. The struggle for control was within a small, socially interrelated class. Political issues were deep and fundamental, intensifying differences between the parties.[9]

At the outset, Colombia, like its neighbors, grouped around Conservative and Liberal collectivities. But the continuation of its bi-party system became a significant variant to the more customary party splintering in Latin America. Early dominance of the aristocracy within both parties set a precedent, for the elite was a closed society into which entry from below was effectively barred. The parties were essentially factional groupings within the small ruling oligarchy. Throughout the nineteenth century the masses were largely proscribed from political participation. The struggle for power was waged within a tight, numerically small group. Revolution and anarchy were common, with irresponsible elements conducting political and civil warfare without regard for the lower classes.

Soon after the turn of the century, dominant oligarchical elements arrived at a tacit *modus vivendi*. Leadership depended increasingly upon the strength of traditional loyalties to maintain an essentially elitist rule. The inner core of the parties was almost impossible to penetrate from below. Localism and geographic isolation enabled the oligarchy to remain dominant, for economic and social forces were otherwise weak and inarticulate. Political awareness spread to the masses slowly. The impact of improvements in communication and transportation was minimized, and the elite proceeded to incorporate mass loyalties within existing party structures.

Suffrage was broadened only reluctantly, and the oligarchy inculcated the enlarging electorate with fundamental Conservative or Liberal ideals. The ever-powerful traditionalist strain in the Colombian mentality permitted the father to pass along to his sons his own political allegiance. Only quite recently, with the masses slightly better educated, fed, and clothed, has there been significantly wider political participation. Industrialization and the rise of a middle class have not yet outrun the shrewd tactical retreat by which the oligarchy has accommodated political leadership to shifting conditions.

Neither Conservatives nor Liberals have yet constructed their parties adequately to adjust to socio-economic realities, and they have not ceased to subordinate the general welfare to narrow class interests. Both, however, have exercised fairly substantial discipline over their organizations which extend down to the municipality. They are controlled at the national level by a convention and a directorate. On departmental and local levels an assembly and directorate supervise party activities. Basic organizational structure has changed little since the end of the nineteenth century.[10]

Grass-roots activities are generally executed by the local party organization, particularly the municipal directorate. Party mechanisms for gaining and retaining control are effective, coming "almost as close as any [in Latin America] in carrying their organization down to the grass roots."[11] Today, greater popular participation places renewed stresses on the organizational efficiency of the biparty system, but the traditional collectivities have succeeded in preventing the advent of a significant third party.

None of the third party attempts have succeeded in capturing public fancy. What have passed as additional parties have been more in the nature of factions or pressure groups, resting upon a variety of economic or social interests. They have generally been fluid, *ad hoc* entities, organized to achieve short-range political objectives. After failing to achieve their goals, they have slipped into oblivion. Both those with an ideological and those with a personalist orientation have failed through an inability to gain a sectional foundation. Despite Colombia's unitary constitutional system—which is advantageous for the gathering of local or departmental support—the minor parties have concentrated efforts on attaining immediate national prominence. Their ambitious haste has caused a diffusion of energies which contributes to ultimate collapse.

Ideological third parties have centered around the Communists and Socialists. The former long operated as the Partido Comunista, then became the Partido Social Democrático, which divided into rival groups in 1947.[12] The Socialists have existed for years on the periphery of national politics. The Partido Popular Socialista Colombiano (PPSC), as it is known today, has long held the conviction that "democratic-liberal" institutions are inappropriate for Colombia. Advocating a profound change in the entire political structure, it has consistently challenged the existing order, to little effect. Its support of the Rojas Pinilla military regime was founded on the hope that he might tear down and then completely rebuild the social and political framework.

Personalist groups were founded in the 1930's when Jorge Gaitán organized the Unión Nacional Izquierdista Revolucionaria (UNIR) and Gilberto Alzate Avendaño the Acción Nacionalista Popular (ANP). Neither man became important nationally until after returning to, respectively, Liberal and Conservative ranks. Other fringe organizations such as the Vanguardia Socialista and the Liga de Acción Política appeared briefly, only to pass, unmourned, without winning national importance.[13]

The traditional parties, for all their doctrinal inflexibility, were able to exercise considerable freedom in making commitments, albeit grudgingly, to emergent social forces. Becoming "aggregative" in nature, they gradually began to articulate the interests of new social elements.[14]

Their deepest doctrinal commitments were to such timeless issues as federalism versus centralism, which cut across economic and social lines. Thus the two parties managed to retain their hold on national sympathies. Members of the lower classes usually sought aid from the party of their families' loyalties, rather than from the as yet erratic interest groups or self-proclaimed third parties.

The Conservatives and Liberals have also maintained a virtual monopoly on talented leadership. Alfonso López first provided effective, social-minded direction upon his ascension to power in 1934. Himself a member of the aristocracy, López recognized the problems of the masses and took actions which branded him as disloyal to his class. A large part of the oligarchy never forgave López his "betrayal." Jorge Gaitán, having returned to the Liberal party, followed López in championing the interests of the masses. The first leader of national prominence to rise from the lower social strata, he was nearing the presidency when cut down by an assassin's bullets.

It is worth noting that López' departure from traditional political lines led to a schism within the Liberal party, and Gaitán's presidential candidacy in 1946 was rejected by party leaders, who nominated a representative of the oligarchical interests and thereby threw away certain Liberal victory. The exceptional popularity of both men with the masses has not since been equalled. Today new social forces are beginning to compete more effectively with the older political groups. A new figure with mass appeal may emerge from outside the major parties, but he will be confronted by the combined power of the existing dual party system. It is improbable that a third party will arise at this juncture to contradict the practice of a century and a half.

A responsible party system implies more than the mere fact that parties are operative. Essential features include non-identification with any one individual, a priority of party principles over personality, a national basis of support, and the subservience of both programs and candidates to law, morality, and effective exercise of popular sovereignty.[15] Conservatives and Liberals have, over the course of time, reflected the first three characteristics. They have generally been associated with deeply-entrenched historical traditions; principles have played a prominent role, and both have enjoyed the characteristics of a national collectivity. But neither has measured up consistently to commonly accepted standards of morality and devotion to the public.

Extreme social cleavages have lent considerable force to mutual party shortcomings. Lack of compromise and the exercise of narrow partisanship have led occasionally to disenfranchisement of an electoral majority. "That rejection of compromise, which . . . drove the country to within a millimeter of disintegration"[16] has proven clearly destructive. Yet neither party has operated on a just, fair basis. Political struggle has been acrimonious and violent. The response of the citizenry has too often been cynical.

After winning power, a party initiates the transformation of the body politic to its own maximum advantage, consolidating its position by reducing the opposition as much as possible. The presidential elections of 1934, 1938, and 1950 found but one party represented on the ballot; in 1930 and 1958, the parties presented but one candidate. Even today, the collectivities are motivated largely to entrench their position by nourishing the ingredients of sectarianism, inequity, and occasional bursts of civil violence, all in the name of the narrow "sacred cause."[17]

Basic party orientation has remained consistent over a long period of time. The Conservatives have been committed to strong unitary government, the interests of large landowners, and a dominant position for the church. Liberals have fought for decentralized republican government, broader suffrage, free secular schools, and increased commerce through free trade. Inevitably, there has been consensus on some issues, but there is little validity to the claim that the parties are essentially the same in outlook. Both have declared themselves on matters of basic principle, and it is fitting to take a closer look at party ideology.

The Liberal party has set down its doctrine frequently. Article I of the 1935 Declaration of Principles, which has recently been reaffirmed, states party respect for the liberty of the citizen. Guaranteeing his rights and accepting state responsibility, the party favors "individual initiatives in all orders of activity, but will always intervene when it is necessary to establish a true equilibrium between the individual and enterprise. . . ."[18] Thus, the party accepts "whatever initiative is likely to succeed, that the territorial property fulfills satisfactorily the social function that corresponds to it, and recognizes labor as the primordial fountain of private property."[19]

In the 1942 Declaration of Principles the Liberals further promised to promote economic development through support of public over private action. Necessary means would include protective legislation, easy availability of credit, and extensive technical cooperation. "Liberalism considers that State intervention must be exercised to impede the formation of a monopoly and to assure that activities . . . be oriented toward a social finality . . . to fulfill the economic functions to the benefit of the community."[20]   As these statements suggest, there is agreement that general welfare must be assured through state intervention.[21]   This is significant as an abandonment of the Liberal tradition of free trade and economic *laissez faire*.

Previously the Liberals had long "claimed to apply the norms of English free trade, in spite of its having been conceived for a country strongly industrialized and not for a people that struggled to achieve independent, universal life. . . ."[22]   By its 1942 admission, the Liberal party rejected its long commitment to *laissez faire,* recognizing that "the intervention of the State must be exercised to obtain the creation of a harmonic national economic system in its internal relations and with respect to the realities of international commerce."[23]

Party doctrine reflects some little confusion on the issue of centralism versus federalism.   State intervention and party responsibility for the common man have been accepted, thus implying a strong central government extending from Bogotá to all levels of national life.   Contradictorily, Liberals have proclaimed a belief in maximum local authority and regional autonomy.   They advocate "an administrative decentralization as complete as may be necessary, delimiting the radius of action of the Nation, the Department and the Municipality. . . ."[24]   In practice there has been little substantial difference between the parties here.   Both have accepted direct intervention by central authorities.   The long Liberal espousal of localism has been pushed aside, although its vestiges remain in various party declarations.

On the church question the Liberals have inherited a position they are reluctant to denounce.   Historically the party has been anti-church, and long demonstrated open hostility.   Yet the Liberals are no longer truly anti-clerical.   In practice they have refrained from attacking the clerical ramparts.   What they have continued to deny is the right of the church to dabble in politics.   The continuing Conservative practice of enfolding the church within its arms has made it difficult for Liberals to remove the cloud of anti-clericalism.   But they have come to recognize the positive contribution the church can make to society.   As Liberal Carlos

Lleras Restrepo has declared, the party difference toward the church is "that *we** believe in the separation of Church and State and they [the Conservatives] don't."[25]

Liberals have sought, above all else, to achieve popular recognition as being unique possessors of progressive, reformist ideals. They take pride in forming a vanguard for a new, more prosperous state. A characteristic view is that of Carlos Lozano y Lozano. "Liberalism is fundamentally dynamic; it is identified with the propelling and impelling forces of the society it conceives as reality . . . [it urges] continual creative evolution, it sustains the concept of human perfectability, from whence proceeds its irreducible adhesion to the autonomy of the spirit and the emancipation of the conscience."[26]

Colombian Conservatives have uttered comparable statements on the importance of liberty and human dignity, but their orientation in the role of the state is dissimilar. Conservatives emphasize order as a prerequisite for government efficiency and national progress. Restrepo Jaramillo has written in *El Pensamiento Conservador,* "Conservatism establishes the social necessity of a hierarchy, imposed by the prestige of merit in a state in which one is permitted to exercise one's self without useless bonds."[27] While the government is at the service of the citizen, it does not necessarily respond to the demands of the individual. Rather, Conservative doctrine expresses the belief that it provides for the welfare of the masses in a paternalistic spirit.

Restrepo Jaramillo, an orthodox Conservative and influential Catholic intellectual, has written that "aristocracy is a necessity of the world," although conceding that it is imperfect. Among the duties of the individual is acceptance of the status into which he is born. Conformity to one's natural station contributes to the maintenance of public tranquillity and is essential for effective party rule. Policy should be decided by national authorities and passed down to the people. The citizenry must accept it as the measured judgment of wiser heads.

While holding that upper-class privileges should be maintained, the Conservatives express it in terms of their own vision of democracy. This takes the form of an emphasis upon the family as the one elemental social force, the rock upon which all individual behavior rests. If civil society is to be perfected, the Conservatives insist that it must come

* The emphasis is Lleras Restrepo's.

through the family. In 1953, when right-wing Conservative Laureano Gómez was directing projected constitutional reform, the basis for all voting privileges and local representation was the family, with both husbands and wives exercising the suffrage. Single adults would have been proscribed from political life, regardless of sex or age.

Another distinguishing characteristic of the party is the militancy of its spokesmen and a pugnacious aggressiveness that turns upon itself as well as the hated Liberal enemy. Conservatives like nothing better than a good political fight; they thrive on it. Quick to leap for the opponent's jugular, almost eager to take umbrage at a minor challenge, they wage all-out political war with no quarter asked and certainly none given. The extreme right-wing element has particularly shown this propensity. Perhaps it is not coincidental that the moderate wing has been less successful politically. As one Conservative puts it, "we love political struggle. It constitutes for us an aspect of cosmic movement, created by God, that brings forth the light, the head, and the harmony of the perennial crash of molecules. . . . We love the river that runs, and travels, and changes. . . ."[28]

Allegiance to the Roman Catholic church is fundamental. The loyal Conservative believes that mutual support of church and state is indispensable for the administration of government and the maintenance of the only religion promising spiritual salvation. To this end the party has rededicated itself through the years. It long found shelter under clerical approval, responding in kind. It is true, while conceding that Conservatives have benefited from religious ties, that many party members are utterly convinced of the inherent validity of this policy. The incorporation of the religious element into political disturbances has been important in respect to the high degree of intransigent antagonism between the parties.

With Liberal anti-clericalism moderating, the Conservatives have gone to increasing lengths to remind the citizenry of what it calls the heretical and ungodly Liberal party. Conservatives defend church-state reciprocity, accusing their opponents of propagating anti-church dogma in the hope of breaking its connections with politics. Liberals are further attacked for advocating civil marriage, with a simple civil contract replacing the sanctity of a Catholic wedding. Conservatives add that their opponents retain a basic hatred of the clergy which weakens the very fabric of

Colombian society, and there are frequent condemnations of alleged Liberal advocacy of divorce, although the latter has remained quiet on the issue.

To summarize, the Liberals urge separation of church and state, religious toleration, popular suffrage, response to the social and economic demands of the masses, and the assumption of responsibility by the central government to provide for the increasing political consciousness of the ordinary citizen. Federalism is supported in theory but has largely been abandoned in practice. In contrast, the Conservatives advocate close cooperation with the church, a generally narrow view of "alien" religious beliefs, limited suffrage defined commonly by heads of family, the maintenance of class privileges, management of politics by a small privileged elite, and a highly centralized governmental structure with local authority strictly subservient to national rule.

As is suggested elsewhere, neither party has pursued its doctrine without perversions that are hardly consonant with formal declarations. The dynamics of national politics cannot be understood merely in terms of party dogma. At the same time, the publicly-avowed positions of the parties must be kept in mind while examining their practical expressions of policy. The Colombian party system may be likened to a voracious jungle in which concession is taken as a sign of weakness, while strength must be matched by yet greater strength and ferocity. Opportunism runs high, yet it is considered a legitimate function of party machinery. Politics becomes a matter of extremes; the dark is midnight black, the light as blinding as a snow-blanketed plain. Between, there is precious little grey.

All this makes the constant stream of charges and countercharges more understandable. To the Liberal, the Conservative is a renaissance-minded reactionary, bent upon retaining power and establishing an elitist rule in defiance of the people's needs, supported by the spiritual monopoly of Catholicism. His own party he considers alive, progressive, selfless, and bountifully endowed with wisdom. On the other hand, a Conservative views his opponent as anarchical, demagogic, atheistically anticlerical, and federalist to the point of state disintegration. Liberals are suspiciously close to communism, while Liberal policy would establish a slavery of conscience, destroying national principles and public morality through suppression of the clergy.

Elsewhere there is allusion to the failure of the parties in the contemporary era. This is detailed in the narrative which will follow. For the moment it may be noted that the disastrous results of extremism urge upon the parties today an acceptance of the forces and demands of economic development. Both collectivities have been guilty of a blind refusal to recognize the latent forces released by industrial and technological development. Both must concede, as Blanksten has pointed out, that "the process of economic development can be regarded as one of the most spectacular forms of Westernization in Latin America during the mid-twentieth century."[29]

The leadership of both parties must heed the admonition of Lippmann who, writing in another context, nonetheless brilliantly observed the evils of political rule by an unenlightened oligarchy. In these words lies a lesson for all Colombian political leaders.

> The wisest rulers . . . know that the responsibility for insurrections rests in the last analysis upon the unimaginative greed and endless stupidity of the dominant classes. There is something pathetic in the blindness of powerful people when they face a social crisis. Fighting viciously every readjustment which a nation demands, they make their own overthrow inevitable. . . . They resist every demand, submit only after a struggle, and prepare a condition of war to the death. When far-sighted men appear in the ruling classes—men who recognize the need of a civilized answer to this increasing restlessness, the rich and the powerful treat them to a scorn and a hatred that are incredibly bitter.[30]

INTEREST GROUPS

Organized groups in Colombia have not yet passed beyond a fairly primitive developmental stage. Until quite recently, the ruling elite mounted concerted efforts to retard the formation of politically effective interest and pressure groups. Oligarchical dominance of public policy went largely unchallenged. The church was the only major group as such, and a systematic differentiation of party and non-party functions was scarcely possible. This has been even more pronounced in the several multi-party systems of Latin America, where parties tend to act as do interest groups in western Europe.[31] With a sweeping social and economic transformation gathering momentum, however, the role of the group has begun to take on importance.

Thus contemporary Colombian politics are increasingly seasoned by the ingredients of group interests. The labor movement is prospering, and a politically ambitious middle class is seeking an outlet for self-expression. An awakening industrial proletariat has been pressing the traditional parties with new and vigorous demands. As group interests gather new strength, they can play a necessary and constructive role in national affairs. For "a polity of countervailing powers becomes a possibility . . . making possible government by decisions as the result of compromise through bargaining instead of by fiat through uncontrolled self-interest."[32]

Associationist Groups.—Of two major distinguishable types, the first is consciously organized, lying outside the formal governmental structure but including political functions among its objectives.[33] Of these, the most prominent is the labor movement. The surge of twentieth-century industrialism in Colombia has only recently given notable impetus to the labor movement. The ruling class has been openly hostile to labor organization; both government and employers have opposed the formation and evolution of trade-unionism. Early organizations lacked effective leadership, and for many years labor's gains have been negligible.

Trade unions began to grow in the interval between the two world wars. Under the first administration of Alfonso López, "national" labor was viewed with some benevolence in official circles, and in 1936 the Confederación de Trabajadores de Colombia (CTC) was formed. The first labor organization, it united some 900 locals representing roughly 100,000 workers.[34] Recognition of a political role came from a union statement that ". . . the Confederation acknowledges that union members, as citizens, have the duty to perform a political role and to be actively occupied with defending their economic and cultural interests in the same way that they are conceded rights by the democratic regime, sovereignty, and the liberal reforms of the Republic of Colombia."[35] The López administration proceeded to admit labor into public affairs, and the CTC dominated the labor movement for more than a decade.

Factionalism arose from a split between Liberal- and Communist-oriented leaders. A schism in December, 1940, marked the beginning of a period of organizational factionalism and rivalry. By the end of the 1940's the Liberal group re-established its supremacy, and the Communists left to set up their own Confederación de Trabajadores de Colombia Independiente (CTCI).[36] At the same time, the CTC was further weakened by the rise of two non-Communist groups.

Under the patronage of the Jesuits and the leadership of Padre Vicente Andrade, the Unión de Trabajadores Colombianos (UTC) was founded.[37] Enjoying the tolerance of Conservative administrations after 1946, the UTC waged a campaign for higher wages and advanced social legislation. Through effective leadership and aided by a temporary reaction against the Liberals, the UTC increased its strength. It drew upon affiliation with the hemispheric Organización Regional Interamericana de Trabajadores (ORIT) and by 1956, a decade after its birth, "unquestionably boasted preponderant influence in Colombian trade-unionism."[38]

In 1953 the Confederación Nacional del Trabajo (CNT) was organized with the moral and financial backing of the *peronista* inter-American confederation, the Agrupación de Trabajadores Latino Americanos Sindicalizados (ATLAS). Hernando Rodríguez, a CNT leader, declared that the movement of Perón was "the greatest and most effective . . . in behalf of any people which has ever been carried out in any country."[39] With the fall of Perón in 1955 the movement crumbled, and the Colombian branch collapsed, after an abortive attempted reorganization under the regime of Gustavo Rojas Pinilla.

There has been general debate as to whether the Colombian labor movement was favorable to democratic values. Since 1958 it has gained in political influence, but it has not yet proved uniformly effective in winning acceptance of its views. Labor's role has been largely that of harassing the government and upsetting the economic order with strikes and demonstrations over both legitimate and questionable issues. Interunion strife has diluted its strength, and the coalition government of Alberto Lleras Camargo has been forced to intervene in labor-management problems.

Management remains reluctant to concede the rights of labor as outlined in the 1951 labor code. Attitudes are shifting, however, and labor organizations are increasingly assertive in their demands for social legislation. The current trend is toward better disciplined organizations accepting free and voluntary membership. Since the fall of the Rojas Pinilla government, the labor movement has eschewed close ties with the administration. Although still in a state of transition, labor is exerting increasing force upon the interplay of political and social forces.

Businessmen and industrialists have formed several pressure groups.

Among the first to appear was an employer's organization, the Asociación Patronal Económica Nacional (APEN), which was founded in the mid-1930's. The economic oligarchy grew more disturbed as workers' groups proliferated under the encouragement of Liberal administrations. In the early 1940's an emerging complex of vertical class groups organized to protect financial and commercial interests. The most influential were the Asociación Nacional de Industriales (ANDI) and the Federación Nacional de Comerciantes (FENALCO).[40]

The ANDI and FENALCO took the lead in opposing "unfavorable" trade and labor regulations. Substantial influence was exerted in urging continued protective tariffs. As Conservative obstructionism increased during the party's recapture of the presidency in 1946, they operated in a marked conspiratorial atmosphere. Party oligarchies lent their support, and, indeed, "the Liberal oligarchy saw itself the dangers of power based upon a resentful populace which had been defrauded and was now without hope."[41]

Not all such groups have been reactionary in nature. The most noteworthy has been the Federación Nacional de Cafeteros Colombianos (FNCC). The coffee-growers, organized since 1927, have drawn official support through tax revenues, but their position has been largely independent. One of the most effective and enlightened interest groups, it has consistently proposed constructive measures of fiscal and credit policy.

A variety of other organizations has cropped up recently, representing cattle, cotton, agrarian, banking, and cooperative farm interests. Their influence has been diffuse, but gradual inroads have been made upon the long-dominant economic oligarchical interests. Among the more prominent are the Asociación Colombiana de Ganaderos, Instituto Nacional Algodonero, Sociedad de Agricultores, Asociación Bancaria, and Federación Nacional de Cooperativas. Of particular recent note was the first National Congress of Agrarian Workers, sponsored in November, 1959, by the Federación Nacional de Campesinos.

Professional and student groups may also be classified as associationist. The former are a type of occupational pressure group with close bonds to the universities. In Colombia the lawyers and engineers have proved of some little influence in recent years. The university students, however, form a more significant pressure group. With universities organized along the lines of the European system, student political divisions tend to parallel those of the major parties. It has been said that the universities serve as a small-scale battlefield of national politics.[42]

The Colombian national student federation has been tightly organized, except for a temporary splintering to form a pro-government faction during the Rojas Pinilla dictatorship. Colombian students have generally been militant; the intensity of participation is high. Within the universities, students exercise power in the selection of faculty members. Sitting on governing administrative boards, they often take united action on such matters as school vacations, the scheduling of examinations, and revisions of the curriculum. The schools provide an important source of young political partisans, with students organizing for political activity that bursts forth under provocations of various sorts.

The student federation admittedly plays an occasionally disruptive role in the political arena, but it would be misleading to characterize it as merely a destructive force. The students must be judged in terms of Hispanic cultural outlook. Colombian youth is impressed at an early age with an awareness of national problems. Possessing a highly-developed sense of responsibility for the lower classes, they regard themselves as an intellectual vanguard of progress. Student intervention in politics is a double-edged sword. The basic desire is for renovation and justice, but their actions occasionally encourage political instability.

Recently the students have contributed a democratizing influence on public policy. Student opposition to the Rojas Pinilla dictatorship was early and determined. Several were killed or wounded in the June, 1954, disturbances. A year later, forbidden by the regime to place flowers on the site of 1954 violence, they formed in protest, again forcing the regime on the defensive. They played a vital role in organizing civil resistance to Rojas Pinilla in the days preceding his flight from the country in May, 1957. "When the dictator was forced out of power, hundreds of students were released from jail. . . ."[43]

Institutional Groups.—Formally constituted agencies with established roles in the political system may be classified as institutional.[44] Of these, none have wielded as much influence as the Roman Catholic church. In Colombia the church has been far more than a performer of spiritual functions. As major landowner and operator of the educational system, it has historically joined with the Conservative party in political affairs.

The close alliance of the church with Spain led in the independence period to strong Catholic domination far beyond the religious realm. Insistent and unbending in its claim to authority, the church was particularly active politically during the nineteenth-century Liberal-Conservative struggle.

A quarter-century ago, Mecham wrote that "from the independence period to the present day religious policy has ever been a prominent feature of party programs, and the recurrent alterations of the political order have always been attended by radical changes in ecclesiastical polity."[45] Forming an alliance with Conservatives, the church helped to force extreme anticlericalism upon the Liberals. Only within the last generation have the two parties shifted to any noticeable extent vis-à-vis the church.

The constitutional status of the church was established in the Constitution of 1886, which with modification remains in effect today. The preamble stated that the document was written and adopted "in the name of God, fountain of all authority, and with the purpose of promoting the national unity and assuring the ends of justice, liberty, and peace. . . ." The state was specifically authorized to arrange concordats with the Vatican "to regulate relations between the State and the Catholic Church on a basis of reciprocal deference and mutual respect."[46] The "Apostolic Roman Catholic Religion" was recognized as the national religion.

The Concordat of 1887 and 1888 further recognized the primacy of Catholicism and assured that the government was "bound to protect and enforce respect for it [the church] and its ministers, leaving to it at the same time the full enjoyment of its rights and prerogatives."[47] The church was granted formal control of education. Revision of these arrangements came as a result of the Liberal-sponsored Constitutional Codification of 1936. Negotiations were reopened with the Vatican, and a new concordat was signed after extensive diplomacy amid great political furor on April 22, 1942.

The church thereby lost much of its formal control over public education. Furthermore, the Vatican agreed to nominate only Colombian nationals as ranking prelates of the local hierarchy. The Colombian president had the right of disapproval; new bishops and archbishops were required to swear allegiance to the Colombian state before the president. In effect, the church position was changed little in a political sense. The written agreement has not been put into practice, except for the selection of higher clergy. The governmental right to control educational institutions has been exercised but weakly.[48]

Revision helped lead to the progressive removal of barriers between the Liberal party and the church. As discussed earlier, the Liberals have made considerable efforts at accommodation. In 1945 a North American Catholic could write that the Liberals seemed "sufficiently respectful" toward the church. In turn, the Archbishop of Bogotá, the Papal Nuncio, and higher clerics have encouraged greater cooperation. At the time of the Concordat of 1942, only local parish priests were divided over apparent conciliation of the Liberals.[49]

Moderation of the church position was interrupted in the years following the Conservative return to power in 1946. Conservatives tightened party bonds with the church, drawing it back increasingly into secular affairs as a pillar of political support. This trend extended into the years of the military regime; only when Rojas Pinilla's authoritarianism proved incompetent and inhumane did the church turn against him. Civilian protest had already risen in early May of 1957, and when the church threw its weight against him, the erstwhile dictator fell resoundingly. Although it is yet too early to make a positive judgment, events since 1957 suggest a renewed effort toward reduced political activity by the church.

The early 1950's were marred by the "persecution of the Protestants," one of the most controversial issues of contemporary Colombia. In the later narrative, considerable attention is devoted to the issue. The civil war that spread through the countryside for over a decade was involved to some extent with religious strife. Both political and spiritual factors were involved and cannot be separated. But this issue will be analyzed later. Regardless of the degree of Church responsibility in this lamentable matter, there is little dispute that the lingering outbursts of rural banditry today are unrelated to religious matters. It is no longer true that the Protestant missionary takes his life in his hands by working in the Colombian countryside.

A balanced view of the role of the church must recognize its valuable work in social welfare. In Colombia as throughout Latin America there has been a perceptible evolution toward a more positive position working for civil and political betterment. As Hermens recently noted, the church has "become increasingly aware of the fact that the apparent or real alliance with . . . the 'unthinking Right' . . . was unnatural."[50] Younger priests, in particular, have grown aware of the need for reform, which through social work and instruction has been directed at "rekindling a faith which through years of insufficient attention has tended to become dormant. . . ."[51]

An excellent example is Colombia's Acción Cultural Popular, operating from Bogotá officers under the immediate sponsorship of the Bishop of Tunja. It was founded in 1947 by Monsignor José Joaquín Salcedo, a young priest just out of seminary. Operating a series of technical schools in mountain areas, the Acción today owns six radio transmitters, one with 50,000 watts. Educational materials and radio receivers are distributed, through which illiteracy and lack of technical knowledge have been reduced. By late 1960, an estimated 150,000 Colombians had been taught to read and write. As Salcedo commented, "We must convince our people that improvement is in their hands, create in them the intellectual need to live better. It is no use just building housing projects. You must teach them to demand light, cleanliness, privacy."[52]

Second only to the church among institutional forces is the Colombian military. Elsewhere in Latin America the armed forces have been considered as a political force. In Colombia, however, a more accurate description is that of an institutional pressure group. "Direct Army intervention in politics has occurred less often in Colombia than in most of the other Latin American countries in the twentieth century."[53] Generally neutral politically, the Armed Forces has obeyed the dictates of the commander-in-chief. In return, presidents have refrained from abusing such neutrality. With but a few exceptions, they have not used the military as a partisan coercive governmental organ.

The privileged position of the military has long been recognized, and successive administrations have coddled the Armed Forces. By 1955 it was possible for an officer to retire after fifteen years' service on a pension equivalent to 50 per cent of his final salary. With longer active duty, he would receive a pension which grew by substantial annual increments. On the enlisted level, Law No. 1 of 1945 required all boys to take eighteen months' obligatory service at the age of nineteen, but many exceptions permit the avoidance of service by paying roughly 10 per cent of one's annual income.[54] Further 1945 legislation reduced political temptations by denying suffrage to enlisted men, while officers on active duty were prohibited from legislative candidacy.[55]

The Colombian military is an autonomous body under domination of its professional officer corps. It has openly espoused no social or political philosophy.[56] Traditionally the minister of war has come from the military, and a tacit agreement has permitted the military share of budgetary appropriations to remain constant. "If the government allows the armed forces to function unmolested and to look after their own affairs, it need have no fear they will seize controls."[57]

The apolitical role of the military must not be overstated, however. There have been occasional outbursts, as the temporary seizure of President López in 1944 during the Pasto garrison uprising. Further, the assumption of power by the military in 1953—its first such intervention in eighty-seven years—cast a pall upon the tradition of nonpartisanship. Especially after the disastrous nature of the Rojas Pinilla government, the military has felt the need of cleansing. This was evident in the behavior of the military *junta* which ruled temporarily following the overthrow of General Rojas Pinilla. The military sense of honor and *dignidad* had been sullied. Today the Armed Forces are, more than ever, dedicated to absolute political abstention, content in the role of protectors of the constitution.

Finally, associations of public workers are forming into interest groups. There has been little significant organization, but today the increased role of the state has permitted an expanding bureaucracy. A growing body of men consider themselves professional public administrators. As in all of Latin America, "government workers no doubt may be regarded as political groups."[58] Government employment has risen substantially. "Hispanic culture . . . has honored bureaucracy for hundreds of years. . . . The intervention of the state in the economy has resulted in an even greater emphasis on bureaucracy in recent decades."[59]

Colombia has long operated without a civil service program, despite intermittent attempts to create a merit system. The controlling party installs its own personnel in office. This has usually been kept within the bounds of moderation, although the Mariano Ospina Pérez and Gómez administrations went rather far to install political partisans within swelling bureaucratic ranks. Besides the absence of a merit system, a civil service has been handicapped by the tradition of decentralized personnel management. Individual ministries are responsible for hiring employees and establishing departmental rates of pay. Patronage is inevitable, with ministries normally overstaffed, undisciplined, and poorly organized.

With the bureaucracy founded on patronage and the whim of individual ministries, organization of public workers is severely handicapped. The very presence of government workers, no matter how diffuse, creates pressures of a wide variety. Inevitably the political processes adapt themselves to such forces. A recent text pointed out that Latin governments "are very much involved in all Latin-American efforts for industrialization."[60] Furthermore, the disproportionate size of the bureaucracy and a failure to maintain high professional standards mitigates against efficient operation of government offices.[61]

Bureaucratic growth has been steady since the 1930's, as a plethora of new agencies has been created to administer expanding welfare programs. The existence of a large, amorphous, but politically interested public service leads to consideration of the role of the state. Colombia in a quarter-century has accepted the idea of governmental responsibility over sectors of national life long considered as within the private sphere. The commitment to state intervention is almost complete. Only the central authorities, it is felt, can sustain "social necessities, social solidarities, cooperative assistance, recognition of the interests of the consumer, effective control of industry, just distribution of property, and restriction of competition."[62]

Only a few of the many agencies can be mentioned here. In 1940 the Santos administration created the Instituto de Fomento Industrial for the planning of industrial enterprises. Activities have included, among others, a rubber-tire company, a tanning extract factory, a fishing enterprise, and a naval construction yard. The smaller Instituto de Fomento Municipal was to operate similarly on a local level. At the same time the Instituto de Crédito Territorial took up the task of rural credit and loans but has tended to grant loans primarily to those already possessing some property and collateral.[63] Through these organs the government committed itself to development, research, and promotion. None of the three, however, has been adequately staffed and financed to achieve measurable results.[64]

Additional governmental organs have grown up. Rural affairs are variously dealt with by the Caja de Crédito Agrario, Industrial y Minero (Agriculture Bank), the Banco Central Hipotecario (Mortgage Bank), the Banco Cafetero (serving the coffee interests), and the Instituto Nacional de Abastecimientos (price controls). In 1959 the Banco Ganadero (Cattle Bank) was added to the list. Further examples of state intervention include the Empresa Colombiana de Petróleos (ECOPETROL), which holds a virtual monopoly over petroleum exploitation, and the national airline, Avianca, which was annexed to the government in 1956.

Colombia has inevitably been faced with the inherent disadvantages of such extensive governmental controls: overlapping authority, inadequate staffing of agencies, intrusion into the private sphere, and bureaucratic inefficiency. Those who are dissatisfied with present conditions argue not for a shift away from state intervention but rather a reform of existing organs. As Ricardo Silva explains it, ". . . modern social justice, in order to be loyally practiced, requires that the State be reinvested with all the powers necessary to intervene, direct, plan and organize the economy, subordinated to the common well-being of those associated with it. The pontifical Encyclicals leave no doubt on the intervention of the State for the just protection of the rights of the workers."[65]

The essence of Colombian politics is formed by many components. Social values of the Hispanic cultural heritage are evidenced in both formal and informal manifestations of the political process. At the heart of the dynamic process is the biparty system. Party determination and execution of policy have been shaped by a variety of forces, including interest and pressure groups. These latter are largely in an early developmental period, although both church and Armed Forces have played an influential role for generations.

The explosive, often-chaotic political events of modern times reflect the constant interplay of these forces within the social framework. Within the last twenty years a succession of governments with differing philosophies have shared an inability to cope with the problems of contemporary national life. The ultimate response is the unique governmental arrangement with which Colombia entered the decade of the sixties. Once this narrative reaches the bipartisan experiment, it may be possible to understand more fully the trials in achieving the status of a modern, twentieth-century state.

Part II

THE FAILURE OF COALITION GOVERNMENT

Chapter Three

BACKGROUND TO VIOLENCE

IN AUGUST OF 1946, smiling, silver-haired Mariano Ospina Pérez took office as the first Conservative president of Colombia in sixteen years. This marked the start of a political breakdown that drew the people under increasingly undemocratic rule. As Miguel Jorrín wrote in 1953, "the antecedent . . . of the grave political problems facing Colombia may be found in the presidential elections held on May 5, 1946."[1] For Ospina Pérez had been elected by minority vote, the Liberals having divided their strength by supporting rival candidacies of Gabriel Turbay and Jorge Eliécer Gaitán. This Liberal dispute had been simmering within the party for the previous decade. The failure to agree upon a single presidential candidate in 1946 was the ultimate manifestation of intra-party strife.

The Liberals had themselves returned to power in 1930 after an internecine Conservative battle opened the way to easy victory for Enrique Olaya Herrera, an enlightened moderate who had been serving as ambassador to the United States. In 1934 a reformist wave brought to the presidency Dr. Alfonso López, a diplomat, businessman, first president of the American Mercantile Bank in Colombia,[2] and representative of the reform-minded left wing of the Liberal party.

Alfonso López was indisputably among the greatest Colombians of the century. When he passed away in late 1959 the nation mourned, and even bitter enemies of long years' standing were silent. López was the first Colombian president to become aware of the changing order of national life. Although himself a wealthy man, he succeeded in making contact with the masses as few leaders have done. A gentlemanly cavalier of the world, López worked intensely and disinterestedly for the people during his first term. Using both audacity and common sense, he aroused strong political passions.[3] For years the *bête noir* of the Conservatives, he was actually less bitterly anti-Conservative than many Liberals. For López, there was at least a place for the opposition and a role it might play.

Dr. López was not the unanimous Liberal choice in 1934. At a time when the Conservatives were notably weak, many Liberals preferred a moderate dedicated to the *status quo*. Wealthy industrialists, who had turned away from Conservatism as being too reactionary, now vied with their employees, also Liberals.[4] Considerable compromise was necessary before a full slate of candidates was chosen, even following López' nomination. In the absence of a Conservative candidate—who would in any event have been soundly defeated—López won easily.

Immediately upon taking office he inaugurated the policy of La Revolucíon en Marcha. Identifying himself with growing political consciousness, he drew up social legislation calling for basic tax revision to shift the burden to the wealthy. In the face of bitter opposition by capitalists and Conservatives, he won a majority in the Congress and proceeded to adopt the 1936 constitutional codification.

Labor reform and social legislation committed the state unreservedly to the principle of intervention. The struggle was bitter, and only in later years was it finally accepted by most influential Colombians. At the same time, however, López faced a maelstrom of embittered opposition which extended into the ranks of the Liberals and contributed to the gradual disintegration of party unity. The most controversial aspect of López' program was, for the oligarchy, "the philosophy of the state which Lopez wrote into the constitution."[5] The dispute centered on the declaration of Article 19 that "public assistance is a function of the state. It shall be given to persons who, being physically incapable of working, lack the means of self-support or the right to demand the same of other persons." Article 20, in accepting the social obligations of property, further shocked the oligarchy. Social interest and public utility justified the expropriation of property. The state for the first time had the power, indeed the duty, to intervene by legislation in operations of private enterprise and to protect the worker from abuses.[6] Small wonder that López, scion of a banking family, became the focus for extreme political passions.

The greatest immediate impact of his reforms came from adoption of a progressive income tax. For the first time the Colombian really had to pay his taxes. Before 1936, "even such tributes as were due were ineffectually collected. *No one paid taxes. . . .*"[7] With the tax scale drastically revised and the collecting process tightened, state income now relied less upon customs receipts than on the direct income tax base. The pathological fear experienced by the oligarchy proved unwarranted, but that class never really forgave Dr. López.

A genuinely dedicated man as well as masterful politician, Alfonso López was essentially a reformer, the "most intelligent reformist of the Liberal bourgeoisie, a competent administrator, pragmatic and dogmatic."[8] He was not, like Jorge Gaitán, a social revolutionary. Practical, realistically hard-headed, distrustful of the very oligarchical elite from which he came, he was the first prominent Colombian to recognize fully both the political advantage and the national necessity of sponsoring the demands of the masses. For this alone, he stands out in contemporary politics.

As his term drew to an end, growing opposition within his party manifested itself by the nomination of Dr. Eduardo Santos for president. Santos, founder and owner of *El Tiempo,* a Liberal Bogotá daily with a hemispheric reputation, had led a group of moderate Liberals and Conservatives during the final year of López' administration to block parts of the president's program. Thus Dr. López opposed the Santos candidacy. The breach between the two Liberal wings opened a bit further.

Santos, whose adult career had been dedicated to journalism, was scarcely the reactionary López made him out to be. Yet he was no *lopista,* but rather an heir to the moderate Olaya Herrera. Santos felt his predecessor had gone too far, too fast. He was not deeply immersed in the needs of the masses, preferring minimal concessions while restoring the pre-López *status quo* where possible. Traditional Liberal doctrine was accepted, but the new thesis of state intervention was not, and specific measures of the López administration were in many cases disapproved. In his own way, Eduardo Santos was firmly committed to democracy. But he viewed it as did most Colombians, and there was an inclination to yield only with reluctance to the pressures from below.

López, enraged at the thought of his reforms being negated, founded *El Liberal* as a personal news organ, and before long its columns and those of *El Tiempo* carried daily invective and diatribe. The outgoing president was unable to block the nomination of his opponent, and in August of 1938 Dr. Santos was sworn in. The López reform era came to an abrupt end, never to return with the force and impetus that had carried it through the vital and heady days of 1934 through 1938.

Although his predecessor had ruled amid daily controversy and bitter dispute, Santos succeeded in restoring a sense of balance and quiet stability to the operation of government. His administration was eminently efficient and generally honest. Economic progress continued, and Santos eventually conceded the inevitability of state intervention with the formation in 1940 of several of the semi-autonomous agencies mentioned earlier, such as the Instituto de Fomento Industrial. As López had predicted, however, Dr. Santos checked many *lopista* reforms.

In many cases this was not difficult, for much of López' effort had been dedicated to propagandizing his program and winning support over determined opposition. Only in the latter part of his administration was he able to devote much attention to the actual operation of the reforms; this was made difficult in his final year following the successes of moderate Liberals in the 1937 congressional elections. With Santos vitiating the effect of many reforms by the simple expedient of ignoring them, Conservative leader Laureano Gómez openly supported the Fascist powers in the columns of his influential *El Siglo* and in the chambers of the legislature. The coming of World War II and the public debate over the relative merits of the Allied and Axis causes helped to blur many of the social issues raised by La Revolución en Marcha.

As Santos' term drew to its conclusion, Alfonso López announced his intention of returning to the presidency. If the Liberals had been divided over the nomination of Santos in 1938, they were now more bitterly rent by personal and political conflict. Santos, in temperament as well as philosophy more moderate than López, worked actively behind the scenes to stop the former president. His followers were determined to prevent another Revolución en Marcha, and they felt confident of success. Alfonso López, however, was not to be denied. Irate over Santos' policies, still rankling over his 1938 inability to stop him, López became involved as never before in political manipulation. Nothing would do but a second term in the presidential palace.

With one of the most bitter intra-party fights in living memory looming up, the Conservatives seized upon the opportunity to rebuild their own fortunes by fertilizing the Liberal seeds of disharmony. Dr. Laureano Gómez, whom we shall examine at great length in Part III, had in the preceding decade reorganized his party as a militant, highly-disciplined organization over which he exercised total command. Among Conservatives, the word of Laureano was law. Those who opposed him were expelled from the party and relegated to political oblivion. Gómez was not especially disposed towards those loyal to him, for unblinking obedience was not only expected but demanded. Anything less was heresy.

A dedicated Conservative of deep rightist beliefs, Gómez had attacked López with almost unbelievable ferocity and tenacity for many years, and his public position toward even the most moderate Liberals was harshly vitriolic. With the Liberal dispute now coming into the public domain, he seized upon it with all the wiles of the consummate politician he was. Aware that neither wing of the Liberal party was in a compromising mood, he heaped coal upon the flames, ever agitating and polemicizing. Would Gómez name a Conservative candidate in 1942? The time was inopportune. Would he support a moderate Liberal? No Liberal was deserving of the presidency. What about the return of López? Gómez announced an armed revolution under his personal command if López returned to office.

At the Liberal nominating convention, the magical figure of López carried the day, sweeping him to the nomination once more. Santos was unable to prevent the nomination, and cries of *"viva López"* and *"el gran reformador"* swept through the streets of Bogotá. Moderate Liberals bolted the party, held their own nominating convention, and chose Carlos Arango Vélez, a Bogotá lawyer. Member of a well-known family and son of a prominent diplomat,[9] he had no real chance of election, and this small chance was not improved by the reluctant support of the Conservatives, who considered Arango Vélez the lesser of two evils. The election was never in doubt, and López returned to office by a margin of 200,000 votes. Even as he did so, it was apparent that the Liberals were "fragmented, indecisive, lacking in the authority to speak for all their membership, much less for the whole nation."[10]

The next four years were genuinely sad for both Colombia and for Dr. López. The man who in his previous term had emblazoned his name on the pages of Colombian history now found himself frustrated, opposed, attacked at every turn. His second term has been called "the reform of the reformer," and he has been charged as having moved back to the political center. This is not entirely fair in view of the obstacles facing him.

To begin with, the legislature was in opposition, where the moderate Liberal wing banded with the Conservatives to block him. Workers grew disenchanted as López proved unable to deliver on the promises of the campaign and of his earlier administration. Wartime shortages and drastic revisions of the international economic picture brought inflation while the tide of prosperity waned. Coffee revenues were reduced, imports were inadequate, and the ranks of the unemployed swelled. Anti-*lopistas,* admitting no responsibility for obstruction of the president's program, attacked him unceasingly for failure to enact his program. The result was a swift diminution in the president's prestige and political effectiveness.

Laureano Gómez, although not carrying out his threatened revolution, was most effective in opposition. Continuing pro-Axis diatribes in *El Siglo,* he redoubled his efforts after the November, 1943, declaration of war on the side of the United States. Popular dissatisfaction grew over a war that the masses little understood. Its impact was felt as the reduction of shipping had far-reaching effects upon the economy. This was something the masses could understand, and Gómez' skillful attacks caused further deterioration in López' position. Dissatisfaction was mirrored in continual cabinet revisions, which in one eight-month period saw five complete changes in ministerial personnel.[11]

López, placed in a virtually impossible position, contributed to his own difficulties by a shift of emphasis. *Semana* wrote, "The young intellectuals who had once discoursed with him . . . were replaced by solid financiers, particularly aware of the poetry of figures. The ministers in López' second government did not become millionaires, but millionaires frequently became ministers. López lost the support of a great part of Liberal opinion. . . ." This was a secondary contributing factor in his difficulties, providing a basis for the argument that López had turned away from his earlier reformism.

New administrative problems also rose up to plague the president. The question of government bureaucracy, troublesome in the most literate and advanced of nations, proved a major burden. Inadequate experience, a shortage of trained personnel, and an undercurrent of petty corruption vitiated the effectiveness of reforms initiated during López' first term. Charges of mismanagement were directed against the government, and there was enough truth in some of them to gain public acceptance of those that went unproved.

The strongest characteristic of practical politics in the 1942 to 1946 period was a noticeable deterioration of democratic practices and moral responsibility. Laureano Gómez, for all the things that will be said about him later, was almost pathologically dedicated to the overthrow of López, and no measure was ruled out in his campaign against the government. The Liberals were blindly immersed in their own disputes, seeking supremacy within the party. Gómez shrewdly played upon these divisions in raising his party toward power over the body of López. Dr. Gómez gathered about him all the forces opposed to Alfonso López—the oligarchy, the land-owning aristocracy, growing industrial forces, the church, and even some of the younger Liberals disillusioned with López' increasing attachment to moderate elements of the same oligarchy. Constant personal attacks, largely unfounded, nonetheless tore at López' character and personal life. When a minor episode suddenly revealed the weakness of official morality, Laureano Gómez swept in for the kill.

The *asunto mamatoco* broke in the summer of 1943 when Mamatoco, a fighter with questionable skills inside the ring and a police record outside it, was found stabbed to death in a Bogotá park. Mamatoco's outside activities included the irregular publication of *Voz del Pueblo,* which decried the status of the urban workers. When the case entered the courts, a Conservative judge began a thorough investigation, and the issue was soon a *cause célèbre* in the press. Investigation implicated the Bogotá police chief and a former director of the national police force; both were Liberals. The scandal heightened when a high police official admitted that he had ordered the killing personally and directed an aide to carry it out.

The Conservative press cried assassin, and the people listened. The late Dr. Fluharty, who was in Bogotá at the time, alleges that the affair involved police graft and irregularities in a "pay-off."[12] Certainly there was Liberal complicity, and it was symptomatic of the low estate of public affairs. Beyond that, it was an ideal issue for the opposition, which played it to the hilt. Dr. Gómez charged the minister of government with personal complicity, and in turn was made the subject of a government libel suit. He was jailed after refusing to defend himself, and mobs formed outside the prison to free him. A vicious police counter-attack left rioters battered but undaunted. Ultimately the canny Conservative was released, but the vilification continued.

As pressures multiplied, it seemed problematical whether López would long resist the temptations of resignation. In mid-November of 1943 he requested permission of Congress to leave the country, in keeping with the provisions of constitutional Article 122. Few believed his declaration that his wife required skilled medical treatment not available in Colombia. The opposition was confident that he would not be back. But they had misjudged their man. He did return, openly tired and discouraged, to take up the duties of his office. Almost at once he admitted his desire to quit, reiterating the statement publicly.

The opposition continued its attack without abatement, including suspicious but purely circumstantial indications that López' son was involved with a woman of questionable virtue and was reportedly the last to have seen her before she was found dead. The story was too nasty and circumstantial to appear in the press, but rumors spread about the city that did perhaps more damage to López than an open attack from the press against which effective defense might have been mounted. The president himself might have withstood such defamation, but the involvement of his family and an ailing wife was too much.

Even the non-political military showed its dissatisfaction. In July of 1944 Dr. López went to southern Colombia to observe army exercises near the border. On the tenth, Colonel Diógenes Gil of the garrison at Pasto took López and several accompanying cabinet members into custody, issued the usual manifesto, and called upon fellow military men to join his cause. The people refused to accept the move, the army remained loyal to the constitution, and Gil himself was arrested, with President López and his ministers freed. The incident only interrupted affairs briefly and was not symptomatic of widespread military discontent. However, it was indicative of a growing feeling of responsibility by the military, according to which they might go as far as to intervene should the political situation become intolerable. The incident mirrored the belief, especially among the younger, foreign-educated officers, that the military itself should be the final repository of national sovereignty, with accompanying duties and obligations. The tradition of military non-involvement in political affairs was weakening.

Finally, on July 19, 1945, Alfonso López had exhausted his store of tolerance and the capacity to absorb attack. Declaring himself in the dilemma of "whether to continue fighting Congress or to resign," he sent his resignation to Congress. The legislators at first refused to accept the move, but were ultimately forced to do so. In August, three years to the month after the inauguration marked by high expectations and increasing political bitterness, Alfonso López left the presidency. Into his place stepped Dr. Alberto Lleras Camargo, who headed an interim government for the remaining year of the term.

Alberto Lleras Camargo, who will reappear in a prominent role later, was at the time a political *wunderkind,* unexpectedly thrust into the presidency at the age of thirty-nine. Despite the handicaps of a politically-prominent family in a nation where family dominance in national affairs is somewhat frowned upon,[13] he had begun at sixteen in the newspaper business, following a setback to the family fortunes. Gifted with exceptional talents as a writer and speaker, he was a prominent man of letters at twenty-five and before reaching thirty had served as cabinet minister during the first López administration. He had served in various diplomatic positions, including the ambassadorship in Washington, fortunately was in Mexico at the Chapultepec Conference during the days preceding López' resignation, and thus had avoided much of the political furor.

Although originally a member of the Santos wing, Lleras Camargo had moved to the *lopistas,* once serving the president as a ghost-writer.[14] However, his loyalty did not include servility; he was very much his own man. Even younger-looking than he was, a lean, hollow-cheeked individual of almost cadaverous appearance, his beliefs were somewhat eclectic. To him, "the French Revolution was the fountainhead of democracy,"[15] and his opponents charged him with undue allegiance to foreign principles of liberty and politics. But it was a time for practical politics, and no one realized it more than Lleras Camargo.

With the nation on the brink of civil war, Lleras Camargo formed the first real coalition government in many years, a Unión Nacional in which three moderate Conservatives held posts. In his final presidential message to Congress in 1946, Dr. Lleras Camargo explained that he had found himself without alternatives. Aided by the majority of the Liberals, some of whom were beginning to regret the forced removal of their old champion, he promised free and open presidential elections for May of 1946, managing to hold down the lid against pressures for the duration of his interim government.

THE LIBERALS FORFEIT POWER

The one-year coalition was not constructive, nor was it really intended to be. Such were the turbulent circumstances that nothing could be asked beyond general maintenance of democratic forms pending national elections. Events proved the Liberal division had not been healed by the withdrawal of the beleaguered López. The result was the return of the Conservatives and the passing of coalition government to their hands.

With the retirement of López, the left wing of the Liberal party passed almost by default to one of the most controversial figures in recent Latin America—Jorge Eliécer Gaitán. To his enemies Gaitán was a rabble-rousing, madly ambitious power-seeker; to his friends he was an inspiring leader, champion of the people, leader of the underprivileged, and opponent of oligarchy. There were elements of all these in Gaitán. He might well have become the dominant Colombian of his generation, but for his untimely death in 1948.

Born on January 23, 1898, to a family of humble surroundings, Gaitán as a youth led a hard life. In 1913 he received a scholarship to the Colegio de Araujo,[16] and from there he continued through university, studying penal law under Enrico Ferri in Italy[17] before returning to the Universidad Nacional as professor of law. In 1924 he wrote *Las Ideas Socialistas en Colombia,* in which he set forth a reform program for the Liberals. Gaitán called for a revitalization of the party by restoring its revolutionary fervor in adapting to a coming movement for social reform and renovation. Throughout his career Gaitán was fully aware of the impact the masses were to play, and he insistently advocated measures designed to improve their lot.

In 1929 he first achieved prominence when a peasant revolt broke out in the Santa Marta banana zone. A congressman at the time, Gaitán looked into the matter personally and, in summer of that year, presented his report in Bogotá. He made clear not only that the peasants had turned against management as a result of unjust treatment but that the army had been turned upon them to put down the uprising. There was a great national outcry against the apparent support by violence of foreign commercial interests, and Jorge Gaitán became the hero of the peasants. At about the same time, rebuffed in his efforts by Liberal leaders, he organized his own Unión Nacional Izquierdista Revolucionaria (UNIR). In the 1930's the UNIR strongly agitated for social reforms, although never succeeding in building up significant strength.

In time Gaitán realized that both his program and ambitions might best be served as a Liberal, and he returned to the party, becoming a member of the left wing. During intervening years he served in various capacities—senator, representative, minister of education, and mayor of Bogotá. In the latter capacity he was considered the best mayor the capital ever had.[18] He practiced law actively, becoming an outstanding expert on Colombian penal law, about which he wrote a perceptive work.

With the departure of López, Gaitán at forty-seven was the one individual with broad popular appeal. A self-made man with a background as lowly as many of his followers, Gatián was a spell-binding orator. A friend once said that he was not a good formal speaker but that he so magnetized his audiences that he became "one of the most powerful agitators in American history. His solutions for great problems were confused and reposed more in intuition than in meditation."[19] Despite his darkly-solemn visage and a slight tendency toward corpulence, he was an exciting, arm-waving, vigorously talented speaker, notwithstanding his faults. His eloquence was not too intellectual for his audiences, and what appeared to be tremendous power of conviction lay behind his basic simplicity of reason. Dramatic, belligerent, implacably anti-conformist, Gaitán was guided by a *mystique* of personal destiny that shaped his words as a champion of the little man, voicing predictions of doom for the "reactionaries."

Looking back with the advantage of hindsight, it is fair to say that he was genuinely interested in reform. There is no way of knowing whether he might have proved an irresponsible leader once in power, but certainly his program was unwaveringly consistent. In 1924 he wrote of man's need to enjoy the fruits of his labor, to live at more than a subsistence level rather than in immutable misery. This statement was not startlingly original, of course, but a commendable view that far too few Colombian politicians appreciated or advocated. In addition to brief service as Santos' minister of education, as minister of labor he "had seized every opportunity to favor the trade unions in their disputes with big business."[20] Germán Arciniegas, an astute if partisan observer, wrote that "no other South American politician can be recalled who had so strong a hold over the masses."[21]

Jorge Gaitán was unquestionably an exceedingly ambitious, opinionated, and egotistical individual in many ways, but that does not mean he would have been prevented from fulfilling proposed reforms had he attained the presidency. His premature death in 1948 was one of the most serious losses in recent Colombian history. Had he lived, the bloodshed and heartache of the following decade might have been avoided or at least lessened.

With President Lleras Camargo dedicating himself to the avoidance of outright civil war, the parties girded themselves for the 1946 elections. The moderate Liberals mistakenly assumed that López' retirement left them in firm control of the party, freeing them to return to pre-López times. Apparently the events of the past decade had made no impression; the moderate Liberals saw their chance to turn back the clock and to negate the tenuous progress of those ten years, following a path basically in agreement with the moderate Conservatives.

In this spirit the party convention nominated for president Gabriel Turbay, a *santista* who had been ambassador to the United States and at one time was foreign minister. Turbay, who was to pass swiftly from national prominence, was also a member of a prominent Bogotá family but suffered because of Syrian ancestry. This made him a *turco,* or one of Levantine blood. Colombians are not noted for tolerance toward people of such ancestry, particularly with the presidency at stake. Furthermore, Turbay was unacceptable to the pro-Gaitán masses and to many *lopistas.* There was no cause for surprise when the dissidents proceeded to nominate Jorge Gaitán.

Only the Conservatives could hope to gain from this circumstance, and Laureano Gómez was not one to miss the opportunity. The Liberals, intent upon their own affairs, paid little attention as Dr. Gómez announced non-participation. Even when he proposed support of Gaitán, there was no great flurry of attention. Gómez had recently succeeded in repairing brief dissension within his own party, and suddenly, a mere six weeks before election day, the Conservatives postulated the candidacy of their own Mariano Ospina Pérez. On March 24, 1946, by a vote of 360-3, the party convention chose its nominee.[22]

Gómez had been astutely aware that, had he run himself, the Liberals would certainly have closed ranks against him. Thus the choice of Ospina Pérez was wise. Furthermore, he was a declared partisan of National Union. In Ospina Pérez' acceptance speech he declared that "not by inheritance, nor by education, nor even by temperament . . . have I been a party man in the sectarian acceptance of the term. I believe that I can do service to the country in following the aspiration for national unity that grows each day until it becomes converted into an unquenchable national institution. Power is not a prize. . . ."[23] With Gaitán and Turbay taking turns flailing one another unmercifully, there was considerable popular appeal to a continuation of Lleras Camargo's approach. The absolute hands-off policy of the government, while infuriating many Liberals, was clearly a wise course for the president, who held to it staunchly.

The Liberals were faced with the necessity of uniting behind one candidate, yet neither wing would yield to the other. The moderates, whose intransigence extended back to Santos' first battle with López in 1938, refused to buckle before a *caudillo* with little party support—despite Gaitán's vast popular appeal. On the other hand, Gaitán saw little cause for concessions of his own. Genuinely distressed when Gómez had turned away from him—for Gaitán had been willing to accept Conservative support—he had momentarily considered a withdrawal.[24] The importuning of ardent *gaitanistas* changed his mind, however. He also realized that Ospina Pérez could slip into office without a majority. The firebrand was confident of his ability to assume control of the entire party once Turbay was defeated. So it was that the Liberals plunged ahead into the darkness, with the choice of a minority likely to prevail.

On May 5, 1946, Colombians cast 565,894 votes for Ospina Pérez; Turbay followed with 437,089; Gaitán, lacking effective organization, was third with 363,849. The contested election showed that the Liberals were clearly the majority party, and Gaitán's personal appeal in the face of opposition by the Liberal machinery was sizeable. The Conservatives, united behind their man, regained the presidency after an election in which their candidate received but 42 per cent of the vote. Laureano Gómez had won a shrewdly-calculated victory of great importance.

The Coalition in Conservative Hands

The choice of Mariano Ospina Pérez seemed to some a happy one, despite his failure to win an outright majority. A member of a prominent Antioquia family that had produced several political leaders, including a Conservative president in 1857, Ospina Pérez had attended Louisiana State University and received an engineering degree. After returning to Colombia he had built up his personal fortune while becoming an honored and admired figure. At fifty-five he was reaching the peak of his powers; intelligent, rather soft-spoken, and unfailingly courteous, he appeared to be the man of moderation Colombia needed. The image sharpened favorably when he stood by his pledge of National Union.

During his campaign Ospina Pérez seemed politically close to the Santos-Turbay brand of Liberalism. At the very least, he made his appeal as the best of several poor choices. Neither immoderate Left or Right, as were Gaitán and Gómez, and without the problems of a divided party such as Turbay had experienced, Ospina Pérez gave promise of leading post-war Colombia from the twilight zone. That he failed to do so was not his fault alone, for the Conservatives and Liberals shared in the guilt.

His task was not an easy one. Election as minority chief was bad enough, and beyond that he faced the Liberal-controlled two-house legislature. At the outset he enjoyed the reluctant approval of all of the Liberal leaders with the exception of Gaitán. The latter, however, was the most important, having swiftly become the undisputed party chief. Gaitán refused bluntly to cooperate with the government, and other

Liberals were far less influential. Turbay went to Paris and died within a year; Lleras Camargo became director-general of the Pan-American Union, then secretary-general of the new Organization of American States; López was inactive politically, keeping to his family and friends; and Santos was personally removed from daily party operations. Thus Gaitán alone remained, and there was no chance of agreement between him and the president.

Not only was the greatest Liberal power opposed to Ospina Pérez but the Conservative Gómez was also. He had remained quiet on National Union during the campaign, but afterwards came out against that principle. The changing relationship of Ospina Pérez and Gómez following the Conservative victory was critical, even as it is today. Many Liberals feared that Ospina Pérez would be a tool of Dr. Gómez. This did not materialize, although Gómez served as foreign minister for nearly two years. The president was in his own way a quietly stubborn man with a mind of his own. While his influence within the party was less than that of Gómez, it was sufficient for him to remain his own master.

As the architects of their party's greatest success in many years, the two men, who had been acquainted personally for many years, observed a tacit public truce. Gómez in particular realized that a break with Ospina Pérez would be detrimental to the party position, and he would do nothing to jeopardize it. Laureano Gómez well knew that the Conservatives were the minority party. The president, on his part, recognized Gómez' supremacy in party affairs, and with a populace of sharply divided loyalties, he dared not risk the loss of substantial Conservative support.

The president swiftly followed his inauguration by inviting six Liberals into the cabinet, thus establishing parity in the twelve ministries. As Ospina Pérez pointed out, this was greater opposition representation than Lleras Camargo had employed during the previous coalition. The new president was forceful in describing his policy of conciliation.

A party government, and especially that of a group, invariably is actuated by and acts on . . . the criterion of serving only partisan interests. . . . It is impossible to serve two masters at the same time: the nation and the party. . . . In Colombia's history we have eloquent examples of what a government along national lines stands for. . . . Under my administration there will be no political reprisals . . . no one will be barred from public office for party reasons; I faithfully guarantee to all the exercise of their natural and civil rights, and I shall . . . see that public liberties are respected.[25]

The president erred, however, in neglecting to consult Gaitán before announcing his Liberal cabinet appointments. Perhaps he did not realize that party control would shift to the fiery leftist. However, the day after the election the latter had announced his formal assumption of party leadership. "The oligarchies and the demi-Liberals caused Liberalism to lose its power . . . [we] must regain it."[26] He also told Alberto Niño, chief of the administration's security forces, "I request that Dr. Ospina and the Directorates of the parties work out with me a minimum program . . . to agree upon collaboration to attain it . . . union should be between party and party, not oligarchy and oligarchy."[27] Ospina Pérez failed to meet with him, however.

At the start of his term, Ospina Pérez moved with great caution, trying not to alienate the Liberals unnecessarily. There is little basis for the claim of Liberal Germán Arciniegas that Ospina Pérez was practicing a sly deception in order to provide the machinery for a prolonged era of uninterrupted Conservative rule. The new president was very much a representative of his party, to be sure, and would have governed without Liberal cooperation had it been possible. But within the unavoidable limitations, Ospina Pérez was willing to work for the national welfare. For all his initial moderation, however, he was out-of-step with the cries of the masses. In the fashion of Santos he preferred to grant minimal concessions while retaining and defending the position of the ruling elite. His greatest error—a limited awareness of the new forces alive in Colombia—was one of judgment rather than of evil intent.

By 1946, social and economic problems had become even more serious. With the close of World War II, Colombia found itself pushed to greater inflation; exports continued to drop as new markets were slow to open. At the same time, imports continued in small quantities while the United States poured products into the regions physically ravaged by the global conflict. Signing of the various peace treaties had not brought an immediate reopening of European markets for Latin American—and Colombian—products. The situation had been aggravated in Colombia by inattention during the 1942 to 1946 period, when political strife had pushed aside more basic economic questions.

A speculative passion seized the country, and "channels of black marketeering and privilege-manipulation of government bureaus had been formalized."[28] Dollars had accumulated through the years when luxury items were unavailable. Excellent coffee crops had lacked outlets in the wartime market, and the product was glutting the domestic economy. The wealthy put their money into real estate, rents were raised, and pressures on the urban proletariat increased. Colombia was trapped in a continually tightening circle of higher prices and static wages. Donald Dozer wrote for *Foreign Affairs* in 1949 that

> . . . the worsening economic plight of the masses of the Colombian people, aggravated by the war and postwar dislocations, was exacerbating already serious social tensions and increasing popular dissatisfaction with the national administration. . . . During the single month of March 1948, the cost of living index for an average working man's family rose by 17.3 points, to a new high of 283.8. . . . Control was powerless to curb speculation and prevent price inflation. However, efforts of organized workers to secure wage increases commensurate with these increases in the cost of living appeared in several instances to be thwarted by government action.[29]

Ospina Pérez was not totally inactive in the face of such developments. In late 1946 he pushed for implementation of the Social Security laws which had been largely ignored since their initiation in the 1930's.[30] Labor authorities were active in adjusting to the demands of young organizations, and the president intervened personally more than once to mediate labor-management disputes, notably in the oil industry. But these measures were inadequate for the gravity of the situation. Continually harassed by sniping from within Conservative ranks and occasional Liberal outbursts, the president was forced merely to hang on and hope for the best. Jorge Gaitán was steadily entrenching his position as undisputed leader of the Liberal party. The masses turned to their old hero increasingly, and he answered them with heated polemics against the government. Thus the shaky National Union tottered toward disintegration.

Gaitán's own position had changed. Before the 1946 elections he had been the leader of the underprivileged, fighting for them against the follies of the oligarchy, whether Liberal or Conservative. The fact that his own basic allegiance was to the Liberal party did not prevent him from attacking Liberal representatives of the ruling aristocracy. But now he was thrust into the position of party leadership, and his allegiance was to the Liberal party as a collectivity. He became responsible for a party program of non-cooperation with the government, thus isolating Liberal cabinet members from party machinery. Responsibility placed him in the position either of advocating policies which the moderate wing rejected or appearing false to his promises to the underprivileged. It was a difficult position and, for Gaitán, a wholly new one. In adjusting to it, he was obliged to become even more vehemently anti-government, and passions were whipped up correspondingly.

For almost two years after Ospina Pérez' inauguration, Jorge Gaitán was the dominant public figure in Colombia. His own efforts to better conditions by political means were unsuccessful. A reformist program of extensive government control of banking and credit, with a State Development Planning Commission attentive to the needs of workers and peasants, was defeated in the Congress, but he remained, with only slight disaffection, the champion of the lower classes, who had long since accepted him unreservedly. There seemed no doubt that he was destined for the presidency. No one had popularity to rival his, and Gaitán's hold on public opinion was so great that civil revolution would have followed any attempt to block his presidency by illegal means.

The year 1950 was some distance away, and peasants and workers were increasingly unwilling or unable to carry on under existing conditions. So the first smoldering outbreaks of violence began in isolated rural areas. This was the beginning of a problem which successive governments have had to grapple with. Even today there is rural violence. Although estimates are no more than rough approximations, modest figures reveal that more Colombians have been killed by brother-Colombians than all of the United Nations dead of the Korean "police action." Contrary to what has been written elsewhere, violent clashes did *not* begin following the Bogotá riots of 1948. Rather, they were mounting in intensity for some months before.

Impossible tensions brought street fighting between Liberal and Conservative partisans, bringing death in many small communities. Groups of bandits began to form, claiming allegiance to one of the two parties. National leaders decried such activities, but their own feuds were merely less violent manifestations of the spirit reflected by the fighting. At the outset, such violence was a purely local affair. There was no direction from Bogotá, but both parties were guilty by implication.

They had brought upon themselves this visitation of gathering fury by their adamant refusal to accept the changes in national life. For the Liberals, Gaitán himself pleaded for moderation. Yet he never had turned away from immoderation in the past, and when his policies were unsuccessful in the legislature, the people saw no other recourse.

The Conservatives took it upon themselves in many localities to persecute the Liberals, justifying their action by claiming to be defending the constitutional order. As the violence spread it took on an increasingly partisan hue over which national party officials had little control. Clashes grew in proportion as the situation was exacerbated by charges and countercharges in the daily press. Victims were described by either Liberal or Conservative journalists as martyrs to their respective party causes, and the opponents were excoriated as brutal, inhuman, and uncivilized.

Ospina Pérez, in his own quiet way a man of implacable determination, immediately set about the organization of forces to put down the violence. The *policía política,* or political police, came into power as an extension of existing security forces. Directed at first against all violence, these elements inevitably became an arm of the Conservative party. Liberals were widely persecuted while Bogotá officials denied charges made in Liberal newspapers. Liberal counterattacks in the rural areas, still planned and conducted by local leaders, contributed further to the bloodshed.

There is some disagreement over the responsibility for the political police, with both Ospina Pérez and Gómez being variously blamed. Most of those to name Gómez as its organizer have also characterized Ospina Pérez as weak and vacillating. However, the president was anything but hesitant. As a representative of the oligarchy he was never noted for the formulation and development of new policies and ideas. New departures seemed unnecessary. Furthermore, he never enjoyed a broad base of support comparable to that of López, Gaitán, or Lleras Camargo.

Somewhat isolated from both the people and his own party, Ospina Pérez was determined to put down recurring incidences of violence at all costs. With that goal in mind he directed the formation of the special security forces. His inability to control violence was no worse than that of succeeding presidents. The very nature of politics in

1946 and 1947 was such that these political police almost inevitably became "shock troops at the service of the Conservatives."[31] The fact is inescapable that responsibility for the organization of such a force, as Ospina Pérez himself conceded, was essentially his, and not Gómez'. Those who pictured Ospina Pérez as reluctant and unsure of himself were only partially aware of the temper of the times and the temperament of the president.

The early part of Ospina Pérez administration, then, was that of a shaky coalition placed under extreme duress. Cabinets were shifting constantly, rival hostilities were sharpened, and Congress either opposed the president or tied itself up in legislative knots. Continued inflation and labor difficulties increased political tensions, with unrest seeking an outlet in violent form. Party irresponsibility grew as extremists became vocal under the leaderships of Gaitán and Gómez. The latter was quietly laying plans for an era of undisputed reactionary Conservative rule. The demagogic appeals of Gaitán further unsettled conditions. Even those like this writer, who believe him to have been the great hope of the Colombian lower classes, must certainly concede that he was essentially a disturbing influence after 1946. Whether or not this was his fault is begging the question.

Gaitán's position was strengthened with the Liberal victory in the March, 1947, congressional elections. The over-all Liberal vote was 805,874; the Conservative, 653,986. Despite its majority of 151,888, the Liberal representation in the Chamber was cut from 80-47 to 73-58.[32] Of equal significance was the domination of *gaitanista* congressmen on the Liberal slate.[33] There could be no possible question of his party leadership, and the doom of National Union was brought nearer. Denouncing coalition government as an unnatural abomination, Gaitán preached a hard line urging the return of true Liberalism and reform.

By the spring of 1948 the situation was even worse. Liberal cabinet members had been withdrawn by Gaitán after the president had ignored a formal list of Liberal grievances. Rural violence was still growing; political police were open partisans for the Conservative cause, while Liberals were killed indiscriminately or driven from their homes after standing by helplessly while officials put the torch to their property. Bands of dispossessed Liberals began to gather in the mountains, fighting back with comparable ferocity and intolerance. Minister of Government

José Antonio Montalvo appeared before Congress to declare that the situation would be met "with blood and fire." The number of those homeless increased, death mounted, and many fled to the cities, while others sought refuge in Venezuela. In Norte de Santander, a center of violence, at least 200 families crossed into Venezuela from the Cúcuta area.[34] In January of 1948 a state of siege was decreed in Norte de Santander.[35]

On February 7, 1948, the citizenry gathered in Bogotá to protest the daily depredations. An estimated 100,000 met in the center of the capital to plead for peace and a restoration of civil rights. Jorge Gaitán, in perhaps the finest moment of his career, stood before the crowd, demanding and receiving absolute silence. As handkerchiefs waved at him, he spoke for all Colombians in a direct appeal to Mariano Ospina Pérez. "Mr. President, we are not here to present economic or political demands. All we ask is that our country desist from a line of conduct that puts us to shame in our own eyes and those of foreigners. We ask this in the name of mercy and civilization. . . . We ask that this persecution on the part of the authorities come to an end. . . . Put a halt, Mr. President, to violence. All we ask of you is the guarantee of human life, which is the least a country can ask."[36]

There was no official response.

The government occupied itself with preparations for the Ninth Inter-American Conference scheduled for April. As facilities were readied for the hemispheric delegations, Ospina Pérez chose to bypass the most popular leader of Colombia by refusing to name Gaitán to the Colombian delegation. Foreign Minister Laureano Gómez, whose supreme control over party apparatus seemed almost equalled by his unpopularity with the masses, became chairman of the conference.

As the delegations gathered in Bogotá in early April, there was an atmosphere of discontent that many diplomats commented upon. Propaganda pamphlets circulated the city. There were rumors of an attempt on the life of the United States Secretary of State George C. Marshall. An attempt to place a bomb in the capitol was foiled. One street mob attacked an automobile of the Ecuadorean delegation.

On Friday, April 9, 1948, Gaitán left his law office in the Nieto Building, barely two blocks from the site of the conference. It was just after 1:00 P.M., and the Liberal, with four friends, was on his way to lunch. As one of his companions later described it, the group was approached by a badly-dressed, heavy man with two days' growth of beard. Gaitán stepped aside, expecting the man to pass through the doorway behind, but he brushed by and turned around. As Gaitán began to walk away from the building, four shots were fired. Mortally wounded in the neck and shoulders, Jorge Eliécer Gaitán collapsed on the sidewalk.[37]

As his colleagues stood in shocked amazement, a lottery-ticket vendor rushed toward the assassin. Another man raced from a side-walk cafe brandishing a chair over his head. A mob gathered, and the killer was pummelled to death before their eyes. The thin veneer of civilization had cracked open; Colombia would never again be quite the same.

Chapter Four

THE BOGOTAZO

The Thin Veneer of Civilization

THE FIRST REACTION of the people was outrage. The assassin's body was kicked and beaten almost beyond recognition with chairs, shoe-shine boxes, fists.[1] The mob magically multiplied in number and set forth to avenge the crime. "An unconscious determination of death and of cataclysm impelled them."[2] They dragged the stripped body through the streets to the presidential palace, to which Ospina Pérez and his wife had returned a few moments earlier from a livestock show on the city outskirts.[3] The march on the palace, which some say included a fervent young Cuban named Fidel Castro,[4] was halted at the gates by the loyal presidential guard. No shots were exchanged, and the demonstrators withdrew without gunfire, leaving the naked remains of the killer behind. But trouble had barely begun. The death of Gaitán was, for Colombia, comparable to the assassination of Austrian Archduke Franz Ferdinand at Sarajevo.

Word spread swiftly, and the growing crowd became hysterical. There were cries of "Death to the assassins! Death to Gómez!" and "Down with the conference! Foreigners go home!" Howling for vengeance in one form or another, the throng went searching for Gómez at the foreign ministry. Not finding him there, they marched on the Capitolio Nacional, where the conference was meeting. Guards were overwhelmed, hundreds jamming into the foyer to begin the task of destruction. For a good twenty minutes they moved through the building, breaking furniture, destroying equipment, smashing out windows. Fires were lit on the outside of the buildings, and smoke was soon curling ominously toward the overcast afternoon skies.

With Gaitán's killer dead, the president guarded, and Gómez somewhere beyond reach, the mobs turned from their mission of vengeance to destruction and looting. Automobiles were seized, and trolley cars by the dozen were overturned and set afire. Other buildings were attacked, store windows smashed in and looted, public parks ripped up, churches desecrated. Carloads of hoodlums sped around the city; spotting a likely target, they would screech to a stop, men spilling out to attack with crowbars and even home-made bombs in hand, shouting "Abajo Ospina Pérez! Viva la revolución!" Violence spread to the suburbs, where Gómez' home was sacked and burned. Offices of *El Siglo* were burned, and the Liberal journals were not spared.

Within an hour of the time Gaitán slumped to the concrete, the mobs were swollen with the addition of the national police, who had immediately gone over to the rioters. The wave of terror and destruction rolled along, and, inevitably, liquor stores were broken into; the mood of the crowd turned murderously nasty as bottles were passed from hand to hand, emptied, and flung through nearby windows. Machetes began to appear, and witnesses in later years even swore that it was a common sight to see peasants honing their instruments on curbstones before turning to the next object in sight. New rumors circulated, notably one that priests placed in cathedral towers were firing upon the people. A new object of attack and hatred was provided. By the end of the day the Cathedral had been seriously damaged, and the homes of both the archbishop and the papal nuncio were nearly obliterated.

By 3:15 P.M. the army was out in force, and property destruction gave way to death. In various parts of the city, mobs were ordered to disperse, then simply to stop. Invariably the response was a concerted charge by the rioters. Shots would be fired in the air to no effect, and then the marksmen took dead aim. Several thousand died before nightfall, and countless more in the dark hours that followed. One eyewitness reports that the soldiers' marksmanship was excellent. "Over half of the several thousand dead I was to see in the next few days were killed in the same way—a bullet through the forehead."[5] Crowds again charged the steps of the palace, falling back after many lay dead on the steps, scattered among the litter of cartridges and shells. Further arms came into rioters' hands, and there was occasional machine-gun fire in reply to the army. A light drizzle had been falling since early afternoon, but it failed to dampen the unleashed fury of the rioters.

Foreign delegates had already been evacuated to safer quarters, and the army turned all its efforts against the mobs as troops from nearby villages began trickling into the capital. Not until Saturday did sizeable forces finally arrive to help the undermanned Bogotá troops. The streets were still seething with turbulence. As the fighting was slowly reduced in intensity by the determined Armed Forces, maids of well-to-do families were seen scurrying along sidewalks with baskets, into which an assortment of articles and food were swept. By 5:00 P.M. the danger to the presidential palace had lessened, and the main center of Bogotá was finally being brought under control.[6] An hour later, as the army fanned out across the city, only small detachments were left in the commercial center, and looting briefly flared up once more. Many of the commercial establishments were burning, and clouds of smoke billowed up into the twilight. Foreign correspondents covering the conference later compared the destruction to London at the height of the *luftwaffe blitz* during World War II.[7] Drunks once more lurched through the disrupted streets, now littered with refuse and merchandise that had been stolen, then discarded. At 10:45 a brief battle ensued outside the Embassy of the United States, and past midnight the skies were red from the flames except where blacked out by smoke.[8]

On Saturday the rioting in Bogotá became minimal as government troops regained control. A pall of smoke hung over the capital throughout the day. Some thirty-five buildings were gutted by fire; the historic church of San Francisco was among those sacked and burned down. By nightfall the city morgue was overflowing with hundreds of bodies, in part a tribute to the army directives to shoot first, asking questions later. Jules Dubois wrote of raising his hands in alarm at the command "manos arriba"—hands up. He turned around slowly to see a practical joker pretending to hold a pistol, laughing gleefully. A day later the same trick was tried on a Colombian officer, who whirled around and dropped his mock assailant with a shot from his .45. Bogotá was hardly the place for practical jokers.

As the capital quieted down, the outburst of pent-up emotion and resentment spread across the nation. For at least a month there was serious fighting in rural areas, after which violence reverted to its earlier form of Liberal versus Conservative. The worst outbreak triggered by the Bogotá holocaust took place in Cali and the surrounding region. In the capital of Valle del Cauca the rebels temporarily triumphed.

A town of basically Liberal loyalties, Cali had seized upon the news from Bogotá, including false reports of a new Liberal government, as an excuse to throw out local representatives of the Ospina Pérez regime. A *junta* headed by one Jordán Mazuera proclaimed the triumph of revolt and assumed the functions of government.[9] The city might have remained under Liberal control indefinitely but for the harshly resourceful measures of an obscure army colonel named Gustavo Rojas Pinilla, of whom much more was to be heard in the 1950's.

Commander of the Army's Third Brigade, Rojas Pinilla learned of the revolutionary government and sent a patrol to the municipal hall, where *junta* leaders were taken into custody and marched to the barracks for a confrontation with the commander. He was brief and to the point; within minutes the leaders were placed under formal arrest and locked up.

Disturbances were greater in the Negro-populated Puerto Tejada, where Conservative sympathies were almost non-existent. A Liberal congressman directed the jailing of legally constituted authorities, several of whom were tortured. Colonel Rojas Pinilla sent a strong force to the area, using necessarily harsh measures to restore order and government. He was equally efficient in pacifying the rebellious *caucano* region. As Azula Barrera wrote some years later, "Rojas was . . . by his attitude and his ways, the strong arm of offended legality and the guarantee that, although forced to relinquish power by a new *golpe de estado,* the traditional forces would be able to think of a heroic reconstruction of the juridical order."[10] The writer, influenced by his affiliation with Ospina Pérez, could not know that Rojas would rule all of Colombia one day under the guise of that same "strong arm of offended legality."

In retrospect, Colombians examined the wreckage and turned to the self-excusing rationalization that the entire episode could be attributed to Communist intrigue. Yet the fact remained that the society had been ailing from top to bottom. The lower classes were not alone in the horrendous outburst. No level of society dared admit that the nation was in a dire circumstance that might cause such an episode; the oligarchy, in particular, sought to identify outside influences as the responsible parties. Thus was preserved the myth that Colombia had been an idyllic, enlightened, and progressive democracy before the untoward happenings of April 9, "Black Friday."

The *bogotazo* was more than a dramatic outpouring of emotion and unrestrained, bestial violence. With the veneer of civilization stripped away, the entire moral fabric of the nation was revealed in its rotting reality. The people were demanding a social revolution in brutal terms.

Only lack of leadership, the unpreparedness of those who might have taken advantage of the situation, the alcoholic excesses of the mob in the capital, the firm stand taken by the President with admirable dignity, and the loyalty of the armed forces averted the overthrow of the Government. . . . Nor did the Church escape. . . . Even the wildest demagogue must have been alarmed to see, after nearly fifty years of peace, the appalling savagery of a mob whose feelings had been constantly exacerbated over a period of time by the preaching of doctrines above its standard of political education against a background of unsatisfactory standards of living.[11]

THE POLITICAL RESPONSE

At 8 P.M. Friday night, seven hours after Gaitán was shot, a delegation of Liberal leaders called upon the president at his palace. Darío Echandía, Gaitán's right arm and, some years before, provisional president during a López absence, was present. Others included party organizer Carlos Lleras Restrepo,* Luis Cano, Plinio Mendoza Neira, and Alfonso Araújo. Several aides were with Ospina Pérez, including Minister of Education Rafael Azula Barrera, who has written his first-hand account of the events. After Ospina Pérez dismissed his advisors, the Liberals proposed that he resign in favor of former president Santos, then in Paris, who as elected *designado* of the Senate was first in the line of succession.

The president, who had been in personal danger much of the afternoon, adamantly refused. "I would do Colombia more good as a dead president than as a fleeing president."[12] He admitted considering several courses of action, but resignation was not one of them. To quit would be an act of virtual treason, he added. He had taken an oath to protect and serve the republic, which he could best do by remaining in office.

* Lleras Restrepo is a cousin of Lleras Camargo.

After a moment of silence Luis Cano, Liberal journalist and a veteran of the political wars, burst forth emotionally that he had great admiration for the president but felt that resignation was the best means of facilitating the end of revolt. Carlos Lleras Restrepo repeated the request that Ospina Pérez resign. Santos could be back from Paris in a day or two. In the meantime, he argued, Darío Echandía could be named minister of government and exercise the reins of administration.[13] The president again replied that he would not consider resignation. The situation was delicate, and he would make no further decision for several hours. In a quiet voice he insisted that his departure would result only in prolonged bloodshed. The Liberals finally withdrew with a promise that Ospina Pérez would keep them informed. Echandía, who had been with Gaitán at the Clínica Central when he died, remained mute throughout the meeting, his eyes cast down much of the time.[14] Unsure of the Liberal request, he was also deeply affected by the death of his friend, perhaps more so than any of the others.

Reports had already arrived at the presidential palace telling of the defection of several towns, including Cali, Puerto Tejada, and virtually all of the Cauca Valley.[15] Radio stations in rebel hands were broadcasting conflicting reports. Some stated that a provisional *junta* was in control. Others claimed that Echandía had already assumed the presidency. There was also a report that Echandía and other Liberals had been taken into the government.

Ospina Pérez remained in his palace through the night, receiving periodic reports from Bogotá and elsewhere. At 8:00 A.M. Saturday morning several generals called on the president to report personally. They declared that the capital was apparently under control, but news from the rest of the republic indicated that violence was spreading and could be quelled only after an extensive military campaign. With all due deference, they advised setting aside the constitution in favor of a military *junta*. Ospina Pérez countered by suggesting a military cabinet under his own direction. They replied that only a *junta* could properly deal with the situation. The president again refused, pointing out that even if it returned the presidency to him after twenty-four hours, it would mean going beyond the constitution. Whatever remedy he adopted, said the president, would have to be in accord with the constitution.[16] He ordered the generals back to their posts, except for pro-Liberal General Germán Ocampo, who was asked to remain at the palace.

There was never any question of army loyalty. True to its non-political tradition, the military defended the constitutional order, accepting the decisions of the beleaguered President. As Ospina Pérez later wrote, ". . . officers and men of the Army, loyal to their oath and faithful to the example of our national heroes, fell—some of them at the gates of the Presidential Palace—defending our institutions against the arms which the police had put in the hands of the mob."[17]

Only a few minutes later Ospina Pérez reached the one remaining alternative. He proposed the restoration of National Union and sent word to Darío Echandía requesting Liberal collaboration in a new coalition. He urged all Colombians of good will, whatever their politics, to unite for the pacification of the nation. The fatigued Echandía, who like the president had spent a sleepless night, called together party leaders for a brief meeting in the offices of El Tiempo, half a block from the spot where Gaitán had been struck down. They accepted Ospina Pérez' offer with the proviso that neither Gómez nor the equally unpopular José Antonio Montalvo would be included in the new cabinet.[18]

Echandía returned to the palace and met with the president to discuss composition of the cabinet. Echandía became minister of government, with General Ocampo named minister of war. General Régulo Gaitán* was named director of the National Police and was ordered to reorganize and re-form that discredited body. Other ministerial posts were divided between Liberals and Conservatives. Just before Echandía's arrival, the president also spoke by telephone with Laureano Gómez, who suggested diplomat Eduardo Zuleta Angel as foreign minister.[19] Gómez said he was leaving by plane for Medellín and would leave the country. Gómez blamed the Liberals for the raging bogotazo, suggesting a conspiracy with the Communists. He was not enthusiastic at the prospect of a coalition government but made little comment. A few years later the two men would be arguing publicly over the decision to invite Liberal collaboration.

The immediate announcement of another National Union under Conservative direction had no effect on the rioting, but in the months

---

* Not a close relative of Jorge Gaitán.

to come it was instrumental in calming the nation. All but a few Liberals responded to Echandía's order for cooperation with the government, and in the major cities, peace was restored. As the effervescent dementia wore off, Ospina Pérez addressed the nation on Sunday night, April 11. He reiterated his determination to ride out the storm. "I have in my hands the banner of legitimacy as President of the Republic, and I promise that it will not have to be removed while a drop of blood flows in my veins. I have never practiced a sectarian policy but rather the most ample and generous that the Nation has known. . . ."[20]

The program of National Union, he proclaimed, enjoyed Liberal support and was in accord with a general agreement whereby the government was reintegrated "with the collaboration of the collectivities in equal proportion. . . ." He concluded with a final appeal for stability and calm. "Peace and harmony will prevail within a short while in all the territory of the Republic; normality will return, and thanks to the common effort, we will reestablish what was lost. . . . Each day brings its own anxiety, and that of today is the anxiety of pacification, of serenity and of a vigorous effort in favor of national reconstruction. Nothing of bitterness, nor of dispiriting pessimism. Standing at the foot of ruins, I [nevertheless] believe in Colombia, and I have faith in you."[21]

On April 12 a telegram from Paris declared Eduardo Santos' approval of the new coalition. He carefully praised the presumed heir-apparent Echandía. "Echandía has saved the liberal honor. He must be blindly supported. If he should fail, the country and the party would be lost. When the country agonizes dishonorably before the entire world, it is impossible to think of partisan interests. The only thing that I consider possible, and which I will serve without rest, is that of providing a broad and solid national union to try to reconstruct the essential bases of Colombian life. . . ."[22]

The Armed Forces broke the back of the rebellion, and the new coalition settled down to the task of restoration. The salving of national feelings was emphasized rather than tackling social and economic maladies that the *bogotazo* had protested. Basic problems were swept under the rug as expeditiously and inobtrusively as possible. All concerned were dedicated to forgetting the holocaust as swiftly as possible.

WHO WERE THE CONSPIRATORS?

In its haste to find a scapegoat, the government directed charges of complicity against international communism. Intrigue by the leftist Venezuelan Acción Democrática was also blamed. Secondary blame was later placed on the Liberals, who responded that the Conservatives themselves had much to gain from the death of Gaitán. The full story behind the *bogotazo* will never be known. That there was some degree of Communist involvement is not seriously questioned.

The indictment of the Communists was all too convenient, and evidence suggests that they were not immediately responsible. At the same time, conspiratorial plans were afoot, and local Reds were swift to take advantage of the situation. President Ospina Pérez wrote in later years that he "ascribed the origin to international communism." He then continued that, as a Colombian, he had "attempted to exonerate the Liberal party for any responsibility for these acts."[23] This was followed by implied criticism of the role the Liberals played following their delegation's visit to the palace.

The Colombian Communists themselves have never wielded much strength. In the 1920's the Grupo Comunista was organized by Silvestre Savisky, a Russian immigrant with missionary enthusiasm.[24] Among its members were many who later became prominent non-Communists, including Gabriel Turbay. The Grupo Comunista later grew into the Partido Socialista Revolucionaria (PSR), which was Communist in orientation but unaffiliated with the Communist International. After several years dedicated to propaganda, it joined the Third International during the Second Congress in 1927 and was soon sending members to Moscow for instruction.[25]

During the banana strike and peasant revolt in which Gaitán sprang to prominence, the Reds reached a high point, after which they declined once again. When Alfonso López stole their social-minded attentions, leader Gilberto Vieira supported the regime. On May Day of 1936 he spoke from the balcony of the presidential palace "in support of the . . . policies of President López."[26] A second drive for prominence began in the early 1940's following the reorganization and reunification of rival labor groups into the Confederación de Trabajadores de Colombia (CTC), which the Reds began to infiltrate. In 1944 the Communists, now called the Partido Social Democrático (PSD), polled 30,000 votes in national elections and won four seats in the Chamber and one in the Senate. This was the high-water mark of their efforts.

Just as López had stolen their thunder in the 1930's, the appeals of Jorge Gaitán weakened the Communist position, and in the 1946 elections "the rout of the Communist Party became complete. . . ."[27] The victory of Ospina Pérez brought a switch in allegiance from Gabriel Turbay to Gaitán, who had previously been denounced as a "Fascist." The 1947 elections were a debacle for the party, which then split as a result of internecine disagreements. After July of 1947 there were three splinter groups: the "official" Partido Comunista of Gilberto Vieira, the Partido Comunista Obrero of Augusto Durán, and a small body of petroleum workers under Diego Montaña Cuellar.[28]

The Colombian Communists, then, were weak and divided at the time of the *bogotazo*. As the chief of security forces later wrote, "Russian Communism does not take seriously this two-fronted, indigenous Communism of ours, and although it uses and directs it without explanations, holds it in contempt which it does not try to hide."[29] The role of the local Reds is only a part of the story, for most allegations charged that planning and direction were exercised from outside Colombia. It would be unwise, however, to give too much credence to pre-*bogotazo* reports of extensive arms shipments from abroad and the concomitant arrival of non-Colombian Communists.

The major source of information that international communism played a major role is again security chief Alberto Niño, a Conservative and a member of the government dedicated to "proving" that the episode was a conspiratorial plot by foreigners. Contemporary Latin America is full of political disturbances in which the Communists have been blamed for failings of the national government. The very holding of the Inter-American Conference was an important cause for the arrival of foreign Communists. Quite naturally there were large numbers in Colombia, and this is not disputed. Such has been the case with many hemispheric meetings; even the tyrannical Venezuelan regime of Marcos Pérez Jiménez in 1954 was unable to avoid the coming of Red trouble-makers.

Public statements by Colombian Communists before the conference have also been cited as evidence that a Communist plot was well-advanced. Typical was a comment by Vieira two weeks before the rioting, when he reportedly said that the Communists felt that "the new political conditions created in the country require a full revolutionary battle of the working class and the people. . . ."[30] But such a statement is typical of Communist leaders in non-Communist states. An examination of Bogotá newspapers at almost any time in recent years includes comparable statements by Vieira and others. Such declarations are in themselves inadequate proof of detailed revolutionary conspiracy.

Charges that the local party organized the affair, then, can be dismissed. Such an allegation, as Galbraith points out, "is not consistent with evidence or the course of events."[31] If the outburst is to be blamed on Communist direction, it must be based upon the events of the riots themselves. The question, then, must be: what was the involvement during the *bogotazo* itself? When the rioting first broke forth, there was no indication of either Colombian or foreign Communists in the mob. Shortly after the first explosion, however, several radio stations were seized, including the Radiodifusora Nacional, which broadcast continuous calls to arms. Communist Diego Montaña Cuellar exhorted his listeners to burn the presidential palace and pillage business establishments.[32] "The leftist revolution has begun! Colombians: the army is with the people. Soldiers of Colombia: join us! Your comrades in Bogotá have done so. Long live the leftist revolution! Colombia is in the vanguard. The revolution of socialism! The liberation of the proletariat!"[33]

The radio stations were perfect outlets for propaganda, and assuredly the Communists used them. Yet there is no certainty that pre-planning was involved. Mobs first gathered without Communist direction, and only some minutes later did Reds begin to appear in the crowds or seize radio microphones to broadcast inflammatory lies. This proves only the revolutionary opportunism of local Communists in seizing upon a situation not of their own making. As time passed they joined the throngs to direct and increase the fury of the populace.

Before Friday was out, a "Tribunal of the People" in Barrancabermeja, Santander, was directing attacks against the clergy. Atrocities in Ibagué and Cartagena included churchmen among the victims. At

Armero, Padre Pedro María Ramírez attempted to calm the crowds, was bodily seized and killed, his church profaned. And in Barranquilla priests were also taken by force and beaten to death. Outrages against the church—a mark of Communist opportunism—were far greater in the countryside, where religious faith had traditionally been more fervent than in the cities. A Soviet banner even flew briefly over the governor's palace in Barranquilla until an army officer pulled it down.[34] "Churches, convents, ecclesiastical colleges, schools and institutions were burned, and the clergy were seized, killed and in some cases, horribly mutilated."[35]

Back in Bogotá the Inter-American Conference had decided to continue, and on April 14, Pan-American Day, meetings reconvened in the Gimnasio Moderno, a high school in the Chapineros suburb. Before the close of the conference sessions were again being held in the partially-repaired Capitolio.[36] United States Secretary of State George C. Marshall first announced that the riots were Communist-inspired, and postponement of the conference "would mean giving to Communism the battle for Latin America." This carried much weight at the time; it is too often forgotten that Marshall later amended this, declaring that the Communists were guilty of taking command of riots after they had begun.

Revolutionary pamphlets circulated, and on Saturday the presidential palace received a hastily-published document accusing the "murderous government of Ospina Pérez" of ordering the assassination. The government then had allegedly blamed the Communists. "A thousand times they lie, the assassins [i.e., the government]. Liberals and Communists, united in this historic hour of the country, will save the democracy, overthrowing the murderous government and creating a revolutionary *junta* to assume power. In the popular militias of the armed people, united liberals, communists and democrats in general will form the popular army to reestablish democracy in Colombia."[37] This was characteristic of several such leaflets, obviously the work of Communists or fellow-travelers. In all likelihood they had been turned out during the night of April 9, probably in the Embassy of the Soviet Union.

With order re-established in Bogotá, an investigation was immediately mounted. In a panic appeasement of the masses, even Scotland

Yard was called in, although their findings were never published. The murderer of Gaitán was tentatively identified as one Juan Roa Sierra, an obscure man who heard voices and was apparently a Rosicrucian.[38] It was generally agreed that the murder was a private affair unrelated either to international communism or internal politics.

The possible involvement of the Venezuelan government and of complicity by Gaitán himself are theories that have never been completely put to rest. The Ospina Pérez government announced having found a substantial check from Venezuelan former president Rómulo Betancourt to Gaitán. Furthermore, Venezuelan news broadcasts had announced several developments of the riots *before* they occurred. There were premature reports of the uprising, its success, and the establishment of a provisional government. Witnesses also reported cries from rioters that Venezuelan troops were crossing the border, although this latter can be dismissed as wishful thinking by exuberant mobs calling for Ospina Pérez' downfall.

This theory continues by claiming that a revolution was being planned, after which Jorge Gaitán was to become head of a provisional government. If not a party to such a plan, Gaitán at least knew of it. At the last moment he became timorous, withdrew approval of the conspiracy, and paid with his life in retaliation by the Communists, who were involved along with Rómulo Betancourt.

This is not wholly implausible and has thus been mentioned despite no more than a few circumstantial indications that it might have been true. It should be pointed out, however, that most exponents of this view have been avowed rightists to whom Betancourt himself was a virtual Communist. However, Betancourt is currently providing Venezuela, during his second non-successive presidential term, with a left-wing, anti-Communist, pro-democratic government of considerable ability.

Betancourt himself admits having been a Communist as a young man. Indeed, he was influential in the establishment of the Costa Rican Communist party under Manuel Mora Valverde. But even in 1948, he had long since broken with the Reds. Colombian allegations of a connection with the over-publicized Caribbean Legion are also unconvincing. This small raggle-taggle band of indiscriminate revolutionaries and political adventurers had long been exaggerated as to power and influence, and its basic orientation was, at best, vaguely liberal. Betancourt's own Acción Democrática (AD) was no more Communist than was he.

There is, then, no sure evidence of Communist complicity. What *is* clear is that the Communists were devilishly adept in using the riots to their own advantage, actively inciting the throngs after the assassination of Gaitán had started the violence. The actual shooting of the Liberal has never been proved as part of a larger scheme. Macdonald has written that the chain of events suited the Communists perfectly. "If they did not arrange the affair, at least they took full advantage of their opportunity to encourage mob violence."[39] Robert J. Alexander, an outstanding North American authority on Latin American communism, states categorically that the insurrection gave the Reds "undeserved publicity." The *bogotazo* was not basically the planned work of the Communists. "They did not have the prestige or influence to cause the kind of thing that happened on April 9, 1948."[40]

The tragedy of the *bogotazo* lay beyond the destruction of life and property, the profanation of churches, the atrocities towards priests, or even bestial violations of defenseless young schoolgirls. Beyond considerations of basic humanitarianism, the loss of Gaitán was not the greatest consequence either, although contemporary Colombia would have been quite different had he lived. The saddest element of the affair was the deliberate refusal of responsible officials to recognize the true meaning of the insurrection. A socially and economically oppressed people were begging for new policies and for a basic understanding of their plight. The common rejection of national reality was a philosophical and temperamental crime for which the political leaders—including many of those still active today—cannot with any justice be exonerated.

Chapter Five

NATIONAL UNION GOVERNMENT

Confusion amid Liberal Ranks

FOR SOME THIRTEEN months following the April rioting, the two parties worked within the collaborative government framework to restore a degree of normality to the nation. As this was gradually achieved, deterioration of the coalition set in. Extremist Conservatives opposed the principle of collaboration in the absence of Laureano Gómez, while Liberal demands also increased. Unsettled socio-economic and class antagonisms made another failure of National Union likely. The Liberal party was held together largely because of the determined patriotism of the hard-working Darío Echandía, the new party chieftain.

Born in 1897 in Chaparral, Tolima, Echandía had been a party leader for years. His presidential aspirations had twice been denied through the party division, which in 1937 and 1942 had left him waiting for a nomination that never came. The Liberals had been split as early as 1929, but knowledge of the fact was confined to the circles of policy makers until the 1937 preparations for the forthcoming presidential elections.[1] The party membership then learned of the division, and it immediately became more serious.

Echandía had been a leading representative of the Liberal left but lost out as the nomination went to the moderate Eduardo Santos. He was still in the reformist branch when Alfonso López ran for a second term in 1942. The rise of Jorge Gaitán again relegated Echandía to second place following the López retirement in 1945. However, he worked closely with Gaitán and was the man who announced the death of the Liberal leader from a window of the Clínica Central on the afternoon of April 9.

In the months immediately preceding the riots he had become increasingly moderate, despite his proximity to Gaitán, and Echandía's standing with the moderate wing was higher than before. When taken into the second Ospina Pérez coalition, he set to work immediately to bind up national wounds, although he tended to share the feeling that restoration of order was the only real task. He became a familiar sight trudging in and out of the presidential palace with a continual air of fatigue and apparent pessimism. Echandía always looked a bit sad and even apathetic, although his personality was *simpático*.[2] With an aura of moral solemnity, he had for years been referred to by admirers in Congress as a "splendid spectacle." As a speaker he was not noted for eloquence but rather for strong, methodical logic.[3]

There were those who felt Echandía was too detached, too much a philosophic dreamer who lacked necessary temperamental fire. But his prestige had been growing, and he was satisfactory to both López and Santos. A man of basic middle-class background, Echandía had firm ideas of liberty, a belief in peaceful evolution, moral rectitude, and personal magnanimity. In the critical period following the April disturbances, he was temperamentally the best man to pull the Liberals back together. If the divided party had any one representative leader, it was Darío Echandía.

The Liberals had others who also aspired to party leadership, and there was a sometimes undignified scramble in laying claim to the mantle of Gaitán. Among those jostling Echandía was the respected Francisco de J. Chaux. At fifty-nine a large man with thirty-five years' political experience, Chaux had been born in Quibdó, a member of the misnamed *generación de centenario,* which included Santos, López, Ospina Pérez, and others. Moving in his youth to Popayán, Chaux was generally recognized as a *caucano.* Receiving a law degree from Cauca University, he was elected as deputy to the departmental legislature, then became representative, and finally national senator from Cauca. He had held diplomatic posts, and was minister of industry under the Conservative government of Miguel Abadía Méndez and the following Liberal administration of Olaya Herrera.[4]

Chaux was an expert lawyer and an eloquent speaker, noted for his overpowering voice and typically-*caucano* rhetoric. After supporting the splinter candidacy of Arango Veléz in 1942, he became a convinced *gaitanista* who worked tirelessly in 1946 for the leftist's campaign. Thus his credentials as a member of the left-wing Liberals were sound, and many considered him the true heir of *gaitanismo*. Like Echandía an obvious presidential aspirant, Chaux was handicapped a bit by his age. Although an impressively serious figure of precise courtesy and a cavalier solemnity, Chaux looked older than he was with a white-fringed pate and very deep-hewn facial lines. Some felt that his day was past, and, notwithstanding three decades of public service, he was less well-known nationally than Santos or Gaitán, or even Echandía.

There were other restive Liberal elements following Gaitán's death. As Echandía was concerned with administrative decisions, many ardent *gaitanistas* looked elsewhere for party leadership. The most notable group was headed by Darío Samper, who had collaborated with Gaitán on publication of *Jornada*. Samper and his followers were opposed to collaboration with the Conservatives, and they were vocal in opposing many of the measures the Liberal party in effect had approved through sharing responsibility with the government.

The congressional session scheduled for July 20 was in jeopardy of postponement, as many of Ospina Pérez' advisers proposed delay in the face of unsettled conditions. In early July, however, the four-man Directorio Liberal Nacional (DLN)—Chaux, Lleras Restrepo, Jorge Uribe Márquez and Parmenio Cárdenas—called on Ospina Pérez to reaffirm their support of National Union and express willingness to work for a return of normality in Congress. Thus reassured, the president announced on July 16 that the session would open as scheduled on the 138th anniversary of the Colombian declaration of independence.

In so doing the president acted in defiance of many Conservatives,[5] and a party convention held at the same time refused to support his decision. It was left to the Directorio Nacional Conservador (DNC) to make a choice. Soon after the close of the convention the DNC decided it could scarcely defy the president at the time and announced support of his announcement.[6] Shortly before Congress convened, representatives of the two parties signed a five-point truce that agreed on the necessity for parliamentary peace and electoral reforms.[7]

On July 20, 1948, the session began with Ospina Pérez urging members to "rise to the height of the historical responsibility of saving the country" by strengthening unity and winning "the veneration of future generations."[8] He announced a program under which employees would share in the profits of private enterprise. Workers from the first day of 1950 would share all profits over 12 per cent from industrial and agricultural complexes capitalized at more than 100,000 pesos.[9] After deliberation the legislators approved the proposal and turned to other matters.

This legislature had been formulated by the 1947 congressional elections, and the Liberals controlled both branches—the Senate by 34-29 and the Chamber by 73-58. Liberals Carlos Lleras Restrepo and Gustavo Romero Hernández presided over the upper and lower houses respectively, with Conservatives Guillermo León Valencia and Augusto Ramírez Moreno in turn exercising the two vice-presidencies. The two chambers began parallel debates on the question of the state of siege declared by the president in April, and discussions centered on the meeting of Congress while Ospina Pérez could constitutionally bypass them by emergency powers permitting rule by executive decree.

The Chamber of Representatives in particular felt that the state of siege was no longer necessary; with Congress in session, executive decrees should give way to normal legislative procedures. The issue cut across party lines. Minister of Government Echandía startled many Liberals by supporting the thesis of continued rule by decree, announcing that the state of siege should continue at least until both houses had passed upon the legality of executive decrees already issued. He noted accurately that the government had carefully refrained from interfering with congressional routine. After threatening to resign, he won grudging party agreement.

Debate on other issues was inconclusive, and in the meantime, Liberal and Conservative leaders were meeting at presidential suggestion to lay out an electoral reform acceptable to all. In late August, Carlos Lleras Restrepo spoke for the Liberals in announcing that he was hopeful of agreement. "A decision between the historic Colombian collectivities on the electoral problem would be truly exemplary and singular in the political history of the country. . . . In a century of partisanship, the two collectivities have been 'radicalized' much more by hates than by doctrines. The title of liberal or of conservative has in Colombia an hereditary character across the generations."[10]

Growing Liberal dissension temporarily interrupted debate of an electoral law, however. Lleras Restrepo found it almost impossible to unify the Liberals despite powerful assistance from Echandía. Amid growing criticism from Darío Samper he resigned from the Liberal Directorate in early September, bitterly charging that the Samper Liberals had conspired against party unity. *Jornada* shot back that Lleras Restrepo had been disloyally directing Liberal oligarchies and "anti-*gaitanistas.*" The dispute weakened Echandía's position in the cabinet, and there were fears that he might be forced to quit the coalition, thus bringing down the fragile National Union that he and the president had been doggedly erecting on precarious foundations.

The basis of the disagreement was the question of the 1950 presidential candidacy, for, as the newsweekly *Semana* pointed out, there were few who could explain differences of principle between the two groups. Followers of the major candidates refused to follow their leaders' demands for party unity, and many anticipated the March, 1949, congressional elections as a potential plebiscite indicative of public opinion. This vote might reveal which Liberal pre-candidate enjoyed broadest national strength.

The Conservatives looked on contentedly as the Liberals squabbled. *Jornada* increased the intensity of its anti-Lleras editorials, while Santos' *El Tiempo* railed at the *gaitanista* journal for irresponsibility, at the same time itself indulging in attacks on Chaux, whom it considered immoderate. The Conservative *El Siglo* and *El Eco Nacional* almost audibly purred over the spectacle of continued Liberal disunity.

In early October of 1948 Darío Echandía attempted to rally the Liberals with one of the finest speeches of his career. In an hour-long address he told the Senate that the fundamentals of patriotic reconciliation demanded continued collaboration.[11] The immediate effect was powerful but short-lived. With his patience finally exhausted, he announced his "irrevocable" resignation from the Liberal Directorate, where he had been a member only a matter of weeks. He declared that Liberal opposition to the government was in effect a vote of non-confidence.

Legislators denied this, but Echandía was adamant and soon presented his terms to the party. He insisted on a two-man directorate composed of Lleras Restrepo and Chaux. Liberal proposals for electoral reform would have to be supported, or the six Liberal cabinet members would retire from politics. The party rank-and-file agreed almost immediately, and the crisis passed, but Echandía's support was as tenuous as that of Ospina Pérez within the Conservative ranks.[12]

Directors of the two parties resumed meetings, and in October presented a sixty-article proposal drawn up by Lleras Restrepo and Conservative Gilberto Moreno Trujillo. Further action stalled, and in mid-November the president invited leaders to the palace in the hope of saving the projected revision. Ospina Pérez was joined by Echandía, Foreign Minister Zuleta Angel, Lleras Restrepo, and Conservative Director Luis Navarro Ospina. Additional impetus came with the news of a Venezuelan military *golpe* against the civilian Gallegos government in Caracas. Ultimate agreement was finally reached, appearing first in the columns of *El Siglo*.

Congressional and municipal elections would be delayed until June of 1949, and new registration of voters would be effected before the 1950 presidential campaigns, based upon the advice of a foreign mission. A revised Corte Suprema Electoral (CSE) would include the membership of the republic's oldest living former president (Alfonso López), the rector of the Universidad Nacional (Liberal Luis López de Mesa), the manager of the Banco de la República (Conservative José Manuel Arango), and the two oldest judges of the Supreme Court (Liberal Ricardo Hinestroza Daza and Conservative Eleuterio Serna). All decisions of the electoral court would be unanimous, except for the final declaration of actual election results.

Before the elections the court would draw up a list of thirty Liberal and thirty Conservative names, sending it to the national registar. He would in turn reduce the list by half, sending one Liberal and one Conservative to each of the fifteen departments to oversee the voting and report departmental results to the court. If the representatives in any one department submitted conflicting reports, the court would act as final arbiter. All decisions would be irrevocable.

Both houses of Congress accepted the accord, and by the time legislators had adjourned on December 16 for the holidays, political turmoil had died down noticeably. The CSE had been installed; a department of immigration created; amnesty for political crimes of April, 1948, accepted; a preliminary statute for the Paz del Río steel mill approved; and a moderate revision of the labor laws enacted. At midnight on the sixteenth, President Ospina Pérez announced the lifting of the state of siege after 251 days. Declaring that order had been re-established, he returned the nation to regular civil processes. New departmental governors were named, although military men were appointed in Boyacá, Santander, Norte de Santander, and Tolima.[13]

Efforts to improve the economic situation in the months after April had been minimal. The Instituto de Fomento Algodonero had been established to protect cotton, the Colombian "white gold." It was to draw capital from a new tax on imported cotton, both as a means of revenue and a curb on national textile industries which imported cotton rather than buying on the domestic market. Five agricultural experimental stations were also set up, with eleven substations and five regular stations for experimental work on cattle.[14]

Other measures were minor; temporary concessions which were made following the first fearful wave of post-*bogotazo* recriminations accomplished little. Executive Decree 1483 set forth a program of land parcellation, but characteristic of the president's narrow approach was his statement that proprietors had to be increased numerically "in the present circumstances."[15] Programs of rural electrification, irrigation, and housing had been started earlier, and there was little change during the remainder of Ospina Pérez' presidency. His approach continued essentially oligarchical. Set in the traditions of his class, he was unable to view events with broad national understanding.

With Liberals disorganized and the government trying to rush back to "business as usual," the lessons of the *bogotazo* had clearly been ignored or misunderstood. Typical of the oligarchical attitude was a series of declarations by the head of the stock exchange in July, 1948. Gonzalo Restrepo Jaramillo reported that political issues were the overriding factors in the April disturbances. Writing in *El Espectador,* he proposed tax reduction as further protection for the upper classes. Once greater prosperity accrued to the propertied, he argued, it would also trickle down to the masses. He asked that the government improve conditions for "those who produce wealth," rather than viewing them as the villains of society.[16]   In short, the oligarchy could do no wrong.

LIBERAL WITHDRAWAL FROM THE GOVERNMENT

Upon their return to Bogotá from the holiday exodus, politicians immediately plunged into preparations for the June elections.   The Liberals became embroiled in new disputes which raged in their newspapers in public view of the entire nation.   The two-man directorate of Lleras Restrepo and Chaux worked together in planning a "grand manifestation" of the party faithful for early February on the anniversary of Gaitán's last public address.   But they were unable to curb the dissension promoted by Darío Samper and his *Jornada* colleagues, who almost daily continued to attack the principle of collaboration.

By the start of 1949 this element organized the *comando de izquierda,* which was independent and critical of the directorate.   Organized by congressional figures including Jorge Uribe Márquez* and Eduardo Camancho Gamba, the *comando* expressed discontent over the electoral agreements and followed the extremes of past *gaitanista* economic declarations.   The complexities of Liberal dissension were underlined when the *comando* in turn was attacked by a joint declaration signed by twenty-four former *gaitanistas.*   In short, having assumed Liberal leadership only after the 1946 elections, the *gaitanistas,* in the absence of their leader, were turning upon themselves.

The official Liberal position was established and enunciated by Carlos Lleras Restrepo, who with the tacit backing of Echandía was proving more effective than Chaux.   Lleras Restrepo had risen to leadership rapidly, and was typical of the new young Liberals who were gradually asserting themselves over the older followers of López and Santos.   Lleras Restrepo was not a rank newcomer to politics, having been an outstanding minister of economy under Eduardo Santos.   An economist and financier, he came to party prominence only in the middle 1940's.

Born in 1908, Lleras Restrepo had gone from academic circles into Cundinamarca politics and then to the national legislature in 1935, where he was first noticed during discussions of public administration and finance.   An avowed *santista* during the López-Santos conflict, he returned to private life in 1942 and was politically inactive until after the 1946 elections.   Following Echandía's decision to take the Liberals

* A former member of the DLN.

into the National Union, Lleras Restrepo was largely responsible for winning party support although unable to sway the opposing *comandos*. An imaginative, implacable parliamentarian of sardonic and biting oratory, Lleras Restrepo was every inch the political realist. An intense, hard-driving man with receding hairline, dark-rimmed glasses, and an omnipresent cigarette that delighted political caricaturists, his methodical economic experience made him a politician of calculation and clear logic.[17]

Emerging from his early appearance as a bright "glorified book-keeper," Lleras Restrepo was easily the most active politician of the post-*bogotazo* period. Accustomed to no more than five hours' nightly sleep, he traveled Colombia almost continually, strengthening ties with local Liberals. Probably no Colombian politician of recent years compared with him as a political organizer and activist. Even so, he made more than two hundred calls on the presidential palace in the first year after the April, 1948, riots.[18] Friends referred to the tenacious, often impertinent, and even insolent Lleras Restrepo as, in Unamuno's phrase, *"todo un hombre."* Echandía once said of him: ". . . that man is a genius. They can make him the doorman of the Directorate, and even there he will still be the central figure."[19]

On January 9, Lleras Restrepo wrote a prologue for the Liberal campaign in *El Tiempo*. He called for a continuation of collaboration with the Conservatives but carefully drew a picture in which Liberals were responsible for advances made following the rioting. To Lleras, only the Liberal agreement to join the government had saved the nation from anarchy, thus the party deserved the voters' support. While saying nothing to force a break with the president, he made clear that Ospina Pérez was far from satisfactory. "The affirmation [of the President] with respect to the fact that the cabinet of national union was constituted after the Army had already acquired full control of the situation, can be no more than a slip of the tongue. But it is impossible to accept his implication of a lack of knowledge or a scorn of the patriotic attitude with which liberalism acceded in lending its cooperation for the reestablishment of public tranquility, the keeping of the legal order and the maintenance of institutions. . . ."[20]

The Liberal campaign was informally opened in late January when Lleras Restrepo and Chaux traveled through the capital with loud-speaker equipment to appeal for votes and build enthusiasm for the

February 7 gathering. On that day crowds began gathering in the early afternoon; rural delegations arrived, and when the meeting formally began in the Plaza Bolívar at 6:00 P.M., some 100,000 were present. The spirit was festive, and band music helped drown out much of the oratory. Chaux, Lleras Restrepo, Uribe Márquez, Samper, and the father of Jorge Gaitán all spoke, predicting a June victory and praising the organizational efforts of Gaitán.

Exactly a week later the Conservatives held a manifestation of their own from the stage of the Municipal Theatre. Loudspeakers carried the proceedings to the crowd outside, as orators reaffirmed support of the president and tried to "rectify" the earlier Liberal speeches. Jorge Leyva and Augusto Ramírez Moreno spoke for their party. Leyva said that "the National Union in its true philosophic-socio meaning is a dead letter, simple fiction, converted into a numerical repartition of public posts, without grandeur or any object to justify it." Ramírez Moreno continued in the expression of dissatisfaction with the Liberal role in government and called upon Conservatives to unite as never before in party activity. "To the Conservatives who hear me: if you are in bed, get up. If you are eating, abandon your plates! Anything else is a timid attitude that does not convince us."[21]

Just as the Liberal campaign moved to the interior, the party was again torn by the resignation of Chaux from the directorate. The move was brought on by the announcement of a rival "national" Liberal convention by the *comando*. Announcing that this formal split guaranteed Liberal defeat in June, Chaux said he saw no possibility of a united party effort. In a public letter to Lleras Restrepo, he announced, "I put in your hands my irrevocable resignation that it may be presented to the *junta* of parliamentarians. . . . This determination is motivated by the fact that after my having entered the Dual Directorate of popular liberalism with the people of *gaitanista* currents, my companions have believed it convenient to form the so-called *comando* that is producing in the country, in spite of words that are pronounced or written to the contrary, a divisionist element of our collectivity. I find myself in complete disagreement. . . ."[22]

Chaux's bitterness was a result of his failure to prevent the fissure despite his own standing in *gaitanista* ranks. But he had moved prematurely, for the declaration of a separate convention was the high watermark of the group now calling itself Comando Popular Nacional or Copulina. In actuality it was less interested in a new party than in obtaining a voice within the Liberal directorate. Once Chaux had resigned, the *comando* immediately demanded a national convention of all Liberals to select an expanded DLN with representative composition. They were unwilling to wait until the regularly-scheduled party convention in December.

The basis of the disagreement centered on the question of deciding the heir of Gaitán once and for all. His friends had been many and varied; Gaitán himself was like a field marshal surrounded by ambitious generals both adoring and fearful. Many *comando* members were legitimate *gaitanistas,* but many of his old followers had preferred to follow the directorate in supporting the coalition government. There was no clear answer to the problem. A gathering of party leaders was held shortly, and the *comando* demands were in effect realized. The directorate was reorganized and expanded, to include not only Chaux but Jorge Uribe Márquez. A national convention was also called for the first Sunday of July.

Campaigning picked up in both parties, and rural party strife increased once more. Armed guerrillas swept down from the hills, attacking government forces or small undefended villages, exercising unrestrained will on the target, then retreating into the rugged vastness of the Andes. Conservative troops responded with destruction or burning of a predominantly Liberal village. This in turn inspired new guerrilla depradations. Liberals and Conservatives turned upon their neighbors. Many a man stood watching his home and field being destroyed, then left to join the nearest group of bandits. The cycle was unending and vicious.

Government measures were stepped up, and there was a gradual indication that Liberal-minded members of the army and police were shunted aside to minor posts. Conservative colleagues passed them in rank and responsibility. With the newspapers leading the denunciations, it was no small miracle that Darío Echandía managed to hold the Liberals in the cabinet. On March 11, 1949, the administration prohibited public meetings for ten days, beginning on April 7. They feared a renewal of the April, 1948, eruption. Public meetings by either party were forbidden, and the ban was to remain in force until after the elections of the third of June.

The Conservatives, with Gómez in Spain and Ospina Pérez neither willing nor able to direct daily operations, functioned smoothly on the well-constructed machinery built so painstakingly by Gómez and now operated by his followers. In early March the Conservative directorate complained to the president of the activities it attributed to the Liberals. "We want to expose before Your Excellency our concern over the climate of violence that liberalism has let loose against our party members. . . . The facts of blood and outrages of all kinds . . . make us believe that this attitude obeys a concerted plan with the object of terrorizing our fellow party members and of arresting the scant but salutary effects that the electoral reform will bring forth in the next [national] debate. . . ."[23]

New Liberal Director Uribe Márquez shot back that the Liberals "find a dramatic atmosphere for the conservative persecution, patronized by the authorities. . . . Liberalism is in need of genuine, Bolivarian guarantees. . . ." President Ospina Pérez' reply to both was a model of circumspection, but scarcely improved the near breakdown of Liberal-Conservative collaboration. "Such an unfortunate circumstance makes more necessary . . . the union of all wills to extirpate from our political customs the appellation of violence and to create an atmosphere of understanding and of tolerance that may impede the criminal spilling of blood and apply exemplary sanctions to those who . . . move against our traditions. . . ."[24]

At the prompting of the president, the two directorates on April 1 signed a "non-aggression pact" in the palace, condemning violence on the part of either party and authorizing conciliatory missions to investigate further outbreaks. The pact proved meaningless. On Easter Sunday the bloodiest battle in some time began in Boyacá. Army reinforcements raced to the scene, and after hours of fighting over forty were dead.[25] The Conservative town of Chita had been razed, and other villages were damaged. Ospina Pérez again appealed for an end to violence, his words falling on deaf ears. He promised to use all constitutional means to guarantee security, and Government Minister Echandía denied that a new state of siege was contemplated.

On April 2, 1949, the Conservatives held a campaign meeting in Bogotá that featured a parade and several hours of oratory. Laureano

Gómez was named the 1950 presidential candidate *in absentia*. A large bust of the party chief gave visual reminder of his dominance. When the sun broke through the clouds in mid-afternoon, the speaker seized upon it in a magnificently ridiculous comment. "God is with us . . . He has sent us a splendid sun to illuminate this splendid gathering. . . ."[26] A half-hour later, when a torrential rain dispersed the crowd, Conservative speakers chose not to call upon God as one of their political activists!

Campaigning was interrupted on May 6 when the six Conservative cabinet members resigned so that the president might reorganize before the coming election. The cabinet was reformed as swiftly as possible, with the Liberals retaining their posts. But a few days later Ospina Pérez fired several Liberal governors from departmental posts, and new repressive measures were adopted by rural police forces. On Saturday, May 21, 1949, the six Liberal ministers resigned *en masse*. Following a protesting Echandía, even local Liberals left their posts. The second—and final—Conservative National Union was dead.

Mariano Ospina Pérez officially accepted the resignations at 1 A.M. Sunday morning, and the eventful thirteen-month experiment was ended. The coalition had been an accidental government, the only possible response to the *bogotazo* that remained within the constitutional framework. The failure of both collectivities to exercise control over their entire membership had doomed the effort to eventual failure, however, and growing turbulence by the start of 1949 rendered even the herculean efforts of Echandía powerless.

The removal of Liberal governors helped to precipitate the Liberal withdrawal, but the atmosphere of the nation contributed to the move. The open partisanship of Conservative governors in Boyacá and Nariño not only proscribed effective guarantees but heightened the ferocity of rural fighting. The president, somewhat inclined to look away from the gravity of conditions in the hope that they would miraculously disappear, also aided the Liberal disillusion. He seemed increasingly inflexible rather than adaptive in a situation requiring both action and considerable political agility.

Shortly before the resignations the president had rejected a series of Liberal demands, including the removal of military officers from gubernatorial duties in two departments. A division of party representation in the departmental secretariats had also been requested. Interestingly, the Liberals had also singled out Colonel Gustavo Rojas Pinilla, commandant of the Third Brigade in Cali, asking his removal on the grounds of violating freedom of speech. Rojas Pinilla had issued a written order to his troops to stop the use of free speech by orators at political gatherings. He also sanctioned the use of force, if necessary.[27]

The letter of demands as released to the press referred to violence by stating that, in view of conditions, ". . . we believe that liberalism should not share any longer the responsibilities of government, and that cooperation has been made impossible because of the lack of a moral base of mutual fulfillment and of reciprocal loyalty on which [National Union] was reached. The president assumes with his party, by his own will and as a consequence of his own acts and omissions, the total responsibility of public management."[28]

The Liberals felt that in all good conscience they could do nothing else. At the same time, despite its inevitability, the move was a radical solution that prolonged national uncertainty. The contradiction that remained was to be heightened by the upcoming voting, with Mariano Ospina Pérez heading an all-Conservative government in a nation that showed its loyalties clearly lay with the Liberal party. The Liberals, although still controlling the legislature, were now utterly removed from the executive on both a national and local administrative level. The moment had arrived for the Conservatives to reassert themselves, and the immediate result was to be the increasing harshness of a minority national administration.

Chapter Six

MINORITY RULE TAKES CHARGE

As the campaign sped toward election day, Conservatives played up their role as unique defenders of the faith. Local members of the clergy joined in, although the highest ecclesiastical figures refused to participate. In April a pastoral letter from Ismael Perdomo, Archbishop of Bogotá and Primate of Colombia, called upon all Colombians for a cessation of violence. Pleading for moderation, justice, and charity, he condemned the growing bitterness of extreme party charges. Using the words of Pope Leo XIII, he wrote that "never was there so much need to promote and conserve concord among the faithful, as in this time . . . and to this noble purpose all should dedicate themselves in accordance with a love of Catholic doctrine . . . quieting the political dissensions. . . ."[1]

The archbishop also addressed his clergy in calling for moderation, warning against a blanket condemnation of the Liberal party. He pointed out that the church condemned so-called philosophical liberalism, but was not necessarily opposed to parties referring to themselves as "liberal." The clergy was ordered to avoid support of either party, no mention of political matters would be permitted from the pulpit, and no candidates implicated in the *bogotazo* should be supported by the Catholic church members. Both the spirit and wording of Perdomo's letter were clear. He carefully noted that the "immense national majority of conservatives and liberals . . . defends the same creed, is educated under identical moral norms, and feels equal veneration for the spiritual jurisdiction of the catholic religion."[2]

Unfortunately, his words were not heeded by all. Two bishops in Santander forbade Catholics to vote for Liberal candidates who might "wish to implant civil marriage, divorce, and coeducation, which would open the doors to immorality and Communism."[3] A joint message from the bishops of Pamplona and El Socorro y San Gil, and the apostolic prefects of Curare and Magdalena, made obvious their anti-Liberal sentiments. ". . . [regarding] the crimes of April 9th past, a group of directors of one of the two traditional parties publicly, in the congress, the departmental assemblies and the convention of that party, showed solidarity with the crimes and sacrileges, without their having been rectified. . . . If those directors come to power in the legislative bodies again, the communist danger that menaces the world would be more imminent for Colombia. . . ."[4]

Liberals responded with objections to such interference, and were forced into their most anti-clerical position in several years. Professed church neutrality was ignored by some clergy, such as those just mentioned, who inferentially sniped at the Liberals as responsible for the April, 1948, riots. Continual association of the word "Communist" with the Liberals also aroused considerable ire. By election day there were scattered examples of open Catholic pro-Conservative campaigning.

The Conservatives, outnumbered 73-58 in the Chamber, hoped for an increase of ten seats, which would yield them a small but adequate majority. This control would permit them to counter the Liberal majority in the Senate, which was not subject to voting realignment in 1949. Voting in 815 municipalities would also decide some 287 deputies for the 15 departmental assemblies, as well as 5900 local officials. Few observers expected the Conservatives to regain control of a Chamber, but the fifteen-seat Liberal majority seemed likely to be reduced.

There were 3,000,000 registered voters, of whom some 65 per cent went to the polls. Elections on Sunday, June 5, were fairly calm, with less than a dozen killed.[5] Extensive official precautions had been effective. Highways were blocked, no liquor was for sale, and armed guards were posted around urban polling places, although absent in isolated areas where they were most needed.[6] The Liberals withstood the Conservative challenge by polling some 890,000 votes to their opponents' 780,000. Both parties increased their popular vote, although the Liberal margin of 110,000 was some 40,000 smaller than that recorded in 1946 congressional elections. The Liberal majority in the Chamber of Representatives, although cut in half, still left them in firm control.[7]

President Ospina Pérez was therefore faced with continuing legislative opposition, with his task hardened by the absence of Liberals in the cabinet. *Time* wrote that for three years he had been treading political cliffs, not once being failed by his "judgment, courage, and silken poise."[8] But the balancing act would be increasingly difficult, and his only public response to the elections was a message of appreciation to security forces "for the patriotic position that you knew how to fulfill with your duty. . . ."[9]

If there were any who doubted that June elections were a prelude to the 1950 presidential race, their minds were put right on Friday, June 24. The next year would be one of continuing political turmoil, in which economic and social matters were forgotten amid some of the bitterest controversy in years. For on June 24, a Douglas HK-109 plane belonging to Avianca touched down at the Medellín airport following a trip from New York City. An assemblage of cheering Conservatives gathered around; the door opened and a dapper figure stepped out. He looked down upon the crowd and raised a clenched fist in the air. Laureano Gómez had returned to Colombia.

At the risk of some little repetition, it might be well to take a longer look at Dr. Gómez before proceeding. Born in Bogotá in February of 1889, Laureano Gómez received his political baptism in 1909 by participating in a popular demonstration against President Rafael Reyes.[10] The same year he organized *La Unidad,* a tri-weekly which first appeared in October,[11] and in 1911 he won his first political office as a Cundinamarca assemblyman. In the years to follow he was on various diplomatic missions and also served in both the Chamber and Senate. He organized dissident opposition to the Conservative Abadía Méndez government from 1927 to 1929, and following the Liberal victory in 1930 he assumed leadership of his party.[12] His matchless party leadership in the next sixteen years has been detailed earlier. In 1936 he and José de la Vega founded *El Siglo* and built it to a position of national influence.

In the Senate, Dr. Gómez acquired quickly his oratorical reputation. A natural fighter, he was soon recognized as the greatest Conservative parliamentarian of his era,[13] and even Liberals conceded his legislative brilliance. His speeches had an explosive, even terrifying capacity that often swept his opposition away in disorganized confusion. The picture of an embattled, red-veined Gómez, right arm outstretched and palm upward, was a familiar and formidable one. One commentator, a native-born German who had observed politics extensively on two continents, wrote that "with the exception of Hitler I have never known a politician who so quickly became angry and lost control of himself, roaring and stamping and using abusive terms and growing so red in the face that everybody expected him to have another stroke."[14] In 1935, when only in his mid-forties, he had suffered such an attack.

Gómez' true political mastery was clearest within his party. Dynamic, tenacious, persevering to the extreme, he was undisputed head of the party, although ideologically a representative of the extremist right wing. *Semana* once wrote that Gómez brought to the political arena methods of opposition typical of the French Fourth Republic, while *Time,* quick with a quip as always, called him a "blown-in-the-bottle Bourbon."[15] Voicing his opposition in continual tones of aggressiveness and violence, he so built his prestige that no Conservative dared oppose him. As unapproachable as an uninhabited fortress,[16] Dr. Gómez was the most unchallenged leader in his party's modern history. Certainly no Liberal of the era won such undivided, unquestioning obedience.

One of the least salutary effects of his methods was the smothering of younger Conservative talent. By 1949, after forty years in politics and twenty as party chief, Gómez' every word was law. Occasional opposition cropped up from such vigorous Conservatives as Ramírez Moreno, Alzate Avendaño, and Silvio Villegas. They broke with the party and tried to form their own. Within a few years this effort had failed, and Gómez took them back into the Conservative ranks.

The party felt with no little justice that he had personally outmaneuvered the Liberals in winning the presidency with Mariano Ospina Pérez in 1946. Liberals, of course, refused to credit Gómez, whom the people called "Laureano" and the Liberal propagandists "El Monstruo"— the Monster. The party was united in supporting Gómez' own candidacy in 1950 if he willed it, and the question was simply that of whether or not he wanted the office. Past experience had shown him to be the rarest of politicians—he was not ambitious for the presidency. The trappings and ceremonies of office meant little to him. He had never shown signs of great envy toward Ospina Pérez, the first Conservative president in sixteen years. What Gómez *did* require was the power of party leadership, especially with the Conservatives in control of the government.

Before the war Gómez had been openly pro-Axis and, on his return from self-imposed Spanish exile, showed an increasing enchantment with the principles of the extreme right. This was a change from his earlier outlook, which in the early 1930's had even permitted a close relationship with Alfonso López. Although deeply Conservative and pro-Catholic even then, his beliefs were such as to draw the fire of the hot-headed, totalitarian-minded Silvio Villegas, who attacked him as "impotent as regards violence . . . even more so in the matter of civil action."[17]

The years brought about a gradual reorientation, and in time Gómez was desirous of "turning the course of the nation away from popular republicanism toward the Hispanic state of Ferdinand and Isabel."[18] A nostalgia drew his thinking toward the ideal of a united church and state, the old dogma of the Two Swords. Guillermo Camacho Montoya, an exponent of *laureanista* ideas, wrote significantly in *El Siglo*, "Each day the yoke of Saxo-Americana [sic] is drawn tighter around our throats. Sometimes the yoke is of steel, sometimes of silk, soft and perfidious. . . . But—all is not lost. There is still heard the voice of Laureano Gómez to tell the truth about the future, to direct us to the road of tomorrow, the Catholic Hispanic Empire.

"And we will go back to Spain. The five arrows of Ferdinand and Isabella, the symbol of Catholic unity, will be our symbol also."[19]

During the war he was dedicated to the overthrow of the second López administration, then he turned his attention to the return of the Conservatives to power. Upon his 1949 return, however, it became apparent that his views had grown even more extreme during his stay in Spain. The result was the dedication of perhaps the most brilliant political activist in Colombian history to principles of reaction. At the Medellín airport Gómez sounded a battlecry by equating Liberals with Communists and referring to anti-Liberal statements of some churchmen as official church policy. Augusto Ramírez Moreno drew his personal approval in a welcoming greeting that boded ill for the future. He promised that "the day the congressional majority (Liberals) attempts to take advantage of its powers, the Conservative members, without help from the government, are determined to close the Capital. . . . Fortunately, the Conservatives number one million stout-hearted, determined men who are moving ever more swiftly toward power."[20]

The return of Gómez presaged a bitterly unyielding battle for the presidency. In the following months, the adroit old Conservative again outmaneuvered the opposition at every turn. Realizing that his collectivity was still in the minority, Gómez insisted upon the strictest discipline, capitalizing fully upon the presence of a Conservative president. Victory would have to be achieved through manipulation. It would require the heightening of Liberal dissension, the imposition of undemocratic measures, or the forcing of a virtual Liberal abdication from public affairs. Gómez planned accordingly.

The Liberals were, if anything, overconfident of their position. Sure of popular support, they thought Ospina Pérez too weak to impose serious restrictions on civil liberties or political manifestations. Secure for more than a decade as the majority party, their fears of Dr. Gómez were not strong enough to cause great concern. They felt the greatest danger was in giving him time to develop some unexpected obstacle that might delay their race to the presidency. Thus they chose to move up the elections several months. This proved a grave error, leading to a series of events that suited Gómez perfectly.

When Congress opened its session as usual on July 20, the Liberal majorities immediately advanced a plan of Gilberto Moreno Trujillo to modify Law No. 89 of 1948, the electoral statute. The purpose was to advance the presidential election from June 29, 1950, to the first Sunday of December, 1949. The Liberals also asked that a new registration and electoral census be delayed until after the voting. Debate centered on the question of the legal status of Law No. 89. The Conservatives maintained that it was a code, which could be changed only by a two-thirds majority. The Liberals countered that it was only a law, thus subject to revision by a simple majority in each house. The controversy was based on purely political considerations, but the legal distinction was important, for the Liberal majorities were less than two-thirds, hence the Conservatives could block reform if the measure under revision were a code.

Liberals argued that No. 89 had been a product of the National Union period, claiming that it was typical of a series of broken pacts made by the government. Conservatives noted that civil war might be risked unless the Liberal interpretation of the "law" were rejected. Luis Navarro Ospina of the Conservative directorate declared that "if liberalism insists, the political struggle will be placed on a different field. . . . [Liberals] assume a useless attitude, which puts in danger the very peace of the republic."[21] Ramírez Moreno, also of the DNC, stated that "the conservative party prefers to die, rather than dishonor itself tracing iniquity of such proportions. . . . Choose, dear friends, between honor and the Constitution, on one side, and dishonor and entombment, on the other."[22]

Growing hostility marked the arguments of both parties. Typical of the immoderation was the Liberal refusal of basic courtesy by being absent from the traditional presidential reception honoring both independence day and the opening of the new session.[23] With the overriding issue of presidential elections moving toward a climax, there was good cause for growing apprehension.

THE CONSERVATIVES TAKE OVER

The Liberals adamantly refused to accept Law No. 89 as a code, and the Chamber of Representatives approved the new election law by a straight party vote of 69-63 after a stormy nine-hour debate.[24] Discussion in the Senate was even more heated, and violence occurred in the form of a shower of inkwells, ashtrays, and books flung back and forth across the floor. The Conservatives then walked out and Liberals approved the bill.[25] The president had already denounced the bill and vetoed it when it reached his desk. Returning the bill to Congress, Ospina Pérez refused to accept the revision of the election date without its passage by a two-thirds vote. Liberal Director Lleras Restrepo accepted the executive response as a renewed stimulus, and both houses passed the measure again in defiance of the veto.

Bitterness turned into even greater violence while the measure was being reconsidered. Sessions had already been disrupted earlier when Alvaro Gómez, a son of Laureano and editor of *El Siglo,* distributed whistles to the Conservatives, who drowned out Liberal speakers in the resulting din. But on September 7 conditions reached a new low when, just after midnight, two Boyacá legislators began trading insults. The Conservative, Carlos Castillo, drew a revolver and fired at his opponent.[26] Others joined in, and the shooting continued while the remaining elected representatives of Colombian democracy scrambled for cover under desks and chairs. When the shooting had subsided, Liberal Gustavo Jiménez lay dead on the floor, and the distinguished young Jorge Soto del Corral and three others were severely wounded. The Conservatives once again walked out, and at subsequent sessions, guards searched the legislators for weapons before they were admitted to the hall.[27]

On September 10 some 15,000 attended funeral services for Jiménez, and four former Liberal presidents joined the mourners.[28] Shortly thereafter, at a banquet feting Laureano Gómez, the alleged killer, Amadeo Rodríguez, was seated at the head table on Gómez' right. He later fled the country after an indictment was issued against him.[29] It was then that a group of young Falangists paraded in acclamation of Gómez, crying, among other things, "Viva Amadeo's pistol!"[30]

In the face of Liberal insistence on a November presidential election, President Ospina Pérez re-vetoed the measure, this time on the grounds of constitutionality, automatically sending it to the Corte Suprema de Justicia for juridical consideration. On September 12 the court received a 103-page, single-spaced typewritten document discussing the measure.[31] At the end of September the court, under the presidency of Pedro Castillo Pineda, declared the electoral reform was in accord with the constitution. Law No. 89, it ruled, was indeed a mere law rather than a code, thus the vote for the reform was proper. A Liberal member of the court stated that politics had nothing to do with the decision. However, the vote approving the Liberal reform was 10-6—the court included ten Liberals and six Conservatives.

Nominating conventions were looming up, and the Liberals met first, on Sunday, October 2, 1949. Some 1300 delegates met in Bogotá to proclaim the candidacy of Darío Echandía. "The Convention proclaims the name of Darío Echandía . . . the convention understands that the program, and those purposes expressed by Echandía as bases of his platform . . . include the guarantee of human rights; defense of the citizen's dignity; establishment of an atmosphere of peace and of concord, of security and of trust; protection of labor; development of national production. . . . The reconquest of power does not imply retaliations . . .

but cooperation of all Colombians for the restoration of democratic order ... peace and justice."[32] Echandía himself called for government action to re-establish faith in social guarantees and promised a government that would eschew party politics in the interests of all citizens. Liberalism, he commented, recognized that "the practical unity of the people professing the catholic religion" made imperative the guarantee to the church of free exercise of its mission. He followed the moderate line on the church question with a forthright statement that the Liberals were wholly and unreservedly opposed to communism.

Ten days later the Conservatives met to announce the unanimous choice of Dr. Gómez. Five hundred blue-ribboned Conservative delegates were present, and at 9:20 P.M. Gómez arrived at the Teatro de Colón, raised his fingers in a Churchillian V, and sat down to hear the oratory. Ultimately he rose to deliver his acceptance with the full power of his rhetoric. He said, "... when Conservative lips proclaim peace, they do so with sincerity. Our hearts are not poisoned with hateful desires to destroy the Christian order and replace it with Communist tyranny. We offer peace in the fullest sense of liberty and justice."[33]

Turning away from implied abuse of the Liberals, he discussed his idea of the *basilisco,* which had recently appeared in *El Siglo.* Based upon a mythological allusion, he had formed it "by a process of cold reasoning."

In Colombia people still speak of the Liberal party to designate an amorphous, shapeless and contradictory mass . . . that can be only compared with or described like the imaginary creation of olden days, the basilisk. The basilisk was a monster having the head of one animal, the face of another, the arms of still another, and the feet of some deformed creation, all together forming a creature so frightful and dreadful that its mere glance caused death. Our basilisk moves with feet of confusion and stupidity on legs of brutality and violence which propel its immense oligarchic belly; with a breast of wrath, with Masonic arms, and a tiny, a diminutive Communist head. . . .[34]

Scarcely a statement of party principles and intentions! Only Gómez could have conceived such an attack upon the opposition and carried it through.

Mariano Ospina Pérez had remained quiet on the forthcoming elections, but his ire had grown with the Liberal insistence on moving elections to November 27, the final Sunday of the month. Official measures began to reflect his gradual shift away from serene ineffectuality. Violence became more extreme in the countryside, and officials openly worked for a Conservative victory. Squads of government supporters, often including criminals and convicts, roamed in search of *campesinos*. They demanded registration certificates, and in exchange gave the country folk "safe-conduct" passes bearing a photograph of Gómez. The text read: "The undersigned President of the Conservative Directory, CERTIFIES: that Mr. ——, bearer of card No. —— issued in ——, has sworn that he does not belong to the Liberal Party. Therefore, his life, property, and family are to be respected."[35]

In some instances the foreswearing was conducted before a parish priest, who then added his signature to the certificate. To the credit of Archbishop Perdomo, he denounced such practices in a pastoral letter. "We order all priests under our jurisdiction . . . to abstain totally from furthering, encouraging, or supporting, directly or indirectly, all activities designed to obtain . . . the accomplishment of political aims. . . . They are likewise to refrain from demanding or advising those affiliated with a given political party to renounce their errors openly . . . we threaten with penalty of suspension . . . those priests who subsequently venture to act contrary. . . ."[36]

An unexpected letter from former president Alberto Lleras Camargo at the Pan American Union created further controversy in late October. He claimed astonishment that, according to Conservative charges, the minuscule Communist party of 1946 was now about to take over Colombia. Insisting that the citizenry would not long hold still under a repressive government, he ridiculed the equating of Liberals with Communists. "The Liberal party, which governed Colombia for sixteen years, cannot be outlawed or proscribed from the country's public life, and I gravely fear that only this [death of liberty] can be the logical consequence of . . . a crusade, if the effort continues to identify it with Communism. It is a terrible mistake and a fatal error that will give no satisfaction to a handful of opportunists. . . ."[37] The government replied with an attack on Lleras Camargo for intervening in internal affairs. He promptly submitted his resignation, which was refused by representatives of the other twenty American states.

There were a few scattered Liberal voices still crying for moderation. Abelardo Forero Benavides, a young proponent of accommodation, told the Chamber on October 24 that the Liberals still strongly desired peace.

"The words of Dr. Darío Echandía must not be interpreted only as an arbitrary political plaything, but rather as an expression of a profound desire for peace on the part of all Colombians."[38] Actually, Echandía was already considering a withdrawal from the campaign. Exasperated beyond further counterattack, appalled at the rising toll in the country-side, he and the DLN met with three of the party's former presidents. On Friday, October 28, Carlos Lleras Restrepo announced the decision in the Senate. Echandía would not run.

Circumstances had made it clear that the electoral court was unable and the government unwilling to guarantee free suffrage. The heat of propaganda and growing violence had forced the Liberals on what they called practical and humanitarian reasons to boycott the election. Echandía feared that "on election day the killing would be so brutal that it would succeed finally in imposing upon the majority the Conservative proposed for President; seeing that there was not the least probability of saving a single life, he decided to abstain. . . ."[39]

The Conservatives were genuinely startled; the president proposed hastily a four-man *junta* composed equally of Liberals and Conservatives, which Gómez, with victory within reach, refused. Members of the DNC convinced Ospina Pérez to withdraw the suggestion. The director-ate members themselves were divided: Gilberto Alzate Avendaño favored a strong government under Gómez, Jorge Villareal mused of a possible postponement of elections, while Silvio Villegas was certain only that the Liberals should not be met by conciliation.

Conditions became even more unique when the Liberals, although re-fusing to campaign for the presidency, continued to sit in Congress. Grop-ing for some desperate means of retaliation, they hit upon the scheme of impeaching the president. According to the constitution, the president had to appear before the Senate if the legislators drew up impeachment charges. Hoping to humiliate Ospina Pérez, the Liberals prepared to indict him for failure to keep the democratic order.

It seems inconceivable that the Liberals either expected Ospina Pérez to come or to bargain with them by making concessions. Certainly they had misjudged the president. Fearful of retaliation, Liberals first sent emissaries to the minister of war, asking for personal protection before delivering a note informing the president of congressional intentions. Within thirty minutes Ospina Pérez struck back.[40] Even before messengers had returned to the Capitolio, police were arriving to remove the legislators on charges of disturbing public order. Later in the day a state of siege was declared. For the next eight years it would remain in effect, a reminder that basic democratic principles were forbidden.

On Wednesday, November 9, 1949, Ospina Pérez issued a series of executive decrees. The first formally declared that public order was disturbed, therefore a state of siege was in effect nationally. The second announced the suspension of the parliamentary bodies. The third imposed press censorship, the fourth prohibited all public gatherings or manifestations, and the fifth granted full powers to departmental governors, permitting them to rule as representatives of the central government. A concomitant suspension of all departmental and municipal legislators was also decreed.[41]

There were five considerations by which the government justified emergency decrees. There were alleged uprisings against constituted authority in the countryside; officials could not provide adequate protection without special measures; grave commotion was current; the government was constitutionally required to take steps; and, finally, the Consejo de Estado had been asked to consider the decrees, and had approved.

Ospina Pérez failed to add, as well he might, that the Liberal threat of impeachment proceedings had provoked his emergency decrees. In an interview with William Payette of the United Press, he declared that there would be no change until the causes that "motivated the problem" were removed. Queried about elections, he replied that the government would fulfill existing responsibilities. He made a point of noting that the constitution did not prohibit elections during a state of siege.[42] This was to become the accepted Conservative position—no constitutional provision proscribed elections under conditions of national siege.

In the cities the news evoked alarm that was reduced when the disciplined military police moved into the streets to enforce a 9 P.M. curfew. A government bulletin declared that "complete calm prevails throughout the country."[43] The Conservatives stepped up their drive for power by striking through the Corte Suprema de Justicia. A 1945 statute provided that a two-thirds vote was needed to invalidate any executive decree. The six Conservative members could block any such measure, thus upholding any and all measures adopted by the regime.

Rightly or wrongly, the statute was a part of the national charter, working in this case to the benefit of the Conservatives. The nine Liberal members* protested to the president on November 12 that the two-thirds requirement was incompatible with the very nature of a state of siege. Conservative members of the court had not been consulted and predictably protested the Liberals' action. The Liberal magistrates, as they probably realized, were doing little more than exercising their pens. The president responded in strong terms: "First I wish to express the surprise of the government in the face of this unexampled occurrence in the history of the country, to wit, that a group of magistrates of the highest court of justice should express an opinion on a juridical matter that has not yet been submitted to . . . consideration. . . . I do not know whether you have realized that in writing me the letter to which I refer you have already disqualified yourself to pass judgment in this matter. . . ."[44]

Army steadfastness was a major bulwark to government control,[45] and the president moved swiftly in completing the strengthening of the now rabidly partisan administration. Some weeks earlier Ospina Pérez had appointed as minister of government a business partner of Gómez, Luis Andrade.[46] The pro-Conservative Consejo de Estado was reshuffled to strengthen its orientation through expanded membership. The comptroller-general was also replaced by a more pliable figure.

The final pre-election assault on democratic sensibilities came two days before the uncontested election. Darío Echandía, who had already announced his refusal to recognize the coming regime, was walking with a group of supporters including his older brother Vicente, a non-politician. Police suddenly attacked the men in full daylight on a Bogotá street, firing for several moments. Darío managed to cry out that his party was unarmed, pleading for arrest rather than murder. When firing ended, Vicente Echandía and four others lay dead. The government deplored the episode but stated flatly that the police had been fired on first, although neither the Echandías nor their friends had been armed.

* Liberal magistrate Belisario Agudelo had just died.

Elections were held on the appointed date; the following morning the Gómez paper triumphantly proclaimed that its founder had won the election with all but 14 of 1,140,634 votes. Trumpeting that it was the largest vote ever given a single party,[47] *El Siglo* declared that a new era had come to Colombia. Indeed one had; the republican era—what was left of it—would come to an end under the extraordinary personal direction of Laureano Gómez. Concerning the elections, *Life* was direct and to the point. Its December 12 issue reported, "For decades Colombia was one country in Latin America which never chose its government with bullets instead of ballots. But by last week . . . her liberty-loving people lost their precious heritage through a relentless power play by the minority Conservative party. . . .

"They recalled strong man Laureano Gómez . . . the main feature of his campaign was a reign of terror in the interior. Liberal towns were shot up. In the last two months 2,000 Liberals were killed, hundreds jailed and other hundreds fled their towns."[48] *The Atlantic Monthly* added its own view: "On November 27, under the most rigid dictatorship in modern history, Colombia elected Gómez president. . . ."[49]

Hemispheric opinion was strongly opposed to the proceedings, and there was even revived talk of Bogotá affiliation with the suspected Madrid-Buenos Aires axis between the Franco and Perón regimes.[50] But the president-elect, the choleric "Angry Man of God," had won his victory. The immediate future was dark; one Liberal predicted the victory would usher in twenty years of civil war.[51] It remained for Gómez to arrange a gradual turnover of key administrative posts to the *laureanistas*. Following Ospina Pérez to a national microphone on November 29, 1949, he consecrated to God the victory he had so shrewdly engineered against the will of the majority. His triumph, achieved against all odds, was both a sign of Liberal disintegration and of a brilliant personal political stroke. Every step of the way Gómez had carefully and unerringly calculated the circumstances and continued along the path to supremacy. Thus he could well take satisfaction in the hollowly humble words directed to his listeners. "I bless God a thousand and a thousand times for having filled my heart with this burning love for my country and for having made my mind grasp a sublime doctrine. . . . I praise God because He has permitted me to walk through the fires of hatred without allowing my heart to become contaminated by it, and has kept it happy, free from the dark shadows of vengeance, pure, without the dregs of bitterness. . . ."[52]

Even Laureano's most ardent supporters would scarcely attribute to him a happy, pure, vengeance-free heart. Germán Arciniegas wisely predicted in early 1950 that the future was dim. "It cost us dear in lives and suffering to gain independence, only God knows what it will cost us now to gain liberty."[53]

Chapter Seven

PREPARATION FOR
DICTATORSHIP

The Liberal Agony

WITH VICTORY secure, the Conservatives attempted to court opposition favor with promises of national concord. Laureano Gómez, realizing his task would be eased by winning even minimal Liberal cooperation, promised an administration dedicated to justice and equitable participation of both parties. He spoke repeatedly of the restoration of peace and respect for human life, adding that the lower classes would be benefited by his economic policies.[1]

His New Year's message restated these promises, while President Ospina Pérez also urged peace, adding that he had always sought "concord among all Colombians. My government has used the best men available; it was not my fault that the other party would not collaborate."[2] A few days before, he had spoken more stubbornly in an interview granted the *New York Times,* predicting that the state of siege would be a long one, for it would remain until all the causes of disturbance were removed.

Liberal cooperation was not easily to be obtained; immediately after the election of Gómez, a formal letter of protest was sent to Ospina Pérez, signed by virtually all prominent Liberals. First came an explanation of withdrawal from the elections. "It cannot be said that the Liberals abstained from exercising rights, but rather that they were placed in a position from which it was impossible to exercise them. When freedom of expression and freedom of the press still prevailed, this was made clear by the party's directing bodies. . . ." With thousands of party members deprived of their registration cards and harassed by partisan governors and unprincipled police officials, Liberal voters "were in many cases totally unable to exercise not only normal political activities but the most elementary rights of citizenship. . . . Coercion of the individual conscience . . . reached unsuspected limits here in what was always considered a land of free men."[3]

Other criticisms included the shooting of Vicente Echandía without cause; doubt as to the quantity of Gómez votes; use of the state of siege when not called for by circumstances; and suspension of Congress when constitutional article 73 provided that "by mutual agreement Congress may transfer to another place and, in case public order is disrupted, may meet at the place designated by the President of the Senate." Ospina Pérez' more recent statements were also attacked, particularly his claim that the state of siege would be used to bring about the curing of national ills. This, they argued validly, was not consonant with constitutional tenets. "The ideas expressed by Your Excellency in yesterday's address altered fundamentally and unexpectedly statements reiterated many times during the first three years of Your Excellency's Administration. . . . We want to make clear that it is perfectly obvious to us that to prolong indefinitely the state of siege, after the causes which motivated it have disappeared . . . constitutes a dictatorship of an unequivocal totalitarian type."[4]

The government, wrote the Liberals, had decreed a state of siege because of internal unrest, yet was now announcing that peace and tranquility reigned. Why, then, should the state of siege not be lifted? "Why doesn't the Government render to Congress the report it must make on what it has done in the interim?" They could only reach the conclusion that the government was not interested in the restoration of civil rights.

In the months between Gómez' election and his inauguration in August, 1950, the Liberal wrath over elections and emergency measures made significant cooperation with the regime impossible. The measure of temporary Liberal unanimity was reflected when Alfonso López broke his self-imposed silence in a declaration to the nation. Speaking in January in defense of his party, López rejected cooperation with

Gómez. Accusing Conservatives of initiating a policy of dismissal of party members from bureaucratic posts, he predicted an army of unemployed Liberals. He demanded "more guarantees be granted and the army be reduced; more respect for citizens' rights and less of a police force; more laws and fewer emergency decrees."[5]

López, both then and later, was more sanguine than many Liberals. Announcing his belief in Gómez' statements favoring concord, he added that this would, of course, not mean collaboration such as the National Union had exercised. In discussing the lengthening list of the executive decrees, López indicated little disagreement with the content. What he criticized was the absence of discussion or explanation made to the public. Urging debate of the decree laws, he said that neither he nor the people even knew whether the president-elect would continue the Ospina Pérez "revolution of order" or might return to constitutional norms of democratic government. He expressed the hope that the new government would eschew ties with both Moscow and Madrid, keeping the clergy out of politics and exercising state intervention for the benefit of the economy.[6]

The Conservatives had offered collaboration of a sort without expectation of Liberal agreement, and as the opposition agonized over the formulation of new policies, the Conservatives responded to López' much-publicized declarations by laying all guilt for violence at the Liberal doorstep. Claiming that rural fighting had actually been started by the Liberals when they returned to power in 1930, the Conservatives asserted that the misfortunes of the National Union were results of Liberal intransigence and provocation. Claiming to carry the banners of liberty and order along traditional paths, they denied intentions of establishing a semi-Fascist system. Luis Andrade, the usual government defender of its position, denied allegations of encouraging rural violence through official partisanship. He openly hinted that Liberals were "still" smuggling in arms from Venezuela for distribution to their partisans.[7]

In March of 1950 *Semana* printed an article by Silvio Villegas outlining the nature of the Gómez government. The commentary had already appeared in *El Siglo* and, therefore, was considered a statement of the president-elect's views. A return to constitutional tenets was promised, but with strong suggestions that reform of the constitution was under consideration. Silvio Villegas, himself a proponent of a corporative system for Colombia, wrote that "once the nation is cured of the wounds opened by demagoguery, popular suffrage and *representative corporations* will function normally, and we will again have a free press, with *prior censorship,** but that fully responsible form such as exists in all the civilized peoples of the earth."[8]

Silvio Villegas also paid homage to Dr. Gómez, writing that he was not in the position of a typical politician needing to prove his merits. "In Conservatism his thoughts are orders. In the full maturity of his life . . . Dr. Gómez will be the first servant of Colombia in the government. A victim of injustice, he will not let anything be done without its being . . . sanctioned [by him]. Foreign to hate, he will be the proper and impartial magistrate . . . with a passion equal to the greatness of the country."[9]

Rural violence continued in early 1950. Away from the major population centers, Liberals were militantly unwilling to accept the electoral verdict, finding the only outlet to their frustrations in continual verbal sniping and outright physical attacks. While there is no clear evidence that party headquarters was directing the violence, there was certainly no disposition to disavow such actions. The government, all political considerations aside, was fully aware of the dangers of continued conflict, yet was unsuccessful even in restricting its growth.

Mariano Ospina Pérez planned a personal trip through the nation designed to calm the people and lay the basis for conciliation. Stiffened government actions in late 1949, however, had robbed him of whatever limited popularity he might have enjoyed. On the trip he was met with open hostility. Crowds booed and jeered him, while anti-government placards were common despite police efforts to remove them. Upon reaching the Caribbean coast, he encountered angry demonstrations and menacing crowds. In both Santa Marta and Cartagena his appearance nearly provoked street riots. At official functions, the arrival of local Conservatives inevitably brought choruses of shouts and accusations of treason and dictatorship. The president was forced to cancel the remainder of his tour.

The official position on violence remained immutable through the final months of the Ospina Pérez term. Luis Andrade, during a con-

* The italics are mine.

valescent stay in Baltimore's Johns Hopkins Hospital, told a United Press interviewer that there were no political prisoners—which the Liberals had *not* charged—and that furthermore there was only minor fighting involving simple bandits. There were, he said, no political implications in the disorder.[10] Commerce Minister César Tulio Delgado reiterated the official line in Bogotá, linking economic development with national pacification. "Only peace is characterized by a fragility like the vase of Sully Proudhom. It is not enough that the government takes custody of it and looks out for it without fatigue. It is necessary that all citizens understand that it is an immense treasure, that there is no right to break it. . . ."[11] In the countryside, however, violence raged with unremitting fury.

As the shock of the fall's events slowly wore off, the Liberals began to realize that no political advantage would come from a policy of complete negativism. The respected *El Tiempo* columnist "Caliban"— Enrique Santos, brother of the former president—proposed that the Liberals make the best of a bad bargain by seeking a middle ground. He felt that positions on issues should be thoroughly aired, with the Liberal party choosing between true liberalism or socialism and the Conservatives between traditional conservatism or Christian socialism.[12] Other Liberals picked up the argument, admitting the absurdity of pretending that Laureano Gómez was not the president-elect. The president of the Caldas Liberals, Federico Mejía, further cautioned that irresponsible voices were urging on party leaders "plans against the public order and constitutional normality"[13] which would further weaken and discredit the party.

Eduardo Santos had returned to active operation of his *Tiempo* in the face of censorship that made daily publication a trying experience. He noted in a signed editorial that "events of the past eight months place on me the duty of taking up again a position from which I thought I had retired. . . . I consider it my obligation to accompany those who are directing and editing *El Tiempo*."[14] He, too, recognized the need for conciliation, and *El Tiempo* responded to Mejía's declaration that the Liberals should be wary of those urging conspiratorial activity: "It is true that for some months there has been some activity by unknown people, provocateurs, and perhaps individuals with special missions which are not hard to surmise in spite of their secrecy, all determined to create disorders with the purpose of compromising the Liberals in a blind venture that would become the pretext for reprisals."[15]

Despite the prohibition on political gatherings, the Liberals tried to exercise party functions once more. On April 3 some 700 party faithful attended a banquet for Santos at which disagreement over compromise raised its head before the confused, indecisive party. Alfonso López was not a scheduled speaker but finally acceded to calls from the assemblage for an impromptu speech. He began with suggesting that the party should not necessarily fear the idea of collaboration. Hoots and protests from the floor interrupted him, and the white-faced former president declared that he asked not agreement but the courtesy of being heard out, after which there was mixed applause and jeering.

Even in the face of conditions demanding unity, the Liberals remained agonizingly divided, still involved to a degree on the question of the Gaitán heir. Carlos Lleras Restrepo was trying to rebuild the party and was making trips through the countryside to meet with local Liberals. Continually questioned about the predicted return of López to political activity, he told interviewers that López himself would make the decision. He denied popular rumors that López was meeting secretly with Laureano Gómez to work out collaboration.

Laureano Gómez in Command

The Liberals continued to struggle desperately over a course of action, but Conservatives under Dr. Gómez' leadership were purposefully driving for virtual political hegemony through use of governmental machinery. Security forces were strengthened in the cities; by mid-summer, Bogotá was patrolled by groups of four rather than two, armed with loaded, cocked Mausers. Plainclothesmen were also in the streets in considerable numbers.[16] In the countryside, forces were augmented by recruitment among impoverished young men eager for the security of a guaranteed daily meal and the unaccustomed sense of authority. Guerrilla opposition was such that one report, although doubtless exaggerated, claimed that a mass of 10,000 Liberal partisans had penetrated from the *llanos* into Boyacá, Cundinamarca, Huila, and Nariño.[17] Gómez found the outgoing Ospina Pérez more than willing to build up rural government forces.

Gómez was also careful to cultivate the favor of the military, without whose help his hold on the nation would have been broken. When the election court verified Gómez' victory in late February, Lieutenant General Rafael Sánchez Amaya, long the chief of the military under Ospina Pérez, was joined by his ranking subordinates to declare loyalty to the president-elect. Dr. Gómez replied that the military was one of the immutably constructive elements of society and that upon its stance depended the public welfare. "If it is intelligent, moral, instructive, effective and heroic, the nation is heroic, noble and illustrious, because the armed forces are the compendium of the nation."[18]

On April 29 Gómez continued his courtship of the military at a military banquet in Bogotá's Escuela Superior de Guerra, where he was the honored guest. Sánchez Amaya, newly rewarded for past services with an ambassadorial appointment to the Court of St. James, swore that the military would be entirely under the orders of the president-to-be following his August inauguration. The military, he noted, would guarantee Gómez the liberty and tranquility necessary to carry out administrative and economic measures. "We do not know what the future holds in reserve, but we know our desires: we want a prosperous and happy Colombia, a country in which are combined, without disturbances, authority and order, liberty, individual guarantees and labor, an authority sufficiently strong so that it may not be bent down before fear, and intelligent so that it does not fall into deceit."[19]

Dr. Gómez, at his suavest in such surroundings, replied with modest appreciation that Colombians always thought of the army as austerely virtuous, dedicated to service of nobility and proven abnegation. The citizens found in the army "the tranquilizing certitude that what is permanent to the country, essential to its glory, and vital for its future, is found secure behind the bronze wall of the armed forces."[20]

The old Conservative was equally adept in reaching basic understanding with church authorities, whose support was second in importance only to the military. The task was not difficult, for he had long cultivated the personal friendship of Archbishop Perdomo. Even in periods of bitterest political invective he had managed to retain Perdomo's confidence. On November 29, the president-elect had gone to visit Perdomo, spending some ninety minutes in private conversations. The following afternoon the archbishop returned Gómez' call.[21]

When Perdomo, who in 1928 had succeeded Bernardo Herrera as primate and head of the Bogotá archdiocese that dated back to 1564, suddenly died on June 3 at the age of seventy-eight, Gómez was quick to lead the Conservative expression of grief, a feeling which the entire nation deeply shared. One should note in passing that the first mourner to call following Perdomo's death was Liberal leader Echandía and other "anti-clerical" Liberals. When Crisanto Luque, the bishop of Tunja, was named by the Apostolic Nuncio on July 17 to succeed Perdomo, it had been preceded by consultation with Ospina Pérez and Gómez, as the Concordat of 1942 specified.

Accurately assuming that Liberal indecision rendered hopes of even partial truce worthless, Gómez gave up all attempts to reach any understanding. Blandly declaring that he expected to serve all Colombians, he offered dissidents the opportunity to join him. "Any Liberal, with or without the official sanction of his party, who proves his sincere desire to participate in his country's government will find that his abilities will be used where the government can use them best."[22] Having thus shifted the burden of non-collaboration to the Liberals, he coldly issued denials of religious fanaticism and Fascist ideology. "I shall try to govern so there can be no just opposition."[23] Those who questioned his sincerity saw an indication of his true feelings when a *Newsweek* correspondent referred to Lleras Restrepo. What do you expect of me, he asked, when such a man has called me an *"asesino máximo"*—the greatest possible assassin?*

Questioned shortly before his inauguration, Gómez went out of his way to promise foreign investors a favorable climate. He was positive in his belief that foreign capital was desired, and he favored circumstances whereby profits could be taken from the country in cash, merchandise, or whatever form investors might prefer.[24] Well aware that coffee income was unreliable, he noted that monetary questions were of primary importance. The low standard of living and mounting inflation created social resentments that sharpened the class struggle, while fiscal speculation was harmful to the development of production. Thus the question of monetary stability was crucial.

---

* Lleras Restrepo remembered no such statement, although admitting he may have said it in the heat of debate.

As we shall see in Part III, Gómez for all his unwise political activities was a shrewd judge of the economic situation, and his regime was to prove as successful economically as it was barren politically.

Embattled Liberals were offered no succor where press censorship was concerned. Typical of the growing harassment was the government prohibition of the publication of *El Tiempo* on July 31 when, after being forbidden to print editorial comment, it placed a commercial advertisement in the same space. The government refused to back down even when the *El Tiempo* director, Roberto García Peña, explained that the newspaper's action was taken after three different editorials for the July 30 edition had been rejected by the censors.

Two months earlier Gómez had told a North American journalist that the newspapers themselves were to blame, besides which he considered the censorship very minor. Comparing press freedom to morphine, he commented with a smile that the drug in the hands of educated people was highly beneficial but that it dare not be distributed indiscriminately to the masses. He felt the comparison with press freedom was an accurate one.[25]

The Conservatives were increasingly assertive as Ospina Pérez suspended the July session of Congress under the state of siege. At the inauguration in August the Liberals were in total disarray. On the inaugural weekend, Alfonso López and Darío Echandía were pointedly out of town. Carlos Lleras Restrepo was also away from Bogotá, and Santos was nowhere in evidence. Liberal newspapers also shut down over the week end. It was ironically typical of Liberal disorganization that even party directives to boycott the inauguration were not universally accepted. Two Liberal magistrates from the court and three council members attended. They were later expelled from the party for failure to comply with the boycott.[26]

At 2:02 P.M. of August 7, 1950, members of the court entered the Salón Elíptico of the Capitolio and were joined shortly by nine members of the sixteen-man council. At 3:14 Gómez arrived and was sworn in by court president José Domingo Sarasty, who was to be Gómez' first minister of government. In an eighty-minute address Sarasty said that those present were witnessing an expression of the national will and that the new president was the legal and constitutional chief of state.[27]

Dr. Gómez, receiving the presidential sash from Ospina Pérez, unctuously told his predecessor, ". . . my gratitude is boundless. I hope to be able to imitate the proofs of courage and virtue so amply displayed by Your Excellency, which saved Colombia."[28] Then turning to deliver his inaugural address, Gómez hinted at even firmer government control with a declaration that the entire nation was tired of politics; he hoped to keep such activities minimal. Without directly mentioning the state of siege or press censorship, he indicated that his intentions put more emphasis on order and calm than on individual rights. He would permit no adulteration of the state institutions, adding that liberty did not lead to truth, but rather the contrary.

Professing a friendship to the United States quite contrary to the Yankee-baiting of an earlier decade,[29] he particularly noted the praiseworthy action of the United States in Korea. A promise to favor business and develop capital must have pleased the oligarchy which was hailing his ascendence with the feeling that the regime would, under a stronger leader, prove a "salutary change."[30] He concluded with the peroration, ". . . we men are only blades of grass in the hands of God. May His omnipotent hand save Colombia."[31] But Gómez was much more than a bending blade of grass, and his government came and went long before a hand of salvation was extended to the ailing republic.

Part III

AUTHORITARIANISM AND LAUREANO GÓMEZ

Chapter Eight

GÓMEZ SETS HIS COURSE

The Encouragement of Business

Laureano Gomez was in direct control of presidential routine for only slightly more than a year, but during that time Gómez pursued his duties with an emphasis on economic affairs. The business classes were deliberately favored. Despite Ospina Pérez' failure to do much along economic lines, conditions favored the advance of the upper classes and prosperous businessmen. The removal of wartime controls in 1946 and booming coffee production brought flourishing prosperity for those who already had substantial funds. Gómez was not disposed to turn back the clock on business and industry, and he tightened the regulation and control of labor.

Wage levels were virtually frozen, with fixed incomes growing meaningless as prices rose. With industrialism and a kind of economic nationalism approved by the Conservatives, President Gómez found ardent supporters for his program. Two cabinet members in particular were most responsible for economic policies—Antonio Alvarez Restrepo and Jorge Leyva. Gómez, himself no economist although astute in business matters, was content to leave the economy largely in their hands, as long as his political and social ideas were not harmed. Alvarez Restrepo had been appointed minister of education in Gómez' first cabinet, but he soon replaced Rafael Delgado Berreneche as minister of economy.

Born in Sonsón in 1906, Alvarez Restrepo had entered business, later became director of the Manizales paper *La Patria* and, while still in his twenties, was elected deputy to the Caldas departmental assembly. Later he visited the United States with various inter-American economic groups, as well as serving for a time as consul in New York City. Jorge Leyva, a thirty-eight-year-old Bogotá lawyer and diplomat, had been appointed minister of public works. One of the young ambitious Conservatives striving for greater recognition under Gómez' one-man party rule, he used his post as a political springboard to greater prominence. Like Alvarez Restrepo, he was influential in the development of economic policy.

Several economic measures were enacted soon after the inauguration. On September 1 the government created a Comisión de Expertos to study the report of the Currie Mission, and on the twenty-eighth a Comité de Desarrollo Económico was decreed to study future economic problems. By December the minister of mines and petroleum concluded steps leading to the organization of ECOPETROL, the oil monopoly.[1] Minister of Economy Alvarez Restrepo, a strong believer in the importance of exchange controls,[2] soon moved to revise existing laws. He announced plans to reorganize the Exchange Control Office. The market for exchange certificates had been slow, with prices at a yearly low of 2.8 to 2.9 pesos per dollar. With coffee prices high, it was not possible to reduce the unfavorable exchange balance. Officials of the Exchange Control authorized $15,000,000 to reduce the accumulated unpaid exchange.[3]

In March of 1951 Alvarez Restrepo announced a new exchange system which made Colombia in effect a free market. An executive decree abolished import licenses and the use of exchange certificates. There was a list of prohibited items, largely luxury articles or products which would compete with domestic products. Automobiles, tires, perfumes, and such were among the forbidden imports. All other products were subject to free importation, unhampered by either licensing or quota restriction. For statistical purposes only they were registered with the newly-organized National Import Registry Office. The new system was, incidentally, consistent with recommendations of the Currie Report.[4]

Terms of the decree, issued by the president on April 8,[5] also set up a 2.5 peso rate of exchange. The former system, employing exchange certificates sold at variable rates, was done away with. To avoid undue upsets, an adjustment was included under which 25 per cent of the coffee exports would be liquidated at the 2.5 rate for six months, the rest at the former 1.95 pesos per dollar. The 25 per cent would increase progressively until reaching 100 per cent. Gómez noted during his first post-inaugural interview that the step was offered in a friendly and constructive spirit, which he was sure the people would share.

Even while the new exchange system was in the process of formulation, the Ministry of Economy was studying the preliminary summary of the Currie Report, prepared by the mission invited to Colombia during the Ospina Pérez years. Its over-all program—which called for a sum of $2.5 billion invested over a five-year period—was placed under close scrutiny. The president's son Alvaro told the press that the administration would dedicate its efforts to achieve sound development as the Currie Mission had proposed. Plans were soon in the works to carry out the development program under a United Nations program of technical assistance. United Nations Secretary-General Trygve Lie had met with Eliseo Arango in New York, and in March of 1951 a United Nations economist arrived in Bogotá to direct the program.

The Gómez government continued the trend toward government intervention through the principles of centralized planning.[6] Alvarez Restrepo was firmly committed to official action within the bounds of an austerity program, and he considered the task to be that of organizing and overseeing activities which would otherwise be ignored or mismanaged by private sectors of the economy. Among his efforts was the organization of a new monetary commission exclusively dedicated to further investigation and consideration of national needs where the government might play a role.[7]

There was no hesitancy in applying for loans, and at the close of 1950 the government received $2,600,000 from the International Bank of Reconstruction and Development for the expansion of the publicly-owned Caldas Hydroelectric Company. The United States Export-Import Bank also contributed $2,500,000 in a loan for the purchase of road-repair equipment from the United States. In January, Minister of Public Works Jorge Leyva also flew to the United States to present the IBRD with the government plan providing for construction of 736 kilometers of new roads and repair of an additional 4,000 kilometers, at a total cost of 163,000,000 pesos, or some $85,000,000.

The government had already set aside 54,000,000 pesos from the 1950 budget of 500,000,000,[8] and sought an additional $26,000,000 as soon as possible. Some 20 per cent of the total cost involved the purchase of equipment unavailable in Colombia. Leyva explained that it was important to reduce the Buenaventura port congestion. First, transportation connections with the Cauca and Magdalena valleys demanded improvement. Furthermore, the burden could be lightened by improving facilities in the Cartagena-Barranquilla region. On April 10, 1950, the IBRD announced a grant of $16,500,000 in a loan for highway construction and maintenance. Some 3,000,000 pesos of the sum would be specifically for the paving of the road leading east from Buenaventura. The rest was to be utilized for similar road improvements near the Caribbean. This was the bank's fourth loan to Colombia and increased its total investment in Colombia to $27,630,-000.[9]

The government applied a regimen of careful austerity and the overall economy moved toward a sounder fiscal position. Gómez had personally ordered a survey of the expense records of government departments, and results indicated that few had been operating within allotted budgets. He then issued a decree providing for a strengthened National Accounting Office and also for periodic publication of departmental expenses. This and comparable efforts led to a reduction of the $520,-000,000 public debt to $501,000,000 by April of 1951. In the same month an unprecedented budgetary surplus of 43,000,000 pesos was announced,[10] much of which was applied against the existing debt in the Banco de la República. Credit was restricted to prevent any decline in bank deposits, and those who had loaned against cash reserves to the legal limit were checked so that they did not surreptitiously exceed the limit.

At Gómez' request Alvarez Restrepo also drew up a new code designed to attract greater foreign investment. An Industrial Finance Corporation was established to provide a channel for foreign investments, empowered to act as trustee for industrial bonds and similar contingencies. On August 3, 1951, the regime decreed that free importation of capital would be permitted in either currency or equipment. It could be re-exported at any time, while undistributed profits could even be registered as imported capital.[11] Gómez was making good on his promise to create a more favorable climate for foreign investment; the welcome sign had duly been hung out for foreign capital. Hoping for greater economic diversification, the regime planned on an increase of available capital.[12]

As the president and his ministers proceeded, it became apparent that the administration was largely concerned with projects beneficial to the upper classes. New investment opportunities opened for those with idle capital, while the economic circumstance of the lower classes was materially unchanged. Along with this encouragement of corporate capitalism came increasing strangulation of the tender young labor movement. Pro-labor laws passed by Alfonso López years earlier were cancelled by executive decree, and independent unions were struck down by both legal and extra-legal means.[13]

Thus economic advances were extended to the oligarchy while the underprivileged continued to suffer. Employers and government agents moved into the labor movement, creating company-controlled organizations which the *bona fide* unions were unable to combat. Independent union gatherings were broken up by troops, while representatives of the Procesal del Trabajo told labor leaders what they might and might not do. "Parallel" company unions led to a growing number of "confessional" organizations closely controlled by the owners. As if this were not enough, there was even greater cause for concern elsewhere. For while the urban lower classes were being denied the right for legitimate self-improvement, their rural cousins were in many cases being denied the very right of survival and of life itself.

DEATH IN THE COUNTRYSIDE

Before the inauguration of President Gómez the fighting in the countryside had a distinct flavor of party strife. However, this progressed toward a combination of simple banditry and opposition to Gómez that was decreasingly related to party allegiance. The transition did not come overnight, and throughout the Gómez era there were both Liberals and Conservatives battling in the respective names of their parties. But the magnitude of turbulence increased, primarily as a protest against economic and social ills.

The new president was more aware of the explosive potential than Ospina Pérez had been. Consequently, he undertook a more determined campaign to put down the fighting. The first move was the selection of Roberto Urdaneta Arbeláez as minister of war. Urdaneta Arbeláez was a sixty-year-old lawyer-diplomat of long experience under both Conservative and Liberal governments. Largely educated by the Jesuits in Spain, a specialist in mercantile law and banking,[14] he had most recently served as head of the Colombian delegation to the United Nations. Returning as head of Ospina Pérez' "shock troops,"[15] he had remained with the understanding that a cabinet post under Gómez would be his. There was little surprise when he became Laureano's first minister of war.

Announcing his determination to end "banditry"—for he never admitted publicly that political overtones might exist—Urdaneta Arbeláez dispatched an expedition into the *llanos,* where the indomitable nomadic *llaneros* had taken power unto themselves in defiance of central authorities. He issued a "Warning to All Citizens" on October 20, 1950, defining as bandits all those who opposed military forces. "Bandits" would include all those of sixteen years and up who hid or fled from government troops. Violators of an 11:00 P.M. to 5:00 A.M. curfew were subject to arrest regardless of sex or age. All those carrying firearms without proper registration of weapons were also outside the law. Summary executions were authorized wherever officers considered it appropriate.[16]

Adopting a measure that the later military regime found equally ineffective, the government flew planes over the *llanos* dropping leaflets demanding evacuation of selected areas. The natives were at first reluctant to leave their ancestral communities, but the military moved into these regions, driving out all inhabitants and burning villages. Before long the dropping of leaflets was awaited with apprehension, and many left their homes before evacuation orders came. The result was the forcing of thousands to leave homes and property behind, taking refuge in other communities where social problems were aggravated by the influx of virtual refugees. The measure was of little value in pacifying the countryside.

The advent of Gómez to the presidency brought no improvement in the situation, as banditry increased substantially in several departments.

Antioquia, in particular, had suffered from numerous raids on cattle ranches and farms. By the end of 1950, violence was such that in Antioquia alone some forty police agents were killed.[17] On December 30, 1950, the president in his New Year's message reiterated that the fundamental goal of the new year was the reconquest of public tranquility. Admitting with more candor than his predecessor that terrorism still existed in sizeable proportions, he declared that his government was working diligently to control violence. Energetic action, he promised, would bring rapid pacification.[18] The National Police also revealed plans to recruit greater numbers in January and create additional training schools.

The next few months saw even greater turbulence, however. Eastern Cundinamarca suffered a series of disturbances for the first time, and by June at least seventy lives had been taken. Party overtones were heard when *El Siglo* charged that the Liberals were stirring up more trouble in conjunction with a forthcoming national convention. Minister of Government José Domingo Sarasty also hinted at party involvement with a statement in May that "the *liberal** effort seems revived, especially in Boyacá where attacks of armed bandits on the populations of Miraflores and Muzo have taken a toll of sixty-four lives in six days."[19] The dead were almost without exception Conservatives, he claimed.

With politics reinjected, Carlos Lleras Restrepo immediately replied that he "would request from the Minister that he concede us permission to talk on the violence without subjection to censorship. If he grants permission, the country will know immediately what we have to say on this particular."[20] Such permission was not forthcoming. Two months later Minister of War Urdaneta Arbeláez spoke on the entire problem at some length, particularly blaming the freeing of hundreds of criminals from prison during the *bogotazo*. Thousands serving long terms for nonpolitical offenses against society had fled at the time of the riots. Little could then be done, for files and records had also been destroyed.

Urdaneta Arbeláez did not blame the Liberals for recently-reported atrocities. However, he openly charged the party with tacit encouragement of the bandits. He felt that only by a renewed declaration condemning violence could the Liberals validly deny a degree of involvement. Thus the political element was reduced by his declarations, yet by no means eliminated.

* The emphasis is mine.

Easily the best description of what was happening was reported by Philip Payne in an August issue of *Time*. His report, which has since been widely reprinted, nonetheless merits quotation again at some length, for it captures the essence of the struggle in the early 1950's.

Liberal guerrillas were in the neighborhood, and the stoutly Conservative residents of San Pedro de Jagua knew well that their homes might be struck next. . . .

At 4:30 one day recently, there was a dull boom in the east. The warning did not save San Pedro. Minutes later a uniformed column approached the village. "Don't shoot!" cried one marcher. "We're the Army." By the time San Pedro's garrison of 18 realized that the column was some 50 bandits in stolen army uniforms, it was too late. "Surrender or die!" the bandits roared, and with one brief volley they dispersed the defenders. Two hundred more bandits, not uniformed, poured into the city, shouting "Long live the Liberal Party!"

The rising sun showed the villagers who their attackers were: mostly country boys, some as young as 14, every one with a good Mauser rifle (a few had automatic rifles), a revolver, a machete, a knife. Commanding the bandits from San Pedro's central plaza was a lightly-built man of about 25, clad in a new *ruana*. This was the storied bandit chief, Tulio Bautista. Guns cracked all over the town. . . .

The bandits found a single Liberal in the local jail, held on suspicion of aiding the bandits. Freed, this man showed Tulio's boys where there were two drums of oil fuel for the local power plant. "If only they hadn't found that fuel," mourned a San Pedro survivor later. Tulio ordered the homes of the town burned, to flush out any possible police ambush, but forbade his men to fire the church or the school. . . .

By mid-afternoon, the bandits were ready to leave. At the cemetery they buried their single casualty with military honors. Then they marched away in good order, leaving smoldering ruins and 24 bodies. The surviving people of San Pedro stayed long enough to bury their own dead, to disinter the bandit's body and throw it away to the buzzards. Then, the civil war's newest refugees, they straggled westward to seek shelter in the nearest towns.[21]

Further Liberal Weakening

From August of 1950 until November of 1951 the Liberals were gradually shifting positions and allegiances, all the while growing more impotent politically. As in previous years, they were divided on the question of total opposition or party conciliation. The newly-christened Junta Popular Liberal, composed of *Jornada* journalists and intransigent *gaitanistas*, strengthened their position by charging the regular directorate with following policies permitting the "Monstruo" Gómez to reach the presidency. The DLN was attacked for alleged failure to consult public opinion, and in September, 1950, the dissidents announced the intention of taking over the Liberal party. Promising to fight privilege and the high cost of living while urging restoration of civil rights, the Junta Popular Liberal was critical of past collaboration with Ospina Pérez. Contradictorily, they were willing to support Gómez himself if, as the manifesto read, "it is true that he is inexorably against crime and impunity, if he dedicates himself to the task of healing the wounds of Colombians, and if he genuinely believes that the greatest need of the Nation is peace."[22]

Carlos Lleras Restrepo replied in the name of the directorate with a series of articles in *El Tiempo*. After defending its nature as representative, he attacked the Junta Popular Liberal as an illegitimate offspring of the party. He argued that the DLN was acting in complete accord with policies approved at the last Liberal meeting. Despite his response, the Liberals were badly divided. Changes in the next few months brought eventual agreement on total opposition to the government, and it was also accepted that subversion ought not to be the chosen path back to political power. The dissidents, however, remained convinced that the directorate, and Lleras Restrepo in particular, were basically rightist and oligarchic, thus were not fit for Liberal party leadership. Although unable to meet Lleras Restrepo's request that they show a single instance in which he had favored the oligarchy, the ferocity of the generalized attack continued.

In November the DLN sent the government a manifesto outlining its abstention from collaboration, as based upon civil, non-violent opposition. The directorate promised to maintain total opposition and virtual inactivity until civil rights were restored. Any who disobeyed would be expelled from the party. Former President Santos added in late December that although the political parties certainly should co-operate with one another in a democratic system, there was no real basis for it in view of the undemocratic Gómez regime.

The debility of the Liberals was underlined by the necessity of returning leadership to its elder statesmen, Eduardo Santos and Alfonso López. Both had stepped out of political retirement only for occasional declarations, but by 1951 the Liberal division was so bitter that both former presidents reached the conclusion that they were needed. Of the younger leaders, only the embattled Lleras Restrepo had been carrying on. It was a sad commentary on party leadership that the rank and file was forced to turn to its distinguished elders for competent direction.

Eduardo Santos, in particular, would have denied that he was returning to the political wars. He had turned down repeated offers to head the directorate with the comment that he was "only a soldier in the cause."[23] As *Semana* explained, Santos was not obsessed with politics, and he had certainly preferred to remain in retirement. With the directorate, Santos believed in abstention, non-collaboration, and total opposition. Normally an advocate of the principle of a loyal opposition, he felt it unworkable under existing circumstances, reiterating instead a four-word slogan: "Faith, Dignity, Abstention, Opposition." Such was the lack of civil guarantees that the only Liberal course was to present a unified front against the Conservative administration. Santos' contribution was not a new approach or change of policy, but rather a reunification of all Liberals around the principles they almost universally accepted.

Those who approved of abstention felt that it was a useful temporary expedient. It could be used as a banner of purity and moral righteousness, and it certainly seemed the course of prudence in view of the lamentable rural situation. There was also considerable hope that the Conservatives themselves might begin intra-party squabbling, and a parallel was drawn with the disciplined Conservative abstention in the late 1930's during the bitter Santos-López dispute. Few were candid enough to admit that the Liberals had never been able to achieve the unity of purpose that Gómez had imposed upon his Conservatives. The difference in organizational strength and discipline between the parties was basic. More perceptive observers realized that, now in the presidency, Gómez might simply strengthen his party until abstaining Liberals disappeared into political limbo.

The Liberals scheduled a national convention for June of 1951 in the hope of smoothing over personal differences. More than 700 delegates gathered in Bogotá's Teatro Imperio on June 23. The directorate, still composed of Lleras Restrepo, Chaux, Echandía, and Uribe Márquez, along with the newly-appointed Delio Enciso, opened the meeting with a call for national unity.[24] Lleras Restrepo, the key figure as the convention opened, was under renewed fire from both *Jornada* and López' *El Liberal*. The latter soon stopped its attacks on orders of López.

The basic issue before the convention was that of a revised leadership which might reunify the party and consider possible policy revision. Many delegates voiced the opinion that the party would be more effective under a one-man directorate, although López, Santos, and Lleras Restrepo had all criticized the idea. The directorate renewed the Santos cry for "faith and dignity" and adopted the slogan of the *antioqueño* Hernando Agudelo Villa, "abstention all along the line, civil opposition all along the line."[25]

Carlos Lleras Restrepo opened the meeting with a speech of four-and-a-half hours, in which he set forth directorate policy in familiar detail. Blaming civil violence on disturbances following the 1947 congressional elections, he held the Conservatives responsible for the bloodshed, as well as the failure of Ospina Pérez' National Union. Liberalism, he suggested, might still be willing to cooperate with President Gómez for the re-establishment of peace, but collaboration was impossible unless civil restrictions were lifted. Lleras Restrepo concluded with a peroration demanding freedom of speech. The next morning the Conservatives replied in a "Manchette" editorial for *El Siglo* that he had called for "rebellion against authority; freedom to conspire; opposition to national concord; freedom to hate."[26] Those who advocated some form of collaboration wondered anew whether there was really much hope.

The convention seemed unlikely to settle much, with both Santos and López initially absent. But, at the suggestion of Lleras Restrepo, Santos was elected to preside over the delegates, and on the convention's second day a motion was passed inviting Dr. López to attend. A twelve-man delegation called upon López, and the following day, June 25, he arrived amid great acclaim, responding with a flag-waving, party-arousing oration that awakened the delegates from their lethargy and defeatism for the first time. He made a particular point of praising Lleras Restrepo and of defending his authority vigorously. By the end of the convention, a new directorate had been selected, composed of López, Santos, and Lleras Restrepo. Thus the delegates left control of the party in the hands of this dominant triumvirate. It remained to be seen whether even their efforts might be fruitful. There was at least a little hope in López' call for constructive, lasting peace: "In the face of a situation of persecution and violence that has not been modified by the present regime, the directorate insists that the best policy for the Liberal Party is one of peace. . . . [Alternatives to peace were] catastrophes of unforeseeable magnitude."[27]

One of the final Liberal holds on political power was the position of Eduardo Santos as *designado,* presumably in line for the presidency should something happen to Gómez. The *designado,* roughly akin to a national vice-president, had long been a subject of dispute. The 1886 constitution had created a regular vice-president, but in 1910 two *designados* were established, each one enjoying a one-year encumbency. In 1945 the Congress removed the second *designado,* who had been serving as president of the Consejo de Estado. In August of 1946, then, Congress had begun electing a single *designado* for a two-year period. Carlos Arango Vélez had been chosen in 1946, and upon his resignation the Liberal majority named Eduardo Santos.

However, no election was held in 1948, and upon this omission rested the question of a legal successor to the president. Laureano Gómez was solely interested in assuring Conservative *continuismo,* but there *was* a constitutional question involved. According to Article 125, "when for whatever reason the congress might not have enacted the election of *designados,* the character of those previously-elected will retain their character."[28] The provision was followed by two asterisks which referred back to an earlier clause removing the provision for a second *designado.*

The Liberals naturally interpreted the constitution to indicate that Dr. Santos still occupied the post for which he had been elected in 1946. Conservatives responded that the 1945 revision had left a loophole in eliminating the second *designado,* and they suggested that, in the absence of elections, the remaining *designado's* term would not automatically be extended. Thus the decision to name a new one should go to the cabinet. Conservatives were clearly on boggy ground, but vagueries of constitutional wording did leave the matter somewhat unclear.

The president settled the question arbitrarily with Executive Decree 2996, which declared the post of *designado* vacant. The decree explained that, with Congress not in session, the cabinet ministers were granted legal sanction to name a formal order of succession. It began with the minister of government, continuing through foreign relations, justice, economy, and war, down to the minor cabinet positions. The thirteen ministers were followed by the fifteen departmental governors. Thus José Domingo Sarasty was the apparent successor, with Gonzalo Restrepo Jaramillo second and Guillermo Amaya Ramírez third. Roberto Urdaneta Arbeláez was fifth.[29] He was soon to move up.

GOMEZ REASSERTS SUPREMACY

With Santos no longer in a position to replace the occasionally ailing president, and the Liberals at their weakest in many years, Laureano Gómez proceeded to consider possible constitutional reforms. Even as he did so, his lieutenants bent their efforts to strengthen the regime while preparing for eventual succession in 1954. Few gave serious consideration to José Domingo Sarasty, an able administrative technician with little political power of his own and no apparent strong ambition. The aspirations of Jorge Leyva have already been mentioned, and there was wide suspicion that Roberto Urdaneta Arbeláez was also eying the presidency, despite scrupulous avoidance of any such suggestion. The most powerful Conservative activist, short of Gómez himself, however, was hard-driving, controversial Gilberto Alzate Avendaño.

Born in Manizales in 1910, Conservative Director Alzate Avendaño had been trained in law and began his political career in the early 1930's when the Conservative party was in virtual political ruin. Working arduously, he rose swiftly to the national position of secretary-general; electoral and organizational details fell largely into his hands. But he began to push a bit too hard, and Laureano Gómez arbitrarily dismissed him from the party. Undaunted, Alzate Avendaño proceeded to organize his own party in Medellín and Manizales, the Acción Nacionalista Popular (ANP). Joined by Silvio Villegas, Fernando Londoño, and the Naranjo Villegas brothers—all victims of Gómez exile from the Conservatives—he tried to little avail from 1936 to 1939 to win away Conservative supporters. Alzate Avendaño mixed authoritarian ideas with a Bolivarian thesis, advocating a type of Nazi state of extreme hierarchy and discipline. Stumping the nation with bellicosity, he won little support. His strength was never estimated at more than 12,000.[30]

Silvio Villegas was a major defection back to the Conservatives, and with the ANP dying, Alzate Avendaño himself was restored to Gómez' favor. Only after the 1946 elections, however, did the heavy-jowled, balding Alzate Avendaño return to full political activity. Although apparently dedicated to the advance of the Conservative party, he was still imbued with his own immense ambition and a tendency to talk in grandiose terms of his personal destiny. His talents as an organizer exceeded those as orator or writer,[31] and the party put him to work once more on strengthening its apparatus. His work was comparable in both intensity and effectiveness to that of Lleras Restrepo for the Liberals.

By 1950 Alzate Avendaño had achieved a major ambition—appointment to the Conservative National Directorate. Refusing a cabinet appointment, he continued to build support within the party. When Gómez took office, the five-man DNC was reduced by two as Jorge Villareal became minister of commerce and Guillermo León Valencia took the ambassadorial post in Spain. Augusto Ramírez Moreno soon went to France on diplomatic assignment, leaving Alzate Avendaño with Luis Navarro Ospina as the only two Conservative directors.

In the face of veteran Conservatives, who distrusted the rising young man, Alzate Avendaño showed in early 1951 that they would have to be dealt with. "I hear the clamor of the peoples," he announced.[32] Few doubted that he was eying the presidential palace in 1954. Improving his own strength by vigorously building up the party machinery at all levels, he prepared for the June, 1951, congressional elections in the hope of putting a large number of loyal *alzatistas* in office. His ambitions were rivalled by the dashing Villareal, another coming power in the party, and when the latter resigned from the cabinet, he returned to the party directorate he had recently left. Villareal realized the inherent power of being a director; the Conservative party statute directed in Article 26, "Members of the national and sectional directories will not be elected for posts of popular representation in the national congress and in the departmental assemblies after having accepted and exercised a post [on the directorate] during the period in which the election is held or six months before it."[33] The ban on cabinet membership by a party director was implicitly understood.

In May, Dr. Gómez announced the postponement of congressional elections from June until September, claiming that he considered injurious to national interests any election in which Liberal representation might be lost. He considered Liberal members "essential for the normal functioning of that body."[34] It was understood unofficially that Gómez entertained mild hopes of Liberal participation. It was not forthcoming.

Congressional elections were finally called for September 16, and the Conservatives compaigned on the slogan of "Reconquest of the Legislature,"[35] scarcely a difficult task in view of Liberal abstention. On August 22 the party read a list of 176 candidates over Radiodifusión Nacional, including such prominent Conservatives as Valencia, Eliseo Arango, Evaristo Sourdis, and Mariano Ospina Pérez.[36] On election day over 800,000 voted, and the all-Conservative Congress was convened in Bogota on October 30, 1951. Since an executive decree had directed that a given number of opposition seats could not be occupied by Conservatives, many seats were vacant. The new Senate consisted of 40 Conservatives, with 22 seats unfilled; the Chamber had 71 Conservatives, with 51 empty places.

November of 1951, at the time, seemed a critical month in the long history of Colombian conservatism, although later events proved it less consequential than anticipated. The month was marked by severe political infighting that was finally resolved only by the direct intervention of Laureano Gómez. The Conservative convention was to open on Monday, November 12, almost two weeks after the legislative organs were to convene.

On Sunday, October 28, news spread through Bogotá that President Gómez had suddenly fallen seriously ill. Gómez' doctors ordered him to take a complete rest; for several weeks, he would be unable to exercise the presidential duties. Officially he was suffering from "overwork," but it was later revealed that he had suffered a serious heart attack. Conservative Director Luis Navarro Ospina was called to the presidential bedside, and it was decided to call Congress immediately so that a new *designado* might be elected. Gómez announced that Minister of War Urdaneta Arbeláez should take over as acting president, and Navarro Ospina was soon carrying the news to Alzate Avendaño, who had already been on the telephone ordering congressmen to Bogotá at once.

By Monday legislators were hurrying into Bogotá, many unshaven and in rumpled clothes. On Tuesday the Chamber of Representatives met and swiftly approved Urdaneta Arbeláez by 83 to 11. At 8:10 P.M. the minister of war himself arrived, and by 9:30 both houses were meeting in joint session, where the final vote was 108-3.[37] By the middle of the next day Gómez had sent official word that he was temporarily leaving his position for reasons of health. On Monday, November 5, 1951, Roberto Urdaneta Arbeláez took formal possession of the acting presidency. Gómez retained his position as titular president.

Among the interesting aspects of the situation was the refusal to follow the recent decree establishing a clear presidential succession. But Dr. Gómez had never intended that Sarasty should replace him; his only purpose was to remove all possibility of a Liberal substitute. As soon as a Conservative-controlled Congress was in session, it was possible to name a new *designado*. There was no particular surprise when Gómez picked Urdaneta Arbeláez. By so doing he had avoided possible dispute among Villareal, Leyva, and Valencia. Gilberto Alzate Avendaño had no desire for a short-lived temporary presidency; his ambitions went further.

The choice of Urdaneta Arbeláez also assured the continuation of existing policies, for the loyal minister of war was in close ideological agreement with the ailing Laureano. A member of the old-guard Conservatives, he had served his country well for many years. Remembered by his oldest friends as a prematurely serious young man with a dedicated if narrow sense of patriotism, his circles were oligarchic ones, and through the years he had become accustomed to an ambassadorial atmosphere. A diplomat who was noted for his talents as a compromiser, he had managed to avoid extremes, and was among the small number of prominent Colombians who had served both Liberal and Conservative governments in positions of responsibility. His bland exterior occasionally approached the point of unctuousness, and he was expected to govern through the use of compromise, negotiation, and ultimate reliance upon the power of Laureano Gómez.

When he took the oath of office, Urdaneta Arbeláez promised a continuing campaign against rural violence. He stated that peace would bring the immediate lifting of the state of siege and the return of complete individual liberties. But despite such words, there was scant reason to suspect any lessening of the oppressive controls Gómez had put into operation. The acting president was to continue in the footsteps of the old Conservative leader, with whom he consulted on major policy matters. Their agreement was complete.[38]

The official machinery was soon to tighten, but a Conservative party struggle had begun as an indirect result of the election of Urdaneta Arbeláez as *designado*. The storm center was Alzate Avendaño, whose relentless drive for power had been stepping on many toes. In the process of assuring the election of Urdaneta Arbeláez in Congress, Alzate Avendaño had unnecessarily irritated the older generation of Conservatives, who still regarded him as a young upstart. They willingly made common cause with younger enemies of Alzate Avendaño and he was outmaneuvered at the party convention when it opened on November 12.

Alzate Avendaño made the mistake of absenting himself from the morning session. The old guard, the *gobiernista* Conservatives, moved opportunistically and elected a new party directorate composed of seven non-*alzatistas*.* Alzate Avendaño, astounded at this development and furious with his own followers, who dominated the convention numerically, struck back by naming his own *tradicionalista* directorate.† Both groups claimed to be authentic, and the ultimate outcome was very much in question. The Alzate Avendaño *tradicionalistas* enjoyed an estimated margin of 206-140 on the convention floor.[39] On the other hand, the *gobiernistas* had, also in Alzate Avendaño's absence, changed convention resolutions to invite a group of "notables" to the convention, most of them known to oppose Alzate Avendaño. Not insignificantly, Alvaro Gómez Hurtado was in the forefront.[40]

The *alzatistas,* self-styled *legitimistas,* agreed to make an appeal to Acting President Urdaneta Arbeláez, who hastily passed the political hot potato to the stricken Gómez. A decision came down from the Olympian heights, naming a six-man directorate composed of four *gobiernistas,* only one *legitimista,* and the uncommited Valencia, who was in Madrid.‡ Alzate Avendaño protested briefly that it was unrepresentative, but he knew there was no appeal to a Gómez decision.

As 1952 neared, Laureano Gómez, despite his fragile health, was moving satisfactorily toward the regime he wanted. The economy was prospering to the benefit of the oligarchy; governmental organs were

---

* *Gobiernistas*: Rafael Azuero, Lucio Pabón Nuñez, Luis Navarro Ospina, Guillermo León Valencia, Jorge Villareal, José Antonio Montalvo, and José Gabriel de la Vega.

† *Tradicionalistas*: Francisco de Paula Pérez, Guillermo León Valencia, and Gilberto Alzate Avendaño.

‡ *Gobiernistas*: Rafael Azuero, Lucio Pabón Nuñez, José Antonio Montalvo, and José Gabriel de la Vega; *legitimista*: Francisco de Paula Pérez.

firmly in Conservative hands; Liberal opposition was disorganized and ineffectual; the swift rise of the bumptious Alzate Avendaño had been checked, without any other Conservative standing out significantly; administrative control had passed to the most reliable of his lieutenants, the competent Urdaneta Arbeláez; and while civil war was still on the rise, it seemed to pose no immediate threat to the stability of the regime.

It remained for Laureano to expound his theories of *hispanidad* and establish the reactionary, corporate constitution that would guarantee an indefinite extension of Conservative rule. Despite the brief revival of Liberal hopes with the return of Alfonso López to politics, there seemed no unsurmountable obstacles to the remaking of Colombia in the Gómez image.

Chapter Nine

AN EMERGENT DICTATORSHIP

THE LIBERALS IN COMPLETE ECLIPSE

WITH THE COMING of 1952, the Liberals prepared a final effort at exercising party responsibility before being completely submerged by the Gómez-Urdaneta Arbeláez apparatus. Alfonso López applied all the prestige of his name in trying to bring about party concord. His strangely-cordial friendship with Laureano Gómez was called upon as well, and for the better part of a year he labored arduously, until autumn brought events marking the eclipse of the party.

The year opened on a thinly hopeful note when Urdaneta Arbeláez delivered a conciliatory New Year's message. Anxious to reduce political and civil conflict, which had troubled him as minister of war, he indicated a willingness to negotiate with Liberals on outstanding issues. He was not about to yield Conservative authority, yet the acting president felt that some small advantage might accrue from talks with the Liberals. With this idea he made a point of speaking well of the opposition: "I would like to make specific mention of the fact that high Liberal party figures—among them Dr. Alfonso López—have demonstrated their willingness to collaborate with the government in its effort to reestablish normality in the nation and a feeling of conviviality among the Colombian people. As regards the present special emergency conditions under which we are living, I would like to state the government is making great progress towards returning to normality. It was to further this aim that we called for the election of our congressmen. . . ."[1]

In February, Urdaneta Arbeláez granted a radio interview to Margarita Olano Cruz of *Diario del Pacífico*. Questions were largely general ones, and Urdaneta Arbeláez took a brief swipe at the Liberals by referring to them as speaking of peace but often doing nothing constructive. He compared this to his own past experience with the Soviet Andrei Vishinsky in the United Nations. He willingly conceded, at the same time, that many Liberals were honestly dedicated to peace, adding that "although the government is concerned over the continuing violence and lawlessness, I do not believe that the stability of the present regime is threatened nor that the progress of Colombia is being deterred.[2]

In the same interview he declared, as other chief executives of Colombia had been doing with tiresomely empty assurance, that violence was "truly" being reduced. "This cloud," he insisted, "cannot darken the clear horizon that is opened to the future of Colombia. Some 99 percent of the 12 million inhabitants the country has, are not worried by the so-called problem of violence. . . ."[3] This underplaying of the proportions of conflict had been preceded only two days earlier by the admission of Minister of War José María Bernal that "civil war" existed in at least eleven of the sixteen departments.[4]

Even as Liberals were grasping at these last slender straws, they could not refrain from intermittent outbursts of criticism that weakened their chances. On January 5, López and Lleras Restrepo issued a joint declaration noting that, for the first time in forty years, nearly twenty-four months had passed without a congressional session (November 9, 1949, to November 5, 1951). The subsequent all-Conservative body scarcely met the usual norms of representation. Altogether, some sixty-five months of Conservative rule had followed Ospina Pérez' inauguration, thirty-four of which were under a state of siege.[5]

Dr. López, stepping forward as the recognized Liberal spokesman, made further declarations at a meeting on February 8 at Bogotá's Hotel Granada. Reiterating the Liberal desire for peace and the solution of political problems, he discussed a recent trip to the *llanos* on which he had spoken with guerrilla leaders, urging them to end the blood-letting. He explained that the initiative for the trip had come from Urdaneta Arbeláez, thus emphasizing that he had not broken party unity by seeking out official permission.

In the weeks to follow, Dr. López busily discussed conditions with government officials and Conservative leaders, but the acting president was acting increasingly like Dr. Gómez. In a state of the nation message delivered on April 19 from the presidential palace, he openly attacked the Liberals without reservation, reviving the charge that the Liberals had destroyed the National Union of Mariano Ospina Pérez through irresponsibility. All subsequent party actions mirrored their disregard for the public welfare, he claimed. It was fortunate for Colombia that conservativism had put the principle of collaboration into operation, but the Liberals had willfully broken it twice. Dr. Gómez had further attempted to revive it, only to see the Liberals refuse even to recognize the legitimacy of the administration.

Urdaneta Arbeláez added insult to injury by refusing Dr. López permission to reply over the national radio network. Perhaps the only prominent Liberal to be undismayed was López himself. From the pages of his *El Liberal* the veteran former president continually urged reconciliation and peace. He held several conferences with the acting president, still hopeful of improving party relations with the government. It was at his urging that the Liberals agreed to support the short-lived "Crusade for Peace" launched in May by Urdaneta Arbeláez and Archbishop Luque.

By mid-summer it was clear that Dr. López' extensive campaign was meeting with failure, and there were recurrent rumors of his impending resignation from the Liberal Directorate. The formal announcement came on August 22, 1952. Explaining that his trip to the *llanos,* talks with the Acting President, and attempted cooperation with the authorities had proved fruitless, López felt that his resignation was demanded. Party accord had proved impossible, and conditions of the state of siege made attempts at party activity worthless. The absence of even minimal improvement made his continued presence on the Directorate unnecessary.[6] Quite rightly, López had concluded that his chance, slim as it had been, was past. There now seemed little that any Liberal could do.

One week later Alfonso López made a final bid for reconciliation with a long letter sent simultaneously to Ospina Pérez, Archbishop Luque, and the Conservative president of a projected Commission on Constitutional Studies, Francisco de Paula Pérez. Surveying the events of the last two years, López reminded his correspondents of Liberal declarations against lawlessness, pointing to his own trip to the *llanos* as proof of Liberal intentions. In referring to his resignation from the Liberal directorate he stated that the government had given no indication of cooperating with him. Adding his continued availability for any measures that might lead to a reduction of disturbance, he made a point of inviting the three men to exert their influence on the Conservative party to bring about enlightened examination of existing problems.[7] López was especially desirous of drawing an expression of views from Ospina Pérez but his fellow former president was, characteristically, cautiously noncommittal. The appeal went unheeded, and the final disintegration of the Liberals was shortly precipitated by the lamentable events of September 6, 1952. The death knell of the party was sounded for the duration of Conservative rule and beyond.

In the morning of the sixth, a crowd gathered to pay homage to five policemen who had been killed in Rovira, Tolima. The bodies, which had reportedly been flogged to death and virtually dismembered by bandits, had been flown to the capital for burial with full honors. Urdaneta Arbeláez was among the mourners. A few minutes after the conclusion of services, a crowd gathered in downtown Bogotá and began menacing the officers of *El Tiempo* and *El Espectador*. Police dispersed the crowd, but later in the day a mob of some 200 began milling about the same newspaper offices.

Shouting "down with the Liberals, down with the assassins," they fired several shots, began flinging stones, and broke into the offices.[8] Starting with *El Tiempo,* the mob destroyed advertising and circulation records, wrecked the editorial rooms, and then smashed the pressroom.[9] *El Espectador* received the same treatment, and then the rowdy band moved to Liberal party headquarters and, after destroying its files and wrecking the offices, set fire to the building, gutting it thoroughly. There was no evidence of the usually omnipresent Bogotá police while this was transpiring. It is also worth remembering that the crowd had formed during a time of considerable unrest when a legal, strongly enforced national state of siege existed.

With dusk falling, the lawlessness spread, reaching a level of uncontrolled political hatred. Alfonso López was at home during the afternoon entertaining friends. He was called, informed of the downtown attacks, and was warned that he himself might be the target of further violence. He sturdily refused to leave the house; by 6:45 P.M., however, ominous cries were heard near his residence, and the veteran politician, his guests, and his young grandchildren prudently left the house.[10] A few moments later a crowd of an estimated fifty to a hundred men approached and entered the building, systematically setting about its destruction.

The attackers were well prepared. Valuable articles and family relics were either stolen or destroyed. The files of the former president, his personal library, and irreplaceable state documents and mementos of his long career were not spared. Decorations from foreign governments and autographed photographs of world-famous personages were smashed. Alfonso López Michelsen, his son, told *Semana* that it was impossible to estimate the damages in material terms. "I cannot do it. [The destroyed articles] were undoubtedly very valuable. . . . But for us the articles were valued in a different, a spiritual way. Among my father's things, in his archives . . . were numerous documents, decorations, flags, testimonials. . . ."[11] Even López-hating *El Siglo* admitted that little but floors and walls remained of the home.[12]

After finishing at López' residence, the mob, considerably increased in size by the addition of hoodlums, moved on to the home of Carlos Lleras Restrepo. The fiery Liberal director, also warned shortly before the attack, took out a revolver and drove the attackers away under fire. They soon regrouped, however, and were in the process of surrounding the house when Lleras Restrepo wisely withdrew. His home was even more completely destroyed than that of López; the mob carried dynamite and, after looting the interior, blew up much of the building.

Acting President Urdaneta Arbeláez had left Bogotá following the morning funeral and was speaking at Funza, an hour's trip from the capital. Informed of developments, he returned at once and by 10:30 P.M. had convened a cabinet meeting. Only Minister of Government Luis Ignacio Andrade was absent, delivering speeches to the south in Huila. A statement was issued calling for serenity "to impede repetition of any similar actions." Deploring the incidents, Urdaneta Arbeláez promised "a severe investigation with the inflexible purpose of establishing responsibilities and applying sanctions." Ospina Pérez also spoke out quickly. "As a Colombian and as a Conservative I condemn emphatically the reprehensible facts. . . . [They are] contrary to the traditions of our people and to the doctrinal principles that I have defended."[13]

El Tiempo rose to the challenge, as might be expected of a journal widely recognized as a great hemispheric spokesman for democracy. After missing one day's publication, it reappeared on Monday, September 8, printing an eight-page tabloid using old presses of *El Liberal.*[14] Material damages to its own plant and offices were irreparable, however, destroying what had been built over a period of forty years.[15]

The Liberals attacked the government party with considerable justification. The very fact that the mob had been permitted to run amuck in the center of the national capital was suggestive of complicity. The police themselves were no better than the looters, who seemingly were assured of non-interference by the security forces. Even more damning was the fact that Dr. López' home was only two doors from the heavily-guarded Urdaneta Arbeláez residence, yet the presidential guard permitted the attack, which was in full view, and no effort was made to stop the destructive proceedings.[16]

Liberal allegations touched on other points. The city fire department had not responded to calls; significantly, it had changed fire chiefs a week earlier. The outgoing chief was known to hold Liberal sympathies. Another charge, which was unsubstantiated, was that Government Minister Andrade, one of the more reactionary Conservatives, had recently told a dinner gathering that the regime could control violence if the Liberals stopped inciting "political" bandits. This could be accomplished only by taking ten Liberal lives for every national policeman or soldier killed by guerrillas.[17]

Even riot-hardened *bogotanos* were disturbed by events, and the acting president responded with vagueries to the representations of two young Liberals, Abelardo Forero Benavides and Francisco Umaña Bernal. On September 13 Urdaneta Arbeláez broadcast, with some embarrassment, that "it is essential that these events be condemned, and I do so expressly. I have already done so in the name of the government the very night of the disgrace . . . a rigorous investigation was ordered that will be assisted by the Procurador-General of the Nation, an illustrious jurist of Liberal affiliation."[18] Returning to the depradations of the *bogotazo,* he reminded his listeners of the destruction of the Gómez home, as if to convince them that two wrongs made a right.

Referring again to the persistent charge that the Liberals were intimately involved with guerrilla activities, he cautioned them against further "aid" to the bandits. Coexistence between civil opposition and armed insurgency was impossible, and he warned that similar events might occur unless the Liberals broke off completely with the bandits. He proclaimed the "inescapable" conclusion that Liberals continued to applaud the violent outrages of their rural partisans while complaining of retaliation. He intimated that there might well be new incidents triggered by the deaths of civilians and soldiers. Ominously, he suggested that the time might be near when government agents "would cease to use all their enthusiasm in order to protect vigorously their own detractors against the indignant reaction of their own friends."[19]

Thus Urdaneta Arbeláez took the offensive in threatening further reprisal against the Liberals. He certainly had no prior knowledge of the events of the sixth, and there is little reason to question the genuineness of his expression of sorrow. At the same time, growing attacks on civil rights were being carried out, often without direct knowledge of the chief of state. In this case, the conclusion is unavoidable that highly placed government authorities, if not Urdaneta Arbeláez himself, were well aware of plans to attack the buildings and homes which suffered on September 6.

Rather than modify existing restrictions, the government harshened its control by decreeing a more rigorous censorship code. All material dealing with matters of public or political order, of security matters, and of economic or international issues involving Colombia had to be approved by the government before publication.[20] Even the Conservative press was subject to the new controls, and only *El Siglo* failed to join with the other journals in sympathizing openly with the attacks on *El Tiempo* and *El Espectador*. *El Diario Colombiano* of Cali, on September 15, printed a long article on the tourist attractions of St. Augustine, Florida, in the space usually reserved for editorial comment. It explained this strange procedure with the wry statement that "for obvious reasons, we welcome to these pages an article on the tourist attractions of a distant city . . . and invite our readers to go in search of new horizons."[21]

Alfonso López and Lleras Restrepo had taken refuge in the Venezuelan Embassy, bringing further embarrassment on Urdaneta Arbeláez. The acting president spoke of their attitude peevishly, saying that no one was persecuting them and that "the government is ready to give them the safety and assurance they want." Criticizing their suggestion that the government was driving them away, he accused the two of deliberately worsening conditions by hinting at persecution. He failed to explain away the fact that the attacks on their homes indicated either that the government was not in control of Bogotá or that it condoned political vandalism.

Notwithstanding Urdaneta Arbeláez' insistence that his presence in Bogotá would have prevented the crimes, none could deny that events had shown the citizenry "the necessity of a moral reconstruction and of a sincere effort in favor of peace and of concord on the part of all Colombians."[22] In the absence of any such effort, there was little hope for improvement. The Conservative *El Colombiano* of Medellín sounded the fears of the people on September 11, 1952: "We are riding a wildly spinning wheel where today's victims become tomorrow's executioners and these, in turn, the future victims. Each victim feeds on the idea of retaliation, so that there will be enough hatred in Colombia for the next 150 years."

On Wednesday, October 1, López and Lleras Restrepo left the Venezuelan Embassy with official safe-conduct passes, flew from Colombia to Jamaica, and proceeded on to exile in Mexico City. With other leaders also leaving the country, party leadership was left to three young caretakers, Abelardo Forero Benavides, José Joaquin Castro, and Alejandro Galves. The National Directorate announced the indefinite suspension of activities, and the party treasury declared the termination of functions. No more contributions would be received. Thus, amid official embarrassment but personal satisfaction, the mounting dictatorship had driven to cover its only significant civil opposition. The Liberal party was grievously wounded, its future questionable. During the days following the attacks of September 6, only one prominent politician had failed to comment publicly. He stayed at home in semi-isolation; it was a happy time for Laureano Gómez.

THE MECHANICS OF OPPRESSION

With the coils of dictatorship tightening about the body politic, coercion and controls became more open. Rural guerrilla warfare led to increasing repression, the open use of force spread, and press censorship became a significant tool of the regime. Violence was tinged with elements of religious persecution, and continued church-state cooperation made it appear even worse. These elements were all woven into the pattern that clothed but failed to hide the reactionary nature of the government.

Censorship, legally sanctioned under the existing state of siege, was slowly extended in scope and efficacy following the inauguration of Dr. Gómez in 1950. After he relinquished active control to Urdaneta Arbeláez, restrictions continued to increase in harshness, motivated in theory by the unending bloodshed in the countryside. Before Urdaneta Arbeláez stepped in, Gómez had issued an executive decree in April of 1951 denying radio newscasters the right to broadcast comments or oral editorials. They were limited to the mere reading of news items, which had to be presented a day in advance for possible revision by the censors.

Under Gómez the over-all censorship was largely a matter of inconvenience, particularly for the newspapers. Political information was submitted to the censors, where it was accepted or infrequently rejected on a fluctuating standard that made the operation highly unpredictable. The nuisance value of the censorship was not too effective as a check on political information that was available to the people. The element of annoyance was greatest in such insignificant matters as sizes of headlines and arrangement of makeup. Even society pages were occasionally tampered with. Only infrequently, however, were papers forbidden to publish for a day or so as punishment for previous "inconsistencies."

Roberto Urdaneta Arbeláez announced when he became acting president that censorship would be minimal, although controls were necessary as long as public order was incomplete.[23] But the criteria by which censorship was applied became noticeably more rigid. In June of 1952 another set of regulations forced *El Tiempo* and *El Expectador* to halt publication for several days, following a government pronouncement that the name of Conservative maverick Gilberto Alzate Avendaño could not appear in print![24] Alzate Avendaño's personal protest to Urdaneta Arbeláez was unavailing. Only when he later recovered status in Conservative circles was his name "mentionable" once more.

During a special mid-summer congressional session, two full days were devoted to debate on the question of press freedom and the maintenance of order. *Alzatistas* argued that regulation should apply solely to articles directly affecting public order. They attacked indiscriminate regulation of any and all subjects. Minister of Government Luis Ignacio Andrade, who was becoming the representative figure of reactionary elements in the regime, sarcastically responded that the government considered total censorship necessary, and would change its position only with the total elimination of violence. He took personal responsibility for the ban of Alzate Avendaño's name, justifying it on the grounds that *alzatistas* were anarchical, irresponsible, and devoted to the upset of the existing order.

The floundering Liberal Directorate also wrote Andrade deploring censorship and asking for a clarification of the government position. Andrade replied with reference to a newly formed committee on constitutional revision. "[The] censorship will not impede the publication of the Commission of Constitutional Studies, nor those who, without being a part of it, want to bring their intelligences to the corresponding deliberations. . . ." The only exceptions would be applied when, "instead of bringing solutions oriented to [reform] . . . they serve as an instrument of agitation and a dispersive force on national opinion. . . ."[25] Once more he reiterated that restoration of peace and order was a necessary condition before press freedom could be granted.

The situation was brought to international attention on August 15, 1952, when the Inter-American Press Association (IAPA) issued a report strongly denouncing the absence of press freedom in Colombia. In a report prepared by the *Chicago Tribune*'s Jules Dubois, the redoubtable *bête noire* of hemispheric censorship systems, the IAPA declared that there was "no more arbitrary and politically capricious censorship exercised anywhere in the Western Hemisphere today." Pulling no punches, Dubois reported that government censorship in Colombia "is enforced by a faction of the Conservative Party with the sole purpose of perpetuating itself in power. The Government does not dare to lift censorship or to decentralize the state of siege, because it would topple in 24 hours."

The government reacted with predictable anger, and Dubois' attack failed to slow the increasing repression of the dictatorial mechanism. Virtual civil war, no closer to extermination than before, provided continuing opportunity for regulation. Furthermore, the regime continued to draw the church into national affairs. Although the clerical hierarchy had intended only to help generally in national pacification, it found itself intimately affiliated with the Gómez-Urdaneta Arbeláez machinery.

When Laureano Gómez took office, the church tended to react similarly to the manner of the business class. It expected him to put down rural fighting and restore national amity while promoting the welfare of the church. Thus the Catholics were willing and even anxious to work with him. During the first six months of his administration the church extended its clerical control of education under government protection. The Colegio Nacional de San Bartolomé, previously operated on a secular basis, was handed over to the Jesuits. In Cundinamarca the local clergy were invited in writing to participate in government direction of the departmental public education. Local inspectors would be named in the municipalities because, said departmental Conservatives, "the Catholic Church needs, now more than ever, to regain its position of vigilance and control of the Catholic education of the Colombian people."[26] Municipal boards of cinema censorship were reorganized, with clerical representatives passing on films as to their moral content.

The year 1951 marked the serious incidence of religious violence, leading to the widespread charges of Protestant persecution by the state. To understand the controversy, a brief examination of the nature of missionary Protestantism in Colombia is necessary. First introduced in 1825 by a Scottish agent of the British and Foreign Bible Society, James Thompson, Protestantism was not permanently represented until the arrival of the Reverend Horace B. Pratt, of the Presbyterian Church, U.S.A., in 1856.[27] In 1877 the Presbyterians founded the American school in Bogotá. As late as 1916, however, Colombian delegates to the Protestant Congress of Panama conceded that the time was not yet propitious for extensive missionary activity.[28]

The Liberal accession to power in 1930 was advantageous for the Protestants, and by the 1940's a large number of evangelical societies were sending representatives to Colombia. A lengthy list of denominations included, among others, the Assemblies of God, the Evangelical Union of South America, the Mennonite Brethren Church, the Wesleyan Methodist Missionary Society, and the Southern Baptist Convention.[29]

The Conservative victory of 1946 marked a new turning point, for the regime adopted a policy openly discouraging further missionary activity. Methods of proselytizing were controlled; Protestant propaganda was forbidden on radio and in the movies, and open proselytizing in the streets was stopped.

Colombian Protestantism, which was recently estimated to have some 46,000 members,[30] developed a missionary approach of strong anti-Catholicism, claiming without documentation that Colombian citizens were confronted by an unknown, unapproachable God. One veteran missionary spoke of the many Roman Catholics who, "having failed to find peace and truth in their religion, have turned away from every faith. . . . [Others,] tired of Rome's demands, are seeking something for which their hearts cry out. . . ."[31]

Protestant criticisms argued that the church was particularly "notorious for the long hold of reactionary clerics upon education."[32] The hierarchy was blamed for reactionary, restrictive intolerance. Experienced observers, regardless of their own beliefs, have found difficulty in accepting such extreme Protestant views as the following, which is fairly typical: "Protestant Christians have been vigorously persecuted in many places by rabble-rousing priests and these acts of violence have been passively abetted by many local governments."[33] The point to be drawn is not that the Catholic hierarchy was or is by any means enlightened in its spiritual activities. Rather, the fact to be emphasized is the tradition of narrowly intolerant antagonism between Catholics and Protestants. Under the strong pro-church policy of Laureano Gómez, inevitable repercussions intensified the bitterness of the religious dispute.

Peasant unrest and the increasing Conservative-Liberal civil warfare inevitably fanned the flames of religious intolerance. Protestant missions in strongly Conservative regions drew increasing criticism for their aggressive proselytizing, and many uneducated countryfolk were willing to accept common rumors that the Protestants were in league with "Liberal bandits." In traditional strongholds of conservatism, violence began to recur in the name of religion. Local priests were upon occasion forthright in upholding the principle of religious freedom. This was not universally true, unfortunately, and the "diabolic confounding of religion with politics . . . one of the most sinister features of the situation,"[34] gradually heightened intemperate passions on both sides.

In March, 1952, the Evangelical Confederation of Colombia issued the first of a succession of documents attacking the church for premeditated persecution. Representing seventeen Protestant denominations, the confederation listed twenty-three instances of persecution in the past three months, including the fatal beating of a Seventh Day Adventist. A May editorial in *Commonweal* took notice of the situation by recognizing recriminations on both sides. While Protestant minorites occasionally invited reaction by public proselytizing that was offensive to devout Catholics, the latter in return seemed unwilling to recognize the rights of individual conscience.

On March 20, a group of children in Ibagué had been harangued by loudspeakers after celebration of a mass, and under the direction of three priests stoned the new Presbyterian Theological Seminary while civil authorities looked the other way.[35] More than a thousand were reportedly involved, with at least sixty window panes smashed. Even the Ibagué citizenry protested the sight of such intolerance urged upon a group of impressionable children.[36] Religious passions continued to rise, and it became increasingly difficult to affix responsibility. The very question of persecution, as Catholic writers pointed out, was difficult to ascertain, for the small Protestant minority was largely Liberal in political loyalty. This was the natural response in view of the attacks directed almost invariably by those of Conservative sympathies.

Attacks by government forces on rural Liberals sometimes included Protestant missionaries, and the situation was intensified while religious involvement grew. The line between political violence and religious persecution was in many cases indistinguishable,[37] thus Protestant and Catholic partisans alike proclaimed respective innocence. Foreign observers found it just as difficult as native Colombians to reach a clear assessment of the rural religious situation.

In the fall of 1952 the respected Luigi G. Ligutti, director of the National Catholic Rural Life Conference in the United States, returned from a visit to Colombia to declare that reports of religious persecution were "greatly exaggerated." The few instances of persecution, he reported, were without either approval or encouragement of high church officials. A few days later the equally respected W. Stanley Rycroft placed before the annual meeting of the Board of Foreign Missions of the Presbyterian Church, U.S.A., an endorsed declaration of the Evangelical Confederation, promising to deliver, upon request, over 700 "documented and investigated" cases of persecution in the previous three years. Obviously, as *Christian Century* editorialized, an investigation was required to reveal the impartial facts.[38] None was forthcoming.

A Swiss observer, touring Colombia in late 1952, declared that the church position had been hardening in the late 1940's and, despite Liberal acceptance of the church's spiritual dominion, considered liberalism intolerable. Thus church influence was exerted firmly on the side of the Conservatives.[39] The growing civil war found excesses that were sometimes tinged with church participation. In Conservative villages, the local priest often helped police in apprehending "heretics," the "enemies of the Church." As he described it, the grisly scenes of Goya were brought to life in all of their stark terror and brutality.[40]

The church, then, was proving in practice a bulwark of the Gómez regime. The civil strife in the countryside, conducted increasingly on the basis of Liberal versus Conservative, was appearing frequently as Protestant versus Catholic. While the coincidence of Liberal and Protestant sympathies exaggerated the picture of persecution, there is no real question that some persecution did in fact occur. Few historic forces are more bitter, more savagely un-Christian than those of religious intolerance and conflict. One of the veritable crimes of the Gómez period was the exacerbation of existing tensions, creating outbursts that reflected no credit to either Protestant or Catholic.

Two brief quotations reflect the blind hatred that was common. In early 1950 a Protestant missionary secretary wrote that "much of the present situation can be laid at the door of the Roman Catholic Church, whose leaders have taken full advantage of the situation to meddle in politics as never before, and to proclaim from their pulpits and through the press that a Liberal vote is a mortal sin."[41] In opposition, Catholics wrote such things as "Protestantism, with its unavoidable and increased destruction, is a social disease, it is a senile debility which finds a way through religious life of a nation. . . ."[42]

The government declared merely that freedom of religion for Protestants was restricted to churches and private homes, while Protestant radio programs were forced off the air. There was no direction of physical attacks by either the church or ranking government officials, but those who violated religious freedom were merely chastised verbally. As David Bushnell saw the situation in early 1953, ". . . the present government has not attempted a systematic suppression of all political and religious liberty, but it is still distinctly autocratic. Moreover, its claim that a full-fledged, country-wide state of siege is necessary to cope with continuing civil disorders is questionable."[43]

Rural warfare was still growing amid recurring episodes of real or imagined religious persecution. In May, 1952, Roberto Urdaneta Arbeláez initiated a "Crusade for Peace" in which he enjoyed church cooperation. Intent upon the restoration of national order, he began a movement aimed at the humanitarian and religious sentiments of the citizenry. He was joined by Archbishop Luque, who called for a national concept of responsibility, of a unified national society without rancorous relations among men. Urdaneta Arbeláez lavished praise on the movement as a "transcendental" crusade devoted to the national welfare and directed against the depradations of "historic materialism."

Supported by an appeal from Pope Pius XII, the church and the Papal Nuncio urged the people to end the violence, which was characterized as a reflection of international disturbances of the day. A major parade was staged in the capital by the church, displaying great fervor for national pacification.[44] But despite initial enthusiasm and the declared support of both political parties and of business and labor organizations, it had little effect. A series of pastoral letters from the ranking clergy of Manizales, Cali, and Popayán[45] failed to sustain the monetary enthusiasm of the "Crusade."

In June the acting president, speaking at the inauguration of a Bogotá housing project, offered what he called a breakthrough in a promise of complete amnesty to those involved in "subversive political activities" who surrendered their arms. Prompt trials and a right of appeal were guaranteed to those over whose heads charges were already hanging. If optimists felt that the proposal might have any effect, they learned otherwise in mid-July when ninety-six young recruits were ambushed and killed by guerrillas in the *llanos*. National reaction was strong, for the youths were non-political teenagers who had just entered government service. But the bloodshed continued unremittingly. *Time* magazine estimated that nearly one-third of the

national territory—including thinly populated sections of the *llanos*—
was in guerrilla hands. And while recent fighting had been heaviest
near Cali, Puerto Berrío, and Riosucio, few sections of the country had
escaped fighting at one time or another.[46]

By this time the government had concluded that there was no possible
threat to their position in the fighting. Urdaneta Arbeláez was more
disturbed by the situation than other leading Conservatives, yet his
efforts at establishing even minimal control had only the effect of
strengthening the dictatorship. As to the religious question, Dr. Camilo
Vásquez Carrizosa of the foreign ministry explained in August, 1952,
that the government gave "guarantees for the freedom of cults. The
government will not permit impunity to any who transgress these
principles, and the authorities, in turn, must prevent and punish any
act injurious to personal integrity, any act which disturbs the religious
conscience of Colombian nationals or foreigners. *But** our authorities
are powerless to prevent the social effects of propaganda."[47]

In July, 1952, Urdaneta Arbeláez issued a decree establishing departmental governors as virtual local dictators. Despite the historic tradition of strong departmental direction through central authorities, he
chose to build up even further the power of departmental officials.
The new decree granted governors the right to name authorities who
had previously been chosen by departmental assemblies. On the local
level, mayors received comparable appointive powers over posts previously filled by decisions of municipal councils. Elections for assemblies and councils had not been held since 1948, and the decree
placed even greater power in executive hands.[48]

The regime further fortified itself by its continuing courtship of the
Armed Forces. Traditionally a nonpolitical institution, the military
had been taking on a political hue as Conservative supporters climbed
over the Liberal sympathizers to positions of rank and seniority. As
civil war grew in magnitude, official treatment of Liberal officers took
on the aspect of a mild purge, and "the army was used to harass Liberals suspected of advocating violent measures. . . ."[49] Liberal officers
increasingly complained of government discrimination. Under both
Gómez and Urdaneta Arbeláez, the Conservatives turned to converting
the army into an instrument of right-wing party rule.[50]

* My emphasis.

In April of 1951 Dr. Gómez granted the military greater prerogatives by a partial reroganization including the creation of the post of commanding general of the Armed Forces. Complete management and administration of military affairs was vested in the minister of war and the commanding general, who were subordinate only to the president. The new post was filled by the fast-rising General Gustavo Rojas Pinilla, the Colombian representative to the Inter-American Defense Board (IADB) in Washington.

After spending some months as assistant chief of staff on the IADB, Rojas Pinilla returned to Bogotá to take active charge of his new post.[51] On September 25, 1952, he was greeted at the Techo airdrome by high ranking colleagues and friends. Minister of War José María Bernal was soon praising Rojas Pinilla in fulsome terms, and on November 4 an official rendering of "homage" was held for the new commanding general and General Régulo Gaitán, who was quietly shelved for political reasons. Rojas Pinilla announced that he had returned home to serve in time of national emergency, with Colombia depending upon the military to "re-establish the dominion of peace and of order."[52]

General Rojas Pinilla, although recognized as an officer of Conservative loyalties, made no overt intrusion into politics. He seemed solely concerned with military questions raised by civil war. In mid-November he made a trip by plane throughout the nation, after which he gave an optimistic appraisal to government authorities in Bogotá. Questioned as to his evaluation of political opposition, he spoke in the best traditions of the Colombian military: "We military do not understand political questions. But we do think that the country is superficially involved with the parties and that the honest attitude of the opposition must be that of leaving aside personalities and receiving opportunities for conciliation that the government sincerely offers them."[53]

He was further feted at the end of 1952 with his promotion to lieutenant general. On December 18 Acting President Urdaneta Arbeláez, his ministers, and some four hundred officers attended a celebration of his elevation to the nation's highest military rank. Rojas Pinilla delivered a short speech noting the nation's confidence in the Armed Forces, adding that the government could rely upon the military to defend national security. Colonel Alfredo Duarte Blum emphasized the loyalty of the Armed Forces: "Whatever dimensions the military forces reach in

Colombia, the attitude toward the State will always continue the same. The body and soul of the people, our devotion for republican and democratic norms is unquenchable, for these norms are the cherished patrimony and common love of Colombians."[54]

And so the violence raged as the government began preparations which would formally remake the state as Laureano Gómez desired. Despite the harassment of the *alzatistas,* there was no political force with both the ability and inclination to stop the imposition of constitutional reform.

Chapter Ten

FROM REFORM TO REVOLUTION

HISPANIDAD AND CONSTITUTIONAL REFORM

MANY YEARS HAD GONE into the formation of Laureano Gómez' political philosophy, and by the time he achieved total power, the so-called "invulnerable Siegfried line of the Conservative Party"[1] was totally committed to a strongly authoritarian traditionalism. Philosophically he was linked to the ideals of *hispanidad* and Catholicism, to a constitutional corporate state reminiscent of fascism. While such an orientation is not common in contemporary Latin America, it has been historically of considerable influence. Gómez' exposure through the years finally led him to extreme reactionary thought and a personal scorn of usual democratic traditions.

During the 1930's there were considerable incursions of Fascistic ideology in Latin America, reflecting to a degree the images of the Spanish Civil War in the Hispanic world. Although European fascism was perhaps too exotic a product to grow deep roots in the Western hemisphere,[2] it had an appeal that struck sympathetic chords. *Hispanidad,* as embraced by General Franco, was narrowly partisan and strongly fascistic, and his *falange* was offensive to many Latin Americans. Yet there was an inevitable transfer of ideas across the Atlantic, and *falange* parties sprang up as byproducts of the Spanish conflict.

The ideology of *falangismo* was based upon an unholy trinity of *hispanidad,* military authoritarianism, and unchallenged Catholicism.

Appealing to national patriotism while attacking the twin "imperialisms" of capitalism and communism,[3] *falangismo* in the late 1930's and early 1940's naturally took the form of support for the Axis colleagues of General Franco. In Colombia, this was agreeable to Laureano Gómez. He had publicly shown loyalty to the Franco regime as early as 1937. During a visit of Franco officials that year, the Conservatives arranged a banquet at which Dr. Gómez stated his approval: "Spain, marching forward as the sole defender of Christian civilization, leads the Western nations in the reconstruction of the empire of *Hispanidad,* and we inscribe our names in the roster of its phalanxes with unutterable satisfaction.... We bless God who has permitted us to live in this era of unforeseen transformations, and who has given it to us to utter, with a cry that springs from the very depths of our heart: 'Up Catholic, Imperial Spain!' "[4]

By the start of the 1940's Dr. Gómez was, as we saw in Chapter 6, firmly pro-Axis in allegiance. John Gunther reported that Gómez' "ideas, his instincts, his sympathies are all bitterly anti-United States."[5] He allegedly organized a small military *falange* within the Conservative party, and his *El Siglo* rendered full support to both Hitler and Mussolini. In 1942 he declared in the paper that Axis control of the Panama Canal was preferable to that of the United States, and officials at the United States Embassy believed him to have received Nazi funds for the construction of a new, ultra-modern plant for his paper.[6] In Spain, where the foreign minister was criticizing Latin American republics for supporting the Allies despite a heritage of the spirit and blood of Spain,[7] there were only favorable comments regarding Laureano Gómez.

The shift of pro-Axis views was dictated by the exigencies of politics, and Gómez somehow escaped the taint that might have been attached to him once Colombia declared for the Allies and accepted the various resultant wartime shortages and restricted international trade. But Dr. Gómez held firmly to his basic beliefs, embodying as they did the values of discipline, order, and authority. Thus he turned with increasing ardor to the example of Spain and in time revealed through public pronouncements his concept as imposed upon Colombian life.

To Dr. Gómez the national system should embrace the unquestioned rule of a landed elite. Bolivarian rule by an elite would permit the elimination of elections, "the scourge of all republics."[8] Gómez was not enamoured of universal suffrage and was perfectly willing to transcend the laws if necessary. "If the law is abnormal or inconvenient, push it to one side. . . . Retain elasticity . . . although the procedure may not always be strictly legal. The letter kills; the spirit gives life."[9]

In a manner of speaking Gómez had slipped back four centuries[10] in his search for an authentic *hispanidad*. Antonio García wrote that Gómez had not merely returned to the past, but was seeking the historical day before yesterday.[11] From the Spanish Civil War he had learned "the methods, the use of violence, the technique of terror, the well-remembered Golden Age of the Spanish Colony. The counter-revolution refined its political objectives during the war: wipe out the Republic and force a return to things as they were in the 'imperial and Spanish era.' "[12] The Franco affiliation with Roman Catholicism also brought open involvement of the church itself, and Gómez believed that the two should be inseparable. He was perfectly willing to take refuge behind the church to maintain an essentially despotic hold upon the people.

The importance of the church connection cannot be over-emphasized. In mounting a counter-revolution casting him as the grand inquisitor of the era, Dr. Gómez became an hispanist morally and emotionally committed to the doctrine of the double sword—church and state. "The political, social, moral, economic, and educational doctrine is that which flows from its natural fountainhead, the Roman Catholic apostolate religion. . . ."[13] In opposing order and discipline against traditions of individualism and anarchy, his authoritarianism questioned the basic principles of democracy. As the Uruguayan Dardo Regules has written, " 'Francoism' acts under different forms, but certain aspects are always present. . . . It encourages strong-armed governments, especially military governments. It accentuates confusion between the Church and State, as a religious policy, and it seeks to coordinate one-man governments against democratic institutions. At heart, it is a movement of distrust in the forces of human relations and human liberties."[14]

In May, 1953, Dr. Gómez wrote extensively and revealingly in the columns of *El Siglo* explaining his view of political society. This is perhaps the best single statement of Gómez' thought from his own pen.

Universal suffrage, inorganic and generalized in all social activities to define the direction of the State, contradicts the nature of society. The management of the State is by definition a product of the intelligence. An elemental observation shows that intelligence is not equally distributed among the members of the human species. In that aspect society resembles a pyramid whose vertex is occupied by . . . an individual of very outstanding position by his intellectual condition. Below are found those with lesser capacities, who are more numerous. Thus continues a kind of stratification of social capabilities . . . abundant in inverse proportion to the shine of intelligence, until arriving at the base . . . which supports the entire pyramid and is composed of the obscure and inept multitude, where rationality scarcely appears to differentiate between human beings and brutes. . . .

This generation must ensure that the anarchic factors encrusted in fundamental institutions be extinguished, else its subsistence will destroy now, as it did before, the greatness of the republic.[15]

As Dr. Gómez' philosophical orientation won its outlet through his personal grip on the nation, he stood forth as an unyielding autocrat under whom Colombia approached the brink of anti-democratic, reactionary authoritarianism.

The actual process of drawing up proposed constitutional reforms began in mid-1952, and in the following months was carefully supervised by the ailing Gómez, who was free to devote his attention to it while Urdaneta Arbeláez executed his policies as acting president. Talk of a national constituent assembly began to circulate. Among the main Conservative spokesmen was Carlos Vesga Duarte of *El Eco Nacional,* while there were Liberals who also hoped for revision. Young Alfonso López Michelsen and Indalecio Liévano Aguirre argued for reform in *El Liberal.*[16] The issue received growing discussion by the press, where the question was initially that of party representation at a constituent assembly, or *constituyente.*

Minister of Government Luis Ignacio Andrade announced in June that measures leading to constitutional revision would be undertaken. "The government has become convinced," he declared, "that revision of the bases of the country's institutional organization is indispensable. There is going to be, consequently, a fundamental reform of the Constitution of the republic."[17] An eleven-man commission would be constituted to study possible reforms.

On July 11, 1952, Andrade sent messages to the party directorates listing the proposed membership of the commission, which would include six Conservatives and five Liberals.* The purpose was to revise the

* Conservatives: Evaristo Sourdis, Rafael Bernal Jiménez, Eleuterio Serna, Alvaro Gómez Hurtado, Alfredo Araújo Grau, and Francisco de Paula Pérez.   Liberals: Alfonso López Michelsen, Carlos Arango Vélez, Antonio Rocha, Alfonso Araújo, and Abelardo Forero Benavides.

law of the land in the light of what experience had taught, "to the end of strengthening enduringly public calm with the firmness that results from the adequate protection of rights and social guarantees. . . ." The Conservatives accepted immediately, while the Liberals promised to study the proposal before announcing its position. They dallied over the issue for some time, and on August 2 the five proposed Liberals received letters from the Conservative appointees announcing a meeting of the Comisión de Estudios Constitucionales (CEC), to which they were invited. After further deliberation, the Liberals chose not to participate.

The Conservatives themselves were not clear in their minds on the exact form that revision would take, and Gómez was content to let them debate the issue. A group headed by Pérez asked only minor changes suggestive of the original 1886 charter.[18] Alvaro Gómez Hurtado, however, reflected his father's ideas in advocating a basically different document, under which the executive would be free of congressional control, the Senate would become a corporate body, and departmental legislatures and municipal councils would be suppressed. Andrade spoke for the official position in saying that the general goal was to maintain the fundamental constitutional structure while redefining the roles of the branches of public power and strengthening the norms of juridical equality with respect to public liberties and national authority. "The idea of the government . . . corresponds to the diverse titles of the existing constitution and to the thesis proposed by His Excellency Dr. Laureano Gómez. . . ."[19]

On October 20, 1952, Urdaneta Arbeláez spoke out on the issue.

One must lament that the distinguished liberals who were designated to form part of the commission abstained from agreement; their presence in the deliberations and the support of their eminent figures would have been beneficial to the government and the permanent interests of the country. . . .

The Government, for its part, feels that the constitutional reform must be delineated within a genuinely republican scope; it understands very well that the new times and the progressive philosophical-political schools that are disputing for the dominion of the world require a renovation in the instruments with which democracy must count, to assure its permanence. . . .[20]

Further information on the mechanics of the reformist process came in December. Announcing that the CEC was nearing the conclusion of its deliberations, Andrade said that its recommendations would go to a new committee which would consult with government officials before publishing a "definitive" edition.

At the end of 1952 Dr. Gómez published his specific proposals in *El Siglo,* which were circulated and discussed in the early weeks of the new year. The presidency, chosen by popular vote, would be strengthened by virtual freedom from congressional control. The executive would not be responsible to the legislature, nor would he be subject to impeachment proceedings. Budgetary power would be unlimited, and there would be virtual dictatorial power in the hands of the president. Thus, wrote Gómez, the existing "conflict between the Legislature and the Executive" would be wiped out—strengthening the executive and weakening the legislature.

The bicameral congress would consist of a chamber elected by universal suffrage, and an upper house chosen by limited suffrage on the basis of corporative representation. The upper house senators would be institutional spokesmen for business, industry, agriculture, cattlemen, labor, government employees, university and professional groups, the church, and the Armed Forces. Its functions would be those of a debating body lacking true legislative responsibilities.

Executive power would also be enhanced by even greater centralization of regional authority. Departmental assemblies would be reformed as "administrative boards" along the lines of industrial societies and would be reduced in number to six members in small departments and eight in larger ones. They would be under the chairmanship of department governors who would continue to be appointees of the president.

Municipal government would also be greatly reduced numerically, thus helping to avoid activities characterized as "garrulous, dilapidated, scandalous." The local mayor—again appointed from above—would preside over groups of from four to eight municipal councillors, elected only by heads of families and mothers. The judiciary, long a target of many politicians, would be reorganized "to preclude political influence." The *procurador general,* named by the executive, would supervise legal work, and there would be tight control of all appointments to the bench.

The church would formally be reintegrated into politics with the nation consecrated as a so-called "Christian Democracy." Proselytizing activities of non-Catholic sects would be rigidly controlled, and the Catholic religion would provide the moral basis upon which the government would determine policy. The press would also be permitted a questionable sort of freedom by operating in accord with government-determined "public service," thus being subjected to official control. Political freedom would be in accordance with *laureanista* lights, with the executive empowered to judge when party activity conformed "to the purposes of . . . state, and operated for the general or public interest."[21]

The regime moved toward the implementation of reform when Urdaneta Arbeláez issued Decree 0029 convoking the Asamblea Nacional Constituyente (ANAC). Various groups were cited, each of which was to select ten representatives and ten alternates. These included the Sociedad de Agricultores, Asociación Colombiana de Ganaderos, Asociacíon Bancaria, Asociacíon Nacional de Industriales, Federación Nacional de Cafeteros, Federación Nacional de Cooperativas, Federación Nacional de Comerciantes, and the labor groups Confederación de Trabajadores Colombianos and Unión de Trabajadores Colombianos. A list of journalists was also requested, and university representatives were to be chosen by rectors of fourteen such institutions. Thus the corporative system was to receive a trial even before the promulgation of a new constitution.

While members of the *constituyente* were being selected, discussion continued on the details of CEC recommendations. Since proposals were not definitive, there was still opportunity for revision after the announcement of the CEC plan. Alvaro Gómez Hurtado gained some Conservative support with the "Plan Galat" which proposed that one-third of the senators be elected by corporations, one-third by municipal *juntas,* and one-third named by the president himself.* Carlos Vesga Duarte suggested a plan under which a departmental *cabildo* would elect one senator, six would be appointed by the president, six would come from the ranks of former-ministers, and one senator would represent each of the twelve separate corporations.

The CEC proposals were finally released in February, 1953, including a senate organized on a semi-corporative system. Sixteen departmental senators would be chosen for six-year terms by municipal *juntas.* In addition there would be fifteen representatives of various corporations. Finally, all former presidents would be included, and the president in office could name a maximum of six more drawn from lists of former cabinet ministers. It now remained for the meeting of ANAC to begin

* For details, see *El Siglo,* December 30, 1952, a special ten-year issue.

deliberations on reform. Executive Decree 0277 convoked that body for April 20, and it was assumed in the meantime that any proposals distasteful to Gómez or Urdaneta Arbeláez would be further revised.

On March 28 the acting president appointed his six representatives to the *constituyente,* and other groups also began selecting their representatives. In early April, convocation of the *constituyente* was delayed until May 11. As the new legislative organs were finally organized, each department was granted a senator, chosen by departmental conventions of the presidents of municipal councils. Other senators were chosen from the corporative groups already listed. These would theoretically represent the interests of economic and institutional rather than political groups. All government cabinet ministers of at least two consecutive years' service would receive a seat for two years following their resignation, thus lending their knowledge and recent experience to the direction of national affairs. In contrast to the Senate, the Chamber would be entirely popular, chosen through regular standards of popular suffrage.

Beneath the national level, the proposed constitution provided for an administrative *junta* elected by a departmental assembly of municipal councillors. The criteria for administration would be purely technical, with partisan politics proscribed. The basic cell of local organization would be the *cabildo,* with members elected by mothers and fathers. Bachelors would be excluded, thus establishing as a criteria for suffrage the belief in the basic irresponsibility of single men. *Cabildos* would elect councillors to municipal organs.

The chief executive, as expected, would have direct authority over regional government through wide appointive powers, and nationally the president was free from legislative commitments. His source of power was the people, thus, so it was argued, his sovereignty would not be impaired by the legislature. Government planning was also integrated under a comprehensive national program beyond which the legislature was not permitted to go. The church position was just as Gómez had urged at the end of 1952.

The scheduled ANAC meeting on May 11 was again delayed, with the rescheduled opening set for June 15, 1953. In the meantime, extraordinary events overnight revised the nature of Colombian politics. This was largely the ultimate result of growing animosity and confusion projected, for the first time, from within the Conservative party.

CENTRIFUGAL CONSERVATISM

With the effective removal of the Liberals from the political scene, the Conservatives began to differ among themselves. The moderates were increasingly concerned with the course of events, and there was a gradual turning away from Laureano Gómez in search of a less reactionary leader. At first there was no open challenge to the party chieftain, but from midsummer of 1952 on, disunity within the party began to grow.

In addition to moderate Conservatives troubled by Gómez' policies, the *alzatistas* were also inclined to oppose the regime. Alzate Avendaño himself had established a strong organizational basis for support when Gómez drove him from the inner circles of the party in late 1951, and many loyal *alzatistas* had followed their leader. In early 1952 Alzate Avendaño moved his undiminished ambition for power to a different level. He prepared for future congressional elections while publicizing his grievances against the government and Conservative hierarchy. In February he expressed his feelings harshly in *El Siglo,* which surprisingly printed the remarks. "I hate the government, I detest its representatives, I scorn the president and his ministers, I repudiate its works, I combat its errors. . . . And furthermore, I share the thesis of the liberal press: I want the state of siege to be lifted, press censorship to be ended, an agreement reached with the bandits. . . . This I have said with equivalent or similar words, as one who previously was one of the chiefs of conservatism and who now is the presidential candidate of his own group." Harsh words, indeed, and perhaps politically unwise, but they were indicative both of his personal rage and of the measure of Alzate Avendaño's driving ambition.

In May of 1952 the *alzatista* Conservatives held their own convention in Bogotá's Teatro Capitolio. Their leader appeared to repeat his criticisms of official policy. Another rival "Conservative Directorate" was named and approved by the 400-odd delegates present. The action was, of course, denounced by the regular Conservative Directorate as unauthorized. Not long after, the acting president issued a decree calling Congress into special session from June 23 to July 12, 1952. By making it a special meeting, he was able to restrict activity to discussion of matters he brought before the body. Thus the legislators dealt only with questions involving regulation of the petroleum industry, revision of the importation of foreign capital, and a reaffirmation of Urdaneta Arbeláez' own position as *designado*.[22]

In August, Gilberto Alzate Avendaño renewed his politicking when it became known that a full two-month congressional session would be held in October. On August 16 in Puente Nacional, Santander, Alzate Avendaño was attacked by the DNC as "traitorous" to the country and the party. The so-called intellectual leaders of subversion—i.e., the Liberals—were also to be punished sternly, the DNC promised. The new congressional session met on October 20, 1952, and there were signs of accommodation between Alzate Avendaño and the government. He realized that bitter opposition would improve his standing with neither Liberals nor Conservatives and certainly would not speed his return to political power. For the government, conciliation would remove a sharp thorn from its side. Thus, in the lower house the *alzatista* candidate for the Chamber presidency, Eliseo Arango, was elected by acclamation.[23]

The acting president hinted broadly during his opening address that it would be unwise for Congress to remain in session too long, especially with the prospect of constitutional reform now in the air. He repeated past statements expressing hope that the Liberals might decide to join the constitutional studies commission, and there was the inevitable reference to violence with yet another promise to control it. The next few weeks were barren ones, and when the holiday recess was taken on December 20, it was apparent that any legislative organ under a Gómez regime was destined for political sterility.

With the opposition of Alzate Avendaño somewhat muted, a more serious threat appeared in growing enthusiasm for Mariano Ospina Pérez as presidential candidate in 1954. The regime was publicly noncommittal, but it was widely recognized that he was not considered a true Conservative by *laureanistas*. Dr. Gómez was not personally antagonistic towards Ospina Pérez but assuredly felt that one of his own ardent supporters would be more loyal in fulfillment of new constitutional forms. There would also be greater opportunity for Gómez to continue direction of affairs, and he remained concerned with his personal exercise of power.

Ospina Pérez played his part perfectly following Gómez' inauguration. For many months he remained in virtual seclusion. After meeting the constitutional requirement of Colombian residence during the first year following his own presidency, he cut himself away from the government by taking an extended trip, first to New York, then on to Europe. In May of 1952 *Semana* noted that he had met with various Conservative leaders assigned to European ambassadorial posts, presumably discussing a possible return to politics. But through his absence, Ospina Pérez neatly avoided public discussion of political issues, thus remaining many things to many people. As the Gómez regime became unpopular, moderate Conservatives increasingly pictured Ospina Pérez as the best hope for a turn away from the reactionary Gómez counter-revolution. Only in July, 1952, did the former president declare, with comely modesty, a willingness to serve once more if called upon. In a letter to Villareal, then serving as Senate president, he said, "If conservatism expresses, in the opportune moment, its will that my name serve as a banner of harmony among Colombians and of sincere, generous union, firm and complete in my party, I would not vacillate in accepting the place that duty will show me and whose fulfillment I would consider undeclinable."[24] Thus he was publicly unassuming, able to withdraw, apparently subject to the will of his party, and—most important to any politician—available.

By the fall of 1952 there were increasing pressures on Ospina Pérez to declare himself, and his silent support grew steadily. But, ever quiet and cautious, the Conservative former president said nothing. For many years he had pursued his goals in the same manner. He smiled and ignored direct questions, continuing activities at a measured pace. When pressed closely about his candidacy, he merely smiled a bit more and tranquilly changed the subject. One observer commented that Ospina Pérez was "phenomenally noncommittal."[25]

By the end of November his undeclared candidacy was strengthened by the equally undeclared support of Alzate Avendaño. The latter well realized that he himself had no chance of winning the presidency in 1954 over the opposition of *laureanistas*. His best course of action was that of strong support for Ospina Pérez and of close identification with him during the 1954-58 term in office. Alzate Avendaño was not a patient man, yet he recognized that circumstances dictated a period of extended preparation and waiting. The presidency was worth even a four-year delay. At heart no more an *ospinista* than was Ospina Pérez an *alzatista,* Alzate Avendaño nonetheless was willing to accept the necessary political expedient. Strange bedfellows are as common in Colombian politics as elsewhere.

Mariano Ospina Pérez continued to straddle the fence, exercising extreme caution in expressing views on Conservative or government policies. His appeal widened, and there were few grounds on which he was open to legitimate attack. The government hoped to derail his candidacy yet was for a time willing itself to don *ospinista* robes if ultimately unable to stop him. The remnants of the Liberal party were also looking on Ospina Pérez as a man who might return once more to coalition government and moderate the harsh reaction of official control. Remembering their collaborative efforts during his presidency, they conveniently forgot the skill with which he had attacked them when politically advisable. They did not recall the lesson of earlier experience, when Ospina Pérez had proven wholeheartedly partisan to the Conservative cause. For notwithstanding his position of relative moderation within his party, Ospina Pérez was a loyal Conservative. He would have preferred ruling without Liberal participation, were it possible.

Only in December did Ospina Pérez finally begin to speak in guarded tones of political affairs. In Cajica, Cundinamarca, he told local Conservative directors that he was fully in accord with the administration, denying the existence of any rift. And as the traditionally pro-Ospina Pérez department of Antioquia praised him, the national party directorate issued a manifesto supporting not only Gómez and Urdaneta Arbeláez, but denying opposition to Ospina Pérez' 1954 candidacy. In early 1953 he began to move into the foreground, although carefully avoiding direct criticism of the government. Traveling extensively in western Colombia, he was received with enthusiasm sharply in contrast to the denunciations experienced on the Caribbean coast during the latter part of his own term in office. On January 10 he said in Cali that the Conservatives "in the name of the nation" should close ranks, pacify the country militarily and spiritually, allow political refugees to return home, and encourage all sects and factions to join in the cause.[26]

The former president, stressing his belief in party unity and attacking those who would divide the Conservatives, was successful in establishing himself as a symbol of Conservative unity and a guarantor of peace. There was still some possibility that *laureanistas* might be forced to accept him, although the approval of Alzate Avendaño was in some ways a liability. In February, for example, Conservative Director Joaquín

Estrada Monsalve made it clear that, while personally favoring Ospina Pérez, he disapproved of the apparent sanctuary the *alzatistas* were seeking in their support of the *ospinista* candidacy.

Ospina Perez had declared his general approval of constitutional reform, but it was generally felt that he did not favor the far-reaching changes proposed. Despite the eclipse of the Liberals, the former Gaitán campaign against the "oligarchy" continued to exert an effect on a large segment of the population. The group saw in government and society "only a wicked conspiracy of the haves versus the have-nots. This feeling basically explains the wanton destruction perpetrated in April, 1948, and until there is a fundamental improvement in the economic condition of Colombia it could still happen again."[27] Thus there was popular support for Ospina Pérez that he had rarely enjoyed in earlier years.

The undercurrent of official opposition to Ospina Pérez was muted until April, 1953. Earlier, as Dr. J. A. Restrepo wrote Professor Fluharty, official opposition took the form of discontented gossiping.[28] In March, despite the interest in constitutional reform and the forthcoming meeting of the *constituyente,* congressional elections were held for the regular Congress. On March 15 more than a million Colombians voted for new representatives to the Chamber of Representatives. Seventy-six of the 132 seats were won by the Conservatives, with the remaining 56 vacant, allocated to the minority. With the anticipated meeting of the *constituyente* near, there was relatively little interest in the voting.

Civilian opposition took on greater substance with Ospina Pérez' formal declaration of candidacy in April. Dr. Gómez immediately let it be known that Ospina Pérez was not acceptable, and the battle was joined. *Laureanista* forces planned a national party convention so constituted that they could dictate a candidate of their choosing. And there was the further alternative of arranging an extension of Gómez' term by the *constituyente,* thus permitting Urdaneta Arbeláez to continue *laureanista* policies.

Ospinistas recognized the threat to their man and, with the excuse of the fifth anniversary of the *bogotazo,* planned a rally on that date. *El Siglo* editorialized that such a manifestation was impertinent, for April 9 was a day of national mourning, not political celebration.[29] Dr. Gómez, whom the *ospinistas* had hopefully invited, refused to attend such an "unfriendly" gathering. Presidential campaigning was premature, he argued, and the government took a dim view of such activities. On April

9 and 10 *El Siglo* raked up the events of the *bogotazo,* attacking Ospina
Pérez for bringing the Liberals into his government in what it termed
political capitulation.

There was little time to waste, and *ospinistas* scheduled the banquet
for April 11. There was great demand for the tickets, although the
government removed posters advertising the affair. Even members of the
government vied for the precious tickets. United Nations delegate
Evaristo Sourdis, a former Ospina Pérez cabinet member, returned from
New York expressly to attend. Those who were present heard Ospina
Pérez take the offensive for the first time. His acute sense of timing
indicated that the time was ripe, and he spoke out against the government with vigor.

The long-time associate of Laureano Gómez charged the regime with
totalitarianism, declaring that no government could long continue in
power with only the mechanism of force and physical coercion. He
made a necessary bow toward the military by praising their attitude during the chaotic days of 1948, implying that they would soon desert the
regime. What Colombia demanded, said Ospina Pérez, was a return to
the "original democratic, *anti-caudillista"* principles of traditional conservatism. Sparing nothing in his open fight with the regime, he turned
to events at the time of the *bogotazo.*

He had, he cried defiantly, been deserted by present Conservative
leaders in a time of crisis. Abandoned by those who should have stood
firm, he was left as sole protector of the nation and its constitutional
order. With Conservative leaders turning their backs, the only solution
to save the nation was to cooperate with the Liberals. Ospina Pérez even
inferred that the Liberals showed more patriotism than the fleeing Conservatives. Referring to Dr. Gómez by name, he said that the party chief
had suggested he resign in favor of a *junta* and then had fled the country
leaving Ospina Pérez to shoulder alone the responsibilities of the crisis.

The former president's hard-hitting attack drew a response from *El
Siglo* on April 14 with a Conservative declaration that it would "defer"
Ospina Pérez' candidacy as divisive to the party.[30] He was again criticized for his allegedly soft position vis-à-vis the Liberals. Only a "strong
hand" could cope with the situation. On April 18 it became apparent that
Ospina Pérez' sallies had gone home, when Laureano Gómez interrupted
his long convalescent retreat to broadcast a defense of his position. In
one of the strongest speeches of his eloquent career, the embattled old

Conservative delivered a ten-page declaration heaping scorn upon his adversary and praise upon himself.

Gómez recalled, not without a large element of truth, that during the Conservative drought from 1930 to 1946, he had fought single-handed for the party while Ospina Pérez was occupied with his own business and family affairs. After organizing the Conservative victory of 1946, he was forced to watch Ospina Pérez exercise a policy of unorthodox conservatism in which he compromised unnecessarily with the Liberals. Renewing old charges that the Liberals were wholly responsible for the 1948 riots, he fiercely denounced Ospina Pérez for granting them a hand in government as a "reward" for actions that left half the capital in rubble.[31]

Gómez also saw to it that Roberto Urdaneta Arbeláez took to the air to criticize Ospina. The acting president's broadcast of April 21 denounced *ospinista* ambitions, reminding his listeners that the state of siege was still in effect, and then attempted to muzzle Ospina Pérez by forbidding further campaigning and political mass meetings. As he put it, agitation from presidential candidacies was "inopportune, extemporaneous, useless and tremendously dangerous." It was on this basis that Ospina Pérez was refused radio time to reply to Gómez. There was a touch of poetic justice in the former president's being forced to print small clandestine leaflets for surreptitious distribution, since conditions of the state of siege had originally been imposed by Ospina Pérez himself. In the pamphlets, he characterized the Gómez speech as untruthful and declared his intention of campaigning in defiance of the government. "They should let me speak," he said, "if they do not fear the truth."[32]

The political future of the republic now appeared dependent upon the outcome of the struggle between the two dominant Conservatives—the shrewd, implacable, dictatorial, and choleric Laureano Gómez, and the quietly strong-minded compromiser, Mariano Ospina Pérez. For one of the few times in his long career, Ospina Pérez was unwilling to compromise. As the battle heightened in intensity, the question was only secondarily one of constitutional reform, and primarily that of ultimate victory for either Gómez and Ospina Pérez. Few realized that the outcome would be dictated by another force, the only one with the inherent strength to pull Laureano Gómez from the pyramid of power he had assiduously erected. That force was the Colombian Armed Forces. Only as long as the military stood fast could Dr. Gómez retain power in the face of Ospina Pérez' challenge, which was after all a perfectly constitutional one.

Government partisans, preparing for the forthcoming *constituyente,* suddenly realized to their astonishment that national reaction was bringing a strong shift of loyalties. Thus, although the *constituyente* members had been hand-picked earlier, the first meeting was postponed for the second time and scheduled for June 15. Even so, a caucus of *ospinistas* on June 12 indicated that the government might find itself in the minority. Ospina Pérez and his followers hoped to elect one of their own as chairman rather than the government's Luis Ignacio Andrade. Their chances were good, but other events were to intervene, rendering the question purely academic.

The survival of the government rested upon official machinery, the sagacity of Gómez, and the power of the military, which remained loyal in the face of national discontent. On April 16 General Rojas Pinilla issued an Order of the Day in which the military was reminded of the need of "not losing serenity in the difficult moments through which the country is passing."[33] Clearly the Armed Forces were the ultimate determinant upon which the issue hinged.

Unwilling Military Intervention

The military basis for the existence of the Gómez regime was the established tradition of nonpolitical interference. The Armed Forces was an autonomous body largely under the domination of its professional officer corps. A few Liberal sympathizers remained in the hierarchy, but pro-Conservatives for some years had been favored by the government. With political disorder growing, those who contested for power were acutely aware of the military. The leader of the Armed Forces was the esteemed but political inexperienced Gustavo Rojas Pinilla. Ultimately he was drawn into the situation very much against his will; national responsibility has rarely been thrust upon such an unwilling and hesitant individual. But for all of Dr. Gómez' exceptional acumen, he was to make the most serious error of his career. In a burst of anger, it would throw him into one of the few situations from which he would be unable to extricate himself.

One of eight generals on active duty in the spring of 1953, Gustavo Rojas Pinilla as the *comandante general* was commander-in-chief of the entire military establishment. Born on March 12, 1900, in Tunja,

Boyacá, Rojas Pinilla was the youngest son in a family of six. He enrolled in the military academy and was commissioned as a second lieutenant of artillery. He went to the United States soon thereafter, studied civil engineering at a small college in Angola, Indiana, and returned home to a military career. He gradually progressed up the hierarchical ladder, fulfilling his tasks with competence if not brilliance. He was not averse to doing business on the side, and a 1936 fitness report said that his "business instincts carry him to the point of sordidness."[34]

By 1945, then a colonel, Rojas Pinilla became chief of the Department of Civil Aeronautics, spending several years in the construction of military airfields. During the *bogotazo* as commander of the Third Army Brigade in Cali, he thoroughly put down insurrectionists although, as already mentioned, his single-minded ruthlessness made him the subject of Liberal attacks and brief political controversy. In 1949 he was for a time Ospina Pérez' minister of communications, and when he returned to regular military duty, his obvious Conservative loyalties contributed substantially to his continuing rise. Rojas Pinilla was a competent professional at his trade, and his colleagues readily accepted him as commander-in-chief.

Rojas Pinilla was not widely known nationally until after his return in late 1952 from service on the Inter-American Defense Board. But his new prominence and the attempts of the government to cultivate his support thrust him into the public eye, and by June of 1953 he was a familiar figure. An apparently modest and unaffected man of simple tastes, he was properly military when necessary, spoke with a "nervous voice of martial musicality,"[35] yet was affable among his colleagues, whom he treated with a spirit of light camaraderie. As his popularity with the military grew, Laureano Gómez made the mistake of treating the man as a potential rival.

In the events that transpired, it is important to remember that Rojas Pinilla was sincerely convinced of the essential correctness of the non-political nature of the military. His own Conservative sympathies were second to his dedication to the upholding of constitutionality. There is little doubt that Rojas Pinilla would ever have turned upon the government had he not been forced to do so as a matter of saving his career. In May he told a *Semana* interviewer, when questioned about a possible political solution,

The solution to the present Colombian political problem has been given by His Excellency Dr. Roberto Urdaneta Arbeláez in his last radio address, guaranteeing the neutrality of the government and official fulfillment of duties towards all, without discrimination of any kind and without complacency for anyone. The basis . . . for the return of institutional normality and the guarantee of vigorous democracy is in the termination of banditry and in convincing the citizenry that its first duty is to revere authority. . . . Democracy is invigorated with the fulfillment of the laws that have been promulgated democratically and in the reverence for dispositions emanating from those who have freely been elected to govern. . . .[36]

As the political tides swirled about Rojas Pinilla, the possibility of armed intervention was increasingly rumored both in Colombia and abroad. As it turned out, Rojas Pinilla himself had been counselling politically minded subordinates against intervention which many felt inevitable and already overdue. An unidentified diplomat commented that Dr. Gómez was in a position to "do anything he wants"[37] as long as the army remained aloof. In a mid-May interview with *Times*man Sydney Gruson, General Rojas Pinilla insisted that "we (of the military) are bound to support the Constitutional Government and we will do so at any cost." He expounded the army concept of defending any constitutional government. Reminding Gruson that for nearly a century the military had been above political quarrels, he returned repeatedly to the "neutral position" the army was maintaining.[38]

On May 22, 1953, Rojas Pinilla spoke on military loyalty in the presence of Urdaneta Arbeláez at the Escuela Militar. "The Military Forces fulfill religiously the norm of Country above all parties. . . . Be sure that the force of arms represented by the generals and by the commanders of all grades, here present, surrounds your person and supports the activities which . . . look for national concord. . . . Trust, Your Excellency, that the campaigns being advanced to divide the Armed Forces will be shattered . . . for firm and sincere union is our force, and upon this force depends the security of the Government, as well as the defense and the future of the Armed Forces and the salvation of Colombia."[39] Officers who urged intervention were not in the majority. Many saw only too well that they could endanger their material benefits in pensions and pay. Rojas Pinilla's personal position was strong enough to ensure that no fractional military group could take action without his approval. In the end, intervention was prompted not by the deterioration of national affairs but rather by an open threat to the military and to Rojas Pinilla himself.

Dr. Gómez, harassed as he was on many sides, saw in the popular Rojas Pinilla a possible rallying point that threatened his own position. Thus he determined to remove the general. In the final analysis, his misjudgement of Rojas Pinilla was the error that drove his regime out of power. Laureano Gómez pushed his man too far, and Rojas Pinilla had the wherewithal to defend himself. Gómez first ordered the general to Germany to inaugurate an airline connecting Hamburg with Bogotá, apparently planning to dismiss the general *in absentia*. It was characteristic of the politically naive Rojas Pinilla that he was willingly following orders until subordinates dissuaded him.

The titular president proceeded to bide his time, although still determined to remove the general. In late May concern was such that the minister of war found it necessary to quiet talk of armed uprising: "There are some people who, without meditating on the absurdity of their ideas, would want the Minister of War and the Army to express opinions to their fellow citizens regarding the political problems between the parties or within the Government party. Nothing would unchain so many evils on the country, on the Government and on politics itself."[40] Dr. Gómez continued to watch for the opportunity to remove his chief of staff. The chance came with a *cause célèbre* that became known as the Echavarría Affair.

Toward the end of May, a junior officer told his superiors of being approached by a wealthy Conservative businessman from Medellín, Felipe Echavarría. He allegedly broached the subject of an assassination plot against Rojas Pinilla and nine others. Acting under orders, the officer went along with the scheme until money and weapons were provided, after which Echavarría was arrested for questioning. Detained in early June by the Security Department of the Ministry of War, he underwent an interrogation that was less than gentle, although whether or not he may have been tortured has never been determined.

Alvaro Gómez Hurtado got wind of the affair and tried to intercede, asking that Echavarría be declared insane.[41] They army refused the plea as well as further pressure from various sources. In late summer Rojas Pinilla retrospectively claimed that the man had not been tortured but was detained "by reason of charges made against him by a junior officer of the Army, to whom he gave arms and money to assassinate ten persons. . . ."[42] Gómez later charged that Echavarría was "barbarously tortured and beaten." In any event, the setting was ready for the final *dénouement*.

On June 5 Laureano Gómez, first learning of the situation and seeing a chance to remove Rojas Pinilla, called the new minister of government, Lucio Pabón Nuñez, to his house. Pabón Nuñez, who was soon to play a powerful role in national affairs, declared that a proper military investigation was being conducted and insisted that the prisoner remain under military custody. In this he was acting with the support of Urdaneta Arbeláez, who did not share the titular president's distrust of Rojas Pinilla.

Spurred to further action, the aroused Gómez on June 13 went to the presidential palace, summoning the cabinet and Urdaneta Arbeláez to settle the issue decisively. Perhaps Gómez was convinced that Echavarría had indeed been subjected to inhumane treatment; be that as it may, he was going to remove Rojas Pinilla whatever the cost. At 10 A.M. that Saturday morning the meeting was held on the second floor of the Palacio de Nariño. Gómez demanded a decree calling for Rojas Pinilla's ouster. Minister of War Pabón Nuñez again stated his disagreement and was supported by Urdaneta Arbeláez. Gómez angrily shouted forth his immediate resumption of full presidential duties; after an absence of nineteen months he was returning as chief executive. Urdaneta Arbeláez raised no objections, calmly saying that it was of course Dr. Gómez' right if he chose to return. The cabinet resigned, permitting Gómez freedom of choice in forming a new one. The ministers then withdrew to attend an affair being given in honor of Minister Rafael Azuero, where they said nothing although they appeared highly disturbed. One minister, however, had stayed behind.[43]

Jorge Leyva, minister of public works and an ardent *laureanista* of considerable ambition, remained to speak with the president. A few moments later he emerged with Gómez' first new decree in hand, naming Leyva minister of war and removing Rojas Pinilla in favor of General Régulo Gaitán. In the meantime, Rojas Pinilla himself was once again absent from Bogotá, vacationing at Melgar, Tolima. He was not, as several have erroneously written, preparing to fly from Bogotá to the United States on a military mission. In the events that followed, the first decisive steps were taken not by Rojas Pinilla but, rather, by loyal officers quartered in Bogotá. While the army sent a plane to Melgar for General Rojas Pinilla, newly-appointed War Minister Leyva was received in person at the Batallón Caldas barracks in the Bogotá outskirts. He planned to announce the removal of Rojas Pinilla, but the military had already learned of the change. Not only had they sent for Rojas Pinilla, but were prepared when Leyva arrived at the Caldas barracks. General Gaitán accompanied Leyva.

Upon arrival they identified themselves and were immediately placed under arrest. At that moment, 1:30 P.M., the fate of the Gómez regime was sealed. The only question was the form in which the Armed Forces would exercise their powers, and that decision was held in abeyance until Rojas Pinilla's return. The Bogotá forces made sure that their control was complete. Dr. Gómez had returned to his home, and he was soon placed under house arrest. Rojas Pinilla reached the capital and, after an immediate meeting with high ranking officers, ordered additional troops into Bogotá and confirmed that Gómez would not be permitted back in power. He turned aside demands that he take power by promising only to decide after speaking with political leaders. Even at this point he was reluctant to step into the presidency.

Rojas Pinilla called on Gómez personally and, as Pabón Nuñez later said, he told the old Conservative, "Dr. Gómez, I admire and respect you like a father, but I am not in agreement, and things must be changed." He promised Laureano and his family guarantees of safety out of the country, to whatever destination they chose. He then telephoned Urdaneta Arbeláez, informed him of the course of events, and arranged a meeting at the presidential palace with prominent political figures.

Thus the General was pushed into command. Had Gómez left him any choice, he would have remained loyal. As it was, the removal of Gómez and the securing of Bogotá had been undertaken and accomplished by officers without any prior consultation. Rojas Pinilla's subordinates would have respected his wishes for non-intervention had Gómez not threatened to remove him. Even as Rojas Pinilla and his party arrived at the palace at 7:10 P.M., he was transparently eager to make arrangements permitting the Armed Forces to withdraw.[44]

Liberal leaders were absent, for most of them were outside Colombia. But Ospina Pérez and Urdaneta Arbeláez were both present, as were representatives of Alzate Avendaño. General Rojas Pinilla first suggested to Ospina Pérez, then to Urdaneta Arbeláez, that he assume the presidency.[45] Ospina Pérez declined, saying that he had no right to the office without having been elected. Urdaneta Arbeláez influenced both by his loyalty to Gómez and his preference for at least the trappings of constitutionality, also refused. He told the general that he could not resume power while Gómez remained the constitutionally elected president. And so, with great reluctance the perplexed Rojas Pinilla finally accepted the inevitable. "As the nation cannot be without a government, and someone must govern, I assume power."[46]

At 10:00 P.M. on June 13, 1953, the national radio network announced the startling news to unsuspecting citizens: "For the peace of the nation and the future of Colombia, we wish to inform that Lieutenant General Gustavo Rojas Pinilla has just assumed the Presidency of the Republic with the unanimous support of the armed forces, the national police, the national directorate of the Conservative Party, Dr. Mariano Ospina Pérez, Roberto Urdaneta Arbeláez and Lucio Pabón Nuñez, and representatives of both political parties."[47]

Later that evening General Rojas Pinilla himself went to the microphones to address the citizenry. It was almost midnight when he explained that the army, in the face of a "tremendous political crisis," had assumed power in preparation for "pure elections."

The Armed Forces call on all Colombians of good will . . . to form a crusade that, faithful to the traditional mandate of the Country, puts this above the parties and puts the common good above the conveniences of castes and of groups. . . .

No more bloodshed, no more depradations in the name of any political party, no more strife among sons of the same immortal Colombia. Peace, Law, Liberty, Justice for all, without differentiations or preference for the classes more or less favored. The country cannot live tranquilly while it has hungry and ill-clothed sons.

The Armed Forces will be in power while the necessary conditions are prepared for the holding of clean elections, from which there will emerge genuinely democratic systems, the legislative rulers and judges, which the Colombian people wish to choose in complete liberty.[48]

So it was that the military reversed its tradition of political abstention. Other than the abortive Pasto *coup* against López in 1944, it had not interfered in government since the nineteenth century. There was to some extent a repudiation by moderate Conservatives of their party leader,[49] for the new government retained a large number of party members. For once the change could be attributed less to the running Liberal-Conservative fight than to gradual fragmentation among the Conservatives. The struggle between an intransigent Gómez and an equally determined Ospina Pérez centered on questions of compromise with the Liberals, as urged by the latter, and on the corporative state Gómez was building.[50]

As *Nation* editorialized a few weeks later, the *coup* was not the usual military seizure in the Latin tradition. Had Gómez continued to organize his corporative state without removing Rojas Pinilla, the army quite likely would not have stepped in.[51] Certainly the only serious threat to an increasingly restrictive and oppressive regime was the military itself. The shrewd old autocrat had so denuded other political groups of power, while stripping himself of any rightful claim to public confidence, that the only remedy was a *golpe de estado* by the military. Reaction to the overturn of constitutional government was initially favorable. "The entire country . . . without any distinction of political or religious, social or intellectual character, expressed its exhiliration. . . ."[52] Only some months later did the bloom of the honeymoon begin to wear off.

In justification of the military seizure, Antonio García later wrote that, for Colombia, there was no other choice. "All forces of resistance to the dictatorship had disappeared, save one. . . . The *coup d'etat* of June 13, 1953, was a blow against the victorious counter-revolution. The Republic could not defend itself in 1953, except in the same way it was created in 1810."[53] As the people gathered in the streets of Bogotá to celebrate, they told one another, in words of their national anthem, that "the terrible night has ended."[54] Unfortunately, they were closer to midnight than to dawn, and the after-midnight hours were to hold unknown terrors of darkness that would sorely try the unity of the country and the very souls of all Colombians.

Part IV

CAESARISM AND INCOMPETENCE

Chapter Eleven

MILITARY RULE AND POPULAR ACCEPTANCE

Binding National Wounds

The heady wine of popular adulation swiftly brought intoxication to the Rojas Pinilla regime. So widespread was dissatisfaction with the preceding government that there were few misgivings over a military government. There had been no civilian institution capable of restricting the power of Dr. Gómez, and military intervention was the only way in which he could successfully be challenged. The general came to power on a wave of excitement,[1] buoyed by fervent hopes of a beleaguered citizenry.

Of the many problems confronting the military government, several seemed of overriding immediacy. The civil war had reached tragic proportions; press censorship and the abridgment of individual freedoms had created an oppressive atmosphere; the activities of the *constituyente* or ANAC and the matter of reform of government were also pressing. Perhaps of the greatest importance was reunification of the populace. Increasing bitterness of the long party conflict had been aggravated by the repressive controls of the Gómez regime. It lay in the hands of Rojas Pinilla to bring a degree of harmony and moderation to the divided people of Colombia.

With the nation emotionally exhausted by the hatreds of many years, Rojas Pinilla was at first successful. His genial nature and quickly-responsive good humor made him attractive to the people; only later did they learn that his affability was tempered with an explosiveness that came with quick anger and a streak of vindictiveness. His broadcast the night of his ascendence spoke of reuniting the citizenry. The next day, Sunday, June 14, he spoke to thronging *bogotanos* from the balcony of the Palacio de Nariño, pleading for the support of his countrymen. "I have arrived at this position . . . without hates, without rancors, with only my heart in my hand to offer to the Colombian People. . . . The Armed Forces will not fail you because our motto is this glorious one: LIBERTY AND ORDER. . . . This Government does not extend to you the clenched fist. It extends to you the full and open hand that you may take it, because it must govern with public opinion. So, public opinion and its support is what must save the country, as it is the support for the Armed Forces. May I invite you to shout: *Viva Colombia,* just and free!"[2]

At the outset General Rojas Pinilla was accessible to the people through frequent appearances. He travelled throughout Colombia calling for unity. With his ministers in Bogotá acting under his direction, the general built substantial personal popularity, revelling in the homage paid by crowds that greeted him as national savior. On July 14, in an extraordinary five-hour demonstration, some 100,000 rode by in a motor cavalcade composed of 1500 buses, 2300 taxis, and 3,000 trucks.[3] The sixteen-mile-long parade, which paralyzed city transportation for hours, passed in an arrangement of the national colors—red, yellow, and blue. Drivers saluted him with a raucous cacophony of horns and sirens.

Rojas also attempted to reduce partisan irresponsibility by mollifying the parties. During the June 14 address he announced that the Gómez-invoked *constituyente* would meet the next day as scheduled. Mentioning the "unconstitutional" activities of Laureano Gómez, he promised that the Armed Forces would seek a "national solution . . . not one along strictly party lines."[4] Thus the ANAC was convened on Monday, June 15, when sixty-one delegates met to receive the new chief executive. He was enthusiastically cheered while walking in full-dress uniform from the palace to the Capitolio, accompanied by some fifty high-ranking officers. Arriving at the elliptical salon, he was greeted by delegate Carlos Alborñoz in the name of the ANAC, which pledged full support. The presidency was declared vacant, after which General Rojas Pinilla was named to fill the post until the end of Gómez' elected term on August 7, 1954.[5] Rojas delivered an eight-minute speech of acceptance in which he affirmed that his government would shelve plans for drastic constitutional reform.[6]

Recalling the events of Saturday night, he stated he had believed that a civilian should head the government. When this proved impossible, however, the republic was suddenly met by administrative chaos demanding prompt action. "Then was the time that I determined to save Colombia from anarchy and to engage all my efforts . . . to the enterprise of redeeming the country, with my conscience tranquil from having done as much as was humanly possible for me to do in that situation that others had produced."[7]

Rojas Pinilla again promised nonpartisan government, adding a statement that revealed his own Conservative proclivities. Conservatism, he told the delegates, had in its program and traditions "fertile norms for carrying to the end a rational and patriotic reform of those aspects that are urged by the demands of modern life. . . . [In] the doctrines of the Catholic Church it has the inexhaustible source of unperishable truth; in the thought of Bolívar, a lantern that is not extinguished. . . ."[8] Two weeks later the general told the Colombian Academy of Jurisprudence that the constitution would in time be reformed, but on a just national basis differing from the corporative document planned by Gómez. He underlined at the same time his intention of instituting reforms and directing policy from outside the sphere of party politics.[9]

Expressions of support flowed in from different elements of society. The Supreme Court—later a target of Rojas Pinilla's reforms—resolved that he might, "with the support of all Colombians," restore normality through honest elections.[10] A few days later the church added its approval when Crisanto Cardinal Luque* urged all catholics that Rojas Pinilla's position "must be recognized and obeyed."[11] In August the general was further endorsed in a letter written by Luque to the exiled Gómez in New York City. The cardinal was unequivocal in his position: "As far as I can know public opinion in its authentic reality, I have the notion that the general feeling is that the juridical situation of the new Government was regularized by the National Constituent Assembly, and that is also my personal conviction."[12]

---

* Luque had recently been elevated to the rank of cardinal, the first in Colombian history to achieve this station.

Rojas Pinilla tried to form a cabinet of broad background, although it was largely composed of moderate Conservatives and military men. With only hard-core *laureanista* Conservatives opposing him, the Liberals also lent support. Exiled party leaders including Eduardo Santos and Carlos Lleras Restrepo cabled their approval. The Liberal Directorate reopened its Bogotá offices, and many were anxious to renew party activity. Liberal publicist Abelardo Forero Benavides spoke of the Liberal goal of national pacification, declaring that Liberalism offered Rojas Pinilla its collaboration in achieving that end. "Liberalism aspires to democratic liberty . . . [as] a civil and republican political party . . .[it] aspires to a Colombia that governs with justice, with equity and with impartiality. A just, generous, upright government has the applause of all Liberals."[13]

The task of pacifying the countryside was still a major one, and strife was far above the level of simple party warfare. Bands of insurrectionists continued to attack small isolated garrisons repeatedly, withdrawing swiftly into the protective mountains. Additional innocent bystanders were driven from their homes almost daily, and in many sectors government troops adopted a scorched earth policy. Reprisals from both sides often touched uncommitted families with barbaric results. By 1953 the elements of banditry and crime had increased significantly. Terroristic atrocities were common.

The Gómez regime had turned a deaf ear to demands for an unconditional amnesty. At the start of 1953 Minister of War José María Bernal had been asked if the year would bring peace. He retorted that it depended on "what you call peace. Up to now the Liberals have not declared it."[14] This was consistent with the government claim that Liberal leaders could end the fighting by commanding it. But that time was years past, and all eyes now were on Rojas Pinilla as he grappled with the problem. Few Colombians failed to realize that the first requirement was restoration of "a sense of security and confidence."[15]

In early July, Gustavo Rojas Pinilla offered amnesty to the guerrillas. It was conditional only in demanding that those who surrendered bring along their weapons, swear to give up warlike activities, and return to their former occupations. Great numbers were soon responding to the proferred peace offering. On July 7 more than 600 surrendered in Medellín alone.[16] Through August the surrenders continued. On

July 22 two rebels said they were arranging the surrender of some 4,000 Liberals who had been in the mountains five years. One, twenty-seven-year-old Eduardo Fonseca, stated that authorities were dealing sympathetically with them. He explained that those he represented would lay down their arms if the government was true to its word. In a matter of days the largest surrender yet negotiated took place.[17]

On August 20 President Rojas Pinilla told a group of foreign newsmen that 90 per cent of those fighting the Gómez regime had already given up and returned to honest pursuits. Total pacification, he announced, would soon be completed.[18] Disinterested observers felt that 10 per cent was more accurate. But the situation was unquestionably improving for the first time in years. At the end of the month, the *constituyente* even recommended an unqualified amnesty, although the government refused, alleging that many weapons were being hidden which could be available in the event of renewed banditry.

By the end of August many more were giving up the fight. The conditional amnesty was widely trusted. Many of the embattled guerrillas themselves had wearied with the years of turmoil. A minimal estimate placed at 50,000 the number forced from their homes and businesses in the preceding three years. The rebels themselves were roughly 20,000 in number. Most of the powerful leaders, such as Juan de Dios Franco, Juan de la Rosa Posada ("The Little Bird"), and David Acudelo Cantillo ("The Triumphant"), had yielded by the beginning of September,[19] and for the present, at least, fighting was reduced.

Although rural violence was temporarily curtailed, modified martial law continued under the state of siege decreed in 1949 by Mariano Ospina Pérez. Press freedom was still restricted. At first General Rojas Pinilla seemed inclined toward gradual restoration of press freedom. Minister of Government Lucio Pabón Nuñez said that censorship would apply only to reports affecting public order. He promised further steps would be taken to minimize the restrictions.[20] In hopes of establishing *rapport* with the new government, the Bogotá Newspapermen's Circle on June 23 sent its greetings to Rojas Pinilla, advocating the repeal of censorship in all forms. "Freedom of the press being one of the firmest pillars of democracy, the Bogotá Newspapermen's Circle is already anticipating happily the elimination of existing censorship."[21] But Rojas Pinilla maintained censorship. He negotiated a voluntary agreement with publishers to exercise self-censorship, avoiding references to violence or political passions.[22]

The president discussed the issue in mid-August at a mass interview granted a large number of North American journalists. Forty-eight were present as he claimed that internal censorship no longer existed except in the department of Atlántico. Elsewhere, he said, self-censorship was left in the hands of the editors. Toward the end of the interview he mentioned that he had ordered an end to censorship of outgoing cables on June 30. Reporters immediately objected that their dispatches had required the censor's official stamp. Rojas Pinilla turned with a flourish to his director of press and radio censorship and directed, "In your presence I repeat to the head of the censorship my order that no dispatch is to be censored in advance."[23] This would apply, he added, to resident as well as visiting foreign reporters.

Less than a week later the government clashed with Gómez' *El Siglo*. It seemed at the time to be merely a natural reaction against the organ of the deposed president but proved to be the precursor of many subsequent government-press disputes. *El Siglo* had printed a vituperative manifesto of Gómez, and almost at once Pabón Nuñez made a nationwide broadcast answering the charges with comparable immoderation. When the paper refused to give the address equal prominence, it was suspended until the speech was printed in full. A communique stated that ". . . since press censorship exists in Colombia its function is not only to forbid but also to indicate to the newspapers the form in which to conduct themselves with the state. . . . The speech of the Minister of Government . . . must be published with the same typographical display that said newspaper used in publishing the texts of the message and the letter of the former president . . . as a rectification of charges made there."[24]

In a stubborn refusal to comply, the Conservative paper first chose suspension rather than surrender. It soon capitulated, however, and on August 22 reappeared with virtually the entire front page filled with the text of Pabón Nuñez' speech.[25] Its difficulties were not at an end, however. In September it drew the fire of government officials who charged it with publishing subversive matter. Punishment was a thirty-day suspension. *El Liberal* of Popayán was also ordered to close for ten days and angrily announced indefinite suspension of publication.

Medellín's respected *El Colombiano* also chose to shut down rather than print government-slanted analyses.[26]

The Colombian press put aside partisan feeling to unite in defense of its basic freedom. The day of the above disclosure the managers of the Liberal *El Tiempo* and *El Espectador* petitioned Rojas Pinilla to lift the ban, which he did on September 29. Further restrictions were also moderated, apparently with a view to the forthcoming Mexico City conference of the Inter-American Press Association. The newly-appointed director of the Office of Information and Press at the presidential palace, Jorge Luis Arango, reiterated that the government was "interested in lifting press censorship and in the full return of legal institutions in the country."[27]

On October 2, 1953, the government announced a national conference of newspaper publishers and editors, and the president lifted censorship for the duration of this "First National Press Congress." Temporary freedom of the press returned to Colombia for the first time in four years. Editors and publishers of every Colombian newspaper were invited; publishing houses and radio news staffs were also invited. The Bogotá meeting, delayed until the end of the month, faced the task of drawing up recommendations for government authorities. They in turn promised to enact a press statute within a few weeks, reportedly permitting the lifting of existing censorship. Hopes were further buoyed after ANAC adjourned when the administration declared that censorship would remain suspended, with "the hope that newspapers will continue to lend the Government their valuable influence toward fulfilling its task of restoring peaceful living among all Colombians."[28]

The first four months of the Rojas Pinilla regime, then, were ones of hope and faith for the Colombian citizenry. The president was already coming into conflict with the nation's press. However, there was no more than a nagging, unsubstantiated suspicion that he might not be heading toward freedom of the press. Otherwise, the situation appeared greatly improved. For the first time in years public opinion was broadly favorable to the government. It remained to be seen whether Gustavo Rojas Pinilla could follow up his initial success with substantial responses to some of the more deep-seated national problems. Certainly he achieved considerable momentum during his first few months.

THE GOVERNMENT STRENGTHENS CONTROL

Within a few months, Rojas Pinilla began to strengthen his position through institutional devices. In retrospect he can be seen as taking his first steps toward military dictatorship. At the time, however, it was not clear that his purposes were other than disinterested. The initial popular enthusiasm inevitably had to cool. Furthermore, whatever his ultimate intentions, measures were necessary to develop a means of governing other than that of executive decree.

Reform of the judiciary was a paramount issue that had been in the air ever since the Echavarría Affair. Following the overthrow of Dr. Gómez, Felipe Echavarría had been tried by a lower court and found guilty of conspiracy. He appealed the case, declaring that the confession by which he was convicted had been extracted by methods of brutality and torture. Rafael Rocha Riaño, the senior justice of the circuit court, reviewed the appeal and on November 4 granted Echavarría an unconditional release, holding that there was question as to the legality of the confession upon which the conviction had been based. He then granted *El Tiempo* an interview to argue that the opinion was based upon a conscientious study and application of the law. Although a Liberal sympathizer, he insisted that politics had not entered into the decision.

On November 11, in Cartagena, the president delivered a scorching denunciation upon the entire Colombian judiciary. Declaring that he had personally heard the confession, Rojas said that there was more than enough proof to justify detention and conviction. He noted that no witnesses to the confession had been questioned, darkly adding that his government was cognizant of large amounts of money being used by the wealthy defendant to obtain freedom.[29] Rojas Pinilla was proud that there had been no government intervention. However, the decision was "the most vilely infamous juridical serpent" in history. Strong words, to say the least.

Having thus disposed of the Echavarría decision to his satisfaction, the president turned his ire upon the entire judical system. He had already shown himself dissatisfied with the system in early executive decrees. He now described it as the "principle obstacle of fulfillment of the government's program." He expressed disgust with judges who yielded to partisanship or financial pressure and suggested that forthcoming reforms should provide satisfactory recourse to punishment for professional misconduct. "While the Judicial Power cannot isolate itself from the partisan camp and rapid and effective processes do not exist to sanction the Judges and the Magistrates who lack the fulfillment of their duties, the administration of Justice potentially is a shameful deception, and will continue being the greatest obstacle to national *convivencia.* . . ."[30]

After delivering his blast the president flew to Providencia Island for a brief rest. On the mainland a squall blew up at once, and on November 13 the sixteen-man Corte Suprema de Justicia resigned. Departmental courts announced their support of the CSJ, although not tendering wholesale resignations. On the lowest level, municipal courts were divided on the issue. In Rojas Pinilla's absence, his minister of justice, Antonio Escobar Camargo, announced that the president had not yet accepted the CSJ resignations but had taken the matter under consideration.[31] The possibility was raised that a special congress might be called in January to study revisions of the judicial system.

Rojas Pinilla soon accepted the collective resignation, hinting that reorganization would be facilitated if other bodies followed the same course. As a result, six members of the Corte Suprema del Trabajo and four from the Consejo del Estado tendered their resignations before the close of 1953. Within a few weeks the president named sixteen new justices, who were sworn in before him on February 5, 1954, in the Palacio de Nariño. He instructed them not only to carry out their usual duties but also to prepare judicial reform which might be sent to the *constituyente* in June.

For Rojas Pinilla this could have been the first real test of his political power. As it developed, he was able to place in the highest court of the land a group of men he had individually selected. Pending possible reforms in June, he had a CSJ presumably obedient to his wishes.

In April political activity picked up in anticipation of the June meeting of the *constituyente.* For some months a new Comisión de Estudios Constitucionales (CEC) had been drafting proposals for ANAC consideration. Meeting first on December 12, 1953, the commission operated much the same as its predecessor, although outlines of their proposals were quite different. No longer would the election of municipal councils be restricted to heads of families, nor would the national executive be so overwhelmingly powerful. The measures which Gómez planned for his corporative system were dropped. Departmental legislatures would be essentially unchanged, in lieu of the Gómez boards of experts under direct supervision of central authorities in Bogotá. Three guiding principles had been set before the CEC by Lucio Pabón Nuñez. The role of the church would be preserved, a new representative legislative body would be organized, and an incorruptible judicial system would be organized.

As issues were discussed in the press, the major point of controversy centered on an alleged strengthening of the position of the church. The CEC was to propose that teaching of Catholicism should become mandatory even in private Protestant or non-sectarian schools; non-Catholic religious celebrations were to be restricted. *El Tiempo* was naturally critical of such proposals, fearing an abridgment of freedom of conscience and of religion.

The issue died down with the growth of opposition, and public interest turned to the choice and method of selection of a president for the 1954-58 term. Although General Rojas Pinilla in his Cartagena speech had denied all intentions of remaining in office, none doubted that he would be the choice of ANAC. In March the war minister, Gustavo Berrio Muñoz, was quoted that the military would "continue ruling the fate of the Republic, headed by their greatest soldier, until the citizens themselves indicate whom to nominate as the successor."[32]

The major question was not so much that of Rojas Pinilla's re-election as that of which party might have the "honor" of putting his name in nomination. Well into 1954, both parties were doing their utmost to constitute themselves as the major source of Rojas Pinilla's political strength, retaining in the back of their minds the hope of wresting power from the military and adopting Rojas Pinilla as their own. Both conceded privately that there was little chance for national elections before 1958 when, as the president often said, "internal peace has been fully restored."

In his dispatch of April 4 to the *New York Times,* Paul Kennedy suggested that the position of the Liberals was slightly stronger. Most of their prominent leaders had returned from exile. In addition, Alberto Lleras Camargo announced at a plenary session of the Caracas Convention that he would resign shortly to return home. After seven years with the inter-American organization, his announced motive was to make room for new blood while becoming rector of the newly organized University of the Andes. Carlos Lleras Restrepo as early as November of 1953 had announced the party's decision to cooperate with Rojas Pinilla. The Liberal policy was to support Rojas Pinilla while putting into action a reform program, after which the party might return to power through open elections.

The Conservatives were less unified. The *ospinista* faction was firmly behind the government and already was trying to call Rojas Pinilla its own. The *alzatistas* were somewhat in the background, but not without influence. Their leader was vocal in supporting Rojas Pinilla in his *Diario de Colombia,* which he had begun publishing in the late summer of 1952. Finally, there remained the hard-core *laureanistas* who were in total opposition to the military government. The bitter old Conservative was raining a deluge of vitriolic letters from his exile in Barcelona, urging supporters to fight Rojas Pinilla with everything at their command. Letters to the clergy attempted to turn the church away from the government, while a series of manifestos were published over the signature of prominent *laureanistas,* excoriating the government in the most outspoken terms.[33]

Rojas Pinilla himself carefully sidestepped efforts to draw him into partisanship. Nominally a Conservative, he refused to admit allegiance to either party. His thirteen-man cabinet repeatedly announced that it was above politics. In November the general stated forthrightly that "it would be sacrilegious for me to exchange the national flag for one of a political party."[34] He belonged not to a political faction, but to the nation as a whole. The president criticized the increasing political machinations of the parties. In June, 1954, he said that both should define their programs clearly, ". . . so that the masses might know in their consciences what postulates they are to defend, and which separate them in the political field; when . . . prejudices of the past are forgotten, they will find themselves equally identified with many things that benefit them equally."[35]

As the June ANAC meeting neared, a disagreement between Liberals and Conservatives developed as to the number of seats the former should hold. With the membership still based primarily on the selection made by Gómez more than a year earlier, Liberal representation was small. The convocation of ANAC was postponed in the interests of reaching an unhurried agreement. In mid-July the president issued an executive decree calling for the ANAC to meet on July 28.

Appearing before the group on that date to deliver an opening address, Rojas Pinilla urged an enlarged representation of both parties as well as admittance of representatives of the church and Armed Forces. He requested that political parties directed from abroad "such as communism" should be outlawed. He also urged the adoption of measures embracing judicial reform, feminine suffrage, and the reorganization of departmental and municipal governments. Rojas Pinilla also committed himself to the principle of state intervention: "To the State falls today a greater responsibility than in the past, because its mission is that of assuring the equitable distribution of riches in accordance with the teachings of the Pontificates and Christian thinkers for whom the beginning and end of all economic activity is man and his transcendent destiny. A society that does not care for its elemental base as the people is not only unjustly built but exposed to the worst dangers."[36]

The *constituyente* was responsive to Rojas Pinilla's wishes and was in the process of becoming responsible for normal legislative functions under the military government. Little attention was given the fact that the act which originally established the *constituyente* had specified that it was not to assume legislative functions. Thus, two days after Rojas Pinilla's address the body passed a bill calling for increased representation. The number of Liberal delegates was increased from thirteen to thirty-three.[37] The additional twenty would be named by the government itself. The regime would also select the representatives of the Armed Forces, and the church would name two members of the clergy. Thus the composition of ANAC became fifty-nine Conservatives, thirty-three Liberals— including twenty named by Rojas Pinilla—and two each for the Armed Forces and the church.

There were several vacant seats in the assemblage. Of the original thirteen Liberals, only six appeared. The *ospinista* Conservatives turned out in force, as did most of the unyielding *laurenistas,* conspicuous in red neckties and gaudy suits. Old Laureano himself was on the continent and was to meet his son Alvaro in Caracas on July 28. Technically the deposed president could sit in the *constituyente* in that role, but he wisely stayed away. The church was not enthusiastic with the prospect of direct involvement in ANAC affairs, and Cardinal Luque refused to permit any participation by clerical representatives. The Armed Forces adopted the opposite view, taking advantage of its new legislative representation.

A few days later, newly elected ANAC president Mariano Ospina Pérez rose to announce that Rojas Pinilla had been elected for the 1954-58 presidential term. He had received fifty-three Conservative and thirteen Liberal votes; eight *laureanistas,* led by Luis Ignacio Andrade, voted for Dr. Gómez. Nine other Gómez supporters and four Liberals abstained from the vote.[38]   On Saturday, August 7, 1954, Gustavo Rojas Pinilla took the oath of office before the *constituyente.* This was his first use of legislative "packing" to exert his will in a "legal" manner. He was to use it again and again.[39]

Thus the expanded ANAC completed its most significant work, the legalization and extension of Rojas Pinilla's presidency. It continued to meet until September 8, when it recessed until July 20, 1955. Late in August it adopted further measures submitted by the executive. After July of 1955 it would assume formal and complete legislative functions, until which time executive decree would continue. The popularly elected departmental and municipal councils would also give way to small administrative councils. These, comprising ten to twelve members, would have two appointees of the president, the remainder being named by ANAC.

Another measure was the extension of suffrage to women. Opinion had been sharply divided; in February the Comisión de Estudios Constitucionales had rejected by a nine to eight vote a proposal to grant women the vote. The *constituyente* reversal reflected Rojas Pinilla's personal support of feminine rights. On August 25 the body unanimously approved the change, adding that women would henceforth also be eligible to hold office.[40]   Before adjourning, the Communist party was also outlawed. On September 3 the minister of government appeared before the legislature to urge the measure. The vote was dotted by abstentions, but on September 4 the measure was passed on the second reading as a constitutional amendment. Four days later a final vote of thirty-six to nineteen passed the measure into law.[41]   Thus, the "political activity of international communism is prohibited."[42]

With the September recess of the Asamblea Nacional Constituyente, complete management of national affairs returned to the executive. For Rojas Pinilla the ANAC session had been most satisfactory. His rule had been legalized for the next four years, and proposals for legislative reform had been granted. He was now able to move ahead without substantial political opposition, despite events in the summer of 1954 which had created some little suspicion of his motives and methods. An unhappy occurrence in June had marked the beginning of the end of the extraordinary kinship that had previously existed between Rojas Pinilla and the masses.

THE HONEYMOON BEGINS TO SOUR

The first serious blow to the president's prestige came with an incident on the morning of June 8, 1954, as a group of students made a pilgrimage to the central cemetery of Bogotá to pay homage to a student martyred in a police shooting a quarter-century before. Presidential approval had been granted the procession. After decorating the grave, however, students returning to the University City outside Bogotá encountered several policemen, who ordered them to disperse. A passing truckload of unarmed soldiers stopped and attempted to prevent difficulties. Increasing excitement led to general confusion, and the police were ordered to fire. The crowd of youths swiftly dispersed, but not before a new martyr-to-be was left dying on the ground. The government, pinning the blame on extremists, imposed an evening curfew of 10 P.M. Public meetings were banned; restaurants, taverns, and movie houses were closed for the night.

The next morning a worse clash took place with even more tragic results. Several hundred students of high school and university age marched downtown in an orderly group, headed for the palace and an anticipated audience with the president. A cordon of soldiers prevented their passage at the corner of Calle 13 and Carrera 7, where they promptly settled down in the street. At this point the trouble broke out, and exactly what happened has never been entirely clear.

Officials later claimed that an unidentified shot from a second story window brought down a soldier, after which the army opened fire.[43] Students claimed that they heard no shot. Be that as it may, the soldiers did indeed begin firing. By the time the skirmish was ended, at least eight students were killed and some forty students and bystanders were wounded. By nightfall the city was once more under a curfew, and the following day, June 10, the University City itself was occupied by troops.[44] The institution had recently gone on vacation, thus the possibility of further clashes was somewhat minimized.

The evening of the second outbreak Government Minister Pabón Nuñez addressed the nation to declare that the demonstration was created by non-student elements, and he directly attacked the Communists for inciting the students. He held responsible the "Communists and political extremists." By the eleventh, more than 200, including many Reds, were imprisoned for questioning. Among those who were rounded up were the party secretary-general Gilberto Vieira, former Universidad Nacional rector Gerardo Molina, and the esteemed Socialist leader Antonio García.[45]

With the populace aroused, Rojas Pinilla could not escape without becoming tarnished. He might have been further criticized had not both party directorates affirmed their confidence in him. On June 12 the president discussed the clash in his first national broadcast in nearly a year. Expressing sorrow at the incident, he promised a vigorous investigation to establish ultimate responsibility. He took pleasure in his own exoneration by the directorates, who had "advised the citizenry against the existence of provocative agents interested in impeding the return of peace, and have jointly offered their support to the Government in its firm purpose of maintaining order."[46] Announcing a period of national mourning, he cancelled the scheduled celebration the next day of the first anniversary of his ascension to the presidency.

Only two events were to commemorate the date. First, all political prisoners jailed before January, 1954, were granted an amnesty. Secondly, Rojas Pinilla himself became the first to receive the *gran collar* of the Order of June 13, a decoration he himself had recently instituted. Rojas Pinilla concluded his address with a call upon Colombians "to support the Government in its irrevocable purpose of giving to this country of ours Peace, Justice and Liberty."[47]

Later in the month he also spoke on the events of June 8 and 9 while addressing a graduating class of ninety-six young men from the army's student officer battalion. He still blamed extremist agitators for the incident. "Juvenile ardor was exploited and directed with facility by a few students known as exalted extremists who . . . could put in movement the carefully thought-out plans to unhinge official prestige and impede its continuing strengthening of the faith that the people have in the Government of the Armed Forces. . . ."[48]

By August there were signs of continued discontent as "in some sections of the country crimes and political persecutions were renewed."[49] The final government report on the student clash was not fully substantiated, and little was clear beyond the immutable fact that the government, driven by a need to excuse itself before the public, had arrested twenty-seven soldiers and eighteen policemen for discharging their weapons without adequate provocation.[50]   In the meantime, continuing clashes with the press gradually diluted the original richly blended potion of Rojas Pinilla's personal magnetism.   One of the major strands running throughout any account of the Rojas years is that of the question of press freedom and censorship.   The general's antagonism to the press grew unremitting as months in power stiffened his attitudes and brought out latent flaws in his character.

It was already apparent, after little more than a year in power, that Rojas Pinilla was not only short-tempered but exceedingly vain and thin-skinned.   Like many military men turned politicians, he had been sheltered from criticism throughout his adult life.   The sudden exposure to public disagreement or disapproval, especially when manifested in the printed page and read by tens of thousands of his countrymen, was not something he was accustomed to.   For a time Rojas Pinilla was only mild-ly irritated, feeling this was but a bothersome situation that could be handled with military dispatch.   Later, both his temperamental reaction and public response became more violent.

At first he adopted measures in a conciliatory fashion, and no doubt thought of himself as the model of moderation.   In February, 1954, Jorge Luis Arango of the Information and Propaganda Office circulated a paper to Bogotá publishers asking unquestioning respect for Rojas Pinilla, national institutions, and representatives of friendly nations.   They were also requested to publish no news that might create any disturbance of peace and order.   The pro-government *Diario de Colombia* accepted the suggestion.   Most of the others responded with editorials citing their mutual privilege and responsibility to differ whenever deemed necessary.

Events soon made it apparent that the government could achieve its wishes only by enforcing its request.   On March 6, 1954, an official de-cree ordered all Colombian papers to "pursue factual reporting."   All those who might "transmit, write, edit, assist in editing or distribute writings or clandestine publications in which legitimately constituted authorities are insulted" were liable to punishment.   Conviction could bring prison sentences of six months to two years and fines from 100 pesos to 50,000 pesos.   In addition, such expressions as "it is said," "it is rumored," and "we have been informed" would be considered disrespect-ful.[51]

The first application came barely a week later when on March 15 the government closed *La Unidad,* a Bogotá weekly. The paper had published a manifesto of Luis Ignacio Andrade attacking the Rojas Pinilla regime as unconstitutional. Laureano Gómez was called the "exiled titular President." *La Unidad* had first appeared in February under the direction of Belisario Betancourt, former editor of *El Siglo,* which was still closed. A few days later *La Unidad* announced its self-imposed suspension rather than operate further in opposition to the regime.[52]

The autumn of 1954 brought a further measure designed to strengthen the regime's immunity from the press. An executive decree made the press increasingly liable to government prosecution. In immediate reaction, a special four-man commission was formed to suggest amendments to the anti-libel decree and lay necessary arguments before the president. Alberto Lleras Camargo and Liberal magistrate Rafael Rocha joined Conservatives Alzate Avendaño and Francisco de Paula Pérez in drawing up six amendments to the government decree. On October 15 the president announced a revised measure generally incorporating their suggestions. Fines were reduced from an astronomical level, while closure was eliminated as a penalty for libel. In case of controversy, arbiters would be the national judiciary rather than the Ministry of Government.

This provided but temporary amelioration, and concerned newsmen met in Cali from October 30 to November 2 at the Second National Press Congress, where a special commission for the defense and preservation of press freedoms was formed. Government representatives proceeded to disrupt meetings, and delegates from independent journals soon walked out. This removed what bare skeleton of organizational defense the press possessed. But if journalists were depressed, they could scarcely anticipate the steps with which Rojas Pinilla later abridged what were considered elemental rights of press freedom.

By the end of 1954, positions were gradually being clarified, and many felt that General Rojas Pinilla was unlikely to pursue democratic ideas. There was a general consensus that 1955 would establish beyond question his dedication—or lack of it—to the precepts of democratic practice. As events transpired, the first six months of the new year were enough to convince all but the least perceptive that Gustavo Rojas Pinilla was pursuing, in his bungling but deviously Mephistophelean way, the goal of permanent personal dictatorsip.

Chapter Twelve

THE HARDENING OF RESTRICTIVE
ATTITUDES

THE REGIME EXERTS ITS DOMINANCE

BY 1955 THE government was settling down into a pattern reflecting the nature of its approach and the intention of exercising its will regardless of conflicting views. There was growing scorn of popular opinion, as the authorities from Rojas Pinilla down felt the strength of their position and took pleasure in pursuing their whims relentlessly. The president himself set the precedent at the start of the year by dashing the ardent hopes of the majority for the removal of emergency restrictions and the lifting of the state of siege. In his New Year's message Rojas Pinilla blandly stated that he had no intention of removing the state of siege during his term of office. This meant that "emergency" measures would be extended until August of 1958, some nine years after first being invoked. The justification was the usual one—that the lifting of controls would bring a return of the electoral debates which were "the equivalent of paving the way for the return of the horrible epochs which we cannot sufficiently condemn."[1] This rationalization proved a common one in the months to follow. How could restrictions be removed, asked the government, while violence still existed?

Rojas Pinilla was beginning to realize, as his advisors already had, that his political strength could never be safely based upon either major party. And so, although still cultivating traditional support where possible, he permitted his own supporters to initiate action for the organization of a new, entirely pro-Rojas Pinilla political organization. From 1955 until his eventual downfall, Rojas Pinilla was periodically involved in efforts to establish a personal foundation of power outside the two major parties. It is perhaps surprising that he waited as long as he did before the question of an official third party cropped up. Early in 1955 *Semana* wrote that Liberals and Conservatives were fearful of a *rojista* party, and there was a feeling that he might "take advantage of the momentary disillusionment or coolness of the masses of the two traditional parties to found a 'force' . . . [using] the platforms announced by the Propaganda Office as a program."[2] *Visión* noted that a third party based on peasants and workers was a definite possibility, especially when military support was assured.[3]

In December, 1954, a group of Liberals and Conservatives met with Rojas Pinilla to propose a third force against "sectionalism and the phenomena of political violence to which the country has been subjected." Members of the groups included Conservatives Félix Angel Vallejo, Carlos Londoño, and Liberals Abelardo Forero Benavides and José Umaña Bernal. Further efforts were directed by Lucio Pabón Nuñez, who was becoming the most powerful and certainly most political-minded of Rojas Pinilla's close advisors.[4] In a radio broadcast he announced the formation of the Movimiento de Acción Nacional (MAN). It was designed as a temporary group with representatives from all sectors of national life. Anticipating critical comparisons with Juan Perón of Argentina, he denied any imitation of foreign models. Only "the truest Colombians" would be accepted into the National Action Movement.

Enjoying obvious tacit approval of the general, Pabón Nuñez proceeded with MAN plans. Its support, according to MAN documents, came from "Conservatives, Liberals, Socialists, and labor organizations."[5] It was briefly encouraged by the announced membership of the Confederación Nacional de Trabajadores (CNT), a *peronista* type of labor organization with strong "justicialist" leanings borrowed from the Argentine labor movement. Its formal affiliation with the *peronista* movement had been established a few years before, through formal membership in the Argentine-sponsored ATLAS.[6]

The CNT had already been receiving Rojas Pinilla's support in its highly competitive battle within the divisionistic Colombian labor movement, having won "juridical" status in 1954, with the minister of labor personally drawing up a draft of its doctrinal objectives. In turn, the

CNT had come out strongly for President Rojas Pinilla. Soon, however, CNT backing became a millstone around the neck of MAN.

A rally and mass demonstration were scheduled for February 26, 1955. Early in the month the Directorate of Information and Propaganda released the texts of two letters pertaining to its formation. The first was sent to the president by the committee heading up MAN. Setting the date of the rally and explaining its purposes, it proclaimed its unswerving fealty to the president. The second letter was a reply from the presidential palace signed, oddly, by Lucio Pabón Nuñez himself. In it the government expressed appreciation but added that such acts were not necessary. Furthermore, "the Government considers it suitable at present to do without the manifestation and assembly that were being prepared. . . ."[7]

Opposition had in the meantime been growing, and the scheduled meeting was further jeopardized by its own propagandizing. On February 7 *Semana* wrote that "placards appeared demanding support of the government, battle against the oligarchies." This led to official Liberal and Conservative orders to all party members not to participate. The meeting was first postponed from Saturday the twenty-sixth until the following Monday, when municipal officials from the entire nation were to gather for the demonstration. This idea was quietly put to rest over the weekend, however, and the demonstration never materialized.

A crushing blow had been delivered on the eighteenth in a Lenten pastoral letter cosigned by forty church leaders. Cardinal Luque condemned the CNT labor group as "Peronist and anti-Catholic," and the CNT affiliation with MAN thus placed the latter under inferential church condemnation. The CNT had refused to accept status as a so-called confessional union, wanting no part of church intervention in social matters. Thus the clergy denounced the group for its rejection of "social teachings of the Church on questions of unionism,"[8] and the influence of the confederation declined for the time.

With the third-party movement temporarily set aside, the traditional collectivities began to revive. With attempts at courting General Rojas Pinilla having proved fruitless, both Liberals and Conservatives struck forth on their own. They were still anxious to curry the president's favor but were less sanguine about their chances, and both—particularly the Liberals—began to seek new political ground. In December the Liberals had met in Bogotá under the chairmanship of Eduardo Santos, and once more Alfonso López was elected party leader. López delivered an address reiterating the Liberal desire to return to constitutional normalcy, since violence was, he alleged, now at a minimum. In February he called a meeting of leaders, and on the twenty-third an appeal to the citizenry was issued to place national interests ahead of those of either party. In a matter of days López unexpectedly resigned, being replaced by a seven-man directorate that issued the statement of policy calling for national unity.

Conservatives tried with more conviction than Liberals to draw closer to Rojas Pinilla, but continued Conservative disunity made the task difficult. The basic split between the supporters of Gómez and Rojas Pinilla remained, and the *ospinista* group was either ardently *rojista* or else, like Ospina Pérez himself, had withdrawn into comparative inactivity. There was a brief sensation in February when Alvaro and Enrique Gómez Hurtado were permitted to return from exile. Jorge Leyva also received permission to come home. Pabón Nuñez told the readers of *El Día* that official unwillingness to sanction the return of Laureano was unchanged.[9]

Considerable maneuvering was going on within Conservative circles. The Pabón Nuñez statement was made shortly after a conference held with Ospina Pérez, who had recently returned from the United States. He and Pabón Nuñez were hopeful of attracting support of the militant Gómez supporters, and overtures were also made to the *alzatistas*. Alzate Avendaño was named ambassador to Madrid, which had the double value of enlisting his participation and getting him out of the country. The regime was beginning to harden its position; opposition was frowned on increasingly. Plans for economic development were running into difficulty, and the regime was not disposed to permit others to point out errors. Almost from the outset Rojas Pinilla had followed the familiar pattern of a new revolutionary government in creating new agencies, staffed with loyal supporters, to deal with economic questions.

Only two months after seizing power Rojas Pinilla had decreed the formation of the Instituto de Colonización e Imigración, with the objective of opening up and colonizing idle land belonging to the government. It also encouraged the establishment of agricultural colonies on a cooperative basis. It received official authority to provide technical advice as well as guaranteeing co-operation with private groups interested in establishing so-called colonization centers. The institute was created with 100,000,000 pesos in capital—15,000,000 to be contributed by the Instituto de Electrificación and by the Agricultural Bank, the government to provide the remainder at the rate of 10,000,000 pesos annually.

On September 1, 1953, he also decreed the Banco Cafetero y de Exportaciones. Initially it was hailed by both coffee exporters and producers; it was to increase cultivation, processing, and the export of coffee, operating on a capital of 50,000,000 pesos. The board of directors was composed of three men chosen by the coffeegrowers' organization and the government.

A further measure proved, in plain words, one of the silliest boondoggles of the entire regime. In September of 1954 Rojas Pinilla decreed the Secretariado Nacional de Asistencia Social (SENDAS), the National Secretariat of Social Assistance. He appointed his twenty-one-year-old daughter, María Eugenia Rojas de Moreno, director of the project. His apparent emulation of the Fundación Eva Perón in Argentina was foolish; at the risk of seeming unchivalrous, one must say that young María Eugenia possessed neither the intelligence, personal flair, nor good looks that Evita had brought to the task in Argentina. She also lacked Evita's unlimited funds.[10]

The declared objective of SENDAS was to aid refugees, workers, and farmers, and an Office of Rehabilitation and Help was created to make reports on social problems. It is too easy to poke ridicule at the organization, particularly in view of the questionable abilities of its juvenile director. It might have served a worthwhile function. However, "conceived as a political tool for the Rojas dictatorship,"[11] it was unsuccessful in bringing real improvement in the welfare of more than a small handful of Colombians. The fact that much *could* have been done, and was sorely needed, makes the relative failure of SENDAS another discrediting mark against the military regime.

The general economy when Rojas Pinilla took power had been prosperous. The combination of intelligent economic policies under Gómez and high returns from the coffee crop had brought the economy to one of its highest levels. By the close of 1953 the coffee exports were valued at $460,000,000, an increase of $750,000,000 over 1952. The New York market price was 66½ cents, and prospects for 1954 appeared bright. In January of 1954 Rojas Pinilla's ambassador to the United States, Eduardo Zuleta Angel, issued a detailed statement showing that world production since 1946 had trailed world demand, with a 1946-52 annual deficit of 1,723,000 bags of coffee. Insisting that the sharply-rising price of coffee could not be attributed to market manipulation, Zuleta Angel pledged all Colombian efforts to encourage a stable price level.

Early in 1954 the government took several anti-inflationary precautions. With living costs rising, the regime decreed the duty-free importation of food stuffs. Required cash holdings of banks were increased by 3 per cent; the regular devaluation of the exchange rate as applied to coffee exports was temporarily suspended.* These measures, it was hoped, would increase production. The government also decreed, on April 1, 1954, a surtax on coffee exports. Minister of Finance Carlos Villaveces announced a tax of $10.00 per 150-pound sack of export coffee.[12] This, the first such measure in a decade, called for a 50 per cent levy on coffee revenues based on sales above a base price of $105 per sack. Thus the tax was adjusted to variable prices above the basic figure of $105 per sack. When the decree was announced, the price on the United States market was 98.5 cents per pound, about 30.5 cents above the government base price. The trend of rising coffee income had been flooding the Colombian market with dollars, thus the government "recuperation" rule would force the exporter to sell a certain amount of dollars to the Central Bank for each exported sack of coffee.

The response of the coffee producers was one of vigorous opposition. Manuel Mejía, longtime manager of the Federación Nacional de Cafeteros Colombianos (FNCC), said that the tax was on too high a level. Small planters who comprised the majority of coffee producers would be seriously affected by the move. In response, Villaveces explained that the measures were necessary to counter inflationary pressures. The added revenue, furthermore, would be used by the government for welfare purposes.

In May, 1954, the regime announced revision in the tax structure. A federal tax of 50 per cent was to apply only to coffee sold at the wholesale price of $115 or more, rather than the previous $105. The revenues would be applied primarily to agricultural rather than industrial development. A total of $3,500,000 was expected to be collected and would in part be used for the purchase from Texas of 200,000 head of cattle. The Banco Cafetero would handle the money, also disbursing funds for rural housing and small-scale public works.

Late in the same month the sale of coffee was bringing as much as 99

* The peso was pegged at 2.3845 to the dollar.

cents a pound in New York City, and the inflationary trend continued. The worried administration had lowered duties on all foodstuffs and staple commodities to help check the rising cost of living.[13] A new executive decree in effect opened the doors to imports, with virtually all restrictions taken away.[14] Importers no longer had to request import permits from the regime.

The existing situation on the all-important coffee market changed suddenly in August when Brazil, harassed by increasing quantities of unsold coffee, took unexpected, sharply deflationary action. The international price level dropped swiftly, and the National Coffeegrowers' Confederation moved to maintain its position by buying large quantities in the hope of holding up prices. Exports decreased with the general hesitancy to ship coffee as prices dropped to 73 cents a pound by the end of September.[15] Imports also rose. In turn the administration reacted once more with a change in policy. On October 22, 1954, a new decree announced eight separate measures to deal with the situation. Import curbs were reinstated, while taxes on over 300 "non-essentials" were doubled from the existing 40 per cent level. Importation of many foods—including wheat, rice, corn, and potatoes—was prohibited. Deposits accompanying applications for import licenses were nearly tripled.[16]

By early 1955 there had been no improvement. The lag in payment of foreign exchange obligations was increasing.[17] Banco Central manager Luis Angel Arango had already declared in November that the national gold and foreign exchange reserves had dropped to $196,000,000 while the national debt had grown by $7,000,000 to $230,000,000.[18] Spring of 1955 brought the realization that inflationary dangers were also increasing. In April the president decreed credit controls, with the Banco de la República ordered to increase its gold reserve from 25 to 50 per cent. Other banks increased from 18 to 25 per cent. New deposits after April 13, 1955, would require a reserve of 40 per cent. At the same time, Rojas Pinilla insisted on continued government spending, disregarding the fact that this was easily the most inflationary force in the country.

A lengthy article in *Semana* in May, 1954, blamed inflation on the increase of purchasing power obtained from coffee exports. Attacking the administration for failing to levy an early and high tax on coffee, saving the revenue thereby accrued, it continued to say that "fiscal crazes" had contributed to the existing circumstances. It proposed three possible measures: devaluation, rationing, and rigid contraction of the domestic economy. Rojas Pinilla and his advisors loftily ignored such suggestions. Nearly two years later, with the economy gasping under an impossible burden, comparable measures were finally taken in desperation.

In June of 1955 *Latin American Business Highlights* attacked the growing incompetence of economic policy. The pressure of the $68,000,000 trade deficit in the first three months of the year brought about a scarcity of saleable goods, and with purchasing power still high, the trend remained inflationary. The magazine repeated the growing complaint against large-scale government spending. The response was the June announcement of a series of further loans granted by a group of French firms. Some $100,000,000 would be used in new public works projects.

RENEWED VIOLENCE HEIGHTENS SENSITIVITY TO CRITICISM

While political and economic problems continued, Rojas Pinilla began to step up the severity of his campaign against the press. Renewed violence was a major cause, for the general's temper had shortened in the face of his inability to control the fighting. Although the early months of the Rojas Pinilla government had reduced substantially the magnitude of civil war, there was a sudden upsurge of fighting in late 1953, when *Semana* reported that "in two Departments there have taken place dangerous incidents which seriously preoccupied the government. . . . In Huila, thieves and assassins . . . in El Valle . . . continuous crimes have taken place."[19]

Guerrilla activities expanded in the following year, and in 1955 the death toll rose even more rapidly, reaching a climax in March with an outburst in Tolima. By March 27 some one hundred soldiers were fighting a pitched battle in which they were outnumbered nearly five-to-one.[20] Rojas Pinilla designated Tolima a "Zone of Military Operations," sending in large numbers of loyal troops. At the same time he began attacking the Communists as responsible for the battle. The natural response of the Reds' Gilberto Vieira was a flat denial: "The Colombian Communist Party has always denounced the interests linked to violence against the Colombian working masses. . . ."[21] By April 12 over 2,000 civilians had been evacuated from the area, and fighting continued until the entire population of little Villarica had been removed and the army was using bombers against the enemy. An estimated 2,000 guerrillas banded together briefly, and property destruction approached a third of a million dollars.[22]

The Liberals in particular responded when Rojas Pinilla blamed the Communists for the Tolima battle, and on May 1 the Liberal leaders wrote to the president applauding government actions in controlling the situation. On the fourteenth Rojas Pinilla replied with a mild speech again singling out the Communists. "The Government did everything within its power to make everyone return to peaceful pursuits. But violence has reappeared among us. It would not be fair to say that this happened because the government has turned away from its policy of peace."[23]

In June for the second successive year there was a student riot in the capital, with trouble breaking out when university students tried to commemorate the death of their friends in June of 1954. Police dispersed them with clubs, injuring three in the process. Students were forbidden to place flowers on the site of the 1954 killings.[24] With disorder both in the cities and the countryside, Rojas Pinilla surprised few by announcing that the *constituyente* would not be convened in July and was postponed until 1956. As Rojas Pinilla explained, "the parliamentary system is the greatest attainment of democracy, but such a system is possible only when a country has achieved a high cultural level and when political parties have become civilized."[25]

When Rojas Pinilla was criticized for preventing the legislative body from meeting, he replied with a speech delivered in Cali on July 20, 1955. He reviewed the situation in the countryside, which he reiterated was the basis for his postponement of the *constituyente* session. "Through the delicate state of public order to which I have referred in preceding paragraphs, my decree was expedited which called off the ordinary meeting of the National Constituent Assembly, without this being considered as scorn or criticism of the patriotism of the distinguished deputies. . . . The government has said on different occasions that the normal functioning of the democratic system is not possible without the existence and interdependence of the three branches of Public Power."[26]

Occupied as he was with various problems, the president found time to pursue his harassment of the press, particularly as he grew increasingly the target of attack. Decree 3,000 of October 15, 1954, had embodied the outline of limitations under which the press operated. The first libel action under its provisions was taken in December of 1954 against Alberto Galindo, a well-known political broadcaster and staff member of *El Tiempo*. Galindo had attacked the extensive military campaign in

Tolima by saying it was directed toward the massacre of Liberals, and he was equally outspoken in attacking military privileges which included commissary purchases and a well-stocked cooperative store. *El Tiempo* was required to publish the long counter-protest of the military.

Galindo's charge of anti-Liberal military operations was unjustified, although the issue of military privileges was well taken. The Colombian military, always pampered by civil government, was being increasingly favored by the regime. In sheer numbers alone, the Armed Forces grew from 14,000 in 1948 to 32,000 by 1956.[27] Budgetary appropriations also attempted to insure permanent military support through the erection of luxurious officers' clubs and other lavish fringe benefits. The military budget, which in 1951 was 2.2 times that of educational funds, rose in the 1955 Rojas Pinilla budget to 3.8 times the sum granted for educational appropriations.[28] And even this was without the additional funds allocated separately to the national police force.

On February 23, 1955, *El Espectador* was ordered to submit all articles on economic affairs to the censors before publication, although this measure was dropped a day later.[29] In March, however, restrictions grew worse. Sam Pope Brewer wrote in a dispatch to the *Times* that Rojas Pinilla was carrying on a two-front war with the press. Newly-adopted measures included the forcing of all radio stations to devote free time to a government news program, while he was preparing to publish a subsidized official paper in competition with the privately owned press.[30]

The new restriction on news broadcasts stirred up considerable criticism, but the regime continued to force a daily diet of fifteen minutes' government news and commentary on all stations. The first night's text attacked the press uncompromisingly. Referring to existing public opinion as "the intolerance of troublemakers" in the press, the government pompously proclaimed, "It is not that the state, with its natural means of defense, to which it has at least as much right as the industrialists of the press have to theirs, is trying to create an artificial public opinion.

"The work of the state, and one of its essential obligations, is to free the citizen . . . especially the middle-class man and the masses of workers and peasants, from the paper dictatorship, the printed despotism, the permanent state of siege with which the press intimidates national opinion. The national reality is not the reality of the newspapers."[31]

Later in March the president expanded his position in a speech at Pacho, Cundinamarca. Insisting that projects of his government would receive support from the common citizenry who could not normally exert their influence, he announced his role as that of the supreme fountain of public opinion. Refusing to lift the state of siege, he culminated the succession of attacks on the press with the hollow comment that, for the good of Colombia, he would not put the government "at the mercy" of politicians and unprincipled journalists.

The next month the regime took another step against the press with the announcement that it would publish lists of government officials designating those who might release news directly to reporters. The number would be small; most of the others would be required to submit information through the Office of Information and Propaganda, thus increasing the strength of the regime's control. Persecution of unfriendly newsmen was also on the rise. The regime decreed an automatic two-year to five-year prison sentence for those who divulged information reflecting "discredit" upon the military. To be sure, the decree absolved those who could substantiate their charges. At the same time, the reorganized judiciary, subservient to Rojas Pinilla, was the ultimate judge of the validity of charges.

April was not only a month of growing restrictions, but of active government persecution of the press. Several newspapers suffered directly: the editors of *Diario del Pacífico* were arrested; the editors of *El Diario* went to jail; *Diario del Quindío* was severely censored; and Bogotá's *La República* was suspended for publishing details of the Tolima insurrection.[32] By mid-summer, prior censorship had been declared over nine newspapers. *Diario Gráfico* and *La Unidad* announced that no further political editorials would appear, while Barranquilla's *El Litoral* suspended publication entirely.[33] Cali's *El Crisol* was required to post a 10,000 peso bond against future libel action.

The list of anti-press actions by the government was long, giving stark evidence of the totalitarian aspects of the regime. Yet these were all dwarfed by an episode involving General Rojas Pinilla's official visit to Quito, Ecuador, during late July and early August of 1955. The ultimate result was the imposition of complete censorship, suspension of publication of the prestigious *El Tiempo,* and a full realization that the government was, in essence, dedicated to the denial of universal rights of liberty and freedom of opinion. If any one event marked the final transition from provisional democracy to outright dictatorship, it was this August, 1955, episode involving *El Tiempo.*

A few days before his official call on Ecuadorean President José María Velasco Ibarra, Rojas Pinilla refused an audience with representatives of the National Press Commission who had come to protest his recent restrictions. *El Tiempo* was singled out for criticism, largely as a result of an antagonistic exchange between Rojas Pinilla and *Tiempo* editorialist "Caliban." Full censorship was decreed on the eve of Rojas Pinilla's departure, at which time he told United States reporters that there would be peace in the country "when I have in my hands certain rebel politicians and newspapermen who do not exercise restraint."[34]

Rojas Pinilla then flew to Quito, marking the first visit by a Colombian chief executive to the neighboring republic.[35] He took a huge retinue of 115, including the next four men in succession to the presidency. Minister of War Brigadier General Gabriel Paris became acting president during Rojas Pinilla's absence.[36] In an interview with Ecuadorean newsmen in Quito, the president charged *El Tiempo* and *El Espectador* with making political capital out of the recent unsolved deaths of three Colombian newsmen. *El Tiempo* had blamed the deaths on assassination, while the government attributed them to a traffic collision. Rojas Pinilla's statement in Quito brought an immediate response from Roberto García Peña, managing editor of *El Tiempo.*

On August 2, 1955, García Peña wired a rebuttal to the editor of Quito's *El Comercio,* Jorge Mantilla. He stated, in part: "According to an Associated Press report, President Rojas declared that *El Tiempo* and *El Espectador* had, for political reasons and purposes, exploited the deaths in a traffic accident of three persons. . . . [This] assassination was not a traffic accident, as they are trying to make it appear; it is being investigated, but the material authors of the crime, now well known to all, have not been arrested and the crime continues to go unpunished. I beg you to make this clarification over my signature. . . ."[37]

The following day Chief of Staff General Rafaél Calderón Reyes called in García Peña and instructed him to print on the front page, for a period of thirty days, a prepared text setting forth Rojas Pinilla's position. García Peña asked for time to consider the directive and present an offer of his own. This was granted; his counter-proposal agreed to publish the government article—in itself a major concession—but only as a direct quotation, accompanied by a statement of the newspaper's position.[38] The government refused in the president's absence to accept the suggestion, and within a few hours police were swarming into *El Tiempo's* offices.

Authorities presented their case on August 4 in a broadcast by Lucio Pabón Nuñez. He explained the official view of the disputed deaths, although the logic of his argument did not remove lingering doubts. The government announced further on August 5 that all outgoing dispatches discussing the affair would be subject to censorship. News agencies learned that their reports would first be cleared by a censor before communications companies would accept messages for transmission.[39]

There were misgivings over the *Tiempo* action, despite Pabón Nuñez' insistence that the decision was unanimously reached by the cabinet. Murmurings within the government were heard; Labor Minister Jaramillo Arrubla even resigned in protest. There was good cause for apprehension; the hemispheric storm of outrage could not have been unexpected. Nonetheless the measure was consonant with Rojas Pinilla's earlier policies. Undoubtedly those who did not accompany the general to Quito were well aware of the explosion to be faced if he returned to learn that no action had been taken by way of reprisal.

Upon his return, the general added his own voice to the dispute. On August 13 he charged the newspaper with being a superstate which encouraged public unrest for its own interests. Accusing it of not living up to the press code of honor, he gave strong voice to what was in reality the weakest of justifications. "The salvation of the nation," he announced, "is the supreme one, and if to save it, it becomes necessary to restrict secondary rights and liberties . . . the government will not hesitate to do so."[40]

With the suspension of the forty-four-year-old *El Tiempo,* Gustavo Rojas Pinilla once and for all established himself as an enemy of the free press. This sore festered painfully for nearly two more years, causing the dictator frequent and sharp twinges. But the fight over the issue was a live one, and hemispheric repercussions made it even more worrisome to the regime.

"Public Opinion Be Damned"

The case of *El Tiempo* brought cries of outrage both at home and abroad. The government organized a demonstration in its favor, which is mentioned with great emphasis by Professor Fluharty in one of his many apologetic passages excusing Rojas Pinilla. On the other hand, some 500 women marched in a demonstration on August 10, including the wife of Mariano Ospina Pérez and the mother of Rojas Pinilla's ambassador to Washington, Eduardo Zuleta Angel. They were dispersed by police with tear gas and fire hoses, although their quiet intention was merely to present a formal protest to the chief executive.[41] Near the close of the month leading political figures also requested the reopening of the newspaper.[42] Their petition included the signatures of Alberto Lleras Camargo and Alfonso López, who gave assurances that they would willingly co-operate with the government if basic rights were recognized.

International opinion was critical; typical of comments from the United States was that of *Business Week,* which concluded a disheartened editorial with the plaintive cry that "Colombia deserves better—and the inter-American community is watching anxiously for signs of a reversal of the trend in Bogotá."[43] On a wider basis the militantly democratic Inter-American Press Association marshalled its forces. Jules Dubois, chairman of the Committee on Freedom of the Press, sent an indignant letter accusing Rojas Pinilla of aping Juan Perón. He took particular umbrage at the newest government step, the control of the press through the rationing of newsprint.

The newly established Empresa Nacional de Publicaciones had been empowered to grant permits for the importation of newsprint. Friendly journals would be given the right to buy newsprint at the official rate of 2.50 pesos to the dollar. Those lacking government sanction would import at 4 pesos per dollar, not to mention an additional 30 per cent tax. An immediate result was the closing of *Dominical,* the Sunday issue of *El Espectador.*[44] The Conservative *El Diario* found itself hard pressed, while international journals such as *Visión* and *Time* were banned.[45] As Dubois noted in his message to the president, "the arbitrary and discriminatory decree of 23 August establishing official control over newsprint imports is another step in the Government's attempt at total subjugation of the press."[46]

Even before Dubois' message the IAPA had gone on record against the Colombian censorship. John R. Reitemeyer, executive committee chairman of the organization and publisher of the Hartford *Courant,* cabled Rojas Pinilla an IAPA plea that "this ignominious censorship, which impairs the prestige of the republic, be abolished. Reitemeyer, finding the situation "doubly distressing" because of Colombia's many years in the vanguard of Latin American press freedom, declared that the measures "had deeply perturbed the free people of the Western hemisphere."[47]

Perhaps the best measure of Rojas Pinilla appeared in a September editorial in the *New York Times*. The piece, "Another Dictatorship," was written at the time of the overthrow of Juan Perón.

It is like an ebb and flow, a systole and disastole, a pattern that unhappily has reasserted itself again and again in Latin America. A military officer steps in to put an end to chaos, frustration, or even dictatorship. He promises that he will soon institute or restore a democratic regime. But "all power tends to corrupt and absolute power corrupts absolutely". . . .

The whole affair ranks as one of the most shocking and disappointing developments in recent Latin-American history. General Rojas Pinilla has mobilized against himself the free public opinion of the whole Western Hemisphere and he will not find it an opponent that he can silence, as he has silenced opposition in his own country. Public opinion counts in the United States, and President Rojas Pinilla can be sure that he has opponents who will combat any tendency to favor the Colombia dictatorship beyond the bounds of strict necessity.[48]

As if in disdainful response, Gustavo Rojas Pinilla the next day announced an "end" of press censorship while reimposing control through a new set of restrictions. Limitations embodied in a new executive decree forbade the publication of any news directly *or indirectly* disrespectful of the president or other chiefs of state. Thus the familiar Latin practice of *desacato* or disrespect was introduced to Colombia. All reports concerning the disturbance of public order were completely prohibited, as was "exaggerated" reporting of the national economy.[49] Violators would be liable to a maximum fine of 10,000 pesos, while imprisonment might also be imposed. Rojas Pinilla declared in self-important tones that "one Colombian is more important than the welfare of any [commercial] enterprise." His threadbare argument held that the press was but a series of business entities devoted exclusively to the individual enrichment of its owners.

The most revealing glimpse of the Rojas Pinilla mentality on this subject came from an exclusive interview with Jorge A. Losada, a Cuban member of the *Visión* editorial staff. Rojas Pinilla firmly denied that the closing of *El Tiempo* meant the end of a free press. "When I reestablished liberty, the newspapermen in an act of spontaneity signed an act that was called a *'pacto de caballeros'* and was described by them as self-censorship, inasmuch as they promised without official intervention not to treat matters that in any form could make more difficult the principal task of my Government in the order of reestablishing peace and full juridical normality."[50]   Once the pact was abandoned, he explained, the government was forced to exercise controls.   Again he spoke of great oligarchic power in the hands of the selfish press owners.   "Far from finding in the Government a hostile attitude toward journalism or against those who exercise it, neither is there an unawareness of the function the press fills in the organization of the society; [but] its critical function must be reclaimed by the government itself, as a useful adjunction of administrative management."[51]   By fall of 1955 it was also apparent that the regime had determined to set up its own paper.   Chief of staff Brigadier General Rafaél Calderón Reyes was to take charge of the Empresa Nacional de Publicaciones which would publish the official journal in addition to being responsible for fixing newsprint quotas.

Previous censorship had been directed by the Office of Information and Propaganda, aided by the Servicio de Inteligencia Colombiana (SIC).*   In operation the new office under Calderón Reyes issued many orders, but individual acts of censorship were effected by minor officials without direct knowledge of higher authorities.   Pro-government editors told Brewer of the *Times* that they often received instructions by telephone calls placed in restaurants and similar public places.   It was impossible to judge the authority or even the identity of the man calling.   Outgoing dispatches were handled as if Colombia were a nation at war.   A decree on July 4 even limited usage to several common languages.   Brewer noted with amusement that this was occasionally circumvented by enterprising foreign newsmen who arranged for clerics to send their dispatches in Latin, to the consternation of telegraph officials.

The clumsily inexorable anti-press campaign continued.   In the absence of *El Tiempo,* the afternoon paper *El Espectador* announced its intention of publishing a new morning paper.   The government forbade it to do so without "meeting legal requirements." *El Espectador* found it impossible to determine the nature of such requirements.[52]   In December suppression was heightened when *El Espectador* and *El Correo* of Medellín were both fined for "calumnies and insults to members of the Government and Armed Forces," as Pabón Nuñez put it.[53]   The alleged

---

* This writer personally experienced SIC incompetence on several occasions.

insults referred to the purported presence of a large number of political prisoners. *El Espectador* had printed a statement of the Committee for the Defense of Political Prisoners declaring that 2,000 had been sentenced in the Cundinamarca-Tolima area alone.

In January of 1956 the regime yet once more considered a revision of the press law. A four-man drafting commission under Eduardo Zuleta Angel drew up the document.[54] Early reports of the draft suggested that it simply transferred the task of sentencing violators from the executive to the judiciary. However, General Rojas Pinilla rejected the draft, and in a letter dated May 4, 1956, he promised personally to study the entire question. "The proposed code," he wrote, "having failed to take in certain elements of major importance that should be subject to foresight and regulation . . . must be returned to the drafting committee so they may duly consider these elements."[55]

A schism within the press itself appeared in late spring of 1956 as pro-government newspapers prepared for the Third National Press Congress. Some ten papers ignored the directive of the National Press Association not to organize the meeting. Opening on June 8, the congress deliberated the press question. In a series of measures it approved the regime's hold over the press. Such was its subservience that delegates even refused to debate a proposal requesting "respectfully" that Rojas Pinilla lift the prevailing censorship.[56] Delegates also established a new National Press Federation designed to license journalists and empowered to expel for misconduct those it deemed objectionable. Tad Szulc reported its similarities to the *peronista* newsmen's association in Argentina. The closing speech, delivered by Lucio Pabón Nuñez, announced the government's approval of the congress. He implied that censorship would not be lifted, adding that "the liberty of expression cannot be absolute and undefined.[57]

In August, 1956, the regime finally revealed its long-delayed newspaper, the *Diario Oficial*. The government-subsidized journal was a completely revamped version of the traditional bulletin printing official decrees and legislation. It was carefully designed for large circulation. General subsidization permitted it to sell for ten centavos* while other dailies were fifteen centavos. With daily editions of twenty-four to thirty-six pages, it included extensive wire service from the United States, its own government-directed Colombian news service, and many comic strips. Cir-

* About two cents.

culation was planned for 200,000 surpassing all competitors. Editor-in-chief was Manuel Mosquera Garcés, already president of the new puppet National Press Federation. The sub-editor was a bureaucrat from the Directorio Nacional de Información y Prensa (DINAPE).

Rojas Pinilla hoped in time to organize government publications on a nationwide basis.[58] Some months earlier he had declared, in discussing the project, that his purpose was "to widen this paper giving an absolutely objective and informative national character, respectful of life, honor, and belongings of the Colombians. . . ."[59]

The president briefly tried to mollify hemispheric criticism by permitting the reappearance of *El Tiempo, El Espectador,* and *Diario Gráfico* under new names. *Tiempo* became *El Intermedio, Espectador* was *El Independiente,* and the Conservative *Diario* was renamed *Información.* The same printing plants and the same staffs, largely, put out the papers; typography and makeup remained identical. President Rojas Pinilla made a further concession in May of 1956 by announcing that *El Tiempo* would be permitted to reappear under its own name. But *El Intermedio,* as it was known, rejected the offer, continuing to publish under that new masthead. Founder Eduardo Santos replied to Rojas Pinilla from Paris that the issue transcended that of one newspaper. He described the threat of the "imperious and irresponsible censor determining beyond appeal what must be hushed up and what may be said and how it may be said."[60]

Thus the press issue flared up repeatedly, taking different forms but always reflecting the essence of Rojas Pinilla's intent to muffle the voice of the press. By 1956 his over-all political orientation was clear, as the nature of the government of the Armed Forces sharpened in focus. Party politics were severely limited. With the legislative body on extended vacation, Rojas Pinilla ruled by decree. Foolishly convinced of his destiny, dreaming idly of Bolivarian grandeur, influenced by sycophants who fed his inflated ego, Rojas Pinilla let no one oppose his will. Where lenient with his officers, he was a stern disciplinarian brooking no opposition by civilians.[61]

Rojas Pinilla's strength rested upon several elements. The burgeoning bureaucracy, beholden to him for employment, was slavishly and opportunistically loyal. The peasants looked to him with growing disillusionment but in prayerful hope that the terrors of civil war might be ended.

In the large population centers his prestige had slipped badly. Only the most pessimistic, however, could have imagined the sad events ahead as Gustavo Rojas Pinilla stubbornly pursued his policies despite all outside advice and opinion. It remained for a series of truly exceptional errors to overcome the characteristic Rojas Pinilla inflexibility.

Chapter Thirteen

MILITARISM IN THEORY AND PRACTICE

Ideology and the Model of Peronismo

Once firmly settled in power, the regime took on many of the trappings characteristic of Latin dictatorship. With Rojas Pinilla, one of the striking features was the gross incompetence with which undemocratic practices were pursued. Several contemporary Latin dictatorships have been directed by extremely shrewd, canny politicians. We need mention only Juan Perón and Anastasio Somoza as examples. But Gustavo Rojas Pinilla was essentially an unimaginative militarist; it was owing to more intelligent members of his government that a form of ideology was created to give the regime a theoretical basis. The major exponent of the official "philosophy" was that gray eminence of the regime, Minister of Government Lucio Pabón Nuñez.

A barrage of statements set forth the basis of the self-styled "Government of the Armed Forces." The regime's self-adulation, particularly given to the glorification of Rojas Pinilla, was apparent in *Seis Meses de Gobierno,* a lavish publication containing speeches by the president and others. Most of the views expressed therein were repeated in following years without deviation. Patriotic declarations of high disinterest praised the Armed Forces for taking power "through a call of destiny, to extinguish fraternal hatred and end the horrors of anarchy . . . to reconstruct the country to the point that political groups [might] return to electoral contests repenting of the errors committed and newly glorified by efforts in favor of national coexistence. . . ."[1]

Throughout his rule the general and his aides forthrightly denied personal aspirations. They insisted upon their dedication to the entire citizenry. In June of 1954 Pabón Nuñez declared that the Armed Forces, when "forced" to assume power, did so "with a criteria of curing grave common ills, not moved by ambitions of cast. . . ."[2] He also insisted that the government had a philosophical orientation of its own, which rested on Christ and Bolívar—and what loyal Colombian could possible object?

Homage was paid to Christ through continuing praise of Catholicism. There was the "necessity that the doctrines of the Roman Pontificates be translated into laws that consecrate the rights of peoples, societies and authority, as in the economic-social life; [we must] reclaim privileges for the Christian family, especially those of the workers . . . returning relations of Church and State to the formulas of the Constitution of 1886. . . ."[3] References to Bolívar, often in the form of hosannas of praise having little to do with current problems, made an appeal to the people through declarations of patriotism. There was a clear attempt to transfer the mantle of the Liberator across 150 years to cloak the Rojas Pinilla regime in respectability.

The attitude of the military, ensconced for the time at the head of the government, gradually turned away in part from past traditions. Still dominated by the professional officer corps, there was a tendency for the first time to espouse political beliefs. With the profession scarcely the best in which to learn the art of governing, too many high-ranking officers felt, as did Rojas Pinilla, that operating the government was simply a matter of commanding. Eduardo Santos explained in *Foreign Affairs* that the very requirements of governing were ignored by the military. "To govern—to govern well—often means to have the courage to rectify a mistake; to ask for and listen to advice; to have patience; and to realize that one owes one's power to the will of the people . . . within the limitations they have established. All this is difficult for the military to understand . . . accustomed as they are to the blind obedience of their inferiors . . . [and] the narrow horizon of their profession, which rarely encompasses the element of humanism."[4]

The economic bases of the regime were pedestrian, with financial policies generally following those of the Gómez years, while lacking the practical competence of the previous regime. Finance Minister Carlos Villaveces announced immediately after the Rojas Pinilla *golpe* that foreign investment would still be welcome, with tariff protection continued and monetary stability maintained "by means of adequate control of credit and of money. . . ."[5] Protection of industry would be upheld regardless of pressures, with agriculturalists and industrialists "enjoying an adequate defense" for their products. At the same time, protection would be "neither indiscriminate nor abusive, but a reasonable protection."[6]

Intervention, as already seen, was accepted as a basis for policy. Official pronouncements suggested that Rojas Pinilla was opposed to the position of the oligarchy and would institute sweeping social and economic reforms. *Economía Colombiana* in June, 1954, set forth the regime's alleged goals as including the end of class struggle, the formation of nonpolitical labor unions, development of backward areas, redemption of the peasant through rural education, modernization of farming, and protection of small business. In effect, such measures would strike at the oligarchy, project the overdue social revolution, and bring Colombia fully into enlightened twentieth-century existence.[7] The statement of economic policies was not equalled by practical application, however.

One of the most common declarations of the government forbade the political parties a significant role until the restoration of normality. In time the regime tried to form its own third party, but in 1954 and 1955, at least, the emphasis was on the government by the Armed Forces as being above petty party politics, ruling from an Olympian pinnacle. Although particularly critical of the Liberals, the regime used both parties for whipping boys of official propaganda. As Rojas Pinilla said in Boyacá in July of 1953, the political parties "neglected with frequency the patriotic ideals that must be the strength of their programs, stimulating discord to lead toward the ruin of the country . . . forgetting that they are tools at the service of the nation and that their ambitions never will be interposed on the future of the Republic."[8]

The government was not interested in the elimination of political parties *per se* but "hoped to regenerate their programs and civilize their methods of struggle."[9] The Liberals were to be granted adequate guarantees to exercise their rights, although allegedly having shown previous reluctance to act responsibly. In May, 1954, General Rojas Pinilla even told North American newsmen that he considered it important to grant the Liberals full political participation. The president quoted from *El Tiempo*: "Liberalism has not demanded a thing other than liberty and justice; it desires nothing but the reestablishment of conditions

necessary to make possible the full exercise of democratic systems. . . .
Liberalism has no ambition other than to see democracy restored in
the plenitude of tutelary rights."[10]

The government at first encouraged Conservative activity, although
asking that it "purify" itself in a return to its traditional nationalist spirit
that Dr. Gómez had "sullied.' Rojas Pinilla said that Gómez had been
a "sick man, who physically found it impossible to govern . . . [who]
rose up from his sickbed to unseat the active President and the Commander-in-Chief of the Armed Forces, the only obstacles that impeded
him from implanting and resolving, over the bodies of the people, the
problem of presidential succession."[11]

While emphasizing its own nonpartisan basis, the government urged
on both parties the acceptance of a period of transition leading to more
fully realized democratic norms. This would mean the reconquest of
Christian feeling and of democratic practices "under the supreme command of a policy . . . for all good sons of the Fatherland . . . it is necessary
for Conservatives to become accustomed to seeing Liberals in public
positions, [and] it is necessary for Liberals to become accustomed to seeing
others arrive at those positions."[12] The government declared itself
friendly to party activities, for as Pabón Nuñez said, ". . . this administration does not offer sacrifices to the bloody altar of any sectarism. We
are sincere . . . and irrevocably anti-sectarian."[13]

Once again, however, practice proved distinct from principle. As the
regime moved in the direction of Caesarism, turning its back on the
people, and announced plans for national reconstruction, there came an
attempt to form a government party in imitation of the *peronista* model.

Similarities between Gustavo Rojas Pinilla and Juan Perón had been
drawn in barbed comments by the September, 1955, overthrow of the
latter. Following his ignominious flight to Paraguay, *La República* noted,
"The dramatic fall of the Argentine dictator proves once more those old
ideas, given new vigor by events . . . that for liberty and order [to] be
maintained, it is necessary that power check power . . . the fall of Perón
carried *profound lessons** for the whole world. . . ."[14]

In late spring of 1956 Rojas Pinilla showed that he had been examining
the *peronista* model in the hope of fortifying his own position. On May
30, 1956, *Sábado* announced the forthcoming proclamation of a Third
Force. A few days later the president met with a group of high-ranking

* The emphasis is mine.

officers and departmental authorities to discuss formation of the group. The actual organization would be controlled by Lucio Pabón Nuñez and the departmental governors.[15] Elaborate preparations were made for the June 13 celebration of Rojas Pinilla's third anniversary in power.

Army, navy, and air force troops were sent early on the thirteenth to the Plaza Bolívar. Banners and posters were in evidence showing a crossed rifle and shovel, bearing the slogan "People-Army-Third Force."[16] At the foot of the statue of Simón Bolívar was a crucifix and eight urns allegedly containing the ashes of Colombians killed in Korea and the domestic war. Rojas Pinilla appeared on a platform near the crucifix and read an oath which the servicemen swore to "in the name of Jesus Christ and in the memory of Simón Bolívar."[17] The men took an oath to fight for the dominance of the Third Force until all Colombians joined its banner. The president declared that he wanted no support from politicians of the two historic parties. Bases of the Third Force would be army and labor.

The following day he administered the oath to groups of youth, labor, agriculture, and women. Perhaps feeling that disillusionment with the two parties remained general, Rojas Pinilla bid for the support of those who had felt their loyalties alienated by the petty party squabbling of recent years. Such was the purpose of his careful representation of the movement as a substitute for traditional liberalism and conservatism.[18]

The president's insistence that the Third Force was more than just another party was illustrated by the slogan "Country Above Parties" erected in three-foot-high letters on the façade of the palace. At the same time he obviously had a political party in mind, all protestations notwithstanding. Tad Szulc wrote in the *Times* that thousands of membership cards were printed at government expense, although they were never distributed. Even a salute was adopted: two clasped hands above the head, representing the unity of armed forces and the citizenry.

Rojas Pinilla hoped for support from the labor movement. It had been developing erratically, and he hoped to win over the workers. The Confederación de Trabajadores Colombianos, founded in 1936, had claimed in its peak year of 1948 some 900 locals and 100,000 members.[19] Communist influence, rather strong at one time, had declined after the *bogotazo,* although in 1951 the CTC itself broke in two. The majority wing, dominated by the Liberals, retained the same name, while the pro-Communist group became the Confederación de Trabajadores Independi-

ente and affiliated with the Red international organization, the World
Federation of Trade Unions (WFTU).[20] The *peronista*-affiliated Confederación Nacional del Trabajo had fragmented, but some of its members remained outside the CTC. There were also several independent
Roman Catholic syndicates, as well as a powerful union of petroleum
workers.[21]

When the CNT was attacked by the church and disbanded following
the fall of Perón, its leaders proceeded to establish the Gran Central
Obrera (GCO), whose membership included large numbers of government workers. Its policies were largely directed by Lucio Pabón Nuñez.[22]
It was hoped that the government might bring together an all-encompass-
ing national labor organization through means of the GCO. The regime
had long been courting labor's rank-and-file; lack of success had not
slowed efforts. As early as 1954 Minister of Labor Aurelio Caicedo
Ayerbe had assured workers that they were of major interest to the president and that "nobody but you will be the beneficiary of this popular
administration that aspires to improve and to ennoble your existence."[23]
As Caicedo Ayerbe told labor, "you already can see that the promises of
the government take effect.... We are marching for a new Colombia ...
[the] government thinks that in social matters, not to advance is to
recede."[24]

Events in 1956 proved that Rojas Pinilla's efforts had failed, and the
Third Force died at birth. The church hierarchy, which had its own
reasons for sharing Liberal and Conservative misgivings, declared its firm
opposition to the movement. In a letter to the president written on June
16, Cardinal Luque stated, "The Third Force is dangerous because,
along with most noble objectives, such as patriotic unity . . . it shows
inadmissible intentions from the viewpoint of the Church's teachings and
the principles of natural law. But what preoccupies most is to see in the
front line as leaders of the Third Force the leaders of movements previously condemned by the Colombian ecclesiastical hierarchy."[25] This final
reference was directed at the presence of former CNT directors.

Luque extended his criticism while attacking the regime for meddling
in the affairs of the pro-Catholic Unión de Trabajadores Colombianos. "The Third Force at the same time constitutes a serious threat
for the trade-union movement, which is inspired by directives of pontifical
sovereigns and which adjusts its activities to social Catholic doctrine."[26]
A final criticism was that of demanding of a heterogeneous crowd an

oath of allegiance to a political movement. A further pointed comment was unmistakably clear: the cardinal reminded Rojas Pinilla of Pope Pius XII's condemnation of Benito Mussolini for requiring a similar oath of loyalty from his Fascist party.[27]

MILITARY GOVERNMENT AND CHURCH SUPPORT

From the very beginning Gustavo Rojas Pinilla followed the tradition of courting church support. While there was little clerical enthusiasm following the first months of the regime, there was a general acceptance that the government was happy to acknowledge. The situation during the Rojas Pinilla regime was complicated increasingly by persecution of non-Catholic religious organizations.

We discussed earlier the role of the church with reference to the problem of rural violence. The hierarchy had attempted to tread a middle road, but the exercise of passions often gripped local clergymen, and control from Bogotá was not sufficient to divorce the church from the conflict. The continuing extraordinary spiritual domination of Catholicism was discussed in mid-1955 by *Semana*. Except for a minority of 3 per cent, it wrote, all Colombians belonged to the church, ". . . have been born and have multiplied under the same moral norms of the Church, or have vitiated its precepts with the same indiscriminate decision, and have repented and ordered masses and built temples with identical fervor, with equal assurance of reaching Heaven. . . ."[28]

Rojas Pinilla was not unaware of the importance of church backing. Eight days after assuming power he was endorsed by the archbishop of Colombia, and he consequently turned aside efforts of the Evangelical Confederation of Colombia urging an unequivocal stand against religious persecution. He told reporters in August, 1953, that Protestants had been mistreated only because of meddling in politics, not because of religious activity. Pressed to issue an unconditional guarantee of the safety of non-political Protestant activities, he would say only that he would permit freedom of worship as set forth in the constitution.[29]

On September 3, 1953, he directed departmental governors to stop non-Catholic religious activity in eighteen regions of the country designated "Catholic Missions Territories." The basis was a 1953 treaty between the Vatican and the Colombian government covering an area of 331,000 square miles containing an estimated 1,000,000 inhabitants. Protestant missionaries might remain in Colombia, but would be penalized if preaching their faith in these areas. The Evangelical Confederation condemned the action in an official bulletin to no effect.

Religious persecution picked up in tempo, and by April of 1955 the Protestants reported that, although less bad than under Gómez, the situation was still serious. A report by the Reverend Henry H. Savage of the Baptist Association named Colombia and Ecuador as the two worst South American countries in terms of religious persecution. In the preceding six years there had been continued confiscation of churches, the closing of 159 Protestant schools by government order, and the death of at least 55 persons by various means.

The church became more assertive and the regime more acquiescent to the eradication of Protestantism in Colombia, which by 1956 was accepted tacitly as official policy.[30] Among the various pressures were those exerted against Protestant schools. The Colegio Americano in Bogotá and its two Barranquilla affiliates, operated by the Presbyterian Church, U.S.A. (Northern), had since its 1869 establishment been taking pupils of all religions on a non-denominational basis. The Ministry of Education threatened to remove official sanctions if coeducational teaching was not abandoned. The school responded by segregating the students, boys on one floor and girls on another. In July, 1955, the ministry accused the school of practicing discrimination, thus violating the constitution. Chapters of Acción Católica distributed leaflets nationally, threatening with excommunication the parents of children attending Protestant schools. Cardinal Luque repeated the warning in a December, 1955, pastoral letter read throughout Colombia.[31]

For some years enrollment in the schools under attack had been nearly 50 per cent Catholic. Although excommunication had been threatened, the schools found that registration remained numerically the same. The Bogotá school anticipated the usual 600-student enrollment for the year beginning in February of 1956.[32] Countless applications for admission announced students' religions as "independents," "non-denominational," or even, waggishly, "buddhists."[33]

By 1956 rural violence was worse than ever, and religious persecution had become wide-spread. High government officials lent their sanction to persecution through declarations equating Protestantism with communism. Rojas Pinilla's New Year's message of 1956 presaged new violence when he announced that captured guerrilla command posts included both Protestant and Communist propaganda.[34] This followed a recent statement by Lucio Pabón Nuñez urging all civil servants to be vigilant against Protestant pastors who were responsible for an "attack on our best national qualities" and the disturbance of public order.[35] Most of the renewed violence was occurring in small villages where town priests dominated local affairs.

The campaign took varying and subtle forms. In Bucaramanga, Santander, both British and North American congregations tore down old buildings in order to erect a new church. The regime then refused to issue a license for the new edifice. The Ministry of Education reiterated its 1955 prohibition of Protestant proselytizing in Colombia. It rationalized that such activity opened the way for Communist infiltration. The Catholic religion, said the government, was the only existing unity in the republic, and any disruption would lead to a deterioration of national morality.[36]

The church-state relationship under the military, then, was a close one. The government tied the church to it as closely as possible, although there were scattered suggestions of less than complete church approval. In October, 1955, for example, the official publication *El Catolicismo* editorialized that church policy did not necessarily imply total solidarity. This was a response to Rojas Pinilla's statement that the church "blesses the government, which in turn protects Church interests and is convinced that the greatest service which can be done for the country is that of aiding the Church in its campaign of Christian solidarity."[37]

There was no real schism, however, until the regime involved itself in one of the most incredible episodes in its annals. This affair, known as the "Bull Ring Massacre," was triggered by events of Sunday, January 26, 1956, during the first bullfights of the season. Alberto Lleras Camargo, by now a principal leader of anti-Rojas Pinilla sentiment, arrived at the Santamaría bull ring to be greeted by a full ten minutes of cheering. A few minutes later the president's young daughter María Eugenia, the head of SENDAS, arrived in the company of several officers and her husband Samuel Moreno Díaz, publisher of Alzate Avendaño's pro-Rojas *Diario de Colombia*. On entering the presidential box they were met by resentful whistling, the Colombian version of booing. After the first bull was dedicated to María Eugenia, to which the crowd loudly objected, she and her party angrily strode from the amphitheatre. Periodic outbursts of spontaneous applause and noisy approval for Lleras Camargo forced him to stand up repeatedly to acknowledge acclaim. The bullfighter who had tried to dedicate his first bull to Señora de Moreno finally quit, to be replaced by the Venezuelan fighter Girón and a visiting Spaniard, Chicuelo. Long before the afternoon was over Lleras Camargo wisely left rather than risk provoking a serious disturbance.[38]

Información was the only paper to mention the incident the next morning, and before the day was out it was instructed to submit all future material for censorship before publication.[39] The occurrence was an affront to Rojas Pinilla and his family, scarcely in keeping with finer Colombian traditions. An editorial in *El Catolicismo* rightly condemned the demonstration, decrying "such a demonstration of a minimal level of culture. . . . A woman is always worthy of respect, much more when her title or position is such as to give her special considerations."[40]

The government made no comment until the following Saturday, February 4, when it warned obliquely that "fitting measures" would be taken against the "political manifestation" of the previous Sunday. The same day the president, delivering a speech in Barranquilla, warned that elections would not be called for some two years, adding that his regime would use force, if necessary, to insure "public tranquility and fraternal viability."[41]

Sunday, February 5, brought bestial brutality and death to the Santamaría bull ring. The most vivid account appeared in a report by *Time.* Before the day of the fight, the government had bought $15,000 worth of seats and distributed them to thousands of police and security personnel. On Sunday they passed through the turnstiles unchallenged while the true *aficionados* were first searched for weapons. Once inside, *rojistas* began cheering the president. Soon the non-enthusiasts showed their feelings by silence or barbed replies. "When the oppositionists were fully identified, the bullyboys opened up. Whipping out blackjacks, knives and guns, they attacked in milling fury. Victims were tossed screaming over guard-rails high above exit passageways; hundreds of others were toppled into the arena. Pistols banged away. The toll: at least eight dead, fifty hurt. . . ."[42]

Other accounts varied as to the number of victims. *Visión* announced eight dead and 112 wounded, while United Press dispatches set the death toll at nine. The brutality from beginning to end was extreme. One witness told the following: "Searching for whatever pretext, for not having joined in the *vivas* for the government, or because someone did not speak, without respect for women, adolescents, or children, twenty or more ruffians would jump on one of the helpless victims.

"Among the sights that I remember is that of a man, who had fallen in a pool of blood and lay absolutely alone in between the cement steps, being dragged by the feet to the bottom, while his head banged from step to step."[43]

The regime stifled reports of the carnage. Only with the departure of foreign visitors in succeeding days did the story become widely known. Only one journal, Medellín's *El Colombiano*, printed an account, and it suffered the consequences as the government moved its censorship office to a spot three miles outside that city, making news reporting almost impossible in the face of taking all copy out of town for approval by the censors.

Once Rojas Pinilla himself referred to the incident briefly in a speech at Vélez, Santander. He declared that "in the future, necessary means to insure that similar happenings will not occur, will be strictly enforced." He characterized the episode as "collective insanity that springs from the low social strata of the large cities."[44] To this *Semana* had the most succinct rejoinder, calling the declaration an expression of "God liberate me from my friends and I will liberate myself from my enemies."

There was no proof of Rojas Pinilla's direct responsibility for the slaughter. Indeed, it seems likely that even the unyielding soldier could not have failed to see the damaging blow suffered from such mass brutality. And throughout his regime, although verbal attacks were directed at political groups, repression was usually exercised against individual violators. One must suppose that he gave no direct order for the extreme action that took place. However, infuriated over the insult to his daughter, he undoubtedly demanded some form of reprisal, and his subordinates took it from there. In their inhuman zeal, they went beyond acts which Rojas Pinilla himself would have condoned. Aside from illustrating the ruthlessness of the dictatorial machine, the incident stands out as marking the start of a complete break between Rojas Pinilla and the Roman Catholic church. For the first time the latter spoke out against him in harsh tones.

El Catolicismo denounced the debacle, editorializing that ". . . one cannot avoid condemning and denouncing those events so openly anti-Christian. . . . It seems that something has halted the advance of Colombia toward the fulfillment of such wished-for promises as peace, justice, and liberty. . . . Responsible parties deserving of reproach should be punished, regardless of their position in the hierarchy."[45] A week later Cardinal Luque further attacked the episode in his Easter pastoral letter, referring to "unmentionable developments that are deserving of reproach and are a manifestation of alarming social decomposition." The primate minced no words in referring to the killings as "unspeakable happenings that merit all our reprobation because of their seriousness and the notably criminal circumstances surrounding them, and because they symbolize an alarming social disintegration." *El Catolicismo* also censured the editorial comment of Rojas Pinilla's son-in-law Moreno Díaz in *Diario de Colombia*. To his description of the episode as "trivial and paltry," it replied that "thousands of witnesses denounce the vengeful spirit in which the riots avenged discourtesy with inhuman cruelty, cowardice [and] a reign of brute force."[46]

This split between the church and Rojas Pinilla was temporarily smoothed over, if not forgotten, by the untimely intervention of the exiled Laureano Gómez. On March 14, 1956, the haughty old Conservative sent a 2,000-word letter to an unidentified priest attacking the Colombian church hierarchy. Warning that the citizenry would not honor priests "who are the supporters and partners of this bloody dictatorship," he compared the situation in Colombia to that of Mexico where the church before 1910 condoned the actions of political leadership and was subsequently discredited. In trying to drive a wedge between the church and the president, he attacked clerical support of the "usurper," extending his denunciation parenthetically to the *constituyente,* which he characterized as a "lamentable group of hirelings . . . which could not absolve from crime the tyrant who pays it."[47]

For one of but a few times, the regime handled the affair shrewdly. The *laureanista* paper *Información* was permitted to publish the letter, a few copies were circulated, and then the paper was briefly suspended. *La Jornada* and several provincial papers also printed the letter, however. Liberal editors were told that they might publish the text, although without editorial comment. On the night of March 22 the government issued a communiqué underlining its loyalty to the church, "rejecting the unchristian bitterness and unleashed wrath of Gómez." Further taking advantage of the opportunity, the president sent his cabinet to call on the primate the next day to pay official respects and express disgust with the letter. *El Catolicismo* criticized Dr. Gómez while reiterating its doctrine that church authority came directly from God and that no man had the right to question it. Gómez' insults were described as "unique in Colombian history."[48]

It was indeed the first time in many years that a militantly Catholic politician had unleashed such an attack. Even the Liberals had never been so outspoken. As an attempt to capitalize on the split resulting from the bull ring massacre, it was a gross miscalculation. Perhaps the choleric Gómez simply lost all patience with the church backing of Rojas Pinilla, venting his displeasure in the usual immoderate terms. Be that as it may, he succeeded in delaying the eventual break between the church and the president. As a result, Rojas Pinilla felt more secure as he turned toward the wave of growing opposition that was beginning to threaten his very existence.

Growing Opposition and Military Reaction

Dissension and opposition rallied following the August, 1955, closing of *El Tiempo*, and Liberals in particular stepped out to assert themselves once more. On September 23, 1955, they held a banquet in honor of Eduardo Santos, who was then in New York City. Some 1350 gathered in his honor at Bogotá's Hotel Tequendama, and several influential Conservatives were present.[49] Alberto Lleras Camargo, the featured speaker, urged his audience to struggle for what "those present had agreed upon calling, in continental language, 'democracy.' "[50] *Semana* reported that not only were Liberals now openly opposed to Rojas Pinilla but that the two traditional parties constituted "a weight that cannot be underestimated."

The banquet was significant in marking the return of Lleras Camargo to Colombian politics after a decade devoted to other activities. On November 14 he began writing a column for *El Espectador*. In that issue and succeeding ones he criticized the government in notably unemotional fashion. He willingly conceded the chaotic situation into which Rojas Pinilla had stepped and admitted that both major parties possessed too willing a taste for power. But, he stated, the continuing state of siege had proved unable to restore peace and normality; instead the regime blamed difficulties on "all Colombians except those in the government . . . with the obligation to reestablish order." The strong centralism of the government was robbing the departments of their sovereignty and in turn was bringing increasingly inefficient government.[51]

Early in 1956 Lleras Camargo told the *New York Times* that the state of siege had become an indication either that the government could not control rural violence or that it was intent upon perpetuating itself indefinitely. "The result is that Colombia has a one-man autocratic regime of force with the disappearance of all methods of people's control over their government."[52] In March, Lleras Camargo was named the Liberal chief in a Medellín party meeting, and he was urged to establish a common front with the Conservatives.

A month later the regime retaliated by sending the secret police, SIC, on a raid of Liberal headquarters. Late at night on April 5 they broke in, ransacked the offices, and collected documents they claimed established a close relationship between the Liberals and guerrilla forces. Lleras Camargo and the secretary of the party directorate, Delio Enciso, denied the charges by retorting that the papers in question were political documents sent to the party from throughout Colombia. Nonetheless Señor Enciso was taken into custody for questioning and was held several days. As might have been expected, the government ordered an official "clarification" published in all papers. Those who refused—*El Intermedio* was one —suspended publication.

Further Liberal activity was held in abeyance while awaiting the Conservative response to an invitation proposing a Civic Front against the government. All eyes focused on the Bogotá meeting of the Conservatives. With the exception of Gómez, all prominent Conservatives were in attendance. A strong group under the rising Guillermo León Valencia urged disassociation of the party and government. The response to the Civic Front proposal was an indecisive three-point declaration. The question of Rojas Pinilla's 1958 successor would be considered at the summer session of the *constituyente,* and the return of Dr. Gómez was endorsed. Finally, all forms of totalitarianism were condemned, with delegates agreeing that the "universal fight against communism" had unfavorably diminished "Catholic, Democratic, and Republican postulates." Mariano Ospina Pérez led the group which advocated using the *constituyente* as the means of returning to constitutional normality. The citizenry was in agreement with this thesis, for even in the summer of 1956 "Colombians were universally opposed to him [Rojas] but were still willing to let the president serve out his term, provided he would allow the holding of free elections in 1958."[53]

Faced with Conservative equivocation, the Liberals remained determined to establish a Civic Front. The Conservatives apparently would take no positive action toward collaboration without a declaration from Gómez. Although a hemisphere away and ailing from a serious heart condition, the redoubtable old Conservative was still the major power of his party. And as he dominated the Conservatives, so had Alberto Lleras Camargo become paramount within the Liberal party. There was only one chance to establish a joint Liberal-Conservative program against Gustavo Rojas Pinilla. It materialized in July, 1956, with an event of historic significance to Colombia. For in that month, Laureano Gómez and Alberto Lleras Camargo met in an obscure little Spanish village to discuss measures that led to agreement between the rival parties and, later, to one of the most startling innovations in twentieth-century Latin America.

On July 18 Lleras Camargo arrived at Madrid and proceeded to Benidorm, a sleepy town in the province of Alicante. After four days' discussion, he and Gómez announced the text of the "Pact of Benidorm." Under the necessity of opposing military dictatorship, the two men agreed on a coalition until national institutions could withstand any possible interference. The pact declared that party unity was of "primordial urgency" to express the people's immense displeasure at the barren shambles of civil government. The pact further called upon party followers for joint action in the "reestablishment of liberty and constitutional guarantees."[54] Lleras Camargo then returned to Bogotá, where he was detained and searched at the airport before being permitted to enter the country he had once served as president.[55]

A few weeks later Laureano Gómez granted a rare interview with *Visión*. He spoke only briefly of the agreement, explaining that it was aimed directly at Rojas Pinilla. Conceding that initiative had come from the Liberals, he added that secret talks in Colombia had preceded Lleras Camargo's visit to Spain. He did not miss the opportunity to praise his own government. "I had an impeccable presidency and I made myself unpopular because in my country it seems that the people do not want things correct. You may say that I prefer being unpopular to being incorrect. And add that the people have the government they deserve. I offered a government that they did not deserve; now they have what they deserve."[56] When it was suggested that he was unduly bitter, he turned angrily to the interviewer. "I am not disillusioned with my political thought, and I remain faithful to it, but I am disillusioned that the people who so mistreated me remain."

Back in Colombia, Rojas Pinilla in a rambling telecast was defending himself against charges of graft.[57] His unrestrained speech had been provoked by a magazine article accusing him of becoming a multimillionaire in office. He, who as chief of staff had lived in a rented house, had allegedly acquired at least nine ranches, cattle numbering in the tens of thousands, and a monopolistic arrangement whereby he supplied the army commissaries to provision the troops. His estate at Melgar was reached from Bogotá by an improved highway that had been unpaved in 1953. Millions had been drawn from the treasury to build a rail spur from Melgar to the nearest trunk line.[58] Evidence received by the Colombian Senate in 1957 showed that Rojas Pinilla's holdings rose from 200,000 to 8,000,000 pesos in four years excluding the assets of his cattle company. Charges also included the forced delivery without collateral of $700,000 in loans to his family and friends from various banks.[59]

Rojas Pinilla's public denial was widely reproduced and circulated. For the first time the public was aware of the possibility that the military government was not only dictatorially incompetent but also morally corrupt. Even more important, this was the first issue to turn high-ranking officers of the Armed Forces against their president. An influential group centered around Intelligence chief Brigadier General Luis Ordóñez was increasingly convinced that Rojas Pinilla was dragging the country down with him. The vituperation of his denials of corruption merely suggested that the charges might indeed be true.[60] Certainly Rojas Pinilla had not ended the civil war of which all were weary; there were signs that the economy was slipping badly; and there was reason to question his leadership, in which they had once held so much faith.

Military dissatisfaction mushroomed further as the result of a nonpolitical tragedy that struck the lovely and lively metropolis of Cali. At 1:17 A.M. on August 7, the 137th anniversary of the historic battle of Boyacá, an explosion literally tore apart the heart of the city. Eighty-two city blocks were damaged, forty-one so badly demolished that they were later rebuilt from the ground up. It was announced that at least 800 were hospitalized and over 400 dead.[61] Shocked Colombians later learned that the death toll ultimately went over a thousand.[62] Property damage was set at 150,000,000 pesos.

Cause of the catastrophic explosion was the detonation of seven army trucks loaded with dynamite. They were part of a convoy of about twenty vehicles transporting ammunition and dynamite from Buenaventura to

Bogotá. The others had continued the trip, while seven had stopped in front of a railway terminal near the center of Cali for the night. Observers later reported that not a single stone was left standing at the terminal. The crater was 85 feet deep and 200 feet wide. A heavy pall of dust and smoke remained for some time; thirteen blocks away the main door of St. Peter's Cathedral was blown off.[63]

In Bogotá, Gustavo Rojas Pinilla lost contact with reality. Taking the national airwaves to read a message of condolence to the governor of Valle del Cauca, he attributed the disaster to political sabotage, to a "treacherous and criminal conspiracy." This, the gravest such tragedy in Colombian history, was called a "crime" resulting from the Pact of Benidorm. Rojas Pinilla promised that "before God and man, the Armed Forces will not rest until the authors of this treacherous and criminal attempt receive exemplary punishment."[64] Three days' mourning were decreed, and the central government was mobilized to assist the stricken city.

Seldom had the general made such a damaging public statement. Military and civilian opinion rebelled against the affront to justice and common decency. Alberto Lleras Camargo spoke for the nation in calling Rojas Pinilla's inflammatory statement "monstrous opportunism."[65] The president found himself forced to retract his statement, and he did so with little grace and equally little success. Denying that he had singled out individuals, he explained, "I do not believe that any fellow countryman would fall so low in political corruption."[66] Stubborn as always, however, he insisted on adding that the explosion could be attributed to criminal rather than accidental causes.

But the damage was irretrievable, and national mourning was replaced by futile anger at Rojas Pinilla's irresponsible petulance. In Bogotá there was talk of forcing his resignation, and hostile military sentiment made his position highly precarious.[67] Returning to Bogotá from the disaster area, Rojas Pinilla called a meeting which on August 15, 1956, brought hundreds of officers to the Teatro Patria. The general's immediate political fate hung in the balance, and he well knew it. Calling upon his colleagues' sense of military responsibility and discipline, he hurriedly proposed a series of conscessions. He promised not to revive the Third Force, to convoke the *constituyente*—which had again been postponed—and agreed to step down from office at the conclusion of his term in 1958.[68] And so he was, for the moment, delivered from political oblivion.

Only the reluctance of the military to force his resignation permitted him to remain, costing Colombia more months of dictatorship.

Reassured by military approval, Rojas Pinilla cracked down on the citizenry. His intelligence service announced the arrest of many who were allegedly spreading the rumor that a *junta* would replace the general. Government machinery began grinding out new propaganda containing a plaintive note of near desperation. Minister of War Gabriel Paris denied that Rojas Pinilla would quit, insisting that "the Armed Forces are loyal and support with restrictions their commander, the general, Supreme Chief Gustavo Rojas Pinilla, President of the Republic."[69] On August 17 Rojas Pinilla himself denied such reports. "The President of the Republic," he said unctuously, "lives in tranquility, fulfilling his duty. He gives no importance to calumnies that are published and circulated in subversive leaflets and through the foreign press."[70]

Announcing the forthcoming publication of a "Red Book of Colombia," he promised to reveal the real "culprits" behind internal dissensions. "We shall prove two things: a Protestant propaganda and a Communist propaganda. That is to say, it seems that the Communists have understood that, to carry out a program, they first have to vanquish the religious beliefs of the people. This is the best interpretation of the facts."[71] In attacking Protestantism and communism he was, clearly, on safer and less unpopular grounds than in specifying Liberals and Conservatives.

And so Gustavo Rojas Pinilla was almost gratuitously maneuvering himself into an untenable position. His course of action since the August, 1955, closing of *El Tiempo* had inexorably carried him beyond recall. His alienation of the church, the ill-conceived Third Force project, the inhumanity of the "Bull Ring Massacre," neurotic denials of personal corruption on a large scale, and calumnies in the wake of the Cali catastrophe—all these actions had alienated the populace irretrievably. If public opinion in early 1953 had been generally opposed to Laureano Gómez, it was now dangerously aroused against the chief of the military government.

The military president was totally isolated, and even temporary support of the Armed Forces was unsure. The military themselves had little reason for pride. The genuine dignity and honor acquired through generations of patriotic dedication to the nation had been largely nullified in the span of a few short years. Its overthrow of a constitutional government in 1953 had seemed justified by Laureano Gómez' attack. Having been placed in a position where enlightened rule might have generated necessary basic reforms, the military had abrogated responsibility by trusting blindly in the false values and personal pretensions of its leader, who was out of his element and unsuited to the administration of government. Yet with circumstances far worse than they had been in 1953, the Armed Forces followed the apparent line of least resistance by saving Rojas Pinilla when the lightest nudge would have plummeted him into the abyss of political exile.

Time was running out, and the general continued to play out his string while trying to shrug aside opposition as "absurd rumors."[72] He could only hope to smooth the roiled waters with gestures of less dictatorial government, while concentrating efforts on reconsolidation of his position within the military. A great North American daily described him well: ". . . few latter-day strong men have been so inept as insistently to oppose or offend the leadership of both major parties, numberless independent civilians, the courts, the press, and—as Rojas has done—both the primate of the prevailing religious faith and a minority religious group. . . . The other Americas can only hope that the Colombian leader will see the light before it flashes upon him like a bolt from a darkened sky."[73] But Rojas Pinilla, headstrong, vain, almost totally cut off from his people, was scarcely the man to see or, more important, to understand even the most blinding illumination.

Chapter Fourteen

DEATH OF A DICTATORSHIP

THE WALLS BEGIN TO CRUMBLE

IN LATE 1956 COLOMBIA hung in a state of suspension. The promised gathering of the Asamblea Nacional Constituyente was eagerly awaited, and on Thursday morning, October 11, it met for the first time in two years.[1] The president appeared at opening ceremonies to praise the representatives' inherent patriotism and request their approval of various government recommendations. Among his proposals was an increase in the size of membership by twenty-five, with new representatives appointed by the executive. He also hoped to draw the cloak of legality more tightly about his policies by obtaining direct ANAC approval of all laws and acts decreed by executive order. Mariano Ospina Pérez, presiding over the legislature, replied with a vague comment on the *constituyente's* patriotism that gave no assurance of support.

As the *constituyente* met on following days, the capital building was surrounded daily by white-helmeted police carrying submachine guns and searching each person before passing him inside. While foreign observers had difficulty in attending the proceedings, Rojas Pinilla packed the galleries with disreputable elements who supported him and heckled those speaking out against the government.[2]

The opposition was sharply critical of Rojas Pinilla's projected expansion of ANAC representation. Alberto Lleras Camargo called the measure an arithmetical scheme to pack the legislative body with government supporters in order to extend Rojas Pinilla's power beyond 1958. The existing relaxation in government restrictions, he said, was simply an effort to lull the opposition into lowering its defenses. The outspoken Conservative Guillermo León Valencia also denounced a newly appointed Rojas Pinilla cabinet as having been largely responsible for reducing the value of legislative proceedings to ashes. He further criticized what he called the government violation of Conservative party principles in its newest plans. Rojas Pinilla, his Third Force a dismal failure, had finally stopped talking of being above party strife and was calling himself a Conservative.

To the surprise of many, the general permitted full expression of views in the *constituyente*, and press controls relaxed to the extent that local newsmen were permitted to report and comment on legislative affairs. Despite several strong attacks against him, Rojas Pinilla continued to permit this degree of freedom throughout the meeting of the *constituyente*.[3] Liberals and Conservatives alike demanded the return of Laureano Gómez from Spain.[4] He theoretically had the privilege of sitting in the legislature as a former president. At the first meeting Ospina Pérez was the only one of eight living former presidents in attendance.* In a letter read on October 20, Rojas Pinilla explained that Gómez might return "if he offers to convert himself into a fountain of unity and not of subversion and disorder." More specifically, he said that Gómez had to "recognize the legitimacy of the present government." This, of course, was out of the question. Even before Gómez could retort from Spain, his followers decried Rojas Pinilla's stand. As *laureanista* Luis Ignacio Andrade put it, "What a horrible document . . . imposing a species of tariff in order that [Gómez] many return to the country."[5]

The battle over the question of Rojas Pinilla's appointing new members to the ANAC was a bitter one. The dispute became sharper on the night of October 23 when Alberto Lleras Camargo and Alvaro Gómez Hurtado walked into the hall together, followed by others who had been boycotting the meetings. Enthusiastic applause and even cheering gave a measure of the popularity of the anti-Rojas Pinilla forces.[6] There was some fear that a refusal to accept Rojas Pinilla's terms would mean the dissolution of the group. In an interview on September 30, 1956, he told the *Times* that he was certain he had enough support to approve government plans. Only later was it revealed that he had added that in the

---

* Absent: Urdaneta Arbeláez, Gómez, Lleras Camargo, López, Carlos Lozano y Lozano, Santos, and Olaya Herrera.

event of rejection of government proposals, he would simply dissolve the *constituyente*.[7]

Rojas Pinilla's estimate proved accurate, and his forces won by a 50-43 margin on November 3, 1956. The addition of 25 new members was authorized, increasing the body to 127. Eight separate votes were required before the bill and all its particulars was adopted. The general hullabaloo from the galleries rose deafeningly whenever the opposition spoke, then died down when a government representative came to his feet. Lleras Camargo and Ospina Pérez were in the thick of the opposition fight. Lleras Camargo declared that Rojas Pinilla's personal whim was the only law of the republic. Ospina Pérez charged that approval of the measure would "hand over to him [Rojas Pinilla] the whole Assembly. We are facing a continuous process of the accumulation of authority in one person alone."[8] When the final tally was announced, Ospina Pérez resigned as chairman in a final gesture of defiance.

Rojas Pinilla announced that he planned to appoint the twenty-five new representatives from professional organizations and feminist groups.[9] This seemed a possible first step toward a corporative state such as Gómez had outlined in detail some four years earlier. However, it is not exactly clear what Rojas Pinilla really had in mind. His main consideration was simply the placement of more supporters in the legislature. The *constituyente* meetings also provided a safety valve of popular passions at a critical moment. Unrestricted debate and press coverage suggested a relaxation of controls that abetted the temporary quiescence that returned to Colombia.

The opposition was not disheartened by the failure to block Rojas Pinilla's expansion of the ANAC. Lleras Camargo explained in an interview with *Visión*: "In the hands of the chief of state is concentrated today all legislative power, which he exercises without limitation; the executive power has not confined its practices to stable norms, although the existing rules can be changed by this very government in each concrete case, and in fact are being changed with unusual frequency."[10] He and other enemies of the regime repeated the accusation that Rojas Pinilla was rigging an extension of his power until 1962. In December, 1956, the president, who had denied such charges, said that his government was building "a new order that guarantees to Colombia her just right to enjoy the benefits of civilization." Speaking at Tunja, capital of his native Boyacá, he called his new order a "just use [of power] to limit the outrages of misunderstood freedom." This was needed "because it is not possible to continue speaking of an individual and exclusive capitalism in a socialized world. . . . Nor can we continue insisting on the romantic principles of freedom when, in our own country, the social problems of the modern era surge from all sides."[11]

With the political situation temporarily under control, it might have been expected that the president could enjoy a few moments of relaxation. However, he was instead faced with a deteriorating economic situation of alarming proportions. For some time the economy had been suffering increasingly as the result of grandiose public works projects and bureaucratic maladministration. The economy was approaching the point of extreme danger. The fundamental trouble—beyond the incompetence of Rojas Pinilla's economists—had been a tremendous national buying spree. When coffee prices fell, two major controls had been initiated. The first had channelled incoming dollars through the Central Bank, which later distributed them to importers at artificial levels of exchange. A licensing system had also been inaugurated, categorizing all imports as essentials or luxuries, penalizing the latter by taxes.[12]

These measures failed. The bank was slow in supplying importers' dollars, and foreign exporters ignored uncollected bills by continuing at the same pace. Reserves began to drop further, dwindling by late 1956 to merely $91,000,000. Coffee revenue poured in—$300,000,000 in the first eight months of 1956—but the situation worsened. The foreign debt, a major headache for United States exporters, reached nearly $350,000,000, with no end in sight. As *Time* commented, Rojas Pinilla was ruining his nation faster than Juan Perón—and without some of the unorthodox and unrealistic *peronista* schemes.

With immense graft and vast expenditures to pamper the military, the economy sailed into dire straits. Repercussions included the delay by the World Bank of a negotiated loan for railway construction. The Cauca valley development project (similar to the TVA in the United States) ground to a stop. Industrialization slowed noticeably. Yet the regime plunged ahead. Jet airplanes were bought, and other purchases of arms included a destroyer for the navy. An apocryphal comment of one businessman explained that "the only thing you can make with a warship is an admiral." A scapegoat was required, and the minister of finance was dismissed. On October 4, 1956, the government named as new minister the forty-year-old manager of Bogotá's Banco Popular,

Luis Morales Gómez. He promptly announced an austerity program that would include military expenditures.

Morales Gómez was very much in earnest, to the surprise of skeptics. The Banco de la República estimated that total government imports were more than 20 per cent of the national total.[13] Devaluation was rejected, but the "pegged-free" dollar was released. Official dollars had previously been sold at 2.5 pesos to importers although the free dollar was going at some 5.1 pesos.[14] In an interview the new finance minister promised to reduce the 1957 budget, with only educational and public health appropriations surviving drastic cuts. He announced a tentative budget of 1,180,000,000 pesos ($203,000,000) compared to 1956 figures of 1,400,000,000 pesos ($240,000,000). Import restrictions were presumably to permit the payment of outstanding debts in eighteen months. Even this referred solely to money owed to exporters and had no bearing on the regular external debt. Morales Gómez hoped to repay some $30,000,000 by the end of the year.

Late in November the government froze prices of imported and locally produced commodities at the October 31 level. Anyone selling restricted items above specified prices would return to the buyer the difference in price and would be subject to a maximum fine of 10,000 pesos. Fines of 1,000 pesos would be levied on those who speculated with prices of domestic products by withholding merchandise to force prices up.[15]

By 1957 there was still little hope that Morales Gómez' measures had come in time. *Business Week* devoted its attention to the problem in its January 12 issue. It felt that Morales Gómez might pull Colombia through, providing that Rojas Pinilla left him alone to work out the solution. "The real question is whether Rojas can afford to let Morales give the economy the dose of bitter medicine it needs. For that is bound to alienate the little remaining support the regime is able to buy with the pork barrel."

Problems were much the same: internal inflation, an immense foreign commercial debt, a decrease in gold and currency reserves, and the rise of the free-market dollar. In reducing Colombia's debt in the United States, Morales Gómez made two trips to New York City in February. On the first he tried to restore lost confidence in Colombian finances, explaining his program and its goals. On the second he handed out certificates covering $62,000,000 in accrued debts.[16] The finance min-

ister claimed that all remaining such debts would be paid off by mid-
February, with 60 per cent of the obligations met by the national treasury
and the remainder covered by 2.5 per cent bonds issued to foreign
banks and exporters guaranteed by the Banco de la República, to be
paid in thirty monthly installments.

By accepting such bonds, foreign clients would in effect be financing
40 per cent of the debt. The $62,000,000 payment, claimed Morales
Gómez, wiped out roughly half of the outstanding debts in New York,
although some financiers felt the actual total had been much higher than
the announced $125,000,000. Morales Gómez' plans were further sub-
stantiated, however, when in February of 1957 the Banco de la República
paid 60 per cent of the commercial debt. The finance minister announced
that Colombia now had a reserve of $90,000,000 to liquidate other debts,
the money accruing largely from his austerity program which had cut
back imports to only $12,000,000 during the final quarter of 1956.

All Morales Gómez' moves underlined tacit admission by the government of over three years of economic mismanagement. The economic
prosperity and financial stability of the Gómez years had been dissipated.
Incompetence had reached such proportions that only drastic measures
held any hope of restoring the economy. Despite measured improvement,
the economy was far from well. The 1957 budget was not reduced as
far as Morales Gómez had promised; it was announced at 1,230,000
pesos, of which the military still received some 20 per cent. In contrast,
appropriations for education comprised but 6 per cent of the total. By
March the peso was again dropping in value and by the end of the
month was quoted at 6.77 to the dollar. The continuing flight of capital
abroad overbalanced the foreign investment capital entering the country,
as money sought refuge in foreign banks. But political questions were
again coming to a head, and before long economic difficulties were the
responsibility of a new government.

The Supreme Series of Miscalculations

The curtain rose on the ultimate series of events with the convocation
of the Asamblea Nacional Constituyente on Wednesday, March 20, 1957.
Augmented by twenty-five new appointees, a chairman was elected to
replace Mariano Ospina Pérez—none other than the omnipresent man-
ipulator Lucio Pabón Nuñez.[17] Once more the galleries were packed
with *rojistas* primed to jeer the opposition. Immediately upon taking

the chair, Pabón Nuñez recommended that a motion be made to study a Rojas Pinilla suggestion to dissolve the body before the official reorganization.

Two days later, after receiving such a motion from the floor, he announced that "the period of the present National Constituent Assembly will end on the 10th of April, 1957. . . . The National Government will authorize the convocation of a new Assembly."[18] On March 23 the opposition walked out when the chairman ruled out of order its attempt to read a new unity manifesto. Representatives had been permitted to read the document over the radio at 7:30 P.M., but only forty minutes later Pabón Nuñez denied their request in the legislature. Prepared by Liberal and Conservative leaders and signed by all but one of the living former presidents, it announced total agreement between the two historic foes. The six-page document, characterized by Lleras Camargo as a "new active rather than passive opposition," said that "the solution to the political crisis" called for "understanding and conjunction of the two traditional parties to present a civic resistance to the systematic destruction of the moral, institutional and judicial heritage of Colombia." It also demanded free popular elections for the next presidential term, promising to "present a candidate who personified this agreement of the two parties.[19]

The *constituyente* soon concluded its meetings and dissolved itself. On March 28, Gustavo Rojas Pinilla decreed the creation of a new Asamblea Nacional Constituyente composed of ninety delegates. Thirty would be chosen personally by the president, the other sixty named by a Consejo Nacional de Delegatorios Electorales, a fifty-one-member body to be chosen by new municipal delegates in each of the departments.[20] No popular elections would be held. These legislative manipulations were intended to give the regime the strongest possible basis for extending Rojas Pinilla's rule. And while he was in the process of organizing his re-election, the opposition took measures of its own.

On April 8, 1957, the Civic Front announced a protest gesture nominating Guillermo León Valencia for the presidency. Their choice was appropriate; Valencia was not only an astute and prominent politician but a fiery individual whose combative nature was apt for existing political conditions. The son of the famed "Maestro of Popayán," poet-laureate Guillermo Valencia and himself once a presidential candidate, young Guillermo had taken his doctorate in law and political science from the

University of Cauca, and in 1933, at the age of twenty-five, had founded the journal *La Claridad*.

Serving as senator and as a member of the Conservative Directorate, he had in his youth been pro-Axis and anti-United States, a loyal follower of Laureano Gómez. More recently he broke with the autocrat, however, and had developed into a progressive Conservative of unquestioned patriotism and general good sense. With anti-government meetings prohibited, his candidacy was officially proclaimed on April 23 from a private home in his native city of Popayán. His acceptance speech urged a return to legality and placed national progress before party activity.

Rojas Pinilla hounded his opponents at every opportunity. Political arrests unwisely increased under apparently indiscriminate orders. On April 9, five women and eleven men were arrested at the graduation ceremonies of Bogotá's Colegio de Nuestra Señora del Rosario. The same day six were also detained for distributing political literature on a Bogotá street corner, including the wife of Lleras Camargo, Doña Berta. The women were released with the apologies of the intelligence service, but the men were held overnight. A further petty incident was the invasion of privacy at the home of Señora Gaitán, widow of the assassinated hero of the masses. She, her daughter, and several students had been honoring the anniversary of his death. Both women and five students were taken into custody briefly.[21]

There was increasing government anxiety when the church opposed it in April. Following the president's ban on opposition meetings, the Archbishop of Popayán, Monsignor Diego María Gómez, invited opposition leaders to his palace on April 20. He spoke with them sympathetically, promising that Cardinal Luque would soon take a firmer stand against the government. One of Colombia's most important prelates, he called the choice of Valencia "fortunate."[22] The auxiliary bishop of Popayán, Monsignor Raul Zambrana, also told an interviewer that while the church avoided identification with political groups, it "cannot disapprove any political movement that promises people civil rights" as the opposition was doing.[23] Luque further indicated his own feelings on April 30 when he refused Rojas Pinilla's request for an interview, writing the president that re-election would be illegal.[24]

The new *constituyente* met in Bogotá despite mounting criticism. The ninety-member body was installed specifically to ratify Rojas Pinilla's re-election until 1962.[25] For the sake of "administrative convenience," the sixty non-appointed members were simply picked by a three-man executive committee comprised of Pabón Nuñez, Julio Roberto Salazar Ferro, and Anacreonte González. Pabón Nuñez was named president of the new ANAC, with Salazar Ferro first vice president and González second vice president. All three were ardent *rojistas*. At the first evening of the session, members were read the proposed bill that would suspend Article 171 and the prohibitions of Article 129 of the Constitution. The former said that "all male citizens will elect . . . the President," while the latter prohibited a chief executive from succeeding himself.[26]

Thus male citizens would not be bothered with voting for the 1958-62 president, and ANAC could re-elect the general. In his opening speech to his selected puppets Rojas Pinilla promised to work for the establishment of "circumstances favorable to the aims of calling the people to the polls before 1962 to elect their representatives to municipal councils, to departmental assemblies and to Congress."[27] Unexpected difficulties arose in a dispute over selection of a *designado*. Lucio Pabón Nuñez, eyeing the job himself, urged the naming of a civilian. Rojas Pinilla, somewhat suspicious by nature and partially aware of the adept operations of the ambitious Pabón Nuñez, preferred a military man to protect his own position. His personal choice was Gabriel Paris, but any pro-Rojas Pinilla general would have been acceptable.

This civil-military crisis inside the regime was more serious than many suspected. When Rojas Pinilla insisted upon a military successor, Pabón Nuñez quit the cabinet and within a few days had left the country. His defection was a serious loss to the regime, a further indication of the internal deterioration of the government. On May 1 Rojas Pinilla held a private meeting with military leaders. He was reportedly unable to answer satisfactorily their searching questions as to why he was engineering his re-election some fifteen months early.[28] Sessions were delayed in the *constituyente* as a special commission outlined necessary amendments to the 1886 Constitution. Later they were passed with only one dissenting vote, and the way was cleared for the re-election of General Rojas Pinilla.

Distasteful as this patently fraudulent move was, there remained a slim chance that Rojas Pinilla might have retained military support to jam re-election down his country's throat. But he committed a final blunder of great proportions. Once again the president showed his faculty for selecting the worst possible course of action, then pursuing it with blind fanaticism. He ordered the arrest and detention of Guillermo León Valencia, who had gone to Cali in an effort to speak on behalf of his candidacy. By this final reckless move Rojas Pinilla sealed his own fate.

The governor of Valle del Cauca, Jaime Polanía Puyo, sent men to carry out Rojas Pinilla's command, putting Valencia under house arrest. Following Valencia's refusal to be taken into custody, confused government forces threw a cordon of troops around the house of Jorge Vernaza, a friend with whom Valencia was staying. The presidential candidate had been accompanied there by his wife, daughter, and four friends.[29]

Protests were immediately registered in Bogotá, and in Cali the students went on strike, although the city remained calm. About midnight of May 1, Valencia decided to consult the clergy. Ignoring friends' advice and allegedly shouting repeatedly, "I am the boss," he stalked from the house, spoke with the lieutenant in charge of the guard, and demanded permission to visit the auxiliary bishop of Cali. After browbeating the young officer into compliance, he paid his nocturnal call on Miguel Angel Medina, holding a long conversation in the palace before returning. He was accompanied by three priests on his trip back into house custody.

At 3 A.M. that morning, May 2, Valencia learned that troops had been ordered to seize him by force. The embattled candidate, reputedly one of the best pistol shots in Colombia, went to the window brandishing a .32-caliber Smith and Wesson, shouting into the darkness that "you will have to take me out either dead or tied up. You know the kind of fight I can put up."[30] As the troops hesitated, citizens began gathering about the house, shouting protests and vilification at the soldiers. Student manifestations began in darkened city streets, and the auxiliary archbishop cabled Cardinal Luque in Bogotá, waking the primate to urge church intervention. The cardinal immediately contacted the presidential palace, and the order was finally given to withdraw the troops. Thus, aided by intervention of citizenry and church, Valencia's dogged brashness won the day. It also slowed the dictator's relentless drive for re-election, whipping up a storm that was beyond Rojas Pinilla's ability to quell.

The crisis deepened in Bogotá later that morning as students demonstrated throughout the capital. Pictures of Rojas Pinilla were smashed on the Universidad Nacional campus, while crowds milled through the broad avenues shouting "Death to Rojas."[31] As opposition further crystallized, students at the Jesuits' Universidad Javeriana were attacked by riot squads using tear-gas bombs and water-jets sprayed from trucks.[32] Demonstrations in the heart of the city were permitted through the morning, but later in the day police dispersed them with clubs and gun butts.

Rumors of military dissension spread once more as Rojas Pinilla appointed six new generals on May 2. Following the release of Valencia on May 3, he stated that, if elected for the 1958-62 term, he might not serve the full four years. It was a move of desperation that mollified no one. The nationwide explosion—a largely spontaneous manifestation of hatred triggered by the Valencia blunder—continued through the week end of May 4 and 5. Rioting spread to other cities and revolutionary councils were set up. A fund-raising campaign was initiated to finance revolution, while students continued to interrupt traffic and hand out "Death to Rojas" signs.[33]

Rojas Pinilla responded by calling out the military. On Saturday night, May 4, troops rolled through the streets of the capital in tanks and trucks, stationing some 35,000 soldiers at strategic points throughout the city. A 9:30 curfew was imposed.[34] General Rafael Navas Pardo, although but a lukewarm supporter of the president, directed the show of force. None were misled by an army announcement that the troop movement was a routine exercise. The entire area around the Capitolio and Palacio de Nariño was surrounded protectively.

Events were now moving rapidly. Rojas Pinilla remained almost neurotically bent upon re-election. His intelligence and judgment could be questioned but not his single-mindedness. For the opposition, nothing but his immediate resignation was acceptable. The Comité Central Universitaria, in charge of the student strike, distributed handbills and conferred with labor leaders, preparing to call for a general strike. From May 4 it was directed personally by Valencia, who had by that time arrived in Bogotá.[35]

The president had not yet exhausted his capacity for error. On Sunday morning the police attacked a church in Bogotá. At La Porciuncula in Bogotá's fashionable Chapinero,[36] its admired priest Severo Velásquez delivered a fiery sermon during high mass. Before a packed congregation, with many standing jammed in the doorways, he cried out: "It is the duty of all Catholics, with the pastors at their heads, to fight against criminals, and not only those from below, but also, and principally, those from above."[37] After services the people streamed outside, some of them chanting "Cristo, sí—Rojas, no." Before the building was emptied, police attacked with a barrage of tear-gas bombs. Tank trucks sprayed jets of red dye into the crowd, staining clothing. Padre Velásquez, his eyes streaming from the tear gas, thundered "a curse on the tyrant, a curse upon the man who has led the nation to this situation!"[38] Ten minutes later the attack was over. Hundreds of shell casings lay on the sidewalks, while the façade of the gothic church was covered with crimson splotches.[39]

As the new week began, Lleras Camargo was also active, forming and carrying out plans for a nationwide strike. Urging leading businessmen and merchants to unite against the government, his persuasion won agreement. On Tuesday May 7, commercial activity was paralyzed in the capital.[40] The same day violence broke out in Cali with troops and citizenry meeting in the streets in a series of clashes. The hospital was soon overcrowded with wounded, and the country club was also pressed into service. Large numbers of teenagers were brutally attacked and seriously wounded when they opposed armed troops with a barrage of rocks. The commercial strike spread from Bogotá to Cali, and daily activities were virtually halted. Physical resistance seemed greatest in the heart of the city, and soldiers were unenthusiastically and half-heartedly attempting to quell disturbances.

Back in the capital the regime was apprehensive about the effect of the strike on the failing economy. Food stuffs were already running low, although crisis-wise *bogotanos* had exercised foresight by stocking up on provisions and canned goods when trouble first broke out. Government vehicles cruised city streets urging the end of the strike over loudspeakers. But the people were in no mood to be cajoled. The enraged president broadcast ineffectually that "the struggle begins from now on with a greater force." The minister of finance disclosed at the same time that merchants refusing to sell their products would be liable to criminal prosecution. The city's largest bank, the Banco de Bogotá, was seized and its clerks drafted into the army. But the strike continued.[41]

Amid the collapse of daily routine and government administrative authority, Rojas Pinilla concluded that his re-election should be consummated. On Tuesday night the puppet *constituyente* met to approve bills revising the constitution, and the next day the general was elected for the 1958-62 term of office. Meeting under the protection of hundreds of soldiers, the organ approved his continuance by 76-1.

The regime then tried to arrange popular demonstrations in its support. Its best was a gathering of approximately 800, who marched quietly to the Palacio de Nariño behind a sound truck trying doggedly to stir up enthusiasm. An hour of speeches in praise of the dictator drew little response.[42] A speech was later delivered by the president in response to his re-election, in which he again promised to step down before the end of his term in 1962. The citizenry did not believe him; more significantly, it paid little attention. Little credence was given his claim that the Armed Forces had renewed its pledge of allegiance.

The only national force which had not yet formally declared its opposition, excluding the military, was the Roman Catholic church. The shameful attack on Sunday assured that the hierarchy would no longer remain silent. Rojas Pinilla heaped coals on the fire with charges early in the week that the church was the major sponsor of the strike, claims that were unwarranted. Miguel Angel Medina replied with an open letter denying the attack in a special issue of *La Voz Católica*.[43] On Thursday, May 9, *El Catolicismo* appeared with a front-page denunciation of the government by Cardinal Luque. The primate formally condemned the regime for "murder" and "sacrilegious profanation" of the churches.[44] He also accused Rojas Pinilla of reneging on his promise not to seek re-election. Church opposition in Cali took a different form when the bishop there called for the excommunication of those responsible for the killing of some fifty rioters on Tuesday.

By late Thursday only Gustavo Rojas Pinilla failed to realize that his position was untenable. As was inevitable, the Armed Forces themselves provided the final stroke which removed him from office. For some months Rojas Pinilla's intelligence chief, General Luis Ordóñez, had been quietly sympathetic to the opposition.[45] When national police chief General Deogracias Fonseca returned from Cali to report the situation there as hopeless, Ordóñez promptly drove to air force headquarters and secured agreement to oust the president. He then continued to the headquarters of the Army Command in Bogotá. The army commander-in-chief, General Rafael Navas Pardo, along with

Ordóñez the key figure of these final hours, met with Conservative leaders to discuss the situation.[46]

Back in his palace, the president remained blithely confident of his ultimate triumph. Insulated from direct contact with events by his omnipresent coterie of sycophants, he spent Thursday evening in his study receiving reports of scattered developments. He discussed them calmly with those present, unthinkingly balancing a pencil on his finger.[47] It was nearly 3 A.M. Friday morning when the military leaders repaired to the presidential study to break the news.

Navas Pardo was the one to inform the general. Ushered into Rojas Pinilla's study, he ignored the others in the room and began at once. "My general, you must leave the country. Things cannot go on like this."[48] The president was unbelieving. In a scene that with minor variations has often been played in various Latin presidential palaces, he argued, pleaded, cajoled, and threatened. Finally Rojas Pinilla faced the realization that his last source of strength was gone. Although in no position to bargain, he nonetheless insisted on being replaced by his old colleague General Gabriel Paris. A final compromise was reached in which a five-man military *junta,* including Paris, took over the government. In the pre-dawn hours General Rojas Pinilla took the national airwaves for a final face-saving message. Few heard the beginning, but before he was finished all Bogotá was listening. "It would be impossible that I, who gave the country peace, should cause the country useless bloodshed." Therefore he would "voluntarily" turn over the government to the *junta.* "To avoid that the soldiers of this immortal Colombia . . . [might] be obliged to defend the orders and the legality [by] making use of weapons, with bloodshed that goes against the postulates of peace, justice, and liberty that I have defended without hesitation since the 13th of June, and because it would be a contradiction that we who gave peace to the nation and sought the harmony of citizens would be the cause of new and painful tragedies, I have resolved that the armed forces continue in power with the following *junta.*"[49] Rojas Pinilla was followed by Cardinal Luque, who expressed acceptance of *junta* rule and appealed to the populace for support.

GUSTAVO ROJAS PINILLA IN RETROSPECT

Even as Rojas Pinilla flew into exile, he neither understood nor cared about Colombian reality. When his plane stopped over at Hamilton,

Bermuda, the former dictator defended his regime as having brought peace to the nation. What about the revolution? "There was no revolution. I decided to turn over the government to military junta. Only a few priests were against me.

"We had a peculiar situation in Colombia. In 1953 there was civil war. Thousands were killed. When I took over, guerrillas asked me to make peace and I did. Everything became quiet and there were no more guerrillas. But recently the priests started making trouble."[50] The tragi-comic fact about such a statement was that Rojas Pinilla had practiced self-deception so long that he largely believed his own words. A few months later he was living with his family in Spain, where he briefly shared with Laureano Gómez the protective welcome of the Franco government.

In the next two years Colombia learned that it had not heard the last of Rojas Pinilla. His later return to the country to "defend his honor"[51] against the charges of a legislative investigatory group was also marked by an abortive uprising, the discussion of which belongs in Part V. The investigatory findings substantiated charges of extensive personal corruption as well as incompetent administration. Everything that was revealed fully confirmed popular suspicions which were whispered about during the latter months of the military government.

Examination of the Rojas Pinilla era must recall the man himself, for he was of mercurial disposition and violent temper, stubborn to the point of pigheadedness. A creature of passions rather than of logic, he was almost impossible to reason with. Subordinates shielded him from public opinion, and the general was usually told precisely what he hoped to hear; his narrow and uncurious mind went no further.

His vanity was boundless. This quirk of personality was given full freedom following his rise to the presidency, and he indulged it fully. Rojas Pinilla was fond of being called the Jefe Supremo, or Supreme Chief. His pictures were distributed throughout the republic. This writer recalls seeing them even in tiny villages near the Ecuadorean border in 1956. Busts were set up in public places. His wardrobe bulged with uniforms, including those of an admiral. Of recent Latin dictators, probably only Perón was as glorious a plumed peacock when in full dress attire. Rojas Pinilla even made presents to friends of wrist watches with his face emblazoned in color on the dial.[52]

Comparisons of Rojas Pinilla with his dictatorial contemporaries are inevitable. Coming to power on a wave of popularity, Rojas Pinilla was in a position to become a true demagogue. While many Colombians are too sophisticated to accept such a leader, the masses are not. One recalls that fifteen years ago the Argentines were considered too worldly to follow a flaming demagogic zealot. Then came the arch-opportunist Perón. Certainly Rojas Pinilla's best chance of perpetuating his rule would have been through cultivation of the masses. But he seldom reached his listeners after the first few months of heady optimism.

The general was so swiftly convinced of his undying popularity with the people that he ceased his courtship. Public appearances, although not infrequent, were somewhat formal affairs at which he was surrounded by sober-faced aides and armed guards. When addressing the nation he spoke over the radio rather than haranguing the crowd from the palace balcony. Indeed, when he tried to whip up the passions of his audience, he failed dismally. In Colombia, where verbal circumlocution and oratorical elegance are much admired and, in the upper classes, widely practiced, the plain words of the soldier seemed sadly lacking. On the occasion of pronouncing his Third Force, he rambled almost incoherently, never truly moving his audience. And the agitated speech denying charges of graft was another example of his inability to invoke the heavens in a thunderous demand for unreasoning support.

Thus he failed to arouse the people; the only emotion he created, again excepting the first few months, was that of scorn. Rojas Pinilla had the drives and desires of the Latin demagogue but not the ability. His failures as a Weberian charismatic leader might not have meant failure as a strongman, however. Those who observed Venezuela's waddling Marcos Pérez Jiménez saw a ridiculous little man weighed down with ribbons and decorations. Yet he was not only ruthless and unscrupulous but an extremely able and cunning politician. The same is somewhat true of Peru's Manuel Odría, who made no pretense of playing the military idol, and preferred to dress in civilian clothes.

Added to Rojas Pinilla's failures as a demagogue, then, were his shortcomings as a politician. Perhaps the greatest of these was his inability to grasp an elemental understanding of public opinion and of national life. When the general entered the Palacio de Nariño as tenant he stepped into a dream world in which he was supported unquestioningly by 90 per cent of the populace, revered by all social classes, and opposed but feebly by a few selfish politicians, newspaper owners, and iniquitous priests. There is little doubt that almost to the end the dictator blandly assumed his position to be as strong as when he was acclaimed on that turbulent day, June 13, 1953.

Those near Rojas Pinilla dared not contradict his judgments. They soon experienced the bitter acid of his temper and learned not to ruffle his extreme sensitivity. The easiest course was agreement with the general. Civilian supporters learned how to placate him, avoiding his irregular questioning with vague generalities. The shrewdest of all, Lucio Pabón Nuñez, had measured the dictator accurately; his handling of the general was adept while building his own strength in preparation for an ascension to power which never materialized.

Rojas Pinilla, then, was both inefficient and inept. His patent attempts to ape Perón were exercises in pathetic futility. Twice a movement to form a government party failed. Where the Argentine was the darling of the *descamisados,* the less organized Colombian labor mass was never wielded as a political force. Rojas Pinilla failed to appeal to them through increasing wages, broadened fringe benefits, extended holidays, and greater social welfare. There was nothing in his government that caused the workers to view the general in any sense as a benefactor. The attempt to make over his daughter in the image of a Colombian Evita was particularly ill conceived.

His economic guidance steered the ship of state into such storm-tossed seas that only today has it emerged into a relative calm. Vast social problems, already aggravated before the general's *golpe,* were further exacerbated during his regime. For there was no really viable government program that translated words into deeds. Rojas Pinilla merely drifted passively, breaking into activity now and again in harsh outbursts of oppression and censorship when he felt his power was being questioned.

His one positive contribution was to bring about the seemingly inconceivable reconciliation of Liberals and Conservatives. Only his evil incompetence would have achieved this. With Protestants and then Catholics forced into opposition, with labor ignored and the press made to suffer humiliation, Rojas Pinilla aggravated his opposition by blundering into situations unnecessarily, thereby providing new causes, new converts, and new opposition. When the cautiously conservative military turned against him, the sands had run out for his tyrannical rule.

All this seems a harsh indictment for any man, yet the power-hungry narcissist was perhaps the most utter failure of any dictator in recent times. It is difficult to recall many incidents in which he did not unerringly choose the worst possible course, then follow it with myopic stubbornness. To give him his due, he seems genuinely to have desired the restoration of democracy and peace when he came to the presidency. But power brought a rapid transformation to his flawed personality; this, coupled with his gross incapacity for administration and the formulation of policy, meant for Colombia nearly four years of destructive mismanagement.

The general was neither the first nor the last Latin strongman to emerge from the ranks of the military. Colombia could conceivably suffer the misfortune of returning to a military government, although it presently appears unlikely. In any event, this lies in the field of speculation. Certainly the imagination is staggered by trying to conjure up a figure as devoid of constructive accomplishment as the protagonist of this section of the study. For those with long memories, many years will pass before another figure can possibly rival the brutal political folly of Gustavo Rojas Pinilla.

Part V

BIPARTY EXPERIMENT IN CONTROLLED DEMOCRACY

Chapter Fifteen

THE TRANSITION TO DEMOCRACY

PROVISIONAL MILITARY GOVERNMENT

IN THE SMALL HOURS of Friday, May 10, the five-man military *junta* assumed power under the nominal presidency of General Gabriel Paris. With Colombians already streaming into the streets joyfully crying "he fell, he fell,"[1] Rojas Pinilla's old colleague and minister of war broadcast a statement maintaining the fiction that Rojas Pinilla had stepped down voluntarily. "The military *junta,* faithful to the declarations of President Rojas Pinilla, whose admirable attitude it praises, exalts, and recognizes as a token of exceptional patriotism and disinterest, promises on its word of honor to call popular elections next year, so that the future President of the Republic will be elected by popular vote and in the form established by the constitution and the laws."[2]

The forty-seven-year-old Paris might have exercised *continuismo* but for the two dominant members of the *junta,* Generals Rafael Navas Pardo and Luis Ordóñez. The former, Rojas Pinilla's army chief, was a stable commander widely considered the most competent soldier in the nation. Born of Cundinamarca peasant stock in 1908, he had, like Rojas Pinilla, trained as a military engineer, receiving advanced training from the United States Army Engineer School at Ft. Belvoir. Reaching the rank of brigadier general in May of 1956, he had become army commander-in-chief in December. Although considered strongly Conservative, he had opposed the policy of passing over pro-Liberal officers in promotions and assignment. To interviewers he was soldierly, candid, and somewhat reserved.[3]

Luis Ordóñez, four years younger than Navas Pardo, had been the quiet center of military anti-Rojas Pinilla sentiment for some months. Among the few who were dissatisfied with Rojas Pinilla's desperate plea for support in August, 1956, he had carefully vitiated the more extreme presidential controls instituted in 1957. "His sympathies were . . . with the opposition and he did only the minimum required to preserve appearances."[4] In early 1957 he often held prominent opposition leaders in his personal office, then escorted them back to their homes. His agents were lax in controlling clandestine activities in Bogotá. Indeed, it was Ordóñez who finally chose the moment to replace Rojas, obtaining the cooperation of Navas Pardo, with whom the ouster was planned and executed.

The other two members of the *junta* had also been members of the Rojas Pinilla regime but in the final months realized that the dictator must go. Rear Admiral Rubén Piedrahita, forty-six, as Rojas Pinilla's minister of public works had been perhaps the most respected member of that administration,[5] a competent, hardheaded professional. Major General Deogracias Fonseca, chief of the national police, had worked with Ordóñez to moderate Rojas Pinilla's more extreme measures, and their joint control of security forces assured street order in the hours following the president's departure.

The five-man *junta* moved swiftly to constitute its government. On Saturday a cabinet was formed to include representatives of both parties. Key members were Conservative Minister of Government Jorge Villareal and Liberal Minister of Foreign Affairs Carlos Sanz de Santamaría. Three of the thirteen ministers were members of the military.[6] Almost at once the *junta* welcomed in principle the tentative agreement of the political parties, which was announced in mid-summer, and Navas Pardo pointedly instructed all military and police forces that under no circumstances would the *junta* remain in office after August, 1958.[7]

Within the first week the government withdrew military units from government buildings and other key areas of Bogotá, declaring at that time that all exiles, without exception, would be permitted to return. On Sunday it gave its "word of honor" that free elections would be held for president and that his inauguration in August, 1958, would bring the retirement of all *junta* members. The Rojas Pinilla organ *Diario Oficial* was closed, to be followed in a few days by the abolition of the National Directorate of Information and Propaganda. *El Siglo* appeared in a four-page makeshift form, its first edition in nearly three years. "Caliban" editorialized that depradations were over, that Colombia "for the second time has won independence and dignity."[8] An effective lifting of censorship was met by wide approval as far away as London. "Colombia has a tradition of honest and independent newspaper reporting, and if the end of censorship proves to be more than a temporary measure, then the order of things may really have changed for the better."[9]

The first week of provisional rule was the freest since 1948's Black Friday. As dictatorial controls were dismantled, the *junta* and politicians alike turned to a mannerly restoration of basic democratic rights. The months to come saw notable restraint and moderation with regard to *junta* activities. This circumstance was aided by the small number of *rojistas* who remained following the ouster of the general. There were initial misgivings on the part of some civilians who feared the emergence of another dominant military figure. Alertness for signs of renewed authoritarianism was understandable in the face of a government composed of former *rojista* officials. The face-saving nature of the transfer of power had further aroused doubts in many minds.

The outspoken Guillermo León Valencia delivered a questioning speech warning that he and Alberto Lleras Camargo were prepared to oppose the provisional regime. "It is not a threat that we are raising before the Armed Forces, because we know that they still hold in their hands the physical capability of killing their fellow citizens, but this fear does not influence us as our support will never come from any fear they may impose upon us, but from the patriotism with which we may hail their positive accomplishments when they occur."[10] At no time, however, did the *junta* give indications of insincerity. Its members realized that without political support they themselves would have been dangerously isolated. The events leading to Rojas Pinilla's departure had shown that national civilian unity was by no means defenseless. "A nation conscious of its own strength would be in no mood to tolerate any change of mind by the military."[11] Further civil disobedience was hardly inconceivable.

The provisional rulers replied to such criticisms with wise moderation. General Paris, the usual spokesman, broadcast new assurances on Friday night, May 17. Repeating the pledge of free elections and a civilian president in August, 1958, he spoke with some dismay of the *junta's* "painful surprise" that some politicians doubted its good faith. He again promised adherence to the "firm decision to do everything within reach to bring the country back to normality." Explaining that he and his colleagues sought to remedy disturbing situations, he guaranteed continued press freedom, even though some journals were giving free rein "to sentiments of rancor . . . incompatible with the purposes of pacification. . . ." The general further appealed to the press to avoid extremism and exaggeration, urging upon it the responsibility regained with the removal of censorship.[12]

In response to criticism of apparent immunity enjoyed by Rojas Pinilla's followers, Paris urged moderation, explaining that the *junta* refused to become an instrument for retaliation which could only create new hatreds. There were nightly incidents in Bogotá as cars sped through the streets firing indiscriminately at passersby, shouting *vivas* to the deposed dictator. During the first week there were several deaths and many injuries. *Rojista*-inspired outbursts increased; small groups of men would enter cafes and bars late at night, order the customers to cheer Rojas Pinilla, and attack those who refused. Police were reluctant to curb the outbursts; only several weeks after the overthrow of Rojas Pinilla did such incidents cease.

Despite wide fears that the provisional government would prove either ineffective or faithless, prominent politicians proclaimed their support. The sturdy but conciliatory approach of General Paris' speech was well-received, and Guillermo León Valencia agreed to "give the military the benefit of the doubt." Civil-military friction was also reduced when Alberto Lleras Camargo announced his firm support on May 20. Calling for calm mediation of all disagreements, he condemned "with the greatest energy" any display of hostility against the military, which was causing many officers to complain of public insults. He threw his prestige unreservedly behind the provisional government: "I personally have faith in the new Government. I have it because the five high military officers composing it are truly representative agents of the Armed Forces. It is a revolutionary provisional Government with the revolutionary task of leading the Colombian nation in the shortest possible time from previous abnormality toward constitutional normalcy. This is how a Government of the Armed Forces can be conceived, under a state of siege but moving in the direction of the reestablishment of order."[13]

Critics of the alleged "soft" policy against *rojistas* learned by the end of May that the dictator would be stripped of all titles. He was separated from military service by a series of formal decrees denying him all honors; the title of Supreme Chief was done away with. As Luis Ordóñez said, "God is the only Supreme Chief so far as we are concerned. I do not think the five of us should try to play God."[14]

The five officers had been unsure of themselves during the early days in power; they leaned over backwards to avoid misleading appearances. While removing any question of *rojista* sympathies, they found it both awkward and difficult to shake up the entire bureaucracy. Before long, however, indecision was replaced by a perceptible shift to positive administration, and the *junta* proceeded to operate with purposeful confidence and efficient dedication. As effective division of authority was worked out, and although Paris remained provisional president, the five men had complete equality. All decisions were reached through majority vote with a show of hands following discussions during which all five spoke. The cabinet of thirteen men, of whom ten were civilians, reported to various of the *junta* officers. Each of these five was expected to have the authoritative opinion on matters pertaining to ministries under his direction.

The regime was aware of its unconstitutional position and served with a heightened sense of responsibility. Luis Ordóñez declared that its greatest difficulty was the very fact of its illegality. "There is nothing in the Constitution to make our existence legal, so we have to be careful to do nothing that would make the situation even more illegal." He was equally emphatic in insisting that the *junta* would return Colombia to constitutional government. "I can assure you that we shall turn over power to a civilian president at 3:00 P.M., August 7, 1958, whoever he may be, and we do not want anything else to do with running the country. I hope his speech will have no more than ten words, so we can hand him the Government without wasting an extra second."[15]

Almost immediately after the fall of Rojas Pinilla, political leaders began examining the institutional problems of the transition back to democracy. But the *junta* held itself above such matters, leaving solutions to those who would be living with them. The military government was more concerned with problems of economic survival. Despite the tireless efforts of Luis Morales Gómez in the final Rojas Pinilla months, the economy was gasping for air. Carlos Sanz de Santamaría, the new foreign minister, said that nearly all income from exports, from industry and bank reserves, and from various loans had been wasted in 1956 and 1957 without any positive accomplishments. Credit was nearly destroyed, large sums of capital had fled abroad, and the peso was but a third of its official exchange rate. "The present bad financial situation," said Sanz de Santamaría, "may require years to correct."[16]

According to private estimates, Gustavo Rojas Pinilla had needlessly cost Colombia some 20,000,000,000 pesos, or about $5,000,000,000. His personal fortune outside the republic was allegedly some $10,000,000.[17] The *junta* named as minister of finance the respected Antonio Alvarez Restrepo, who had been responsible for the fiscal policies of the Gómez regime. It was his unenviable task to pick up the pieces and attempt to re-establish a sound economy. On May 31 Alvarez Restrepo announced the coming devaluation of the peso for July. In a speech to the National Congress of Merchants at Cucutá he proclaimed the need to eliminate the official exchange rate of 2.5 pesos to the dollar, referring to it as "a corpse across the road, whose pestiferous emanations are those of contraband with all its consequences."[18] The difference between the official rate and the existing free rate of about seven to the dollar had cost perhaps 10 per cent of the income from coffee sales through extensive smuggling.

Expert advice suggested a high rate of 5.5 pesos per dollar, but Alvarez Restrepo was reluctant to more than double the rate. At the same time he faced pressure from coffee producers who favored absolute free exchange for their dollars. Devaluation was accompanied by dollar certificates issued on the basis of exports. This permitted the government to keep some control over movement of the peso. Exporters sold their dollar earnings to the Central Bank, which in turn sold dollar certificates to importers at a rate designed to stablize the free market. The result for the rest of the year held the free rate at about six to the dollar, with certificates at five to the dollar.[19]

Devaluation helped sweep away the clutter of import and fiscal regulations which had made corruption easy for speculators under the Rojas Pinilla maladministration.[20] The exchange scale was slowly increased by steps, with the coffee rate beginning at 3.75 to the dollar and gradually rising as the economy adjusted itself. In order to assist the people in adapting to the revisions, on June 22 Minister of Labor Raimundo Emiliani announced a decree ordering public and private companies to increase workers' salaries as of July 1. Those with monthly salaries of no more than 400 pesos ($58.00) received a 15 per cent increase, while those with incomes of 400 to 1000 pesos were granted a 10 per cent boost. Even this was barely adequate in view of the devaluation.

Before the close of June the cost of essential foodstuffs nearly doubled, and the decreed salary increases proved inadequate in the effort to avoid discontent. The government was adamant in its view that further raises were economically unsound, and it held firmly to its policies of austerity. Attached to the same decree was a provision for family subsidies, whereby workers received a premium for each of their children after October 1. The regime proceeded to set aside 4 per cent of its payrolls for these subsidies, as well as an additional 1 per cent for a national apprentice institute established to provide technical training for young workers. Companies proving hardship from the pay increases could be exempted from compliance for as long as twelve months.[21]

The immense foreign commercial backlog of $442,900,000, owed largely to United States creditors, pressed upon the government relentlessly. One of the first actions of the *junta* was to request an expert study by both the International Monetary Fund and the International Bank for Reconstruction and Development. Initially no new loans were asked; Colombia had already received some $110,000,000 from the IBRD, largely for the development of transport and power. Foreign advisers urged immediate action, devaluation, and a limitation on private credit while the national budget was balanced.

Implementation of general austerity was rapid. Before the end of June the budget was slashed by a reduction of nearly $20,000,000 in military expenditures.[22] The corrupt public works program of the dictator was severely curtailed, with the exception of a few partially completed projects. Notorious examples of graft included the several roads under construction to link the various farms and plantations which Rojas Pinilla had acquired, rail spurs serving the same purpose, and the partially constructed power plant at Paipa on the central plateau.[23]

Austerity was directed at the control of inflation and a tightening of credit. Uncontrolled printing of currency was stopped; it had increased the money supply by 1,000,000,000 pesos in the past three years. The government began pulling money out of circulation by decreeing that the Central Bank would retain payments collected through earlier deposits for import licenses; it was not permitted to re-lend the money as before.

Mandatory private bank reserves for deposits were increased from 14 to 18 per cent.

International credit was restored through a variety of measures. In July, Antonio Alvarez Restrepo negotiated a loan of $60,000,000 from the Export-Import Bank, and an additional $27,000,000 was provided from private North American sources to pay off individual exporters and re-negotiate the backlog of commercial debts. The European debt of about $40,000,000 was arranged through a schedule of payments set up on a basis of 20 per cent cash and thirty-six monthly payments beginning in January of 1959. Comparable agreements were established with North American creditors, and by the end of the year Alvarez Restrepo reported that the Rojas Pinilla foreign debt had been reduced from $442,900,000 to $122,000,0000.

This improvement had been further aided by decreed limitations of imports. The flow of nonessentials was controlled through a ban on luxury items, while essentials were placed on a free list. An October decree established that the full value of any import had first to be deposited in the Banco de la República. Previous deposit requirements had been only 15 per cent. The tight-money policy made it difficult for importers to provide 100 per cent earlier deposits on goods that would not arrive for two or three months following issuance of the license. The monthly average of imports dropped from $42,000,000 to $26,000,000 by December, 1957, and the dollar and gold reserves were up to some $120,000,000.[24] In April, 1958, further restrictive measures were introduced, cutting the monthly average to $18,300,000.[25]

Emphasis was placed upon substitutes for imports, for Colombia had been spending $72,000,000 a year for the purchase of agricultural commodities. Although credit to industry and commerce was sharply decreased, banks were encouraged to make agricultural loans to help increase sagging agricultural productivity. In November of 1957 the government decreed a land reform designed to improve farming methods and make the land more productive. Lands were classified, and at the start of 1958 all farms over 50 hectares (120 acres) were required to cultivate 15 to 25 per cent of their land, on penalty of stiff fines for non-compliance. An independent agency was established to enforce the decree. The United States provided further assistance through a loan of excess agricultural commodities valued at $5,000,000.[26]

The 1956 and 1957 budget deficits of roughly 200,000,000 pesos ($33,-000,000) were regarded quite rightly as dangerous, and the 1958 budget was balanced at 1,400,000,000 pesos ($233,000,000). Even this was 300,-000,000 pesos higher than originally estimated. Significantly, appropriations for education were doubled to 140,000,000 pesos ($26,000,000). By early 1958, what had been an essentially healthy economy seemed to be picking up measurably. The cost of living, which had increased 14 per cent in the last six months of Rojas Pinilla's regime, was rising less than 1 per cent a month. The peso, although not completely stabilized, settled at a little above six to the dollar, and in December, 1957, Antonio Alverez Restrepo told interviewers with some satisfaction of his accomplishments, although adding that several years of further austerity remained ahead.

By the close of 1957, the *junta* had the situation well in hand and had overcome doubts as to its intentions. Civil liberties, uncensored press, dedication to democracy, and free activities of the parties had all contributed to its high regard in the eyes of the people. Scrupulously playing no politics, entering such affairs only when the politicians reached an impasse, the *junta* clearly intended to leave power in August, 1958. Lleras Camargo put the matter succinctly when asked about the popularity of the provisional government: "Very simple. They have kept their word."[27]

Bipartisan Political Agreement

The major burden for the restoration of democratic rule fell to responsible political leaders. The *junta* itself was in no position to arrange a new political establishment even had it been so inclined. The Liberal-Conservative opposition to General Rojas Pinilla, as enunciated in the Pact of Benidorm, required extension to include the exercise of responsible government. Thus the key figures in negotiating a mutual accommodation of the parties were necessarily those who had stood out in the fight against Rojas Pinilla—Alberto Lleras Camargo, Guillermo León Valencia, and Laureano Gómez, the latter still in Spain. The historic Benidorm agreement, it was agreed, was the basis for more lasting institutional agreement. However, a split within Conservative ranks complicated the picture.

The agreement signed in March, 1957, had committed the parties to further collaboration during the return to constitutionality. Dr. Gómez had refused to accept the manifesto, although some of his followers had expressed adherence. The Conservative division, which had begun with Mariano Ospina Pérez' opposition to Dr. Gómez in 1953, had shifted while growing even more bitter following Rojas Pinilla's *golpe de estado*. Significant numbers of *ospinistas* had joined the military regime, and acrimony heightened following the dictator's resignation. The *laureanista* Comisión de Acción Conservadora had proclaimed Gómez the "sole chief of the Conservative party," and both factions planned "national" conventions.

Cooler heads finally prevailed, and following several days of unpublicized meetings, leaders of the two wings signed a pact on June 3. The moderate and rightist elements agreed to hold a joint convention at the end of the month, at which they would endorse Guillermo León Valencia as their presidential candidate. Signatories agreed that the pact would "ratify the adherence" of all Conservatives. The document was signed by Conservative action *laureanistas* and members of the moderate *ospinista* Conservative Directorate.[28]

With the Conservative breach closed, the next step came in July with the formation of a joint commission for the study of constitutional reform. An eight-man body drew up a twenty-two-page document explaining an arrangement whereby the parties would share government equally for the next twelve years.[29] The puppet *constituyente* would be dissolved, and congressional elections were set for November 24, 1957, with presidential balloting on May 4, 1958. The *junta,* pleased with the agreement, immediately declared the dissolution of the *constituyente* while decreeing the election dates.

Despite the June pact of the Conservatives, however, there was considerable truculence on the part of the Gómez camp. It had refused to serve on the bipartisan commission which drew up the political agreement, and the resultant impasse forced further direct discussion with Laureano Gómez. Alberto Lleras Camargo accordingly flew once more to Spain, and the two men met in Sitges, some fifty miles from Barcelona. The intermediary for their second historic interview was Camilo Vásquez Carrizosa, a former Gómez minister of agriculture. On July 20, 1957, Lleras Camargo and Gómez drew up the Declaration of Sitges, which Lleras Camargo read to the nation upon his return to Bogotá on July 29.

The Sitges agreement was aimed at drawing closer the two parties and establishing a lasting foundation for party coexistence. Of more immediacy, it served to recognize the continuing influence of the aging Conservative chieftain who was determined to play an important part in political developments. The declaration outlined a proposed constitutional reform providing for complete parity in all branches of government. The agreement would remain in effect for twelve years, during which time the presidency would alternate between representatives of the two parties. The parties would be equally represented on both national and local levels. Details of the election of legislators were not arranged, but a national plebiscite would be held in presenting the proposed bipartisan arrangement for approval. Basis for the agreement was the joint struggle for the restoration of democratic processes and the absolute termination of violence.[30]

Alberto Lleras Camargo, architect of the plan, was greeted with demonstrations of enthusiasm upon his return to the capital, and public interest assured that the *junta* was disposed to permit the proposed plebiscite. In August the Declaration of Sitges was put into effect, scheduling the plebiscite for December. Any citizen of twenty-one or over would be eligible to vote. There was some disagreement as to the constitutionality of such a plebiscite, but its proponents explained that reform was essential before national elections could be held. Party conventions would draw up lists of candidates to be chosen in congressional elections. Alberto Lleras Camargo referred to the time as one of "democratic convalescence." "The agreement of the parties should not be seen as an armistice, the better to plan new battles, but," he argued, "to eliminate it for twelve years."[31] Thus the party leaders, "rightly reluctant to start up the old political game again while partisan passions were still bitter, hoped to get back to parliamentary rule by pledging themselves to share power."[32]

The slow advance toward democracy under this Frente Nacional was still impeded by Conservative disunity. The Gómez and Ospina Pérez wings were not truly reconciled; both were less than enthusiastic about sharing administrative parity with the Liberals. The inflated bureaucracy was still 90 per cent Conservative, and there was natural reluctance to accept increased Liberal participation. Recurrent talk of an administrative career service also disturbed many Conservatives.

Despite the assumed agreement on the candidacy of Valencia the Comisión de Acción Conservadora was unhappy and began speaking of a possible nomination of extreme rightist Jorge Leyva, once Gómez' minister of public works and also briefly the minister of war at the time of Rojas Pinilla's *golpe*. There were two factors at the root of the disagreement. Most of the long-standing bureaucrats were *laureanistas* who had survived the Rojas Pinilla years and were antagonistic to the moderate *ospinistas*. Even more importantly, Gómez himself had developed strong personal antipathy to Guillermo León Valencia and was reluctant to grant Conservative approval to the firebrand from Popayán.

On Saturday, October 5, 1957, Laureano Gómez returned to Colombia once again. The man who stepped back into national politics was a gaunt, aged figure leaning heavily on a cane. Such was his health that he spent some time in Cali before continuing to the thinner atmosphere of the elevated capital. However, the dominating character and diamond-sharp intellectual brilliance were undimmed, and the doughty old autocrat was still a powerful political figure. Coincident to his return was the convention of the moderate Conservatives, who restated their support of Valencia. A week later the *laureanistas* planned their own convention in Barranquilla, and Conservative disunity was underlined by a manifesto specifically objecting to the Valencia candidacy. It declared that "there is not even a shadow of legitimacy" in the convention of the moderate wing, and the forthcoming rightist convention was the "legal" one by virtue of its convocation by Dr. Gómez.

With the rift widening, Alvaro Gómez Hurtado asserted that his father's was the only doctrinaire conservatism, denouncing *ospinistas* for supporting Rojas Pinilla until late 1956. Only the *laureanistas* were true Conservatives, while the moderate wing was characterized as impure. Valencia, it was recalled, had at first been affiliated with the dictatorship and thus was unacceptable as a national Conservative representative. Critics were told that, while Dr. Gómez had indeed agreed to constitutional reform and the plebiscite, he had not agreed to Valencia's candidacy. Reminded of the June pact with the moderates, the *laureanistas* simply replied with more attacks on Valencia. The moderates, aware of Gómez' power, explained that they were not opposed to him but refused to have further dealings with Alvaro Gómez Hurtado, who had unyieldingly led his father's supporters in Colombia during the exile of Dr. Gómez.

The Gómez convention was held in Cali after a delay of several weeks, and it attacked both Valencia and the moderates fiercely. Dr. Gómez heightened the divisive situation by turning his still formidable rhetoric against the *ospinistas* in a bitter denunciation that brought the delegates to their feet repeatedly. Better a divided Conservative movement, he cried, than a pact with the "impure, insincere opportunists" of *ospinismo*.[33]

Revitalized by the return of their champion, the Gómez forces in early November took the offensive with a sweeping attack that included the Liberals as targets of their wrath. On the night of November 16 Gómez' directorate broadcast a declaration implying Liberal responsibility for the continuation of the ten-year-old rural violence and banditry. The Liberals, it was argued, had also been trying to take advantage of the Declaration of Sitges for narrow partisan purposes. The Liberals had "presented to the country a new policy, the extent of which we cannot yet define," but one which differed "substantially" from the previous Liberal-Conservative agreements.[34] The declaration included a demand for *junta* postponement of the plebiscite scheduled for the first day of December. Such a delay would let the citizens "form new judgments" concerning the alleged new Liberal policy "diametrically opposed to that which served to draw up the constitutional reforms" embodied in the plebiscite.[35]

The *laureanistas* asked congressional elections before any plebiscite, and added that elected Conservatives would then present a list of names from which the Liberals might agree upon a presidential candidate. It was a shrewd move, for Gómez was confident of greater support with the people than the moderate wing. By electing the majority of the Conservative congressmen, he could assure the nomination of a presidential candidate other than Valencia. The call for congressional elections before any plebiscite left him in a strong bargaining position; it was really immaterial to him whether the plebiscite was held first, while most of the Frente Nacional supporters were convinced that the electorate should first pass judgment on the proposed reforms.

With the Conservative schism widened even further by the formation of a small Falangist-oriented element under Gilberto Alzate Avendaño, who denounced the principle of coalition government, there was growing discussion centering on the possible candidacy of Alberto Lleras Camargo. Although Lleras Camargo had already rejected such suggestions by his stated preference for a Conservative president, many Conservatives felt that "the situation of Conservatism is so dramatic that only Alberto Lleras, a Liberal, can unite us. . . ."[36] Certainly the ailing Gómez, his will power as unquenchable as ever, would not accept Valencia, while the possibility of gaining wide support for Jorge Leyva was slim. Most considered him an unprincipled opportunist of the first order.

The Liberals carefully stood aloof from the Conservative dispute. Carlos Lleras Restrepo, plunging unstintingly into the organizational matters of politics once more, was attempting to tour the entire nation to urge upon Liberals the necessity of supporting constitutional reform, of burying old rancors and political animosities. The afternoon following Gómez' bitter speech, Alberto Lleras Camargo scrupulously avoided any direct reply while arguing that reform was obligatory. Declaring that a postponement of the plebiscite would bring inevitable chaos, he directed his party to continue propagandizing on behalf of the constitutional amendment.

In November the situation grew critical. Dr. Gómez, irked by Lleras Camargo's refusal to recognize him as the sole leader of Conservatism, again called upon the *junta* to postpone the plebiscite, and the old warrior was on the verge of wrecking the Frente Nacional movement. His mounting anger at the support *ospinistas* had immediately given Rojas Pinilla in 1953 was almost boundless, and an abortive plot by diehard *rojistas* tested the mettle of the *junta* at almost the same time. Political dissension had nourished the hopes of Rojas Pinilla's remaining followers, and their plot, which had been nurtured since July, included wide dissemination of clandestine pamphlets. This propaganda, charged the *junta,* was designed "to make the people feel they are being deceived by the Government." "By means of heavy correspondence and special emissaries," the conspirators had further attempted to convince the exiled Rojas Pinilla that "his presence in the country was essential that he might reassume power."[37]

The government, revealing the existence of the plotters on November 18, said that nine conspirators had been arrested and that paid assassins connected with pro-Rojas Pinilla officers had been directed to create chaos by means of the murder of Lleras Camargo and the *junta* members. Arrests continued for nearly a week, and the necessary sternness of the government aroused anxieties of a return to military dictatorship. Certainly the depradations of Rojas Pinilla at his worst returned to the minds of those who preferred to view the years of dictatorship as an abortive episode which could not be repeated.

The church, which since June had been firmly advocating free elections, reiterated its position in a statement signed by the five Colombian archbishops, declaring that Catholics were "obligated to vote in the national plebiscite according to their consciences."[38] As a wave of uneasiness swept the capital, the *junta* reluctantly stepped in for the first time. With negotiations in danger of complete collapse, the military called in party leaders to plead for a reconciliation of views instead of plebiscite postponement. A series of meetings were held in the palace, with political representatives and *junta* members present. The government insisted on agreement of some sort, and after nearly sixty hours' discussion, a compromise was effected.[39]

To accommodate Dr. Gómez, it was agreed to postpone any decision on presidential candidacy until 1958, following the election of a Congress. Thus he won the one concession he most desired. The *junta* would convoke congressional elections in March, and the decision on Valencia would be "submitted to ratification by the Conservative and Liberal members of the next Congress."[40] With his price thus paid, Gómez agreed to the December plebiscite. His previous position on that vote was but a tactical position he willingly yielded in return for the opportunity to exercise personal power of veto through elected *laureanista* Congressmen.

The way was clear to hold the historic plebiscite, and at 8 A.M. on Sunday morning, December 1, Colombians began moving to the polls for the first free exercise of the vote since 1949. Colombian women were voting, one of the few measures instituted by the Rojas Pinilla regime which was retained. Feminine reaction was not uniform, and many hesitated to exercise suffrage either through force of habit and tradition or because of the idea that the men's vote would somehow count for more. However, a number of feminist leaders campaigned widely urging women to vote, and the importance which the church gave the voting was an additional impetus.

The final form of constitutional revisions included several new items. Perhaps the most important of these was the formal establishment of bipartisan government, specifying an equal number of cabinet posts, as well as equality in departmental and municipal assemblies. A further provision called for the popular election of congressmen in 1958 to restore that nonexistent legislative power. The *junta* would be legalized as the provisional government until the August return of civil rule. Equal rights were established for both sexes, Catholicism was recognized as the national religion, and a minimum of 10 per cent of the national budget would be allotted to education. Life tenure would be granted all justices of the land's highest court, and a nonpolitical civil service would be established.[41]

There had been an intensive campaign to urge participation. Pamphlets, posters, newspaper advertisements, and radio broadcasts had asked the people to exercise their rights, with both public and private groups working to get out the vote. Buses were provided in many cities to carry voters to the polls, while sound trucks toured the streets reminding the people of the voting. It was carried out in a mood of elation, and population centers showed a festive attitude on the part of the voters. Pink indelible ink was placed on voters' fingers to prevent double voting, and many who had never cast a ballot before proudly displayed ink-stained fingers as testimony to their exercise of suffrage.[42]

National optimism was high as early returns registered overwhelming approval, and on Sunday evening thousands gathered outside the presidential palace to greet the smiling Lleras Camargo and five *junta* members. General Paris told the throng that they had shown national unity in what were "the cleanest elections the republic ever had." The nature of the reform would carry Colombia "to a post of extraordinary magnitude among the free peoples of America."[43] Final results clearly reflected the unanimity of the voters, who endorsed by nearly eighteen to one the compromise designed to end crippling strife and put the nation on a new road.[44] Of the 4,397,090 total vote, 4,169,294 approved the reform. Only 206,864 were negative, while 20,738 cast blank ballots and 194 were annulled for irregularities.[45]

The negative votes were more than a token expression only in Boyacá and the two Santander departments. The former included followers of Tunja-born Rojas Pinilla, while diehard Santander was the remaining stronghold of unreconstructed Conservatism of a more reactionary brand than that of major national leaders. Even so, the "noes" in that region were less than one-third of the departmental total. *El Tiempo* recorded with satisfaction the complete success of the plebiscite, pointing out that in Bogotá, the political heart of the nation, only 5,000 of the more than 350,000 votes rejected the amendments.[46]

Many Colombians spoke informally of the initiation of a "second republic," and there were wide hopes that effective politics would be radically changed. Technically there was no such change, for there was neither a "first" nor "second" republic. But there were grounds to hope for improvement. The *New York Times* editorialized that the Colombians were desperately demanding lasting peace with democratic government. "They have had more than enough of internecine conflict and of dictatorship. They are a politically conscious people." Nor could Alberto Lleras Camargo be overpraised. "It was his ideas, his skill and patience in negotiation, his prestige with all Colombians and his unselfish patriotism that made the agreement . . . possible. Dr. Lleras Camargo has long been one of the towering figures of Latin America. He has enhanced his already high reputation."[47]

Interviewed by *Visión* shortly after the plebiscite, Lleras Camargo spoke of the great experiment he had ardently advanced. His words deserve quotation here.

> Trying an experiment without precedent in other nations, it is very difficult to predict how it may develop. Naturally those of us who propose the thesis of government by joint responsibility of the two Colombian parties are sure that it will have to execute policy without stumbling and with great benefits for the Colombian political culture.
>
> But we realize that an infinite patience will be needed as well as a spirit of transition and of permanent agreement to be able to give Colombia a government of peace for twelve years, so that a new generation can take advantage of that truce in preparing to administrate the country in correct form and without sectarianism.[48]

REFORM AND PARTISAN POLITICS

In the months from December until the following August, a succession of upsets threatened the delicately-wrought bipartisan agreement. On several occasions it was on the verge of collapse. In the period immediately after the plebiscite, popular optimism ran high, but politicians more realistically recognized the obstacles still to be surmounted. The most practical danger was the torpedoing of the system by Laureano Gómez. Should he win the majority of the Conservative seats in Congress, the very selection of a candidate would become difficult. There were also those who questioned whether the principle of parity would prove feasible in practice. Certainly none denied that the system was far from foolproof.[49] Lleras Camargo readily admitted that problems were not insignificant. "No one has thought," he conceded, "that other courses could be harder—for example, living eight years under a state of siege. But we have just done that, and I do not see why we cannot now coexist peacefully, rebuilding the country for twelve years."[50]

With the continuing return to constitutional government requiring the holding of both congressional and presidential elections, the *junta,* by the close of 1957, was beginning preparations for the March elections. They would select departmental and municipal officials as well as national congressmen. On December 11 the regime transferred Minister of Interior Jorge Villareal to the justice ministry, while Brigadier General Pioquinto Rengifo, governor of Antioquia, replaced Villareal. Major General Alfredo Duarte Blum was dropped from the cabinet. In trying to insure the success of the elections, the *junta* thus put the Interior Ministry in neutral hands with its transfer of Conservative Villareal to a less critical post. The removal of Duarte Blum was effected to maintain the existing ten to three division between civilian and military cabinet ministers.[51]

Elections were called for Sunday, March 16, 1958, with 80 senators and 148 representatives to be chosen. A complicated quotient system of proportional representation had been worked out in accord with the proposals approved in December, and some 4,000,000 Colombians were eligible to vote. Registration became heavy in the days preceding balloting, and a last-minute rush forced registration officers to remain open sixteen hours during the final three days.[52] Concern evoked by light registration in earlier weeks was removed, and all indications suggested wide interest.

The three-way Conservative division continued, with each faction campaigning extensively. *Laureanismo* represented itself as pure doctrinal conservatism, reiterating throughout Colombia the fact that it had remained opposed to the Rojas Pinilla government through four years of military dictatorship. The *ospinistas* replied that their moderate position reflected the future of the party, arguing that *laureanismo* proposed to turn back the clock on social and economic reforms. They ducked the issue of collaboration with Rojas Pinilla where possible; occasional references lamely explained that their participation had moderated dictatorial repression until its final months.

Ospinismo further tried to capitalize on the considerable popularity of Guillermo León Valencia, reminding the people of its approval of the man who along with Lleras Camargo had engineered the ultimate unseating of Rojas Pinilla. Militant *alzatistas,* whose campaign was the most ferocious and vigorously uncompromising of the three, openly opposed the Frente Nacional and supported Jorge Leyva, while returning in kind the venomous sarcasm of Laureano Gómez. Backed by a few anti-Gómez rightists and scattered *rojistas,* the Alzate Avendaño forces criticized agreement with the Liberals and espoused a Conservative re-conquest of power.

Alzate Avendaño aroused little enthusiasm, while the Gómez candi-dates were generally stronger than those of Mariano Ospina Pérez. For the Liberals, there was little serious disagreement; most of their cam-paigning was devoted to getting out a large vote. In striking reversal of the traditional Conservative unity and Liberal factionalism, the Lib-erals were effectively united behind Alberto Lleras Camargo and the Frente Nacional. An extreme left sector calling itself the Frente Liberal Popular attempted to campaign separately under *gaitanista* banners[53] but found little support.

Campaigning was concluded by March 6, at which time a *junta* prohibition against further public manifestations took effect until after the voting. Excitement was kept within reasonable bounds, and on election day Colombians again voted in large numbers. Incidents of vio-lence were few, even in turbulent Valle del Cauca and Tolima. Polling places closed at 4:00 P.M., and before the end of the day two major trends were apparent.

The Liberals piled up large majorities over the combined Conserva-tive totals, and the latter were confronted with the fact that they re-mained the minority party in Colombia. At the same time the *laurea-nista* group won a smashing victory over its rivals. Of the 3,650,606 total votes, the Liberals outpolled the Conservatives by 58 to 42 per cent, with 2,105,171 votes to the Conservatives' 1,545,435. *Laureanismo* took 915,886 Conservatives votes, compared with only 340,106 for *ospinismo* and 287,-760 for the rightist dissidents. The Gómez faction won in thirteen of the departments, with 59 per cent of the combined Conservative vote. The rightists themselves outpolled the *ospinistas* in three departments.[54]

The Conservative outcome left Colombia without a presidential candi-date for May. The aging Gómez had no personal desire to be the candidate, although he had won a Senate seat easily. As the leader of the victorious group, he would have a major voice in naming the coali-tion candidate. Valencia, who had been tacitly accepted by the Liberals as the nominee, was for all practical purposes thrown out of the race. When the electoral complexities of divided rule were worked out, Gó-mez had won 26 of the 40 Conservative Senate seats and 40 of 74 in the Chamber of Representatives. Pre-election estimates that the composition of Conservative representation would decide the 1958-62 presidential choice were borne out. Gómez' clear victory created a deadlock which had to be broken; failure would be critical.

Thus Valencia, only a year earlier the symbol of the national fight for liberation from dictatorship, had been shunted to the sidelines, although elected senator. At first he refused to admit the shattering of his hopes, insisting his candidacy was still valid while refusing to accept the nomination of any rival Conservative aspirant. Such were the realities of politics, however, that his candidacy wilted under the harsh rays of the relentless Gómez will. Gómez' commitment to the defeat of Valencia led Alberto Lleras Camargo to admit that insistence on Valencia would provoke civil war. Once again the fate of the republic hinged on agreement between Lleras Camargo and Gómez, and while the *junta* stood by watchfully, the two dominant leaders, neither of whom wanted the presidency, entered into further negotiations. Luis Ordóñez declared that if there were no president in August, the *junta* would nonetheless step down, handing over the government to a congressional *designado*.[55]

Lleras Camargo had rejected the thought of his own candidacy in December, 1958, saying that the only presidential prerequisite was that of the total honesty. "Little by little we are going to reconstruct our national institutions from the ground up."[56] However, on March 31 he read before a Liberal meeting a letter from Gómez proposing that the Liberal himself become the candidate. The Conservative opined that only Lleras Camargo could resolve the impasse, and his only proviso was the stipulation that the 1962-66 president be a Conservative. A special meeting by the Liberals agreed upon the condition, and Lleras Camargo's candidacy seemed assured, although he had not yet agreed to it. While Lleras Camargo had enemies, particularly in rural areas of strong Conservative sympathies, he was clearly the best available man.

Apparent agreement was endangered less than twelve hours later when the April 1 edition of *El Siglo* denounced the Liberals for having refused to consider Conservative alternates to Guillermo León Valencia. Crowds were already in the streets to celebrate the resolution of the problem when Gómez' paper hit the streets. Liberals were appalled, and another party meeting was called at which a permanent commission was named to consider further nominations when and if Dr. Gómez proposed another name.[57] Gómez' earlier decision in favor of Lleras Camargo had drawn a swift and heavy flow of protests into party headquarters, and even the powerful *caudillo* drew back in the face of accusations of having sold out the party to the Liberals.

Again the parties buckled down to the task of selecting the nominee, and the rest of the month was dedicated to the urgent search. On April 12 agreement seemed near when the two parties extended the bipartisan agreement from twelve to sixteen members while picking Conservative businessman Hernando Gómez Tanco as the candidate. But he promptly declined, and the impasse again rose up. Dr. Gómez submitted a list of eighty names to the Liberals, but while they met to consider the list, prospective candidates dropped by the wayside, and with elections only three weeks off, no solution was in sight.

Continual changes in position and reversals of policy would have been farcical had not the subject been so grave. Both Gómez and Lleras Camargo were caught up in uncontrollable political eddies. On the fifteenth a bipartisan *llerista* movement built up, only to be scuttled when Gómez found his own party temporarily out of control. At an acrimonious Conservative meeting Dr. Gómez was denied by a twenty-eight to twenty-seven vote full powers to negotiate the candidacy with Liberals. Moderates again raised the name of Valencia, and it was once more rejected.[58]

Another switch on the sixteenth led to agreement on Lleras Camargo, and the Liberal was expected to accept over the week end. Dr. Gómez managed to reunite his party to the extent of accepting Lleras Camargo. "If my voice deserves to be heard," he roared, "I raise it to ask support for the candidacy of this illustrious Colombian."[59] Once more happy demonstrators filled the streets of Bogotá; it only remained for the Liberal to accept. On Saturday night, Alberto Lleras Camargo refused the nomination.

He announced that a Conservative candidate was preferable, and the issue was so critical to the nation that such a solution had to be found. He felt his own activities in the previous year made it inadvisable to shoulder the responsibility of steering the nation back to political normality. The mood of the nation was one of disappointment and swiftly grew dangerous. Ominous demonstrations were held in several cities; in Medellín an estimated 300,000 demonstrated, during which time two were killed and four injured.[60] The *junta* reiterated an earlier directive to all public officials to hold themselves absolutely neutral while providing complete guarantees to politicians and citizens alike.

Further rallies were held urging Lleras Camargo to reconsider, and on Thursday night, April 24, he reluctantly yielded to public demand. In a radio speech he accepted the nomination while resigning as Liberal party leader. "I consider myself obligated to represent both parties equally," he explained in submitting his political resignation to the Liberals. Guillermo León Valencia made the choice virtually unanimous by freeing his supporters and repeating his personal backing of the Frente Nacional.

Lleras Camargo and Gómez had been around and around in the political revolving door so many times in recent weeks that some feared yet another reversal. However, the decision this time was irrevocable. Crowds again gathered in the streets, waving banners and pictures of Lleras Camargo, and stripping foliage off palm trees. Students turned their coats inside out, formed a snake-dance, and chanted "Lleras! Lleras! Lleras!"[61] Thus the question of the presidency was settled; May elections could be held and Lleras Camargo, in turn, would be inaugurated in August. Unfortunately, the political atmosphere had become strained during the weeks of disagreement, and yet one more obstacle presented itself.

On May 2, a small group of disgruntled military officers planned the overthrow of the political establishment. At 3:00 A.M. Friday morning panel trucks were sent out to seize *junta* members and also Lleras Camargo. General Paris was driven away to military police barracks, clad only in robe and pajamas. Navas Pardo, warned of trouble by a sentry shot, unsuccessfully tried to flee his home over the garden wall. Luis Ordóñez delayed his captors some twenty minutes to deliver a verbal rebuke, but then was taken away under guard. Formidable Deogracias Fonseca was equally noisy, and had to be carried off bodily to the waiting truck.[62]

The seizure of Lleras Camargo, critically important to the insurrectionists, began smoothly. At 4:00 A.M. he was awakened by his watchman, and a moment later a warning phone call urged him to leave his home. As he finished dressing, however, two armed lieutenants entered his home and took him into custody. By an ironic twist, however, the rebels drove past the presidential palace on the way to the barracks and were stopped by the army guard for speeding. Lleras Camargo was recognized and immediately was freed while his captors were placed under arrest. He continued into the palace and spoke to Colombia over the national network.[63]

The rebel blunder in losing Lleras Camargo was followed by the failure to capture the fifth *junta* member, Admiral Rubén Piedrahita. He had been forewarned by a call from Public Works Minister Julio Roberto Salazar Ferro, who lived next to Fonseca and had seen his forcible removal. Piedrahita thus escaped by his fire escape and soon joined Lleras Camargo at the palace. The two immediately contacted loyal troops, ordered planes to fly over the Bogotá military barracks, and sent a thousand infantrymen backed up by artillery and tanks to the barracks. Continuing broadcasts woke the city to the danger, and the military rank and file also responded to calls for support. Rebel leader Colonel Hernando Forero, disillusioned by lack of support and the dangers of unequal battle, surrendered his captives without bloodshed and was granted asylum in the Salvadoran embassy.

Colonel Forero later said his insurrection was a "romantic movement in protest against the *junta* because it is a weak government."[64] The uprising, which had been a complete surprise to the authorities, would have postponed elections and established a new military regime under Forero. Its only support came from a few close friends plus a small portion of the 500-man military police force in the capital. The *junta* immediately broadcast a pledge to hold elections on Sunday as scheduled, "even if it costs us our lives."[65] The capital was placed under heavy guard, and all vehicles entering Bogotá were stopped and searched.[66] There was complete outward calm and the return to an atmosphere characterized earlier as "fair."[67] Rights of *habeas corpus* were suspended only briefly, until the arrest of all those implicated.

Lleras Camargo's election on the fourth was opposed only by the token candidacy of Jorge Leyva, who opposed the bipartisan plan although conceding Lleras Camargo's victory in advance. When the votes were tabulated, Lleras Camargo had received 2,482,948 votes to Leyva's 614,861.[68] The 3,097,809 total votes, half a million below the March balloting, was considered good in view of the nature of the vote. Since the anti-Frente Nacional vote in March had been less than 300,000, the doubling of the extreme rightist vote appeared an expression of rebellion by hardcore Conservatives against party support for Liberal Lleras Camargo. Bogotá remained calm, but violence elsewhere took thirty-one lives and injured nine others.[69] In a broadcast after voting ended at 4:00 P.M., the president-elect asked for no victory celebrations which might arouse further bitterness.

The weeks remaining before the inauguration were fairly quiet. Public demonstrations honored the *junta* for its patriotism and dedication to the restoration of civilian constitutional rule. While its patience had thinned more than once before the interminable political squabbling, the ultimate establishment of a bipartisan system under Lleras Camargo proved a worthy reward. In July the newly elected Congress convened as the first regular legislative session in nearly nine years. The 116th National Congress, it took up the past nine years' decrees under the state of siege. With the Senate under the presidency of Laureano Gómez, the president-elect was provided legal sanctions to operate the government until the lifting of the state of siege, which he promised as one of the first orders of business.

On Thursday, August 7, 1958, the external transition back to constitutional order was completed with the inauguration of Alberto Lleras Camargo. The ceremony was attended by the diplomatic corps, members of Congress, Cardinal Luque, and high-ranking officials. Appropriately, Lleras Camargo was given the oath of office by Laureano Gómez. Thus the untried experiment in controlled democracy under bipartisan rule began, directed by the architect of the plan, one of Colombia's most illustrious sons. It remained to be seen whether even Alberto Lleras Camargo could make the system work. As the president himself had said not long before, the new president would have to be "a magician, prophet, redeemer, savior and pacifier who can transform a ruined republic into a prosperous one. . . ."[70]

Chapter Sixteen

THE FIRST YEAR OF BIPARTISAN RULE

LLERAS AND NATIONAL PACIFICATION

ALBERTO LLERAS CAMARGO returned to the presidency at a time of crisis; the future of the republic depended in large part upon his guidance and wisdom. The bipartisan experiment was basically different from the attempts at coalition in the 1940's, when Conservatives maintained most positions of authority. For the first time the president was compelled to stand above party, with the two collectivities equally responsible for the formulation and execution of policy. There should be little of the usual opportunistic politicking, else the carefully constructed edifice would tumble in ruins. If any man could make the extraordinary experiment work, it was Lleras Camargo.

The new president brought prestige and an almost universal respect to his office. His career from early adulthood, as described in Part II, had provided a series of varied experiences which now led to the most demanding task of his public life. Lleras Camargo the man was quietly unassuming to the point of shyness; a small, almost frail-looking man, his friends knew him as a witty conversationalist of keen intellect. A voracious reader whose high sloping forehead typified the caricature of an "egghead," he possessed a dispassionate mind which applied logic to all problems. His reverence for facts was an inheritance from his days as a working journalist.

Although proud of his personal library, Lleras Camargo was no ivory-tower scholar immersed in his books. Fond of horseback riding and hunting, he was also a familiar figure on the Bogotá Country Club golf course. Neither was he lacking in personal courage. In January of 1956 he and the other members of his foursome were fired upon while golfing. As his friends dove to the ground, Lleras Camargo scoffed: "Ridiculous! Why would anybody shoot at me?" He was about to continue playing when further shots by the unidentified marksman convinced him of the danger.[1]

A man of personal frugality and unimpeachable honesty, Lleras Camargo had refused his monthly pension from the Rojas Pinilla government on the grounds that his 1945-46 presidential term was not based upon popular election. And following his return to Colombia in 1954 from the Organization of American States, he became the unsalaried rector of the experimental new University of the Andes.[2] Lleras Camargo was also a man of conviction, and his talent for compromise did not include retreats from principle. As head of the Colombian delegation at the San Francisco United Nations meeting in 1945, he was one of two who voted against the Soviet veto proposal in the face of great-power abstention. "My Government is opposed to the veto. How can I abstain?"[3]

Lleras Camargo was acutely aware of national problems, yet his viewpoint was that of a man who had served a regional organization at the highest echelon. The breadth of his outlook was apparent, for example, in an address delivered at a special meeting of the Inter-American Economic and Social Council in Washington. "The world is passing through a great revolutionary stage. . . . Vital is the question of how the administrative action of each State may be coordinated to enable the international agencies to render them the greatest possible service. . . . If we fail to realize that we are living through a revolutionary period, we shall continue to react . . . with the outmoded attitudes, methods, and equipment of the past, and we shall unwittingly suffer the consequences."[4] Later in the same address he referred to the necessity of Latin effort. "If all the people of the Americas could be converted into men of our times, the human aggregate would be the most powerful moral, political, economic, and military force the world has ever known. A nation cannot bridge the gap by itself."[5]

As incoming president, Lleras Camargo was the greatest exponent of the bipartisan plan. Constitutional reform along his lines was imperative, for controlled democracy could operate with comparative freedom, leading in time to true democracy. Colombia had yet to learn that "majorities, merely because they are strong, do not league together against the minorities, even when these are richer or happier."[6] The constitutional reforms could prepare the nation for the responsible exercise of democracy. "If they are applied well, if they are carried out with the agreement of the two parties charged with governing the country, no emergency measures should be required."[7]

It would be a mistake to underrate Lleras Camargo's abilities as a practical politician. During the years of Liberal conflict between López and Santos, Lleras Camargo had served both men in highly responsible positions. In 1945, when Dr. López had become the center of political turbulence, Lleras Camargo was out of the country on diplomatic duties and was perhaps the only Liberal far enough removed from the political wars to exercise the provisional presidency, as he did until 1946. The Frente Nacional was founded on the cooperation of the traditional parties, yet he believed that new movements could flourish under it. A new political party would do so, although not being included in the proportional representation in public office. The very structure of reform was designed "to make impossible the struggle for power between the two traditional parties . . . while institutions are restored and the political life of the country soothed. . . ."[8]

One of his two major problems was that of national pacification. He promised to devote himself to the procurement of "order, austerity, good administration, and the moderating and rational effect on the play of republican institutions, under which Colombia has had its most fortunate epochs."[9] Recalling his own boyhood when his widowed mother had been forced off family lands in Boyacá by political terrorists,[10] he declared in his inaugural address that a major aim was putting an end to civil war. The nation was told to prepare "for an intense campaign of pacification."[11] While explaining that he had no new plan to end the violence, he emphasized that the causes of disorders were diverse and, even after a decade, not fully understood. "My country—and with it the parties and public powers—does not know all the causes of this extremely complex phenomenon, which certainly includes economic roots and motives. . . . [But] there must be more effective efforts in continuing the struggle against violence."[12]

The lifting of the state of siege would be declared once Congress began to deal with the decade of legislation by executive decree—which it did upon meeting in July. As he told *Visión* following his May election, the first sessions of Congress, even before he took possession of the presidency, should dedicate itself to that problem. In his inaugural message Lleras Camargo reiterated his intention of lifting the state of siege so that "normal democratic institutions" might function once more.[13] Moving swiftly following his inauguration, Lleras Camargo named his cabinet of thirteen, with one military officer and six representatives of each party. Among the key appointments were Conservative Guillermo Amaya Ramírez and Liberal Julio César Turbay Ayala as ministers of government and foreign affairs, respectively.

On Monday, August 18, 1958, the president declared that the state of siege would shortly be lifted, and on the twenty-seventh, Amaya Ramírez appeared before Congress to read the decree. He stated that "public order is reestablished and the state of siege suspended.[14] As Liberals and Conservatives joined the enthusiastic cheering of the packed galleries, the decree removed emergency measures in all territories and eleven of the sixteen departments. Modified restrictions were established in the disturbed departments of Caldas, Valle del Cauca, Cauca, Tolima, and Huila. Their departmental governors were granted extraordinary powers "with the exclusive object of reestablishing order in those areas where disturbance still exists." Thus, the constitutional suspension decreed by Mariano Ospina Pérez on November 9, 1949, was removed nearly nine years later. Legislation returned to the hands of Congress, formal press controls were removed, executive rule was again subject to constitutional checks, and citizens were free from arbitrary arrest.[15]

The fight against guerrilla warfare, which had degenerated into sheer lawlessness, remained a task of great magnitude. The government estimated that some 280,000 had died in the past dozen years as a result.[16] This warfare had briefly slackened in the early months of the Rojas Pinilla regime but soon revived. The situation had not been minimized by the *junta* efforts. Valle del Cauca had been particularly hard hit in 1957 and 1958; it was here that Rojas Pinilla's security forces had come to identify themselves with bandit elements known as the Pájaros Azules or Bluebirds. The Pájaros, originally partisan Conservatives, had persecuted foes of the Rojas Pinilla government, creating hatred which manifested itself in the murder of seventeen Pájaros in Cali immediately after Rojas Pinilla's ouster while army and police stood aside.[17]

In less than a year the *junta* had appointed eight different governors in Valle, to little avail. Raiders gathered in the night, plundered coffee *fincas,* then withdrew unopposed. The densely forested region in which many small plantations were located made eradication of such banditry exceedingly difficult. Probably the one encouraging sign was the fact that no deaths were reported during the day of the plebiscite on December 1, 1957. The same could not be said during the subsequent congressional and presidential elections.

During his first year, Lleras Camargo adopted military policies not unlike those of his predecessors. Rural garrisons were reinforced with personnel and equipment, while small mobile units were employed, somewhat ineffectually, to airlift troops on short notice from one trouble spot to another. Toward the close of 1958, however, it grew apparent that additional measures were necessary. The government adopted exceptional penal procedures to judge the bandits and made plans to establish a rehabilitation penitentiary on Isla Marítima to re-educate convicted bandits in the hope of re-incorporating them into national life. A major propaganda campaign was initiated to mobilize public opinion in the search for rural peace.

Outbursts were reduced, and in April of 1959 the minister of war announced that violence was nearing an end. On May 1, 1959, the president told the nation that pacification was virtually complete. Minister of Government Amaya Ramírez also informed the Senate that the daily average of deaths was but 4; in the first six months of 1958, it had been 15.2 a day.[18] Two days later his words proved tragically premature with the rebirth of strife in Tolima, Caldas, and Valle. Within a few days some fifty were dead, and a noticeable resurgence continued, with Tolima recording 206 deaths by the end of the month.[19]

During May the count nearly tripled the combined total of March and April. The administration immediately adopted further measures. Governors were authorized to provide rewards for information leading to captures, and peasants for the first time were permitted personal arms for their protection. Local judges received additional power, and the government refused to renew the period of grace when it expired on June 26. *Junta* policy had pardoned all those guilty of political crimes if they promised to live within the law henceforth.[20]

Plans had been made to establish the major rehabilitation center on a small Pacific island eighty-five miles off Buenaventura. Instead, the government purchased the privately-owned island of Gorgona, over a hundred miles southwest of the same port. Necessary prison buildings were built, while the crowded mainland jails waited impatiently to ship out their prisoners. The growing rate of convictions—Valle alone had 359 in July[21]—pressured workers to complete facilities swiftly. Although unprovoked attacks came, there was noticeable improvement in July. Military action became more effective, while the government had also speeded the process of trial and sentence. By the end of Lleras Camargo's first year in power, figures revealed a 63 per cent decline in violence.

The new president did not restrict himself to the improvement of military and penal measures. The bands of guerrillas still included those who had been drawn in through personal or political hates, and dispossessed *campesinos* were wreaking vengeance for loss of property. There were also homeless thousands in the cities on the brink of starvation who contributed inevitably to increased metropolitan crime rates. Soon after taking office the president established the Department of Rehabilitation and with its manager, contractor José Gómez Pinzón, drew up an extensive building program providing for the construction of modest but necessary roads, bridges, airstrips, and telegraph stations in remote areas. An important result was a measurable increase in employment.[22]

The directing Council of Rehabilitation also worked for the strengthening of rural security forces, and refugees trekked back to ancestral lands from large population centers. With new employment opportunities awaiting them, production was also bolstered; new mountain roads opened up virgin lands to development. Toward the end of 1959 some 100,000,000 pesos helped facilitate the return of an estimated 8,000 families to useful, productive life.[23] The Colonization Department of the Agricultural Bank also began opening up new regions for those who failed to return to their native areas. In February, 1959, colonization authorities announced the availability of 300,000 hectares in the Ariari Valley, Meta intendency,[24] and in the following months there were renewed efforts to aid colonists through eased credit and low-cost commissaries.

As Lleras Camargo's first year drew to a close, the effort at pacification had brought considerable improvement, although the violence was far from eradicated. Linked with the restoration of order, however, was the problem of a small minority of *rojistas,* and the reappearance in Colombia of the general himself helped stir up political passions.

THE RETURN AND TRIAL OF ROJAS PINILLA

The continued presence of a few uncompromising followers of the exiled dictator brought forth demands for stern government prosecution, which many would have transformed into political persecution. Alberto Lleras Camargo appealed to the spirit of moderation by refusing to undertake political reprisals. "A government that wants to and must return to the constitution, cannot take executive means to force justice; the government may intervene to promote and help facilitate the action of justice, but must not pretend to substitute for it."[25] At the same time, disturbances during the *junta* government had indicated that elements still existed which were wedded to the idea of promoting the dictator's return. As sporadic rumors of Rojas Pinilla's return to Colombia upset internal peace, the legislature chose to prosecute the general for crimes against the nation.

On September 25, 1958, a National Investigation Commission formally requested the Chamber of Representatives to file criminal charges before the Senate, which was constitutionally empowered to sit in judgment of former presidents. By a 107-7 vote the Chamber agreed to present charges of Rojas Pinilla's "abuse of power" and obstruction of "due process of law."[26] Rojas Pinilla, who was admittedly anxious to return, announced from Spain that he had not been contacted by the government but hoped to return with the official guarantee "that I be given the means to defend myself and, as I have said repeatedly, that the people be permitted to listen to what I must say. . . ."[27]

The former president maintained the fiction that he had left power of his own free will, intimating that he would return soon. Speaking in Barcelona shortly before his flight back to Colombia, he declared that the Frente Nacional was at best a temporary arrangement. "As for the pact, the Conservative press assures that it is not to be fulfilled. The Liberal Party has taken for itself the lion's share and left the mouse's share for the Conservatives. The pacts of Benidorm and Sitges were cemented in personal promises of Gómez and Lleras without consulting the people, on the pretext of avoiding party strife, strife which I succeeded in avoiding during the four years of my government because I followed the Christian and sincere policy of coexistence among the popular masses of both parties. . . ."[28]

Such was Rojas Pinilla's continued self-delusion. Nothing had changed; he saw no reason for the people not to welcome him. Perhaps with the thought of arousing Conservative opposition to the government, he predicted that the country was moving toward complete Liberal hegemony. "Lleras improved the position of the Liberal party more than Laureano Gómez did that of the Conservative party. Laureano Gómez only lives to continue the persecution of those Conservative chiefs who were his victims until June 13, 1953, when I rose to power."[29]

On Sunday, October 12, seventeen months to the day after his ignominious flight, Gustavo Rojas Pinilla returned to Colombia. He was booed by a small crowd during a short stop at Barranquilla, and at Bogotá he landed amid a heavy detachment of security guards. Only a few friends were on hand, and he was speeded in a bullet-proof Cadillac to the home of Jaime Polanía Puyo, a former member of his government and the father-in-law of Rojas Pinilla's son Carlos.[30] "I am not coming to recover power or as the head of any political group," he declared. "I come to defend my honor."[31] Denying charges of enrichment in office, he maintained the alleged legality of his election by the puppet *constituyente* to the 1958-62 presidency. He began issuing pompous "communiqués" from Polanía Puyo's residence, the first of which denied the competence of the Senate in judging him. He held that only a military court had jurisdiction over any legal proceedings against him.[32]

The Senate proceeded, nonetheless, to prepare its case. On October 16 a subcommittee on investigations and procedure signed an order calling him to testify before the Senate on the afternoon of the twentieth. Rojas Pinilla refused to appear, however, repeating his unfounded claim that the constitution did not permit the Senate to sit in judgment, although that body specifically had power to do precisely that. "I cannot recognize this farce, conceived in hate, vengeance and vain haughtiness."[33] Five days later the government forced his compliance by sending a squad of armed police to the Polanía Puyo residence and escorting Rojas Pinilla on a four-block walk to the Communications Building, where the subcommittee was meeting. The entire area was blocked off with tanks and half-tracks.

Sitting with Senators for some two hours before he was permitted to leave, Rojas Pinilla was questioned only ten minutes. The occasion was essentially a token gesture showing government ability to force his appearance. Most of the interview consisted of idle conversation over coffee. Polanía Puyo later told the press that Rojas Pinilla had emphatically refused to give testimony and would continue to do so. This refusal lay the grounds for further suspicion that his motives in returning involved a possible recovery of power, although the aging, gaunt man seemed hardly one to direct a *golpe*.

During his exile Rojas Pinilla had been receiving assurance from friends that many would welcome his return to power.[34] On Wednesday night, December 3, the former president was arrested as Alberto Lleras Camargo announced a state of siege after learning the existence of "a subversive plan to overthrow the legitimate authority . . . under the personal direction of General Rojas Pinilla." Citing permission of the Consejo de Estado to declare emergency measures, he announced complete military support while characterizing the emergency decree as a "most repugnant decision." "Persons dangerous to public order" had already been arrested, he declared, adding assurances that Congress would *not* be shut down. He requested it to remain in session beyond its scheduled December 20 recess and declared his hopes of restoring constitutional guarantees shortly.[35]

Explaining that a revolutionary *coup* had been planned, Lleras Camargo ordered troops into the streets of the capital, while Rojas Pinilla was speeded to Barranquilla and thence aboard the frigate *Capitán Tono,* where he was held incommunicado in the Caribbean. The uneasy interlude was marked by some fifty arrests within a few hours, including a handful of congressmen and several intimates of Rojas Pinilla. SIC, the intelligence service, revealed that bands of terrorists had been moving into Bogotá. Plans called for them to invade Congress, break up meetings, and loot downtown stores. Special agents were to assassinate some 200 political and military leaders. The military would step in, retired *rojista* officers would return to active duty, and the people would be told of a "popular revolution."[36]

The citizenry promptly united behind the administration, and the swift action in anticipating the plot succeeded completely. On January 13, 1959, the president lifted the state of siege in all but the five departments where rural violence continued. This contrast with the previous actions of Ospina Pérez, Gómez, and Rojas Pinilla who had maintained rule by decree for nearly a decade, was not lost on the people. January was a month of public displays in support of the president. The complete lack of public support sounded the final death knell to Rojas Pinilla's hopes. It remained for the Senate to continue its proceedings. In the months to follow, this display of apparent justice and fairness set a standard which was received with admiring approval throughout the hemisphere. At the same time it raised questions which were better left unanswered and could have little purpose but to exacerbate bitter political memories.

With preparatory groundwork completed, the trial itself began at 4:04 P.M., January 22, 1959. It was the first time since 1867 that such proceedings had taken place; at that time General Tomás Cipriano de Mosquera had been convicted of setting up a monopoly on the sale of salt.[37] The Senate was not trying the former dictator for criminal charges, but for abuses which could lead to a sentence depriving him of his civil rights. If convicted of what were termed political crimes, he could then further be judged by the Corte Suprema de Justicia on criminal charges, which could sentence him to a maximum prison term of twelve years. Essentially, there were two charges: inappropriate and illegal exercise of power and the violation of the constitution with the purpose of increasing his personal patrimony.

Rojas had three defenders: Jesús Estrada Monsalve, who had served on his Consejo de Estado; Liberal Senator Carlos V. Rey; and Conservative writer and legislator Daniel Valois Arce. The interrogation was directed largely by Carlos Lleras Restrepo, who had been elected to the Senate and was again serving as Liberal organizational leader. The government spent some eight weeks carefully laying out its case, and Rojas Pinilla himself took the stand. Senators saw a stooped, hollow-cheeked man in an ill-fitting double-breasted suit who meekly addressed them as "Honorable Senators" and was in turn called "the accused." Under questioning he admitted that his fortune had increased substantially in office, although he maintained this was solely through "gifts" from Colombians and foreigners. The cattle company his family had formed had neither kept books nor paid taxes; Rojas Pinilla had filed no income tax returns. The dictator, aged well beyond his fifty-eight years, gave stumbling replies to many questions. His answers were vague, his memory apparently poor.[38]

The Senate had previously declared that its object was to determine "whether or not he was unworthy by reason of the deeds that he has executed. . . ."[39] Investigators soon finished with their questioning, and the trial entered its second phase, which brought into the open, the smouldering political hatreds that reached back more than a decade. Carlos V. Rey began with a series of violent charges against the Gómez regime, and this was followed by the accusation of Daniel Valois Arce that Dr. Gómez had known in advance of plans to assassinate Jorge Gaitán in 1948. Calling Gómez an "accomplice" in the murder, he declared that he was making a sworn statement that the Conservative had learned of the assassination plans in advance. In a three-hour diatribe he told stunned congressmen that Gómez had come to power "on a mountain of corpses," while his presidency had navigated "in an ocean of blood."[40]

Rojas Pinilla's lawyers, their defense rendered worthless by the thorough documentation of Senate charges, determined to turn proceedings into a farce during which controversies of past years would be raked over. The defense maintained, without substantiating the charges, that General Rojas Pinilla, while on a military mission to London, had somehow seen the long-suppressed Scotland Yard report, which allegedly named the "intellectual assassin" of Gaitán. There were hints that it was Gómez, and the lawyers promised that Rojas Pinilla would reveal the name. He never did so, however, and the contention was not supported by evidence.

The atmosphere was charged with concern following such charges, and Valois Arce caused greater consternation with the unlikely charge that he had seen Alvaro Gómez Hurtado in the company of the assassin Roa Sierra before the murder. The killer had been unknown in political circles at the time, and it seemed extraordinary that Valois Arce might even have recognized the man. Gómez Hurtado was also known to have been in Switzerland as ambassador on that date, yet Valois Arce refused to withdraw his statement.[41]

Rojas Pinilla was permitted to make a statement, and he turned belligerent once more with characteristic immoderation that further damaged his cause. For some forty hours, in ten four-hour sessions, he put on a rambling, illogical, largely irrelevant display. One magazine was led to comment that, had he acted as his own lawyer throughout, he "would have been condemned and sentenced for homicide."[42] Accusations hurled at political enemies served no worthwhile purpose. Typical was the flare-up of temper when he noted during an interval that

Carlos Lleras Restrepo and Alvaro Gómez Hurtado had begun a private conversation. Rojas Pinilla immediately told Lleras Restrepo that Alvaro had ordered the burning of his home in 1952. Such a charge, even if true, was entirely beside the point and was given without evidence. Once more feeling became bitter.

There were grounds for criticizing the entire proceedings, although government dedication to the judicial and constitutional processes was praiseworthy. The acting president of the Senate disgustedly cut off Rojas Pinilla after forty hours, and, although understandable, this was an unwise move in view of public interest over charges concerning the Gaitán assassination. The public was left in some doubt, for there was still the possibility that Rojas Pinilla knew who had arranged the murder, as he claimed. The likelihood that the former dictator could contribute anything pertinent was slim, but with the issue once raised, the course of prudence dictated patience in bearing with Rojas Pinilla's inanities until suspicions were proved or discredited.

Furthermore, as several newspapers commented, the nature of the charges against Rojas Pinilla avoided any implication of those involved in varying degrees with the dictatorship. Prominent *ospinistas* and other political figures had been active during the years between 1953 and 1957, and any thorough investigation of Rojas Pinilla would have brought such connections to light. The bullring massacre, the student shootings, lavishly-endowed official publications, and the alleged concentration camp of Cunday might have soiled many more reputations, including those of the members of the *junta*, who had been decorated by Lleras Camargo when he received power from them. Liberal Juan Lozano recalled, as one example, that a former mayor of Bogotá had been prosecuted and jailed for the use of government funds to organize *rojista* demonstrations. He was quickly released when a *junta* member sent a letter testifying that the mayor had been ordered to appropriate such funds by higher authority of an individual who was still nationally prominent.[43] Rojas Pinilla himself had raised the issue in stating, "If there is honesty, you must bring here without exception all those persons who collaborated with my government."[44]

Certainly Rojas Pinilla was highly unpopular at the time of his overthrow, and the abortive December insurrection further discredited him. Thus condemned by public opinion, the citizenry spoke of many repressions and illegalities far more serious than those of which he was accused by the Senate. But once proceedings had begun in earnest in January, there was little choice but to pursue the matter to its conclusion. A further incident stirred feeling in mid-February when the widow of Jorge Gaitán abruptly rose to her feet in the gallery to cry out that the Senators sitting in judgment were themselves accomplices in many crimes of past years.[45]

The final verdict was announced on Wednesday, March 18, following a six-hour secret session. At the end of the trial's thirty-fifth session, the Senate found Rojas Pinilla guilty. He was condemned by a 62-4 vote of acting "in violation of the national constitution" and by a vote of 65-1 of "abuse of power by improper conduct in the exercise of the office of President." Six Senators were absent, and eight who opposed the Frente Nacional abstained. The verdict was then referred to a committee which would draft the sentence.[46]

Following a recess for Holy Week, the Senate reconvened and voted on April 3 to strip Rojas Pinilla of political rights, military honors, and monthly pensions. He was barred from voting, holding public office, and further military duty. With the long acrimonious proceedings thus concluded, records were transferred to the courts, where he was still liable to charges of "common crimes." It was probably fortunate that further turbulence was avoided by letting these charges die a quiet death. Whether or not the Senate proceedings had been valuable was debatable, but in any event the conviction completed the process. Nothing further could be gained by extending the prosecution.

The Economic Revival

Throughout this year of national pacification and the removal of the spectre of Gustavo Rojas Pinilla, the administration was exceedingly active in tackling crucial economic problems. Despite the general improvement through fifteen months of *junta* efforts under the direction of Antonio Alvarez Restrepo, there was much to be accomplished. The progress of industrial development was uneven, agricultural production was discouragingly slow, and there had been little success in diversifying export products. Dependence on coffee for more than 80 per cent of export income continued; there was also a need to develop substitutes which would reduce the flow of imports, particularly food stuffs and raw materials. The fiscal deficit was still large, and inflation was an omnipresent danger.

Like Laureano Gómez a decade earlier, Lleras Camargo realized that economic planning should be in the hands of competent trained economists. Thus he revived the National Planning Council under his own chairmanship. An advisory group organized in 1949, it had been of minor importance for some years, but under Lleras Camargo it was directed to undertake sound long-range planning. The key section of the council itself was its Planning Department, which had the dual responsibility of preparing recommendations for the council's study and for drafting specific recommendations on items requested by the council. The research staff of some fifty professionals were soon immersed in studies of widely varying natures. At the outset, it worked on specific recommendations by which Lleras Camargo might create general stability of internal and external trade while increasing agricultural and industrial production as rapidly as proved economically sound.[47]

On September 4, 1958, Minister of Finance Hernando Agudelo Villa read a three-hour policy statement to assembled congressmen. A declaration of problems and intentions, it was designed to protect and encourage productive investment while exercising fiscal control through penalties discouraging speculative investment. Investors in agricultural pursuits would be particularly favored through easy credit and official cooperation of relevant organs. Increasing credit would be made available for the stimulation of manufacturing and production of basic consumer goods. A scale of tax exemptions was promised to encourage further the diversification and expansion of export commodities. The government also promised increased taxes on unproductive properties and buildings.[48]

Proposed social reforms testified to Lleras Camargo's belief in evolution rather than revolution. Budgetary priority would be given to matters of "social interest," and the income tax would be revised to shift the burden to the wealthy. Commercial and industrial enterprises would be asked to accept price and wage control which would permit occasional balanced increases.

The congressmen reacted favorably, showing an increased awareness that aid to lower income groups would also help stabilize the national economy. It was also evident from the speech that Lleras Camargo was firmly wedded to the principle of government intervention. He proposed in effect complete administrative control over all phases of economic and fiscal policy. Semi-autonomous organs would exercise diminished authority, with direction and responsibility clearly originating from the cabinet itself.

Having thus outlined its proposals in a general way, the administration turned to the adoption of specific measures. Notwithstanding plans to increase production and diversify the economy, the major effort was necessarily dedicated to basic fiscal problems of restraining inflation, establishing a favorable balance of trade, and paying back more of the outstanding foreign obligations. The administration continued the *junta* program of austerity, and by holding down the flow of imports, gradually built up its reserves. Heavy shipments of coffee, although at declining prices on the New York market, enabled the foreign exchange reserves to climb by November, 1958, to $170,000,000, the highest in nearly three years.[49] Three international loans totalling $370,000,000 were negotiated,[50] and before Lleras Camargo had been in office six months, an estimated $300,000,000 in foreign commercial debts had been repaid.[51]

The results of rigid austerity were apparent in a favorable balance of trade for the year of $86,000,000, the best in twenty years.[52] Colombia was one of only five Latin nations to enjoy a favorable balance. Reduced government spending and the tightening of credit also brought the increasing cost of living within less unreasonable bounds. Where the overall cost had increased 25 per cent in 1957, it was held to 8 per cent in 1958.[53]

The picture was not entirely favorable, however, and by the start of 1959 *Visión* commented that, despite measurable improvement, the only real clouds on the horizon were unquestionably economic.[54] Commitments had been incurred which would consume some $125,000,000 of 1959 income, and new loans were necessary to maintain effective import control. Even so, it was estimated that imports would have to rise to a minimum of $28,000,000 million per month if industrial expansion were to continue. The imbalance between the cost of living and the wage level was causing some discontent; typical of several minor disorders was the March smashing of department store windows in Bogotá as a protest against an increase in bus fares.[55] By the end of that month a reorganization of import restrictions helped in part to offset the increased cost of living, with the official rate of exchange hitting 6.4 to the dollar.

Hernando Agudelo Villa announced an official readjustment of salaries to meet rising costs, although there was some press criticism that the government was showing a "simplistic manner" in dealing with austerity and its consequences. In April, 1959, the administration moderated import controls, authorizing the abolition of a 10 per cent exchange remittance tax on various items. Import authorizations in April reached their highest level since September, 1957.

By August of 1959, with Lleras Camargo's first year a matter of record, the peso rose to 7.8 to the dollar on the free market, a contrast to the January low of 8.3. Credit had been sufficiently stabilized to permit progress in development, and the International Bank for Reconstruction and Development sent a representative to Bogotá to discuss requests for new loans. He announced that Colombia's credit had been completely reestablished. There was brief concern in July, 1959, when imports suddenly soared to $37,500,000. This was offset in part by an improvement in coffee prices, however, and in August imports dropped down once more.

Problems of low agricultural productivity, lack of diversification, and wasteful use of the soil plagued Lleras Camargo much as they had his predecessors. There was official encouragement of crops other than coffee, hoping both to promote diversification and to provide Colombia with an enlarged domestic supply of basic food stuffs. In February, 1959, the Banco Central released 90,000,000 pesos through relaxation of control of bank reserves, making them available for agricultural loans. It was "another attempt by the Colombian Government to provide much-needed agricultural credit and reflected the emphasis being given to promoting agricultural production."[56]

On May 10 the Senate introduced a new customs tariff designed particularly to promote agricultural development. Although some 700 items were added to the tariff list, duties were eliminated on agricultural machinery and fertilizer. At the same time, new taxes were levied on many agricultural imports, thus encouraging increased domestic production.[57] The United States also helped materially through an extension of the sale of surplus agricultural commodities under the provision of P.L. 480, helping to relieve temporary food shortages without relaxing import controls on foodstuffs. The Export-Import Bank provided further assistance in the form of loans and credits.[58]

The emphasis on diversification brought increasingly favorable results through 1959. Wheat production rose 18 per cent, barley 25 per cent, and soya 100 per cent.[59] Cotton was rising sharply, and by mid-1959 the crop was a record 155,000 bales, an increase of 48 per cent over the previous year. Banana production reached 30,000,000 stems, compared with 28,000,000, and cattle-raising received new impetus through the creation of the Banco Ganadero, which was authorized 100,000,000 pesos of capital for livestock improvement. An appropriation of 600,000,000 pesos for agricultural development testified to official interest in the over-all problem.[60]

The emphasis on austerity prevented the administration from initiating widespread social reforms. Although the activities of the Department of Rehabilitation had helped relieve the pressures on the cities, conditions were still poor, and workers were vocal in their criticism. The government arranged a series of so-called "gentlemen's agreements" with major producers in the hope of controlling the gap between wages and prices. Workers' cost-of-living index, based on 100 for 1954-55, had climbed by December, 1956, to 133.5, but by November, 1958, had risen only to 143.6, with most of the levelling off coming after May, 1958.[61] Workers were nonetheless caught uncomfortably in the squeeze between wages and prices, and Lleras Camargo was faced with a succession of labor disputes during his first year.

Following his election in 1958, Lleras Camargo had told interviewers that he was sympathetic to the free organization and operation of an independent labor movement, and he indicated that the experimental nature of the Frente Nacional would not hamper Colombian labor. He felt that strong syndicalism was important for the strengthening of the salaried workers. Furthermore, he recognized constitutional guarantees of the rights of labor "to organize and to make a legitimate defense of interests by commonly held rights, such as the strike." "I could not impede," he added, "even if I wanted to—and I do not—the proper organization of the workers, with full independence and freedom of legitimate activity."[62]

As austerity gradually pressured the middle and lower classes, discontent began to assert itself in the form of open and organized labor protests. In June, 1959, a long-simmering protest by bank workers led to the declaration of a nation-wide strike on June 8. Employees had been demanding concessions which included fringe benefits and a wage increase of 20 to 50 per cent. The government tried to avoid a strike by declaring banking a public service, thus rendering any stoppage illegal. The Asociación de Empleados Bancarios ignored this move in calling the strike, and leaders exerted responsible control, thus avoiding any incidence of disorder. After two days the president agreed to act as arbiter and to review the demands. He was personally sympathetic with demands for a wage increase and had already recommended that strikers not be dismissed.

The strike pitted the collective organizational strength of the CTC and UTC against the powerful ANDI, which was urging bank employers not to yield. With the dispute largely a test of strength over the right to strike, Lleras Camargo's attempted neutrality left him in the middle, his administration endangered by growing tension. Bank workers were among the lowest paid employees in Colombia; their demands would have established a monthly minimum wage of 250 pesos or $31.25. Public sympathy was with them from the start and grew when the government had attempted to prevent the strike.[63] The bankers bent before the pressure of public opinion to the extent of conceding further social benefits but adamantly refused to yield to wage demands. It remained for Lleras Camargo to decide the issue.

In mid-July the president announced his decision, which granted higher minimum salaries on separate scales. Skilled and unskilled workers in major cities would receive a minimum 350- or 250-peso monthly salary. In other cities, workers would be similarly classified, with wage minimums set respectively at 300 and 200 pesos. Additional raises were set up on a sliding scale, and fringe benefits were included. A longer period of notice was required for dismissed employees, annual bonuses were increased, and career employees were guaranteed a chance for advancement "in the event of vacancies in positions superior to their own. . . ."[64] Perhaps the best measure of Lleras Camargo's success was the fact that neither management nor labor was fully satisfied, yet both respected the decision without serious protest.

Summer of 1959 was marked with continual labor unrest, and by August more than a hundred various disputes had been handled by the administration. Hardworking Minister of Labor Otto Morales Benítez settled a serious dispute raised by Cali sugar workers when 1400 returned to work on June 18 after a thirty-day strike. He also managed to reconcile opposing views in avoiding strikes threatened against the oil, rubber, and tobacco enterprises.

Labor discontent was such in July that the administration released a statement calling for mutual understanding and responsibility to the national welfare. Lleras Camargo explained that, while compromise was important in seeking solutions, the employers should have the right to dismiss workers when there were valid reasons. Workers, at the same time, deserved protection from arbitrary decisions. Furthermore, while the right to strike was constitutionally valid, only those unions directly involved should participate. He strongly opposed the extension of sympathy strikes which could cripple an entire region.[65]

The president's position had been enhanced by successful handling of the ominous bank dispute, and his responsible approach to labor questions was further underlined by his actions toward the striking Riopaila sugar workers in August, 1959. At the Riopaila mill near Cali, workers grew dissatisfied with union leadership and directed their complaints not to proper labor authorities but to the company management. Union leaders were contractually protected, thus management could not dismiss them. The workers promptly struck; under such circumstances they were not legally justified, and ninety-two were dismissed. Mediation was being undertaken when workers at neighboring sugar mills called sympathy strikes, and 70 per cent of the sugar industry in the heart of the sugar-producing region was paralyzed.

Following disturbances in the streets of Cali, Lleras Camargo broadcast his condemnation of the Valle Federation of Workers, which was responsible. Workers were asked "to scrutinize carefully" the actions of those leaders who had called the sympathy demonstrations. Two government mediators took up the question of the dismissed Riopaila workers, while sympathy strikers were permitted to return to work within a specified time limit. Those who refused were not rehired.[66]

In August the minister of labor further explained to Congress the official view that improved labor-management relations were mandatory. The administration "considered unionism a new means of achieving advances in the Colombian social struggle," but at the same time felt obliged to caution against factionalism that would weaken collective action. Business circles were less than pleased at what they considered the enunciation of a soft policy toward labor; recent stoppages were regarded as unjustified, yet seemingly sanctioned by the government.

Such a reaction was natural for management; the oligarchy was still very much alive, and its rule, which had been unchallenged until the 1930's, had been strengthened when the Gómez regime had virtually demolished the national labor movement. The fact remained that, while the government was naturally somewhat uneasy about antagonizing organized workers, it also realized clearly the importance of a responsible labor movement. This could scarcely develop without permitting a chance to exercise authority while meeting on a level of equality with the leaders of management. Only through practice could organized labor learn its rights, duties, and obligations as a significant sector of national life.

After his first year, Lleras Camargo, through reliance on intelligent economic advisors, had brought a marked resuscitation to the economy. The situation was still far from enviable. Perhaps 5,000,000 still lived in hunger, while an equal number barely managed to reach the lower fringes of an adequate living standard. An elite of less than 5 per cent controlled some 40 per cent of the national income.[67] Lleras Camargo had yet to close significantly the gap between segments of the population. He warned the people that public expenses would continue to be carefully controlled, applying austerity against the "most constant causes of inflationary tendencies."[68] However, economic accomplishments indicated beyond doubt that, while the country was not booming, it was "working towards a stabilized level which will allow . . . [it] to grow without going into bankruptcy or falling prey to internal disruption and political turmoil."[69]

A broader view of Lleras Camargo's first year reflected growing political and economic stability upon which he might build. Formal party activity had gradually returned, but not until 1959 did either the Liberals or Conservatives undertake significant efforts. Then they began their own period of transition during which there was almost continual shifting of positions and jockeying for influence between rival factions. By the time Lleras Camargo's second year was well under way, the parties were once more intimately involved in national political questions.

Chapter Seventeen

THE RETURN OF PARTY ACTIVITY

SHIFTING POLITICAL ALIGNMENTS

IN POLITICAL TERMS, the second year of the bipartisan experiment began in July, 1959, when Congress convened for its regular sessions. Party and factional alignments were somewhat blurred, for a flurry of activity in the months immediately preceding the session had shown continuing Conservative division, and the Liberals themselves were far from monolithic agreement.

One could identify five separate Conservative factions, with alliances and membership in a state of flux. The "legitimist" Gómez group was in the majority and bore the responsibility of collaboration with the Liberals in the government. The *ospinistas* or "republicans" were somewhat more dedicated to moderate reform while hoping to take over control from Laureano Gómez. A small group of individuals remained wedded to the fortunes of Guillermo León Valencia, who after leading the fight against Rojas Pinilla was now cut off from power, although continuing his support of the Frente Nacional. Two right-wing elements were also vocal: the extremists under Jorge Leyva, and the Falangist-oriented followers of Gilberto Alzate Avendaño, who had their own plans of social and economic reform.

The *leyvistas* and *alzatistas,* in short, were in basic opposition to the Frente Nacional. *Laureanistas* and *valencistas* firmly supported the bipartisan government. *Ospinistas* accepted the experiment but wanted control of Conservative participation in government. Initially the *valenc-*

istas had joined with the followers of Ospina Pérez but soon broke away because of *ospinista* sniping at the government in opposing the Gómez dominance. Jorge Leyva had also banded with Ospina Pérez for a time, but his forthright antagonism to the government rendered continuing cooperation difficult. If all this seems confusing, it was no less so to the Colombian citizen.

The significant rivalry was between the Gómez and Ospina Pérez elements, and the Lleras Camargo government found it increasingly difficult to remain on good terms with both. Lleras Camargo's neutrality was disturbing to Gómez, who demanded recognition as the only legitimate Conservative director. At the same time *ospinistas* demanded greater participation in the government. Early in 1959 Lleras Camargo appointed several *ospinistas* in the hope of drawing them more directly into the administration. In June, however, José María Bernal announced an Ospina Pérez reversal in policy, calling for opposition to the Frente Nacional. Bernal further demanded the resignation of the newly appointed *ospinista* cabinet members, Minister of Development Rodrigo Llorente and Minister of Education Abel Naranjo Villegas.

Both submitted their resignations as directed, but they wrote to Lleras Camargo that they considered the Bernal declaration a purely political maneuver and were cutting themselves off from the Ospina faction. The president promptly asked them to stay in office, which they did. This development had no immediately discernible effect, but it did the *ospinistas* little good. It was only too apparent that the move had been dictated in the hope of winning further recognition from the administration.

The "national" Conservative convention held by *laureanistas* in June emphasized the irreconcilable Conservative division. Renewing his efforts to strengthen control, Gómez circulated through his directorate a letter calling for the adoption of a social-economic program. It stated Gómez' basic insistence that party interests should be set aside completely until the government had restored a full measure of economic and political stability. Noting Gómez' firm approval of administration policies, the letter discussed the role of the parties in the democratic experiment. It was held that bipartisan government was not diluting Liberal and Conservative doctrines. Rather, it was drawing upon the best of each party's doctrines in formulating a truly national policy during the sixteen years of bipartisanship. By 1974, both parties would return to a full and partisan advocacy of all their traditional beliefs. Conservatives were urged to adopt a general plan dealing with land redistribution, education, increased production, and electrical expansion. Significantly, there was no discussion of the problem of rival factions within either traditional collectivity. Yet this was one of the government's greatest difficulties in making the experimental system work.[1]

The *laureanista* circular brought a further strengthening of its position, and several influential Conservatives changed allegiances. Even the Leyva directorate, despite its opposition to the government, declared that the *laureanistas* appeared more responsible than the *ospinistas*. Leyva was, at the time, spending five days at home under police guard for his refusal to testify before the Senate in connection with the Rojas Pinilla case.

As Congress opened, the Frente Nacional was hampered by opposition from Conservative factions, now including the *ospinistas*. Amid a variety of problems, two issues stood out. The first was proposed modification of constitutional Article 121, which would limit executive power during any state of siege. The second dealt with the principle of *alternación* which, although approved by the people in the 1957 plebiscite, had not yet been ratified by Congress.

Despite the government's comparative strength, the adoption of neither measure was assured, for a two-thirds vote was required, and dissidents could block any proposed reform by uniting in opposition. Revision of Article 121 was intended to prevent any future president from assuming virtual dictatorship under the provisions of a state of siege. The modification would require that Congress be called into session immediately after any executive declaration of emergency rule. It would meet daily until the restoration of civil guarantees, and executive decrees with which it disagreed would be sent to the Supreme Court for judgment.[2] Existing rules stated that the president could decree martial law only after promising not to reverse previous legislation and to call a legislative session *when possible*. But the experience with Ospina Pérez in 1949 proved that this was no effective check on executive rule by decree, for in that instance he had forced the legislature to recess and never called them back.

Discussion was intermittent for several weeks, and renewed political activity postponed a decision, although as early as September there had been preliminary approval from both parties. The proposal was ultimately held for "further consideration," effectively shelved for the duration of the congressional session. The *alternación* bill, however, stirred up more trouble before the government finally won. Opinion was clearly divided, and politicians felt strongly about it one way or the other. Along with political *paridad, alternación* was the basic principle upon which the government was operating, and ratification was necessary or the entire Frente Nacional movement would have collapsed.

The government worked arduously to gain approval, while Laureano Gómez exerted all his influence in its behalf. He warned that opposition to *alternación* was tantamount to calling for a rebirth of ideals and practices "destined to reestablish dictatorship, destroy the peace, and disturb the era of greatness standing open before Colombia."[3] On the political level, Gómez was also understood to believe that a convincing victory on this issue would strengthen his hold on the Conservative party, enabling him to increase his majority in the March, 1960, congressional elections.

Major opposition came from *ospinista* Conservatives and a new Liberal faction led by Alfonso López Michelsen, the son of the former president. López Michelsen led the public campaign against *alternación* for several weeks,[4] arguing that, with the Conservatives obviously the minority party, Liberals should not be expected to turn over the presidency in 1962.[5] This, of course, was a form of political opportunism based upon the desire for a return to partisan politics.

Congressional opposition was led by the *ospinistas,* who argued that alternation would prevent a full exercise of democratic rights for sixteen years, thus leading to the selection of presidents through the operation of party discipline and the dictates of political leaders. The point was well taken in view of the dissident ability to prevent a two-thirds vote on any issues about which the minority factions could agree. At the same time, the advocates of the Frente Nacional had long recognized and accepted the fact that it was operating on the basis of a controlled democracy. Full-fledged exercise of democratic political rights should not be trusted, it was felt, until completion of the extended period of national recovery. Congressional deliberations turned for a time to a variety of less important matters, but in September a final vote was taken, and the legislators approved ratification of *alternación*. The amendment was accepted and attached to the federal constitution.[6]

September was marked by further Conservative activities. On September 19 and 20 the *laureanistas* held another gathering at which minority elements were defeated on every issue. The *ospinistas* and *alzatistas* tentatively agreed for the first time to select a joint directorate under which they would make a renewed effort to oust Dr. Gómez, but they were thwarted in their efforts to include the other two party factions. Valencia refused to accept their opposition to the Frente Nacional, although he voiced personal misgivings as to some of the administration's methods. The self-styled "independents" of Jorge Leyva also refused to cooperate, even though they were firm in their opposition to Gómez. Leyva feared that an alliance with the more numerous *ospinistas* and *alzatistas* would leave him without the opportunity to voice his own independent views.

Undaunted as always by opposition, Laureano Gómez continued on his own, praising both the administration and what he called the faithful adherence of the Liberals to the bipartisan pact. In October the old man suddenly delivered a blow that shook the government and provoked nation-wide political dispute. Speaking before more than a thousand loyal *laureanistas,* he attacked the Corte Suprema de Justicia as "infamous" and "prevaricating." He refused to take further part in political duties until action was taken to remove the national seat of "miserable jurisprudence."[7]

His violent outburst, almost ten years following a similar attack on that court in the fall of 1949, was provoked by a decision in a libel case involving one of his sons, Enrique Gómez Hurtado. The editor of *El Siglo,* Enrique had brought suit against *ospinista* Silvio Villegas, editor of *La República,* which opposed the Frente Nacional. Feeling had already been strong, for Villegas had at one time been an effective member of Laureano's political machine. The episode was triggered by a *La República* charge that Enrique Gómez Hurtado had used government influence for commercial purposes. Enrique took the matter to the courts, and when *La República* could provide inadequate proof of its charges, Villegas was found guilty of libel.

Villegas in turn carried the case to the Supreme Court, where the decision was in effect reversed on a technicality. The court upheld the other decision in finding the newspaper guilty of libel but ruled that Villegas himself had not been directly involved, thus could not be held guilty. The ruling was legally correct, and seemingly called for a new suit against the individual responsible for the story itself, Efraín Motatto Avalos. Dr. Gómez, however, preferred to attack the court itself. In effect, he raged, the highest court of the republic had ruled that a crime had been committed yet refused to criticize or punish the man ultimately responsible. How, he asked, could the highest legal body refuse to punish crimes it admitted had taken place?[8]

Such were the pressures brought to bear that five of the ten Conservative justices—all *laureanistas*—submitted their resignations. Congress also began to discuss the issue, although many Liberals found the process of interfering with the judiciary distasteful. In the latter part of the month the administration appointed a two-man committee to draw up effective judicial reform removing it from political influence. Previously, the twenty magistrates had been nominated by the executive and elected by the legislature. The new plan, which required another constitutional amendment, gave the president ultimate authority. The court itself would select candidates for appointment, submitting the list to Congress where one third of the names would be eliminated; the chief executive would then make his choices from the remaining names. Terms would extend for eighteen years, with the body being partially renewed every six years.[9]

There was some protest in Liberal ranks, and Darío Echandía even offered to resign as party leader, a measure which was answered by a strong vote of confidence. The dispute became so caught up in political controversy, however, that no further action had been taken by the end of the congressional session on December 16. There were warnings that a special session might be called to consider the matter in January, 1960, but post-holiday campaigning for the March elections was so active that the session was postponed, with the issue of judicial reform still hanging fire.

The final months of 1959 saw an increase of political activity, with the congressional session providing an ideal sounding board for speeches and declarations. The newly-formed *alza-ospinista* Conservative element continued to drive for power and was increasingly subject to the criticism that political opportunism was dictating its policies. In late October it held a new gathering at which Gómez' methods were criticized.

This meeting marked the end of the loose affiliation between Guillermo León Valencia and the *ospinistas*. When the meeting adopted resolutions which did not clearly praise bipartisan government, Valencia rose to deliver a speech of protest. He was denied the right to speak and immediately walked out of the hall, followed by a handful of supporters. He later read the same speech on the Senate floor, speaking of his personal friendship with Ospina Pérez but criticizing the presence of scattered former *rojistas*; Valencia also feared the influence of Gilberto Alzate Avendaño, whom he strongly mistrusted.[10]   Alzate Avendaño in the meantime had been asserting himself with characteristic force within the councils of the *alza-ospinista* alliance.

In November this new group, which posed a serious threat to Gómez' Conservative dominance, released a manifesto attacking the government for violating the original bipartisan agreement in two ways. First, the selection of a Liberal rather than Conservative president was criticized; second, the administration was accused of excluding minority representatives from appointments. This latter charge was totally in error, for Lleras Camargo had done everything possible to deal justly with the warring Conservative factions.

The constant political in-fighting and maneuvering among Conservative factions continued until the brief respite brought by the holiday season. Preparations were being made for the critical March elections. At the same time, the Liberals were also showing a division of opinion, although their disagreement was far less confused and bitter than that of the Conservatives. Until mid-1959 the party had been rather quiet, while Carlos Lleras Restrepo continued to strengthen its local units behind the scenes. Suddenly Lleras Restrepo dropped out of politics for personal reasons, withdrawing from the Senate to leave on an extended European trip. He was replaced by Darío Echandía, who in August of 1958 had been elected *designado* with the support of majorities of both parties in the Congress.[11]

The only real Liberal disagreement came from a small minority known as the Unión Popular Nacional (UPN), organized and directed by Alfonso López Michelsen. Its directorate was formed by López Michelsen, Alfonso Barberena, and Juan de la Cruz Varela. Essentially a leftist branch of the party, the UPN espoused somewhat radical reformism not unlike that once advocated by Jorge Gaitán, whose spectre still hung over national politics to some degree. Although the UPN directorate claimed that it was but a group trying to influence the adoption of a new Liberal policy for economic and social development, it seemed most interested in propagandizing beliefs while increasing its strength within the party.

By the close of 1959, then, various factions within both traditional parties were girding themselves for the forthcoming elections. Several different issues were to be contested, all of which made the vote one of the most significant in contemporary Colombian affairs. It remained for the Colombian people to give expression to their wishes.

THE CONGRESSIONAL CAMPAIGN

With elections foremost in their minds, the various factions proceeded to set forth their views. The tone had already been established by Lleras Camargo in early November when he welcomed the participation of all elements but urged them to explain their programs fully. Declaring that the public had a right to know exactly what was proposed, particularly by those opposing the government, he called for responsible campaigning on issues rather than personalities. Further, he welcomed the opportunity for an electoral restatement of the decision expressed in the 1957 plebiscite regarding the party truce.[12]

The Conservative intra-party struggle began in earnest even before the close of the year, and the *laureanistas* based their campaign upon the defense of the Frente Nacional. Efforts were launched with a Bogotá banquet on December 10, where Alvaro Gómez Hurtado and others appealed for continuing support of the administration. Citing the recovery of the economy and the stabilization of national life, the *laureanistas* declared that only they could properly represent the Conservatives in the bipartisan system. As Belisario Betancourt said in a campaign address, "We demand the vote because we have the certainty that to elevate the people's level of living is required. . . ."[13] Furthermore, a vote against Dr. Gómez would be tantamount to rejection of the Lleras Camargo administration.

The majority faction looked for its greatest strength in rural areas, where approval of the Frente Nacional was firmly established through the reduction of banditry. Optimism was further strengthened by the belief that neither Ospina Pérez nor Alzate Avendaño would be effective campaigners in the provinces. Ospina Pérez had never been particularly adept in communicating with the masses, while Alzate Avendaño had been espousing his own individual brand of reform in rather intellectual terms, which made his appeal seem slight outside the population centers.[14]

However, such calculations proved somewhat inaccurate. The *alza-ospinista* front, despite its earlier trips to the well of opportunism, was gradually acquiring new strength. The prestige of Mariano Ospina Pérez had never been higher. Remaining in the background following Lleras Camargo's inauguration, he had avoided erosion of support through public exposure, such as Dr. Gómez had been experiencing. He was further strengthened by the increasing desertions which were riddling the already small *leyvista* group, for most of the defectors were opposed to Gómez and had joined the *alza-ospinistas*.

Dissident Conservatives consistently drew larger crowds than their opponents, and they were hard at work on the local level. Their emphasis on rural campaigning reflected the decision to meet Gómez on his own ground, where the *laureanistas* had least expected a challenge. Both Ospina Pérez and his rather improbable ally participated actively, and their attacks on Gómez were virulent. Jorge Leyva was also busy in the provinces, although few paid him much attention.[15] Conservative sympathy gradually shifted toward Ospina Pérez as the result of his personal campaigning. With unlimited funds at his disposal, the sixty-nine-year-old former president proved most effective.

Never having entered politics seriously before his 1946 election, Ospina Pérez had enjoyed limited party support during his presidency, partly because of an unusual succession of upsets. His years out of office had given him increased stature in the eyes of the public; it was almost as if a revered elder statesman had suddenly reappeared. The errors of his presidency were forgotten, while efforts to fight the repressions of Gómez in 1953 and Rojas Pinilla in 1957 were fresher in many minds. Never an eloquent orator, Ospina Pérez shone as an improviser at informal gatherings, and he had become much more adept at political tactics. His striking personal appearance, which Dr. Gómez had scornfully called "the elegant silhouette of the financier," added to his impact on the *campesinos*.[16]

Ospina Pérez was supported by clearly defined groups. Many veteran Conservative politicians joined his cause rather than subordinating themselves to Gómez direction. The oligarchy, of which Ospina Pérez was more representative than Gómez, favored his bid for Conservative power. His credentials could scarcely have been better, and the wealthy coffee growers, in particular, backed Ospina Pérez. He provided a clearly preferable alternative to Lleras Camargo's pro-labor social reform, which they regarded with mistrust. Certainly Ospina Pérez' agricultural, banking, and money policies were in accord with their own interests.[17]

As elections neared, the story of the Conservative campaign was increasingly that of the *alza-ospinistas*. Opposition to Gómez' cooperative efforts with the Liberals, which had already been registered in the vote for Leyva's presidential candidacy in May, 1958, increased among the hard core of conservatism. The increased tempo of the dissident campaign struck repeatedly at Gómez' accomodation of the rival Liberals. Its effort to wrest Conservative control from Gómez was based in essence upon a premise that would have been unthinkable only a few years earlier. Laureano, throughout his lengthy career, had remained first and foremost the indomitable *caudillo* of the right to whom traditional elements of the party clung approvingly. But the remarkable change of orientation which Gómez took following his return from exile had not been understood or accepted by many doctrinaire Conservatives.

Notwithstanding the years of intransigent reactionary Conservatism, Gómez was first a patriotic Colombian, and he was too astute not to realize in 1957 that the Lleras Camargo bipartisan agreement was necessary. There was no other means by which the country might rebound from the extremism which had reached its zenith under military dictatorship. Thus his immense political talents had turned to full support of and collaboration with Alberto Lleras Camargo and the Liberals. In the 1960 campaign, his opponents recognized the erosion of his prestige within the party and played the issue to the hilt.[18]

The embattled *alza-ospinistas* were aided by a surprising apathy on the part of Dr. Gómez. Even allowing for limitations imposed by the infirmities of age and recurrent heart trouble, there was considerable surprise when Laureano took little part in the campaign. Certainly this was in direct contrast to his forty-year career of political struggle; it seems best explained by his realization that his popularity had been seriously damaged by the necessary collaboration with the government. Whether he may have anticipated this when making his basic choice to support the Frente Nacional is not really important. Without his approval the bipartisan plan would have been doomed before it began. Indeed, its successes could be attributed more to Gómez than anyone else, excepting only Lleras Camargo.

Gómez defended his collaboration with the declaration that the return of peace and democracy had demanded support of the Frente Nacional, and he made no apologies for his personal role. With more than a little pride, he defied his opponents to imagine what disasters might have been visited on the republic in the absence of such an agreement. He warned that support of Ospina Pérez meant a return to one-party hegemony and the deadly political rivalries from which death and deprivation had stemmed.[19]

Observers felt that Gómez' control of the Chamber was not endangered but that his margin would be substantially reduced. Gómez stated that a significant loss in strength would provoke his resignation, for he refused to play a minority role within his party. "Any retrocession in the results which we might interpret as discrediting [our] leadership . . . would leave the party no choice but to grant me desired permission to rest from my labors."[20]

Disunity on the Liberal side was less extreme, but the small leftist faction of Alfonso López Michelsen had become vocal as the campaign unfolded. Unlike the sons of Laureano Gómez, the younger López had not followed his father into politics but had pursued a career as a writer and professor. Only in 1958 did he enter politics at the age of forty-five, declaring his opposition to *alternación*.[21] Calling for a *"recuperación liberal,"* López Michelsen accepted the thesis of divided government but refused to accept a Conservative as the 1962 president. Following his return to Bogotá in November after the death of his illustrious father in England, he planned a convention for January at which *alfonsistas,* as his followers were called, praised the benefits of the Frente Nacional while criticizing the operation of both *paridad* and *alternación*.

The *alfonsista* convention adopted a motto of *"salud, educación y techo,"* and its convention set forth a plan suggesting virtual socialization in these areas of health, education, and housing. Budgets were to be modified so that greater resources would flow into a national development program. New agricultural and property taxes were proposed, and a pro-labor outlook was adopted, which included the legalization of strikes in the public services.[22] The general orientation of the faction was similar to that of Gaitán, as indicated earlier, and called for policies generally to the left of the administration.

The brilliant López Michelsen, whose reputation as a writer was based in part upon his widely-praised *Los Elegidos* in 1955, was a progressive and a reformer, but not essentially a true revolutionary.[23] He represented social and administrative reforms which fell short of a transformation, yet proposed to move more swiftly than the Lleras Camargo government. López himself explained that he intended to restore a popular and autonomous character to the party. He reiterated his fear that a Conservative president, while that party was supported by a minority of the voters, would be a national misfortune.

As *Semana* observed, this represented an effort to return to a forceful, dynamic "popular liberalism" requiring a charismatic leader of the Gaitán stripe. Yet López Michelsen was a very different type of person; his campaigning was an attempted resurrection of his father's political style, but it often failed to strike fire.[24] In arguing that he would adopt more effective reforms as swiftly as possible, however, he aroused the interest of his listeners. The increasing impatience of the masses for reform found a ready outlet in *alfonsismo*. The faction was faced with a campaign task of overcoming suspicions of political opportunism, and it is fair to say that the dissidents were, on the whole, sincerely and patriotically wedded to their declarations. Although Echandía and the National Liberal Directorate tended to underrate the new movement, it profited by a strong appeal to Liberal sympathies. Not only was there a call for more progressive action, but there was the constant reminder that the Conservatives, once awarded the presidency, might renounce the Frente Nacional and restore their hegemony to national government.

In January, 1960, the Liberal division became more noticeable when Gloria Gaitán de Valencia, daughter of the assassinated Liberal, announced with her husband an attempt to revive *gaitanismo*. The announcement was received calmly but gave a further indication of discontent with national Liberal leadership. She denied any affiliation with López Michelsen, although her denunciation of the party for turning its back on the principles of true liberalism sounded rather similar. Further dissension was aroused by a dispute between party leader Echandía and Juan Lozano y Lozano, an independent-minded Liberal whose political commentaries were widely-read in the columns of different publications.

Lozano y Lozano had been chosen unanimously by a departmental convention in Tolima to lead its slate of candidates. When he refused to give an unconditional promise to maintain liberalism within the framework of the Frente Nacional, however, Echandía chose to crack the whip of party discipline by peremptorily striking his name from the Tolima slate. Lozano y Lozano reacted by presenting his own Tolima candidates as an alternative to regular Liberals, and the politically inactive Carlos Lleras Restrepo, Echandía's former colleague and friend, delivered a strong denunciation of the Echandía leadership. The latter further aroused opposition by permitting the candidacies of influential members of the press, although working newspapermen had traditionally stood outside that form of political participation. Both miscalculations were to cost the party. The experienced Echandía should have known better.

For a full three months the campaign swept back and forth across Colombia. At stake were the 152 seats in the Chamber of Representatives, as well as all the bipartisan *colegiado* bodies in the 16 departments and 890 municipalities. More than 5,000 Colombians would be elected to office.[25] Several issues were being contested. Within the parties, the important question was the extent of the popular appeal of dissident groups. For the Conservatives it was a matter of whether leadership could be won away from Dr. Gómez. As already suggested, prospects seemed good for a resurgence of the *alza-ospinistas*, although the faction was not expected to overcome the Gómez Chamber majority, and control of the Senate was not at stake. The major issue seemed to be whether or not the dissidents might increase their strength to the extent of bringing about Dr. Gómez' threatened resignation as party leader.

The Ospina Pérez—Alzate Avendaño alliance, along with the loss of ground by Jorge Leyva, helped to clarify the confused Conservative picture, with only two groups showing any real strength. The national significance of the struggle was the question of which faction would name the 1962 Conservative president and who would work with Lleras Camargo. Members of the government feared a possible replacement of Dr. Gómez, for he had worked easily with Liberals within the administration. The strength of Liberal dissidents was also watched with interest. While there was no possibility that López Michelsen might win control from the party regulars, any sizeable demonstration of *alfonsista* popularity would be a severe affront to the Echandía leadership.

Beyond such questions of factional control, the issue was one of popular satisfaction with the Frente Nacional.[26] Adherents of the government hoped for a renewed vote of confidence and were anxious about the showing of *laureanista* Conservatives.[27] Despite the atmosphere of general conciliation throughout the republic, the divergencies of approach and emphasis would be decided at least temporarily by election results. A somewhat apathetic public response to the campaign suggested a diminishing interest in personal appeals and the attractions of political personalities. Typical of a certain disillusionment with personal oratory and empty promises was the formation of a Frente Boyacense in that department which called for concrete programs rather than political opportunism.[28] *Semana* went so far as to suggest a wide abstention on election day. Whatever the outcome, political leaders were keenly aware of the high stakes involved.

Elections Demolish the Status Quo

Official preparation for elections was directed at the maintenance of public order, and Alberto Lleras Camargo took all possible measures to insure the unfettered exercise of the vote. In January he met with Minister of Government Jorge Enrique Gutiérrez Anzola and departmental governors to make arrangements for avoiding any form of official partiality. The president was determined to hold to a completely democratic and honest electoral procedure. A month later he conferred with Minister of War Rafael Hernández Pardo and commanders of the eight military brigades to clarify beyond question the military responsibility for the maintenance of peace, official nonintervention, and the avoidance of coercion in any form.[29]

The administration held itself aloof from the campaign, other than urging a large turnout to express confidence in the bipartisan pact. In his one speech during the course of the campaigning, Lleras Camargo declared that the full sixteen-year period of bipartisanship was required before Colombia returned to fall party activity.

The Frente Nacional, constitutionally and politically, is not conceived as an adventure of four years, but as a long and glorious chapter in the history of Colombia. . . .

Sectarianism of government parties, which has been eliminated as a pest to our political life—although perfectly acceptable institutions in countries of high civic cultures—has the fault [in Colombia] of creating the habit of trusting to persuasion or direct political action on the people, in the support of the *official* machinery . . . calculated to destroy all possibility of free competence to its adversaries. . . . The country has resolved to end this form of slavery, but present political conduct nevertheless harkens back to its old antecedent.[30]

The maintenance of public order through the campaign, a testimony to the effectiveness of government authority, concluded with Lleras Camargo's election-eve appeal for a serene example of suffrage which would be an "unequivocal demonstration that the people can govern in Colombia."[31] On Sunday, March 20, 1960, the people responded with the calmest and most peaceful election day in history. Returns were even slower than usual in being counted, and on Sunday night the only substantial reports came from Bogotá, where an early tally found the Liberals leading and the two major Conservative factions running a close race.[32] On Monday morning, however, Colombia awoke to a series of unexpected and widely significant results which called for a complete re-evaluation of the political picture.

Pre-election calculations were rudely upset as the complacency of majority party leaders was shaken to its very roots. To begin with, the *alza-ospinistas* won a smashing victory over Laureano Gómez. For the first time in his career, the *caudillo* of the Conservatives had been clearly repudiated by his party. His majority, rather than being reduced, was wiped out, with the dissident forces winning thirty-eight seats in the Chamber to thirty-seven for the *laureanistas*. Only one candidate from the Leyva slate won office.[33] The final count showed the Ospina Pérez— Alzate Avendaño duo winning 53 per cent of the party vote, Gómez taking 42 per cent, and Leyva the remaining 5.[34]

In the Liberal contest, dissident strength also exceeded the predictions of even the most sanguine *alfonsistas*. The forces of López Michelsen won 20 per cent of the Liberal vote and captured fourteen of the seventy-six party seats, the other sixty-two accruing to the official Liberal slate.[35] The Liberals easily outpolled the Conservatives in their national contest, but both parties registered a 40 per cent reduction in their totals from the levels registered in the 1958 congressional elections. This reflected a third major electoral development, for extensive abstention was the most striking feature of all the unexpected results.

Of an estimated 6,725,000 eligible voters, only 4,400,000 had taken the trouble to register; of these, 2,200,000 cast their votes. Voter abstention had been virtually 50 per cent.[36] This climaxed a trend toward abstention that had been growing ever since the return of free elections. The December, 1957, plebiscite had attracted 4,400,000 voters; the March, 1958, congressional voting registered 3,600,000 valid ballots; the May, 1958, presidential returns were 3,100,000; on this occasion only 2,200,000 filled out their ballots.[37] The diminishing returns had been easily explainable until 1960. The historic significance of the 1957 plebiscite had created greater interest than congressional elections. Presidential balloting was lighter with Lleras Camargo virtually unopposed. However, the 1960 abstention was less facilely explained. Election post-mortems were, without exception, groping for explanations.

The strength of party dissidents was apparent. Feeling was growing that politicians of the majority groups were envisioning a gradual return to earlier conditions, rather than working for true and lasting national reform. This resulted in a general turning away from traditional leadership. The Conservative rejection of Dr. Gómez resulted from factors suggested above, of which the most important was the feeling that he had yielded too many concessions in working with the administration. The surprising showing of the Liberal dissidents testified to the lasting appeal of *gaitanista* formulas to the masses, an appeal which had gained additional impetus from tactical miscalculations on the part of Darío Echandía.

But it was the abstentionist bombshell that most confounded commentators. There were some, including a few members of the government, who considered the small turnout a direct blow at the prestige of the Frente Nacional. Juan Lozano y Lozano felt that "the colossal abstention is a severe vote of censorship to the government."[38] From obscurity the croaking voice of Gustavo Rojas Pinilla claimed that the abstention combined with *ospinista* success signified the correctness of his own former policies. He told *El Siglo* that "the electoral triumph . . . is mine, especially since in the victorious [Conservative] lists are my ministers and many friends. . . ."[39] There was no official comment, although an unidentified member of the administration declared that the situation was in a state of flux, adding that the government was challenged by circumstances created by the results.[40]

The best interpretation of the abstention suggested less a public apathy than a broad demand for a more vigorous pursuit of reforms through the instrumentality of the bipartisan arrangement. The astute Gonzalo Restrepo Jaramillo, until recently an advocate of Valencia, said that the abstentionists were in effect "asking for a return to the truth."[41] The abstention was not a significant protest against Lleras Camargo and his system—indeed, the president had received virtually no criticism during the three-month campaign. The public was seeking to express its desire for greater seriousness and political responsibility on all levels.

There was no little fear that the evolution of reform was being stalled through the political machinations and personal ambitions of political leaders, presaging a likely return to former political ways. The people were especially concerned with the selection of new and younger men to implement a true and effective reform. The uncommitted middle sector of the voters, a floating group without close ties to either party, had felt impelled to abstain even in the face of Lleras Camargo's call to the polls. The depth of feeling was suggested by the pride with which many abstainers displayed their clean, un-inked fingers. It was worth noting that the enthusiastic abstainers in the cities included many of the university students, who had been ardent supporters of the Frente Nacional and continued to admire Lleras Camargo. As *Semana* said, many of those who abstained appeared more *llerista* than Lleras Camargo himself.[42]

The over-all picture, then, projected the desire of the people to continue the movement away from the political history of the recent past. This is further examined in the next chapter. As for the immediate practical results of the startling voting, events had turned the political scene upside down. The defeat of Dr. Gómez brought a swift rash of resignations by *laureanista* members of the government. The loss of majority control made replacement by *alza-ospinistas* inevitable. On Tuesday, March 22, Laureano Gómez accepted defeat in a document declaring that the election signified a renunciation of his leadership. Elections meant that his brand of Conservatism "can direct only a group, not represent the whole party. Thus we must withdraw."[43] Rejecting suggestions of reaching a compromise with the victors, he emphasized continuing adherence to the bipartisan plan, which remained "the best thing for Colombia."[44] His statement released his followers, leaving them at liberty to follow whatever leadership they chose.

Before the close of the week the *laureanista* offices were shut down; yet many were reluctant to accept Dr. Gómez' decision, preferring to fight on. With their majority still intact in the Senate, there was a feeling that the battle was over, but not the war. *Laureanista* Minister of Government Jorge Enrique Gutiérrez Anzola claimed that the *alza-ospinistas* were not representative of a national Conservative consensus, and he argued for a special all-Conservative plebiscite, an extraordinary proposal which received little support.

A better assessment came from another *laureanista* cabinet member, Minister of Mines Alfredo Araújo Grau, who conceded that voters had taken responsibility for the party from Gómez but had not vested it in anyone else.[45] But for the retirement of Dr. Gómez, a bitter and divisive struggle might have been conducted over an extended period. His voluntary renunciation of power cast immediate responsibility into the laps of Ospina Pérez and Alzate Avendaño, almost by default. Ospina Pérez, who had hailed the results as giving him power to join the administration in forming a truly "authentic" Frente Nacional, immediately issued a call for all Conservatives to give up their personals "isms" and to accept his leadership for the formation of a unified, cohesive Conservative party. It remained for the elements to reconcile their disagreements on such matters as court reform and revision of presidential powers under a state of siege. More than mere personality differences were involved.

On March 28, Ospina Pérez and Alzate Avendaño set up as headquarters a new *"casa conservadora"* in Bogotá. A three-man directorate included Eliseo Arango and the two architects of the triumph over Gómez.[46] The latter two met with President Lleras Camargo on the thirtieth and for more than two hours discussed necessary tasks of reorganizing the government. Economic and social problems also received attention. The new Conservative leadership promised support of bipartisan government, believing the Frente Nacional necessary for continued stability and order. Showing greater responsibility than had been evident in political maneuvering during the preceding months, they agreed upon the necessity for close understanding with the Liberals. It was agreed to freeze the *status quo* temporarily, until Lleras Camargo returned to Colombia from a visit of state to the United States and Canada, at which time he would meet to discuss the necessary readjustment of government structure.[47] The cabinet, which had resigned following elections, was also retained until the president's return.

With Gómez defeated largely because of his support of national conciliation, the two who had engineered the event now committed themselves to a similar effort; they were now in a position to decide the future of the Conservative president in 1962, pending agreement of the Liberals.[48] As for the Liberals, new direction was indicated with the resignation of Darío Echandía in the wage of the disappointing Liberal effort. Withdrawing from party affairs "for a rest," he named a five-member committee to direct the party pending a national convention. Its most influential members were Jorge Uribe Márquez and Adán Arriaga Andrade. Interestingly, one of the five was a woman—Carmenza Rocha[49]—a sidelight which further testified to the gradual political transformation. The exultant López Michelsen, in the meantime, refused to enter either the government or a new Liberal directorate and cited returns as proof that the day of the oligarch was nearing an end.

The March elections had so confounded the previous political *status quo* that the following weeks were filled with confusion. The voice of the people dictated sweeping political re-evaluations. For those who interpreted the popular will with the greatest perception, the reward would be national leadership in the challenging years just ahead.

Chapter Eighteen

TOWARD A NEW COLOMBIA

As THE BIPARTISAN government passed through its second year and then entered 1961, there were both favorable and unfavorable hints of what the future might hold. Economic progress was noted in various sectors, and the extremism of the 1940's seemed less characteristic under the experimental governmental arangement. At the same time, a growing dynamism marked the interplay of social and political forces, and responsible authorities were confronted with renewed demands for progress and reform.

LLERAS CAMARGO AND AN EXPANDING ECONOMY

In late 1959 and 1960 the administration turned increasingly to economic and social measures. Through a substantial improvement in its credit rating, Colombia presented an enlarged but balanced budget for 1960. It called for a total expenditure of 1,891,000 pesos, some 90,000,000 above the 1959 budget. The Ministry of Public Works received 20 per cent, Finance 19, War 17, Education 10, and Public Health 5 per cent. Over 60,000,000 pesos were allotted for rural rehabilitation and pacification, while a bond issue of 200,000,000 was issued for development projects including railway and highway construction, shipping, and air facilities.

Restoration of credit permitted the administration to seek further loans abroad. By September, 1959, the debt to North American exporters had been cancelled, while obligations elsewhere totaled $207,000,000, of which $129,000,000 was owed the Export-Import Bank. Jorge Franco Holguín, youthful director of the National Planning Department, impressed bankers favorably during a visit to the United States, where he arranged further financing of industrial expansion by $103,000,000.[1] The Export-Import Bank granted a $25,000,000 credit to the Banco de la República for maintenance of the flow of basic imports from the United States, and the International Monetary Fund provided a $41,250,000 standby credit agreement to help stabilize the exchange market.

Continued controls through 1959 maintained a favorable balance of trade, and imports were held to $28,000,000 a month until the final ninety days of the year. In 1960 the government further reduced the supply of dollars available to importers, planning to limit monthly imports to $30,000,000.[2] Broad economic progress during the year permitted an increase of imports, although the monthly average reached $34,000,000 by September, 1960, leading to an unfavorable balance of trade.[3] Controls were tightened once more, and by the end of 1960 the monthly average for the year was down to $32,000,000.[4]

National fiscal affairs received further impetus in August, 1960, when a mission headed by North American Ambassador Dempster McIntosh and Planning Director Franco Holguín negotiated two loans totaling $70,000,000. The Export-Import Bank authorized further credits of $45,000,000, a major portion of which would purchase United States equipment and machinery for a dozen penetration roads to five new colonization areas. Additional credits for $25,000,000 from the new Development Loan Fund underwrote local expenditures on the twelve roads, as well as providing financial support for the five-year program designed to resettle some 50,000 in designated "colonization" areas. In November the International Monetary Fund also granted Colombia a stand-by fund of $75,000,000 for a twelve-month period ending in November, 1960.[5] The previous year's fund of $41,250,000 had not been called upon.

With fiscal underpinnings strengthened, the agricultural sector also advanced from 1959. Signing of a new International Coffee Pact in Washington in August, 1959, set the Colombian quota at 5,959,000 bags. Two months later the twenty-first annual convention of the Federación Nacional de Cafeteros Colombianos declared support of the pact. There was sentiment for the elimination of existing taxes on coffee exports, but the FNCC limited itself to a request for official assurance of continued market stability plus generous credit.

The close of the 1959 marketing year in September showed a substantial rise in coffee exports. Sales totaled 6,543,493 bags as compared with some 5,000,000 bags in 1958. An estimated 4,500,000 bags were held in storage. By the end of the calendar year, export data showed that coffee income still provided nearly 80 per cent of the foreign exchange. Prices averaged but 45.22 cents per pounds as compared with the 1958 average of 52.34 cents. However, the quota agreement had permitted increased sales, and there was an over-all 17 per cent increase.[6]

However, 1960 proved less successful, as coffee moved sluggishly throughout the year. By September, there was a decline, of 12 per cent from 1959. Exports fell 297,829 bags short of the national quota because of a mediocre crop year and problems of port congestion. *Hispanic American Report* quoted coffee authority Pedro Bernal as saying that the Colombian desire to maintain sales prices at all costs had been translated into increased North American purchases of cheaper African coffee.[7] Colombia's estimated $500,000,000 investment in coffee was such that a drop of one cent per pound meant a loss of $8,000,000 in exchange earnings. Diversification remained urgent if the over-all economy were to become more stable.

Diversification was moving slowly, although particular encouragement came from a significant rise in cotton. The 1959 production more than doubled, rising to 65,000 metric tons from 1958's 28,000 tons, when 8,000 tons were imported.[8] By December 1959, 100 tons of surplus cotton were sold to Europe, and the 1960 surplus was scheduled for shipment to Japan. The Instituto Nacional Algodonero estimated a surplus of 10,000 in the first six months of 1960. The increased supply also permitted expansion of processing plants, and import licenses were issued for textile factory machinery. Cotton consumption in the processing plants had already risen 8.6 per cent in 1959, and 1960 production rose an additional 10 per cent.[9]

In the first half of 1960, as events developed, national production permitted the export of 6500 tons, and by the year's end nearly 20,000 tons had been shipped abroad, netting an estimated $9,000,000 in foreign exchange. With cotton becoming of increasing economic importance, the Instituto Nactional Algodonero and the Federación de Algodoneros established an export fund to cover possible losses incurred from selling at low world market prices. Each organization contributed the equivalent of 80 pesos per ton.[10]

Bananas also brought increased income, and a general surge was strengthened in mid-1960 when the national subsidiary of the United Fruit Company, the Sevilla Fruit Company, bought 20,000 hectares of land near the Caribbean port of Turbo. Turbo was considered relatively free from the seasonal hurricanes which through the years had brought substantial losses to the Santa Marta plantations. United Fruit, in keeping with its new hemispheric policy, contracted for fruit grown in the area by private planters.

Petroleum production also brought additional exchange dollars. A record average of 159,343 barrels daily was set in August, 1959, with the Cicuco field alone increasing its average by 15,000 barrels. Cities Service reported a new producing well in El Carare, and the Shell Oil Company found commercial oil in western Antioquia. Completion of the Cartagena refinery made the republic self-sufficient in oil for the first time, although it was still necessary to import aviation gas and special lubricants. This translated into an annual saving of $18 million.

The daily average for 1959 rose to 146,000 barrels, 18,000 above 1958. There was a 15 per cent increase in the region of exploitation as a dozen companies signed agreements with the government. In reversing past policies, the administration encouraged exploration by foreign firms. Already second only to Venezuela in Latin American production, Colombia hoped to increase its importance as an international producer. The lower Magdalena Valley was of particular interest although foreign enterprises warned that no great increase in commercial production could be expected for at least two years.[11]

Development and exploration continued. In September, 1960, the minister of mines and petroleum reported to Congress that government-owned ECOPETROL had drilled thirty-seven new wells and expected to double the quantity of natural gas. Construction of new storage tanks was scheduled, and 1961 improvements on the Barrancabermeja refinery permitted ECOPETROL to meet all domestic demands for aviation gasoline and lubricants, saving an additional $2,000,000 in foreign exchange annually. By the end of 1960 the government reported the year's average as 7 per cent above 1959, nearly 50 per cent over production in 1955. Some $46,000,000 came into the coffers from petroleum exports. Furthermore, "planned developments in the oil industry and in the petrochemical industry were expected to add substantially to the growing importance of Colombia's oil and oil products in the global exchange market."[12]

Industrial development moved erratically; encouraging signs came from the Paz del Río steel mill, long an uneconomic operation. It had incurred many of the difficulties predicted by the Currie Mission in 1950 but by 1959 was nearing full production. Figures showed a 61 per cent gain by the end of the year, and Colombian steel imports fell to 150,000 tons. By the end of 1960 production had doubled that of 1959,[13] and the nation hoped soon to eliminate all steel imports. At the same time the first zinc factory opened, and the government signed a contract for development of the El Cerrejón coal deposits in Goajira, which had a known potential of 35,000,000 tons and an estimated capacity of 175,000,000. An anthracite concession was also granted to the Miami Basic Metals and Coal Corporation near Puerto Berrío in mid-1960.[14]

Vast potentials unfolded with the effort to complete the 420-mile railway running from the port of Santa Marta to inland La Dorada, some 80 miles from Bogotá. Extensive government expenditures were added to foreign and domestic credits to hasten completion, thus linking the capital to the Caribbean by land for the first time. Imports which had previously passed through the Panama Canal to be unloaded at Buenaventura on the Pacific could now flow directly to Bogotá, and the fine Santa Marta port seems likely to supplant Barranquilla in importance.

Completion of the line in late 1960 meant the opening of millions of fertile virgin acres along the Magdalena River, which the railway parallels for many miles. Possible deposits of petroleum, coal, and iron ore were subject to investigation, and further advantage will accrue from the ready connection between northern cattle lands and the central highlands. Previously the cattle were driven long distances overland, and the quality of Colombian beef suffered thereby.

After its first eighteen months in office, the Lleras Camargo government passed beyond its early series of near-emergency measures to present extensive plans for long-range development. On February 24, 1960, Alberto Lleras Camargo announced an ambitious program sketching the lines of economic progress for the next several years. With basic stabilization realized, he reminded the people that this had been "not the goal, but rather the point of departure for economic development." His cry was for an across-the-board stimulation of the economy.

The address, pointing well into the 1960's, set forth as its basic requirement an increase in national living standards. While income would be increased, a sounder and more just system of distribution would be sought.

Recognizing the importance of bringing economic progress to the greatest possible number of citizens, Lleras Camargo called for a production increase of 5 per cent, which in twenty-five years would double per capita income. The existing 3.5 rate was "completely insufficient" to meet the extraordinary population growth which had recently risen above 2.5 per cent annually. This in itself meant an increase of 150,000 to the labor force for each of the next five years.

Increased productivity, while demanding cooperation from all economic sectors, was keyed to productive investment. This required an annual 8 per cent increase in public and private investment, thus raising the proportion of invested national income from 16 to 20 per cent. A major goal was the further reduction of imports and diversification of exports. The yearly expenditure on imports was nearly $100,000,000, and the economy could scarcely progress while such a condition existed.

Lleras Camargo also emphasized agricultural production, noting that in the past thirty years it had risen only 14 per cent as compared to 66 per cent for industrial production. He promised a new source of long-term agricultural credit, in addition to further efforts by the Caja de Crédito Agrario to stimulate the opening of virgin territory. He proposed tax revision levying a 2 per cent charge on untilled rural land holdings, thus penalizing owners who refused to work productive soil.

The administration asked for increased public and private foreign credit, which would be devoted to power, transportation, land distribution, and comparable projects. New laws were already being drawn up by the Planning Council to guarantee permanence and stability to foreign business enterprises. "Attractive conditions" were being designed to draw an additional $80,000,000 a year from foreign exchange. Furthermore, new petroleum legislation was under study to increase the national share of petroleum profits, while capital which had not yet returned from its flight abroad during the military dictatorship would be protected through a "general amnesty and climate of productive investment."[15] In June, 1960, the government revealed its 1961 budget as 2,382,000 pesos and tentatively anticipated a 1964 budget reaching 2,757,000,000 pesos.[16]

Thus the lines were laid out within which development would be pursued in the near future. Time was a factor, for the general program could hardly solve national problems in quick order. By the start of 1961, however, the bipartisan government had succeeded in restoring the economy to a point from which significant progress might proceed.

Despite a variety of political difficulties to be discussed below, the economy "was characterized by continuing stability and a reasonable rhythm of growth. . . ."[17]

THE DYNAMISM OF SOCIAL FORCES

While economic progress was being recorded, the many elements of Colombian life reflected the interplay of old and new social forces. A perceptible trend toward moderation was emerging from the traditional areas of religious and military influence, but the demands of labor and agriculture, still in the formative years of adolescence, were not characterized by responsible judgment. Thus the traditional inhibiting influence of church and the Armed Forces receded, and the government was increasingly subject to pressures from unions and the rural workers.

The overthrow of Gustavo Rojas Pinilla had marked an important turning point in church-state relations. At that time it was still true, as Herbert Matthews had written some years earlier, that Colombians were "deeply hurt at the idea of foreign missionaries . . . coming . . . to convert this profoundly Roman Catholic people to Presbyterianism, Seventh Day Adventism or whatever it may be."[18] Small children were still familiar with the chant "No queremos Protestantes"—we don't want Protestants—of which a typical verse follows:

> We don't want Protestants,
> They have come to Colombia to corrupt us;
> We don't want Protestants,
> Who soil our fatherland and our faith.[19]

When Rojas Pinilla was removed, *Christian Century* remarked cautiously that the treatment of Protestants in coming months would be a test of the genuineness of alleged religious freedom. "Whether good or bad, the next events will be a true index to see whether Christian freedom really figures in the intent of the new liberators."[20] During the *junta* government there were continued propagandistic barrages. Monsignor Luigi Ligutti was driven to repeat his plea that an objective examination of the situation be undertaken. Richard M. Fagley offered the concurrence of the Evangelical Confederation: ". . . a positive solution for the clear-cut disabilities imposed by arbitrary decree would contribute to religious freedom and social harmony far beyond the confines of Colombia, in situations where restrictions persist. The worldwide implications of such anachronisms need to be pondered by Protestants and Catholics alike."[21]

The position of the church shifted following the death of Cardinal Luque on May 7, 1959, at the age of seventy. Luque, as bishop of Tunja before becoming Colombian primate in 1950, had brought pride to Colombians when he became the first to be elevated to the rank of cardinal. He was, however, strongly conservative in outlook, and the subsequent appointment of Luis Córdoba Concha as archbishop of Bogotá brought a younger, more progressive, and social minded outlook to the top of the hierarchy. In December, 1960, Concha Córdoba was among four prelates named to the Sacred College of Cardinals, when the number of Latin American cardinals was raised to eleven.

Son of former president José Vicente Concha, the new primate had studied in Europe, become proficient in languages, and established himself as one of Colombia's most erudite clerics. Consecrated as bishop of Manizales by Archbishop Perdomo in 1935, he won a reputation for the promotion of religious and cultural life in a broad spirit of humanism. An acute student of religious disciplines and one of the nation's leading Latinists,[22] he had achieved distinction at an early age and, during nearly twenty-five years at Manizales, had worked continually for peaceful spiritual-secular relations.[23]

As archbishop of Bogotá he began "executing a revised format of Catholic-Protestant relations, initiating an intensive program of Church indoctrination and education. Maintaining that the best protection against Protestant appeals was a thorough knowledge of Catholic dogma, he proceeded on the assumption that Protestant inroads indicated a failure by the church to revivify the faith. Local clergy were urged to make more arduous efforts to increase general social consciousness. At the same time, he undertook efforts which led to a public conference of priests and Protestant ministers in Cali in December of 1960. This extraordinary meeting featured addresses by both groups in discussing a defense against communism and the general problem of religious unity.[24]

The atmosphere was charged with official disapproval of the former unholy alliance of local officials and priests. Protestants had practiced a more sensible form of proselytizing, finding that converts could be made without engaging in anti-Catholic attacks. The Evangelical Confederation cut short its bulletins which had informed the world of the Protestant plight while inflaming relations needlessly. No longer could it be written, as a few years earlier by a European observer, that Protestant missionaries failed to understand "that their presence in a Christian country demands more tact than their work among the savages."[25]

As the religious question subsided, there was a military reawakening to constitutional responsibilities. The restoration of government to civilian hands was received by the military with a renewed determination never to intervene again. In May, 1958, president-elect Lleras Camargo had delivered an eloquent address to a military gathering at the Teatro Patria. He gave an acute analysis which might well be pondered by the military the world over. The quality of his declaration deserves substantial quotation here.

Politics is the art of controversy *par excellence,* the military that of discipline. . . . Maintaining the Armed Forces apart from public deliberations is not a caprice of the Constitution but a necessity of its function. If it enters into deliberations, it enters armed. There is not much danger in civil controversies when the people are disarmed. But if someone has at his disposal a machine-gun, a side arm, or the Armed Forces, with which to resolve a dispute when agreement is lacking or he loses patience, deliberations will go to extremes, become more violent, and become unreasonable. . . .

The Armed Forces must not deliberate in politics, because it has been created for all the nation, because the entire nation, without exceptions of group or party or color or religious beliefs, but rather the people in entirety, have given them arms, have given them the physical power with the duty of defending their common interests, have given them special rights, have freed them from many rules that govern civil life, have granted them the privilege that they be judged on their military conduct, and all this with one single condition: that of not entering with all their weight and their force to fall upon innocent citizens. . . .[26]

The military engaged in its fight against rural violence with renewed vigor, and a reduction of civil warfare highlighted the spread of moderating attitudes. Disturbances continued intermittently, but the political elements were largely eliminated. Remaining participants were undisciplined bandits, mostly youths of twenty-five or less who remained violently dissatisfied with the general return to tranquillity. Remembering little but rural warfare, these harsh young men constituted, as Lleras Camargo remarked, one of Colombia's worst problems. "They grew up knowing nothing but robbery and murder. As the rehabilitation program spreads we shall be able to salvage some of them."[27]

In September, 1959, the capture of bandit leader Alberto Cendales, who had *rojista* connections, helped to hasten the elimination of political overtones.[28] The government campaign continued on a wide basis. An

October promise by War Minister Hernández Pardo of "peace as a Christmas present" was grimly contradicted by a bandit attack on a Tolima farm on December 21, where thirty-one were killed. The president announced a final and decisive effort at pacification, using all available resources of the state. Although conflict continued, Minister of Government José Enrique Gutiérrez Anzola was able to announce an over-all reduction of 50 per cent in 1959. Ten new jails were nearing completion, and the Gorgona Island facilities were expected to house one-third of the 25,000 prisoners jamming 163 antiquated buildings on the mainland.[29]

In 1960 Lleras Camargo directed what were intended as final steps in removing this aberration. A peace-planning commission detailed a sharply increased military program, particularly in Tolima, a center of turbulence. Parcellation and colonization of lands was stepped up to absorb unemployed *campesinos,* and 50,000,000 pesos were authorized for expenses. There were two continuing aspects to the problem. As already indicated, the political flavor had been largely removed, and the number of participants sharply reduced. The citizenry had lost all patience and clamored for an end to disturbances.

At the same time, the fanatical lawlessness of the remaining handful of bandits was such that complete pacification—all official declarations to the contrary—remained distant. Scattered incidents will continue indefinitely. In September, 1960, nine were killed and nineteen wounded in an attack at Puente Nacional, Santander.[30] A few days later there was an attack at Bucaramanga, leading in October to a temporary state of siege in a portion of Santander, and in January, 1961, a new attack in Tolima claimed the lives of several innocent villagers. Recent statistics show that the monthly death toll in 1958 was 367.5; in 1959 it was down to 177.2. While 291.8 bandits were captured per month in 1958, the figure rose to 353.5 in 1959.[31] For relatives and friends of the 2,127 who died in 1959, the favorable reduction of bloodshed was small consolation.

In further attempts to eliminate the causes of dissatisfaction in the countryside, the government undertook agrarian reform in the 1960's. Its undertaking was first noted in the summer of 1960 when the Agrarian Bank—Caja de Crédito Agrario—announced the investment of 141,500,000 pesos (some $22,000,000) beyond its usual agricultural credit program. Some 100,000,000 was provided for the purchase of farm equipment and agricultural supplies at Caja de Crédito Agrario supply stores throughout Colombia. An additional 8,000,000 pesos were channeled into increased production of basic food stuffs, notably wheat, corn, and potatoes. In July further impetus came with the arrival of a North American technical mission from the Department of the Interior.

The mission, regarded as a response to Lleras Camargo's pleas during his April visit to Washington, was particularly concerned with the drafting of a general plan for the distribution of public lands for colonization. The Caja de Crédito Agrario negotiated an agreement with Boyacá authorities to colonize some 100,000 hectares, with settlers coming largely from landless families. Credit was provided for housing and farm supplies; plots were parcelled out in 50-hectare segments. Further road and school construction was promised, and the over-all project was comparable to five previous such efforts initiated by the government.[32]

While such efforts were continued by the executive branch, Lleras Camargo sought comprehensive agrarian legislation in Congress. He named a twenty-man commission in September, 1960, to study all existing legislation and proposed reform. Composed of representatives of all significant political groups, the commission was headed by Liberal Carlos Lleras Restrepo. Factional representation was rendered incomplete by the refusal of five *laureanista* members to participate. Remaining members met and swiftly passed a resolution providing for a national agrarian institute, advisory council, fund, and regional autonomous corporations to administer the program as ultimately adopted.[33]

Forty-four days later the commission presented the president with its final proposals. Approved unanimously, it attempted to integrate and order the various existing or proposed reform plans, aiming at equitable land distribution, a higher standard of living for peasants, and a system whereby uncultivated land would be put into production. Ignoring the fact that the national land problem was less that of too few small farms than the unproductive utility of such land, the commission detailed a plan by which land in excess of given amounts would be expropriated by the government and redistributed.

All plots under 300 hectares would be unaffected, but above that a percentage would be taken by the government. Plots from 700 to 800 hectares would suffer 90 per cent expropriation, and above 800, 100 per cent would be taken. It was estimated that less than 5,000 owners held more than 300 hectares. Commission Chairman Lleras Restrepo pointed out the further qualification that only lands essential to national agrarian needs would be expropriated, while others would be exempted where not suitable for intensive farming. Payment would be made in both cash and bonds. The latter would be divided into Class A, paying 7 per cent interest with fifteen-year amortization, and Class B, paying 2 per cent with twenty-five-year amortization.[34]

Public discontent with living and working conditions was more vocal in urban areas. The unions, cited in Part I as among the interest groups most rapidly developing political and social influence, became instrumental in a series of strikes which disrupted the economy. In mid-1960 there was a brief interruption when public transportation drivers protested against a rise in the price of refined oil products which drove up gasoline prices five cents per gallon. A government study noted that the effects on individual taxi and bus drivers would be slight, but in several cities they struck temporarily for a return of previous prices or permission for a fare increase, which the government denied.

A more serious stoppage began on August 5, 1960, when lengthy negotiations broke down between petroleum workers and the management of the Colombian Petroleum Company, controlled jointly by Texaco and by Socony Mobil. Labor Minister Morales Benítez had been meeting with representatives since May, but by August agreement had been reached on fewer than half of the 184 separate worker demands. Two thousand employees left their jobs, and on August 16 the Federación de Trabajadores del Petróleo issued an ultimatum calling for an agreement within twenty-four hours. The resulting nation-wide strike presented the government with a grave crisis, as Minister of Mines and Petroleum José Elias del Hierro warned that only thirty days' oil was on hand.[35]

More than 6,000 petroleum company workers joined the sympathy movement, and the president, declaring it Communist-inspired, threatened full legal sanctions. Strikers soon returned to work, and compromise was finally reached on September 5 following a final presidential threat of intervention. Later in September a bank strike created an even more difficult situation. Once again the moderate Lleras Camargo was driven to characterizing the underlying motives of certain labor leaders as being Communist-inspired.

Beginning on September 13, 1960, the bank strike ensued following the expiration of the twelve-month agreement negotiated the previous year after presidential intercession. Bank employees demanded higher wages and fringe benefits such as life insurance and housing. The major dispute centered over union demands for a single collective contract for the entire banking industry. Bankers insisted on individual agreements at each bank with the individual union. The government called the strike illegal because of the "public service" nature of banking, and three-fourths of the strikers returned to work following an official back-to-work order. Banks went on a four-hour day.

Most of the major cities were affected, and in several instances strikers clashed with police. A special congressional committee was named, which arranged a presidential meeting with labor and management leaders, and on the twenty-third the strike ended. The government guaranteed that no dismissals or pay cuts would be permitted, and the parties to the controversy accepted a conciliation period to be followed by an arbitration court including representatives of bankers, employees, and the government. It was not until November, 1960, that the arbitration commission submitted its decision. Management demanded that the award be submitted to the highest court, as the agreement permitted. After further controversy this was finally accepted by the unions, and all employees returned to work.[36]

The final months of 1960 saw strikes or threats of work stoppages in textiles, soft drinks, tires, and even Bogotá television actors. A presidential press release attributed general unrest to Communist agitation, noting in particular the intransigence of several labor leaders in apparent defiance or ignorance of the wishes of union members. Undoubtedly there were some small elements involved, and the influence of the Cuban Revolution was also partially responsible. Nevertheless, causes for disturbances were wider. The serious problems of the urban proletariat had been alleviated but slightly, while a growing consciousness of unity and political strength translated union demands into action.

Nor were the unions devoid of responsible leaders, many of whom guarded against possible subversion of the workers' movement by foreign influences. In November, 1960, the Confederación de Trabajadores Colombianos expelled six affiliates, an unprecedented move in Colombian labor history. The powerful Federación de Trabajadores del Valle—which included both industrial and agricultural groups in Cali—was removed, and five in the Bogotá area were also expelled, among them the Textiles Monserrate and the Sindicato Unificado de la Constitución.

Both the CTC and the UTC had also rejected a request from the Confederación de Trabajadores de Cuba to endorse a salute to the Castro revolution. The Colombians responded that the revolution has departed from its original objectives by following the dictates of international communism.[37]

REGIONAL COOPERATION

In moving toward a new Colombia, the administration became the first in many years to take broad interest in hemispheric affairs. Aware of the benefits of regional cooperation, a concerted effort was made to strengthen ties with neighboring states. The subject of increased exchange of persons and ideas was quietly broached by Foreign Minister Julio César Turbay Ayala at the conference of foreign ministers at Santiago, Chile, in August, 1959. He stopped at both Lima and Quito for further discussions on the way home, and soon after his return to Bogotá had conversations with Venezuelan Foreign Minister Ignacio Luis Arcaya.

The movement led to the organization of binational study commissions with Panama, Venezuela, and Peru. Commissions agreed to discuss improved economic, cultural, and commercial relations. There was also a veiled hope that talks might lead to a variety of regional agreements. Colombo-Venezuelan ties were particularly important, for among the problems of the Lleras Camargo government was that of brisk illegal border trade which provided a major source of unregistered free market dollars in Colombia.

The government had tried to cut down on smuggling since taking office, particularly with regard to coffee contraband. The long, thinly populated border area was also being used for extensive illegal cattle dealings. Venezuela was believed to receive up to 600 head of cattle daily, paying more than double the price the cattlemen received on the Colombian market. *Visión* reported that Colombian smugglers earned $100,000,000 annually through these illegal negotiations.[38]

While Colombian and Venezuelan authorities decried such activities, by 1960 it was estimated that contraband in manufactured goods alone was worth $70,000,000 from Venezuela and $10,000,000 from trade across the shorter and less remote Ecuadorean border.[39] In October, 1959, a different dispute arose. The practice of borrowing labor had been common, with Colombians working in Venezuela much as Mexican *braceros* do in

Texas. Accusations of mistreatment and discrimination were made by Colombian workers, and President Betancourt immediately ordered an investigation. A possible diplomatic crisis was avoided through a moderate attitude of responsibility on the part of both nations. Turbay Ayala declared Venezuela blameless, pointing out that inadequate enforcement of the existing 1943 border agreement was responsible.

That agreement, which had suffered in effectiveness through inadequate staffing and personnel, was examined jointly by the two governments. The foreign ministers drafted a new agreement directing both countries to undertake an immediate census of bordering areas, and extensive publicity was planned to fully inform all employers who might be involved. Six-month permits would be issued to passenger vehicles, while residents would receive thirty-day permits for border crossing. Consulates were more heavily staffed, and the two ministers agreed to meet again in April, 1960, at which time effective implementation would be re-examined.[40]

Colombia continued to pursue closer regional understanding, and in December, 1959, Turbay Ayala travelled to Rio de Janeiro for talks with Brazilian Minister Horacio Lafer. Newly formed binational commissions began to meet, and in early 1960 discussions with Panama planned the point at which the incomplete Pan American Highway would meet at the border in crossing the wilderness of the Darien jungle. The agreement also established a joint effort against the tropical diseases which road builders would encounter. A February sanitation treaty was signed, with comparable agreements negotiated with Venezuela, Ecuador, and Brazil.[41]

Shortly thereafter, an extension of the international highway system was planned in talks with Ecuadorean and Venezuelan ministers of public works, and from May 9 to 13, 1960, the Colombo-Peruvian commission held its second meeting in Bogotá, outlining plans for cultural exchanges, joint development of resources, and the mutual reduction of import duties. Studies were proposed for a closer integration between national markets, and the commission recommended a permanent committee to initiate measures proposed by the meeting.

Further discussion was undertaken for the improvement of regional transportation facilities. The Flota Gran Colombiana, a joint shipping fleet organized by Colombia, Ecuador, and Venezuela, had become a binational enterprise after the Pérez Jiménez regime had withdrawn

Venezuelan participation in 1953. Talks were directed toward possible reintegration of Venezuela, and new documents established free access to ports of the three nation for Flota Gran Colombiana ships. Talks with the United States were concomitantly undertaken to bring about a renunciation of a proposed retaliatory tariff on goods shipped from the United States by the fleet.

Comparable measures discussed a possible Flota Aérea Gran Colombiana which would include Panama, Colombia, and Venezuela. It planned adaptation to the jet age by converting to new equipment and facilities, which could more easily be financed through joint efforts. It was expected to involve only international air travel. Participants were optimistic and planned at a later stage to approach Ecuador and Peru in extending the arrangement.

Economic connotations were contained in the December, 1960, announcement by Minister of Communications Misael Pastrana Borrero that the republic would join the fledgling Latin American Free Trade Area. In the hope of increasing minor exports, such as meat and several products of light industry, the administration thus committed itself to drawing up a list of manufactured articles and raw materials to trade with other members. The Free Trade Area, modeled after the European Free Trade Association, had been approved in February, 1960, at Montevideo by seven Latin republics.* The basic hope was, of course, effective regional economic integration, hopeful of significant trade expansion and concomitant economic diversification.

Thus Colombia moved into the seventh decade of the century giving indications of a change in outlook and a governmental effort to reshape the nation in consonance with its necessities. But the forces of change were powerful, and misdirection could lead into more extreme solutions. The ultimate test would unavoidably be the innate understanding and political skill by which the leaders of the nation attempted to channel the dynamics of an increasingly complex society. As a result, the political precursors of the future implied far more than a mere question of party dominance or the ascension of any given individual. The immediate task was the preparation for the presidential succession in 1962. Events suggested rather strongly that ranking leaders were still dedicated primarily to personal advancement and only peripherally interested in the fate of the republic.

* Argentina, Brazil, Chile, Peru, Paraguay, Uruguay, and Mexico.

Chapter Nineteen

POLITICAL PRECURSORS OF THE FUTURE

Obstruction and Opportunism

Unexpected results of the March, 1960, congressional elections had startled politicians, and the consequences included a more disorderly alignment of factions. None of the intraparty power struggles were resolved; instead, internecine feuding increased in ferocity. Individual leaders battled on both sides of the political fence to solidify their strength. Motivated by an opportunism founded on desire for personal ascendency, political leaders pursued a labyrinthine web of shifting alliances and revised policy positions. Governance of the nation was left in the hands of the president, who struggled vainly to win constructive support in Congress.

Lleras Camargo's immediate task was a reorganization of the Frente Nacional cabinet in the wake of elections. He reshuffled Conservative representation, attempting to divide the six party seats between followers of Gómez and of Ospina Pérez and Alzate Avendaño. Gómez persisted in his avowed retirement, however, and *laureanista* appointees declined to join the cabinet, suggesting instead their replacement by *alza-ospinistas*. After a few weeks, however, the real intent of Laureano Gómez became doubtful as his followers continued political operations. By July it was widely believed that the old warrior was planning a political comeback.

In withdrawing from responsibility for government policy, he hoped to turn discontent against the Ospina Pérez faction, thus strengthening his own position in preparing for the 1962 elections. With little likelihood of agreement between the two Conservative groups, it seemed that a struggle for total control would permit the winner to name the Conservative presidential nominee in 1962. Gómez hoped in the meantime to recover control of the Chamber.

In August the *laureanistas* stepped up their assault, accusing Ospina Pérez and Alzate Avendaño of opportunism in joining the Frente Nacional after having conducted the March campaign on explicit opposition to bipartisan government. The two were also criticized for having supported the Rojas Pinilla dictatorship during much of its time in office. The administration was called upon to refuse *alza-ospinistas* all participation in the government, a suggestion which Lleras Camargo rejected on the grounds that the bipartisan agreement provided for cabinet representation of the majority faction of each party.

The feuding Conservatives paused briefly in September to attempt a reconciliation, as party workers and the rank-and-file saw that a lack of party unity would endanger the otherwise certain selection of a Conservative president in 1962. *Laureanistas* made the first overture in proferring what was termed a return to historic party principles. Agreement was suggested on the selection of a candidate; a joint economic policy would be formulated, and concord would be sought on a congressional proposal to limit presidential powers during a state of siege.

The *alza-ospinistas,* recently rechristened as the "Christian Democratic" Conservatives, replied by accepting all proposals but that one dealing with the limitation of presidential powers, substituting a proposal for a joint committee to smooth factional differences. Surface agreement soon evaporated, for the two were sharply divided on the issue of overriding importance in party calculations: selection of the 1962 presidential candidate.

Gómez Conservatives suggested two alternatives. The first proposed selection of a nominee in December of 1961, holding a convention of all congressional Conservatives. With a greater majority in the Senate than the *alza-ospinistas* enjoyed in the Chamber, *laureanistas* would be assured of control. In lieu of this proposal, they offered to hold a nominating convention following the 1962 congressional elections, hoping to recover control of the Chamber and re-establish a majority within the party. The opposing wing ignored both suggestions.

Throughout this period Alberto Lleras Camargo was laboring to bring some semblance of order out of party anarchy. In June he had commented sadly that Colombia was becoming a "silent nation," with political groups "leaving the Government with the representation of everyone and without the power to influence anyone."[1] For the first time he reportedly warned of a possible resignation if party leaders persisted in their self-seeking opportunism. In November, 1960, he shook up the cabinet again, insisting upon representation of both Conservative factions. Virtually demanding cooperation from both groups, he named four *alza-ospinistas* and two *laureanistas* to the fourth cabinet since August, 1958.[2]

Even the president's prestige proved unavailing, for the *laureanista* appointees sought approval by their congressional representatives, and it was denied. On top of this, confusion was compounded with the unexpected death of Gilberto Alzate Avendaño on November 26, 1960, from complications following minor surgery. Always a political activist of the first order, Alzate Avendaño had been gaining dominance over the septagenarian Ospina Pérez, and his sudden demise further beclouded the issue. The death brought a further development as Dr. Gómez, who had been working quietly behind the scenes, emerged with public declarations—his first since meeting defeat in the March elections.

The Conservatives were, therefore, badly divided. Both elements were guilty of self-seeking politicking. Both inside Congress and out, the *laureanistas* blocked concerted action wherever possible. The Ospina Pérez forces, on the other hand, had shifted ground substantially after winning elections on a platform opposing the bipartisan government. Although remaining critical of certain aspects of official policy, the *alza-ospinistas* eagerly accepted cabinet positions and attempted to strengthen their faction through official means.

The Liberals were involved with equally serious problems of a somewhat different nature. The immediate retirement of Darío Echandía after the elections left the Liberal majority temporarily leaderless. A national convention was convened in July, at which Carlos Lleras Restrepo was offered party leadership. Like Dr. Gómez, he had been exercising a bogus political "retirement," and he turned down the Liberal directorship, suggesting a seven-man executive board which was speedily adopted.

Lleras Restrepo did agree, however, to accept nomination for *designado,* which would place him first in the line of presidential succession behind his cousin Alberto Lleras Camargo. By the end of 1960 his political strength was substantial, and there were more than a few rumors

that he would assume the presidency following a resignation by Lleras
Camargo. Lleras Restrepo was careful to retain personal freedom of
action by refusing formal party leadership in July. Among other things,
it permitted him to avoid taking a public stand against the dissident wing
of Alfonso López Michelsen.

Following the elections the dissident leftist Liberals had held their
own convention in May and adopted the name Movimiento de Recuperación Liberal (MRL). Repeating campaign criticisms of the "oligar-
chically-dominated" Frente Nacional, the younger López refused a cabinet seat for his faction, scoffing at the prospect of a Conservative president of a Liberal-minded electorate. Echoing the cry of "Salud, Educación
y Techo," he promised a series of broad social-minded proposals for the
congressional session opening in July. An expression of sympathy for
the Cuban revolution was also voiced.

López Michelson expressed confidence in the progressive outlook he
attributed to Carlos Lleras Restrepo, and he promised constructive cooperation, although refusing to attend the regular Liberal convention.
Urging new leadership upon the Liberals, he staunchly denied that his
own MRL was a party as such. His purpose, López Michelsen insisted,
was to achieve a reorientation of Liberal party principles. At the same
time he announced the intention of running an MRL presidential
candidate against the Frente Nacional in 1962, and when Congress convened in July, the MRL position proved important by holding a balance
between the other regular Liberals and the divided Conservatives.

Congress opened its session on July 20, 1960, and immediately mirrored
the contradictory positions of the factions. President Lleras Camargo
urged the legislators to avoid a "decline of the Frente Nacional" which
would "lead only to national disorganization, anarchy, and the progress
of extremist movements of the Right or Left."[3] In August he again addressed a joint congressional meeting, outlining the accomplishments of
his first two years in office. It was only too plain that progress had come
largely through executive activity. Congressmen had taken little if any
significant action on the wide variety of social and economic measures.
The president noted that the political situation was beyond his capacity
to control, and he called for renewed patriotism from Congress.

The lawmakers first took up the question of electing a *designado,*
and weeks of political invective prevented the matter from coming to a
vote. Only on August 31 was Lleras Restrepo finally elected in the face

of *laureanista* abstention, when the MRL reversed its first decision to oppose him. Indicative of prevailing obstructionism was the *laureanista* announcement that it had no objection to Lleras Restrepo, yet it delayed legislation by refusing to vote for him. Under the Senate leadership of Alvaro Gómez Hurtado, *laureanistas* merely continued their attacks on *alza-ospinismo.*

With the *designado* question resolved, attention turned to a bill proposing revision of constitutional Article 121. Presidential powers were to be limited during a state of siege, and the executive would be required to convoke Congress at once following any declaration of a state of siege. If he failed to do so, Congress could itself call a special session and, by a majority vote of both houses, could force any presidential decree into the judiciary, where the decree would be automatically suspended unless acted upon within six days.

Controversy raged until late in the fall. As Conservative politicians hurled epithets across congressional aisles, regular Liberals made it clear that they would not honor *paridad* by accepting a Conservative president in 1962 unless Article 121 were revised. Anticipating a possible Alzate Avendaño candidacy, they demanded assurance of constitutional protection against arbitrary extension of Conservative rule through exercise of decree powers under a state of siege. The November death of Alzate Avendaño did little to reduce Liberal insistence on amending Article 121.

When more than three months of congressional activity failed to bring agreement, new rumors circulated that the president might see his task as impossible and submit his resignation. Agrarian, judicial, and fiscal reforms were among "necessary" measures which had not even been studied. Strongest opposition to the amendment of Article 121 came from *alza-ospinistas,* who called for a revised proposal. Lleras Camargo finally directed a new appeal to the Congress, calling upon renewed political responsibility while reminding the nation of its past experience with party intransigence. He openly criticized partisan obstructionism and urged a revival of the spirit with which the experimental government had been launched. Only the MRL, which remained opposed to the Frente Nacional, failed to receive the presidential appeal with praise.

By November an amended Article 121 was approved in the Senate, after further interruption by an unprovoked *laureanista* attack upon Lleras Restrepo. The measure passed by a ninety-three to three vote.

In the Chamber the *alza-ospinistas* threatened to block the proposal but finally relented in mid-December, and the long-delayed reform became law. Termination of the congressional session led to a muting of political activity in early 1961. The Conservative division remained broad, however, while the López Michelsen faction held power disproportionate to its electoral strength.

An additional political event was the return of Carlos Lleras Restrepo to the political wars. Long known as a rather social-minded figure somewhat to the left of center politically, he drew increasing strength from those who, while admiring the exceptional presidential talents of compromise and moderation, felt that Lleras Camargo was moving toward reform less swiftly than he might. There was talk of Carlos as "Lleras II," whom some regarded as more forceful than his cousin. Lleras Restrepo gathered strength through the closing months of 1960.

Characteristic was a taunting cartoon appearing in *El Siglo* in October. It pictured Lleras Restrepo with a handful of balloons showing his role as *designado,* chairman of the commission for agrarian reform, leader of the Liberal party, head of the Liberal Senators, president of the Celanese Company of Colombia, and member of the directing *junta* of a Bogotá bank. He was shown pointing a demanding finger at Lleras Camargo's sole balloon, the presidency.[4] Any doubt as to Lleras Restrepo's strength was further dispelled by the mounting attacks by *laureanista* in Congress and the pages of *El Siglo.*

Political activity more and more resembled the bitter power struggle of earlier years, as the majority of national leaders again turned their backs on past lessons—much as they had done after the 1948 *bogotazo.* Alberto Lleras Camargo maintained his lofty perch atop the volcanic situation, and lesser men adroitly countered one another's moves in such a way as to create virtual paralysis of the political process. There was little more for Lleras Camargo to do other than to continue his reforms through executive action. He had brilliantly won a breathing spell for Colombian democracy, but the course of the future depended upon the responses to problems and demands lying beyond the completion of Lleras Camargo's term in August of 1962.

AN EVOLVING POLITICAL CHALLENGE

Revival of acrimonious political partisanship casts a pall over the future of the two-party system in Colombia. In truth the system has not properly functioned under conditions of full democracy since the early months of the Ospina Pérez administration in 1946; the accomplishment of significant measures under the bipartisan agreement has been the result of executive action under the direction of Lleras Camargo. Effective party participation through the legislature has been absent. Factional disputes among both Conservatives and Liberals have approached the point of inevitable splintering into a number of minor groups representative of relatively small segments of public opinion.

The *laureanista* faction will likely remain loyal to its aging champion as long as Dr. Gómez lives. Alvaro Gómez Hurtado perhaps can be expected to assume eventual leadership, yet his own lengthy career gives little reason to anticipate his attaining a truly national position of leadership. *Alza-ospinistas,* at the same time, are reassessing their position following the death of Alzate Avendaño. The aloof and occasional direction of Mariano Ospina Pérez cannot long continue to uphold the myth of representing unified national conservatism.

The Liberals, still clearly the majority party, may be expected to retain at least a façade of national unity, thanks to the reappearance of Carlos Lleras Restrepo on the political scene. But Lleras Restrepo will be hardpressed to maintain a consolidated party, particularly should a Conservative assume the presidency in 1962, as the bipartisan arrangement promises. Certainly he will be forced to move toward the Left, bringing a Conservative reaction that cannot be predicted.

The "gradualist" approach to national problems—although the only course open to Lleras Camargo—places increasing demands upon the public. The pressures of the urban proletariat and the emerging labor movement are increasing, and new vigor will be imparted to leftist elements. Sentiment behind the Movimiento de Recuperación Liberal should not be underestimated; forces may indeed drive the former president's son from his present position. It is within these elements of the Left that those sympathetic to the Cuban revolution are exerting themselves.

In October, 1960, an MRL demonstration drew some 20,000 to Bogotá's Plaza de Bolívar. Many of the speakers wore Communist party ribbons, spoke in support of Fidel Castro, and urged destruction of the bipartisan administration. Extremist activity was also recorded a few weeks later in Cali, where a United States flag was burned before a small crowd.[5] López Michelsen was led to denounce pro-Communist elements within

the MRL, expelling several members while attacking Castro for betray-
ing the goals of his revolution. The MRL founder also rejected platform proposals including withdrawal from the Organization of American States, denunciation of the church, extensive collectivization, and
confiscation of foreign enterprises.

As long as a large proportion of the Colombian masses remains in
need of social reforms and economic betterment, the appeal to extremism
will remain, growing in intensity with the passage of time. Increased
disillusionment with the traditional parties can bring a strengthening of
a movement toward what is euphemistically termed "revolutionary" as
contrasted with "parliamentary" democracy. A further outlet for such
discontent could be the miniscule movement of Jorge Gaitán's daughter,
Gloria Gaitán de Valencia, and her Socialist husband, Luis Emiro
Valencia. They succeeded in attracting a following in the 1960 meetings,
organized under the name of Movimiento Popular Revolucionario
(MPR). Even today, there is Liberal eagerness to slip under the mantle of
gaitanismo. The impact of the extraordinary *caudillo,* whether demagogue or patriotic reformer, is not yet dead.

Apart from party considerations, a striking feature of contemporary
Colombian affairs is the continued dominance of veteran political figures.
Such were the repressions of the Gómez and Rojas Pinilla machineries
that, for nearly a decade, political activity was largely closed to aspiring
younger politicians. With the flight of Rojas Pinilla in 1957, returning
leaders were those of the 1930's and 1940's. A few of the familiar figures
have passed from the scene. Alfonso López died in late 1959 at the age
of seventy-three, and Gilberto Alzate Avendaño, long prominent although barely in his fifties, died in November, 1960. Eduardo Santos
returned to political retirement in 1957, and Darío Echandía withdrew
following the failure of his leadership in 1960 congressional elections.

A review of today's most prominent names includes Lleras Camargo,
Lleras Restrepo, Gómez, Valencia, Ospina Pérez, and López Michelsen.
With the exception of the last, each of these men has been politically
prominent for at least two decades. Cabinet ministers and congressional
figures are largely technical administrators or loyal followers of veteran
leaders. Yet Colombian politics must look to a new generation of leaders. Indeed, the 1962 presidential sash will likely fall about the shoulders
of a man not mentioned in this chapter. Leadership must come from
such young men as Jorge Franco Holguín, thirty-five-year-old director

of the National Planning Department. The future belongs to his generation, not to that of Laureano Gómez (born in 1889), Mariano Ospina Pérez (born in 1891), or even the younger Alberto Lleras Camargo.

Attention might be given to a recent comment made by Franco Holquín. When questioned concerning the fact that many of Lleras Camargo's economic advisors were young, he responded, "We feel that we are modifying the [political] terms in which Congress discusses projects." He and his compatriots were less interested in politics than in efforts "to promote capitalism, or we will not go through capitalism at all, but will jump from the feudal stage into socialism."[6] In early 1960 a Conservative leader was asked to suggest the best man for the 1962 presidency. He reportedly replied, "Alberto Lleras."[7] This was the highest form of political compliment to the president, but it also illustrated the crying need for vital new blood in the Colombian body politic.

Semana published a grim feature story in 1960 entitled "Sleeping Beauty of the Tropics," in which the need for new personalities and energies was underlined. The magazine printed a column of major world news headlines, first for 1949, then for 1959. The second column presented a comparison of Colombian headlines. *Both* 1949 and 1959 included the following items: Echandía heads Liberal campaign; Gómez considers retirement; political chiefs call for pacification; talk of diversification continues; coffee provides 80 per cent of total export values; illiteracy demands reduction.[8] Here was but further testimony for the necessity of progress under the leadership of an untested younger generation.

The outlook, then, calls for a generous portion of skepticism, yet is undeserving of unmitigated pessimism. The unique bipartisan system has made positive contributions to national politics. Despite its inherent artificiality, the political balance has aided immeasurably in the conduct of local administration. It has functioned quite successfully on this lower level, where issues are discussed by representatives of the two parties with a view to the general welfare.

Elected officials have come to realize that their political rivals may well be reasonable men with other than petty partisan interests at heart. *Paridad* has reduced local opportunism and inflamed rivalries have been salved; the heritage of cooperation has been established, cutting across party lines. Local leaders have long lacked experience in political cooperation.

For departmental and municipal officials, the experience of divided government has helped lead away from explosive political violence.

Whether the constitutional agreement will continue until 1974 is highly problematical. The two men most responsible for its temporary success—Lleras Camargo and Gómez—will assert decreasing influence after 1962. Anti-Frente Nacional sympathy has grown within both parties. Among the modulating sharps and flats of shifting political opinion, the forces opposed to the Frente Nacional have generally fallen into two groups. The first has held to an opportunistic belief that a collapse of the system will bring a restoration of party hegemony; the second believes that a period of four years of controlled democracy is adequate to prepare Colombia for a return to full political freedoms without reviving the concomitant excesses of earlier years.

Whatever the ultimate duration of bipartisan government, an accurate appraisal can only be made when the artificial arrangement draws to a close. Perhaps the nation will have learned from the lessons of the remarkable constitutional experiment. Future governments would be wise to recognize that "a healthy awareness and freedom of political action are to a considerable extent dependent on such socio-economic factors as literacy, education, satisfaction of physical needs to some moderate level, and the possiblity of fulfillment of social aspirations."[9]

One must hope that the nation is developing the basic understanding of democracy that Alberto Lleras Camargo outlined in an address to the National Press Club in Washington on April 8, 1960. As the president told his North American audience, democracy "is not doomed merely to repair from time to time the ravages wrought by despotism. Democracy must hold fast not only to its intrinsic soul-liberating goodness but also to the capacity it may possess—and does in itself possess—to produce greater well-being and broader justice."[10]

Notes

CHAPTER ONE

1. Preston E. James, *Latin America* (3rd. ed.; New York: The Odyssey Press, 1959), p. 99.

2. United States Department of Commerce, Bureau of Foreign Affairs, *Investment in Colombia* (Washington: U.S. Department of Commerce, 1955), p. 3.

3. James, *Latin America,* p. 135.

4. United States Department of Commerce, Bureau of Foreign Affairs, *Basic Data on the Economy of Colombia* (Washington: U. S. Department of Commerce, 1957), p. 4.

5. *Ibid.*

6. *Ibid.,* pp. 4-5.

7. James, *Latin America,* p. 101.

8. Vernon Lee Fluharty, *Dance of the Millions: Military Rule and the Social Revolution in Colombia, 1930-1956* (Pittsburgh: University of Pittsburgh Press, 1957), p. 21.

9. For contradictory figures of competent authorities, see James, *Latin America,* also Pablo Vila, *Nueva Geografía de Colombia* (Bogotá: Liberia Colombiana, 1945), p. 89.

10. *Basic Data,* p. 4.

11. Lyman Bryson (ed.), *Social Change in Latin America Today* (New York: Harper & Brothers, 1960), p. 38.

12. Joaquín Piñeres Corpas, *Síntesis del Conflicto entre la Ciudad y la Provincia de Colombia* (Rome: Instituto Internacional de Sociologia, 1951), p. 27.

13. W. O. Galbraith, *Colombia: A General Survey* (London: Royal Institute of International Affairs, 1953), p. 87.

14. Lauchlin Currie, *The Basis of a Development Program for Colombia: Report of a Mission, The Summary* (Washington: International Bank for Reconstruction and Development, 1950), p. 8.

15. *Ibid.,* p. 10.

16. *Ibid.*

17. Fluharty, *Dance of the Millions,* p. 212.

18. Arthur Preston Whitaker, *The United States and South America: The Northern Republics* (Cambridge: Harvard University Press, 1948), p. 47.

19. James, *Latin America,* p. 99.

20. Germán Arciniegas, *The State of Latin America,* trans. Harriet de Onis (New York: Alfred A. Knopf, Inc., 1952), p. 157.

CHAPTER TWO

1. Rosendo Gómez, *Government and Politics in Latin America* (New York: Random House, 1960), p. 36.

2. William Marion Gibson, *The Constitutions of Colombia* (Durham: The Duke University Press, 1948), p. 359.

3. See the excellent discussion by John Gillin, pp. 28-33, in Lyman Bryson (ed.), *Social Change in Latin America Today* (New York: Harper & Brothers, 1960).

4. Frank Tannenbaum, "A Note on Latin American Politics," *Political Science Quarterly,* LVIII, No. 3 (September, 1943), 418-19.

5. Frederick B. Pike (ed.), *Freedom and Reform in Latin America* (South Bend: University of Notre Dame Press, 1959), p. 121.

6. *Ibid.,* p. 70.

7. Harold Eugene Davis (ed.), *Government and Politics in Latin America* (New York: The Ronald Press Company, 1958), p. 186.

8. William W. Pierson and Federico G. Gil, *Governments of Latin America* (New York: McGraw-Hill Book Company, Inc., 1957), p. 317.

9. Russell H. Fitzgibbon, "The Party Potpourri in Latin America," *The Western Political Quarterly,* X, No. 1 (March, 1957), 7, 10.

10. Jesús María Henao and Gerardo Arrubla, *History of Colombia,* trans. J. Fred Rippy (Chapel Hill: The University of North Carolina Press, 1938), p. 539.

11. Fitzgibbon, "Party Potpourri," *WPQ,* p. 17.

12. Robert J. Alexander, *Communism in Latin America* (New Brunswick: Rutgers University Press, 1957), p. 250.

13. "El Undecimo Partido," *Semana,* December 4, 1948, pp. 9-10.

14. Gabriel A. Almond and James S. Coleman (eds.), *The Politics of the Developing Areas* (Princeton: Princeton University Press, 1960), p. 481.

15. For a fuller discussion, see Federico G. Gil, "Responsible Parties in Latin America," *Journal of Politics,* XV, No. 3 (August, 1953), 333-48.

16. Gerardo Molina, *Proceso y Destino de la Libertad* (Bogotá: Biblioteca de la Universidad Libre, 1955), p. 255.

17. Félix Angel Vallejo, *Política: Misión y Destino* (Bogotá: Editorial Cosmos, 1954), pp. 218-20.

18. Partido Liberal, *Programas y Estatutos del Partido Liberal Colombiano* (Bogotá: Departmento de Propaganda, 1944), p. 25.

19. *Ibid.*

20. *Ibid.,* p. 33.

21. For a lengthier treatment, see Lilo Linke, *Andean Adventure: A Social and Political Study of Colombia, Ecuador and Bolivia* (London: Hutchinson & Co., Ltd., 1945), pp. 145-48.

22. José Antonio Osorio Lizarazo, *Gaitán: Vida, Muerte y Permanente Presencia* (Buenos Aires: Ediciones López Negri, 1952), p. 9.

23. Partido Liberal, *Programas y Estatutos,* p. 25.

24. *Ibid.,* p. 26.

25. W. Stanley Rycroft, "Bitter Struggle in Colombia," *Christian Century* (February 1, 1950), p. 141.

26. Carlos Lozano y Lozano, *Ideario del Liberalismo Actual: Conferencia Pronunciada por el doctor Carlos Lozano y Lozano el 14 febrero 1939* (Bogotá: Imprenta Nacional, 1939), p. 23.

27. Gonzalo Restrepo Jaramillo, *El Pensamiento Conservador: Ensayos Políticos* (Medellín: Tipografía Bedout, 1936), p. 246.

28. *Ibid.*, p. 255.

29. Almond and Coleman (eds.), *Politics of the Developing Areas*, p. 469.

30. Walter Lippmann, *A Preface to Politics* (New York: The Macmillan Co., 1933), pp. 282-83.

31. Almond and Coleman (eds.), *Politics of the Developing Areas*, p. 502.

32. K. H. Silvert, "Political Change in Latin America," from the American Assembly, *The United States and Latin America* (New York: Columbia University Press, 1959), p. 79.

33. George Blanksten, "Political Change in Latin America," *American Political Science Review*, LIII, No. 1 (March, 1959), 108.

34. Miguel Jorrín, *Governments of Latin America* (New York: D. Van Nostrand Co., Inc., 1953), p. 293.

35. Moisés Poblete Troncoso and Ben G. Burnett, *The Rise of the Latin American Labor Movement* (New York: Bookman Associates, 1960), p. 83.

36. *Ibid.*

37. John Joseph Considine, *New Horizons in Latin America* (New York: Dodd, Mead & Company, 1958), p. 231.

38. Poblete Troncoso and Burnett, *Latin American Labor Movement*, p. 86.

39. "New Peronista Maneuvers in Colombia," *Inter-American Labor Bulletin*, IV (January, 1954) 3, as quoted, *ibid.*, p. 85.

40. Vernon Lee Fluharty, *Dance of the Millions: Military Rule and the Social Revolution in Columbia, 1930-1956* (Pittsburgh: University of Pittsburgh Press, 1957), p. 70.

41. Antonio García, *Gaitán y el Problema de la Revolución Colombiana* (Bogotá: Artes Gráficas, 1955), pp. 300-1.

42. Blanksten, "Political Change in Latin America," *APSR*, p. 116.

43. William Sylvane Stokes, *Latin American Politics* (New York: Thomas Y. Crowell Company, 1959), p. 80.

44. Blanksten, "Political Change in Latin America," *APSR*, pp. 106-7.

45. J. Lloyd Mecham, *Church and State in Latin America* (Chapel Hill: The University of North Carolina Press, 1934), p. 141.

46. W. O. Galbraith, *Colombia: A General Survey* (London: Royal Institute of International Affairs, 1953), p. 47.

47. Miner Searle Bates, *Religious Liberty: An Inquiry* (New York: International Missionary Council, 1945), p. 222.

48. Linke, *Audean Adventure*, p. 140.

49. Peter Masten Dunne, *A Padre Views South America* (Milwaukee: The Bruce Publishing Company, 1945), p. 229.

50. Pike, *Freedom and Reform*, p. 98.

51. *Ibid.*, p. 225.

52. The *New York Times*, September 18, 1960, p. 5.

53. Stokes, *Latin American Politics*, p. 120.

54. "Símbolos Patrios," *Semana*, May 16, 1953, p. 18.

55. Stokes, *Latin American Politics*, p. 132.

56. Edwin Lieuwen, *Arms and Politics in Latin America* (New York: Frederick A. Praeger, Inc., 1960), p. 168.

57. *Ibid.*, p. 169.

58. Blanksten, "Political Change in Latin America," *APSR*, p. 108.

59. Stokes, *Latin American Politics*, p. 400.

60. Pierson and Gil, *Governments of Latin America*, p. 402.

61. *Ibid.*

62. Carlos Mario Londoño, *Economía Social Colombiana* (Bogotá: Imprenta Nacional, 1953), pp. 269-70.

63. Fluharty, *Dance of the Millions*, p. 203.

64. *Ibid.*, p. 60.

65. Ricardo Silva, *Los Trabajadores ante Los Partidos* (Bogotá: Editorial Antares, 1955), pp. 38-39.

CHAPTER THREE

1. Miguel Jorrín, *Governments of Latin America* (New York: D. Van Nostrand Co., Inc., 1953), p. 291.
2. W. O. Galbraith, *Colombia: A General Survey* (London: Royal Institute of International Affairs, 1953), p. 128.
3. Lucas Caballero Calderón, *Figuras Políticas de Colombia* (Bogotá: Editorial Kelly, 1945), p. 29.
4. Austin F. Macdonald, *Latin American Politics and Government* (New York: Thomas Y. Crowell Company, 1949), p. 381.
5. Vernon Lee Fluharty, *Dance of the Millions: Military Rule and the Social Revolution in Colombia, 1930-1956* (Pittsburgh: University of Pittsburgh Press, 1957), p. 53.
6. Samuel Guy Inman, *Latin America: Its Place in World Life* (rev. ed.; New York: Harcourt, Brace and Company, 1942), p. 233.
7. Kathleen Romoli, *Colombia: Gateway to South America* (New York: Doubleday & Company, Inc., 1941), p. 284.
8. Antonio García, *Gaitán y el Problema de la Revolución Colombiana* (Bogotá: Cooperativa de Artes Gráficas, 1955), p. 272.
9. Macdonald, *Latin American Politics,* p. 386.
10. Fluharty, *Dance of the Millions,* p. 65.
11. Macdonald, *Latin American Politics,* p. 387.
12. Fluharty, *Dance of the Millions,* p. 72.
13. Arthur Preston Whitaker, *The United States and South America: The Northern Republics* (Cambridge: Harvard University Press, 1948), p. 88.
14. Caballero Calderón, *Figuras Políticas,* p. 62.
15. Whitaker, *U. S. and South America,* p. 88.
16. José Antonio Osorio Lizarazo, *Gaitán: Vida, Muerte y Permanente Presencia* (Buenos Aires: Ediciones López Negri, 1952), p. 25.
17. Caballero Calderón, *Figuras Políticas,* p. 51.
18. Mont Follick, *The Twelve Republics* (London: Williams & Norgate, Ltd., 1952), p. 328.
19. Osorio Lizarazo, *Gaitán,* p. 320.
20. Macdonald, *Latin American Politics,* pp. 388-89.
21. Germán Arciniegas, *The State of Latin America,* trans. Harriet de Onis (New York: Alfred A. Knopf, Inc., 1952), p. 161.
22. Macdonald, *Latin American Politics,* p. 389.
23. Rafael Azula Barrera, *De la Revolución al Orden Nuevo: Proceso y Drama de un Pueblo* (Bogotá: Editorial Kelly, 1956), p. 163.
24. Alberto Niño H., *Antecedentes y Secretos del 9 de Abril* (Bogotá: Editorial Pax, 1949?), pp. 2-3.
25. Arciniegas, *State of Latin America,* p. 160.
26. Garcia, *Gaitán,* p. 313.
27. Niño H., *Antecedentes y Secretos,* pp. 11-12.
28. Fluharty, *Dance of the Millions,* pp. 90-91.
29. Donald Marquand Dozer, "The Roots of Revolution in Latin America," *Foreign Affairs* (January, 1949), p. 283.
30. Ricardo Silva, *Los Trabajadores ante Los Partidos* (Bogotá: Editorial Antares, 1955), p. 249.
31. Arciniegas, *State of Latin America,* p. 160.
32. "La Fuente del Poder," *Semana,* June 4, 1949, p. 5.
33. "Gaitán, Party Mender," *Newsweek,* June 23, 1947, p. 50.

34. Follick, *Twelve Republics*, p. 331.

35. José María Arboleda Llorente, *Historia de Colombia* (Popayán: Editorial Universidad del Cauca, 1952), p. 224.

36. Arciniegas, *State of Latin America*, p. 161.

37. Osorio Lizarazo, *Gaitán*, p. 294.

CHAPTER FOUR

1. "Bogotá Berserk," *Newsweek*, April 19, 1948, pp. 48-49.

2. José Antonio Osorio Lizarazo, *Gaitán: Vida, Muerte y Permanente Presencia* (Buenos Aires: Ediciones López Negri, 1952), p. 297.

3. Jules Dubois, *Freedom Is My Beat* (New York: Bobbs-Merrill Company, Inc., 1959), p. 81.

4. *Ibid.*, p. 82.

5. *Ibid.*, p. 91.

6. Rafael Azula Barrera, *De la Revolución al Orden Nuevo: Proceso y Drama de un Pueblo* (Bogotá: Editorial Kelly, 1956), p. 365.

7. Germán Arciniegas, *The State of Latin America*, trans. Harriet de Onis (New York: Alfred A. Knopf, Inc., 1952), p. 162.

8. "Bogotá Berserk," *Newsweek*, April 19, 1948, pp. 48-49.

9. Azula Barrera, *De la Revolución*, p. 415.

10. *Ibid.*, p. 418.

11. W. O. Galbraith, *Colombia: A General Survey* (London: Royal Institute of International Affairs, 1953), p. 133.

12. *The Political Situation in Colombia: The Opposition and the Government, April 9, 1948-April 9, 1950* (Bogotá: n.p., 1950), p. 27.

13. Osorio Lizarazo, *Gaitán*, p. 303.

14. Azula Barrera, *De la Revolución*, p. 370.

15. *Ibid.*, p. 363.

16. *Ibid.*, pp. 398-99.

17. *The Political Situation in Colombia*, p. 29.

18. Osorio Lizarazo, *Gaitán*, p. 305.

19. Azula Barrera, *De la Revolución*, pp. 403-4.

20. Joaquín Estrada Monsalve, *El 9 de Abril en Palacio: Horario de un Golpe de Estado* (3rd. ed.: Bogotá: Editorial ABC, 1948), p. 85.

21. *Ibid.*, p. 94.

22. Azula Barrera, *De la Revolución*, p. 421.

23. *The Political Situation in Colombia*, p. 30.

24. Robert J. Alexander, *Communism in Latin America* (New Brunswick: Rutgers University Press, 1957), p. 243.

25. *Ibid.*, p. 245.

26. Stephen Naft, as cited in Alexander, *Communism in Latin America*, p. 247.

27. *Ibid.*, p. 249.

28. *Ibid.*, p. 250.

29. Alberto Niño H., *Antecedentes y Secretos del 9 de Abril* (Bogotá: Editorial Pax, 1949?), p. 28.

30. Rafaél Larco Herrera, *Por la Ruta de la Confederación Americana* (Lima: n.p., 1948), p. 151, as cited in Vernon Lee Fluharty, *Dance of the Millions: Military Rule and the Social Revolution in Colombia, 1930-1956* (Pittsburgh: University of Pittsburgh Press, 1957), p. 101.

31. Galbraith, *Colombia*, p. 132.

32. "Bogotá Berserk," *Newsweek*, April 19, 1948, pp. 48-49.

33. Dubois, *Freedom Is My Beat*, p. 81.

34. *The Political Situation in Colombia*, p. 28.

35. Galbraith, *Colombia*, p. 133.
36. Dubois, *Freedom Is My Beat*, p. 112.
37. Azula Barrera, *De la Revolución*, p. 405.
38. Fluharty, *Dance of the Millions*, p. 103.
39. Austin F. Macdonald, *Latin American Politics and Government* (New York: Thomas Y. Crowell Company, 1949), p. 392.
40. Alexander, *Communism in Latin America*, p. 250.

Chapter Five

1. "Historia de una División," *Semana*, October 2, 1948, p. 5.
2. Lucas Caballero Calderón, *Figuras Políticas de Colombia* (Bogotá: Editorial Kelly, 1945), p. 37.
3. *Ibid.*, p. 43.
4. "Parcelación Liberal," *Semana*, September 25, 1948, p. 8.
5. "Congress Without Riots," *Newsweek*, August 2, 1948, p. 42.
6. "Convención Conservadora," *Semana*, July 17, 1948, p. 5.
7. "Congress Without Riots," *Newsweek*, August 2, 1948, p. 42.
8. *Ibid.*
9. *Ibid.*
10. "Radiografía Electoral," *Semana*, September 11, 1948, pp. 6-7.
11. "Boletín de Crisis," *Semana*, October 9, 1948, p. 10.
12. *Hispanic World Report*, November, 1948, p. 10.
13. "El Acuerdo," *Semana*, December 16, 1948, pp. 8-9.
14. *Hispanic World Report*, January, 1949, pp. 9-10.
15. Carlos Mario Londoño, *Economía Social Colombiana* (Bogotá: Imprenta Nacional, 1953), p. 135-37.
16. *El Espectador*, July 18, 1948, pp. 3-5.
17. Caballero Calderón, *Figuras Políticas*, p. 211.
18. "Cabeza de Oposición," *Semana*, June 11, 1949, p. 12.
19. *Ibid.*, p. 11.
20. "Prólogo de una Campaña," *Semana*, January 15, 1949, p. 5.
21. "Movilización Conservadora," *Semana*, January 29, 1949, pp. 6-8.
22. "Retozos Liberales," *Semana*, February 26, 1949, pp. 5-7.
23. "Horacios y Curiacios," *Semana*, March 12, 1949, p. 6.
24. *Ibid.*
25. *Hispanic World Report*, May, 1949, pp. 10-11.
26. "Manifestación Conservadora," *Semana*, April 9, 1949, p. 7.
27. "Derrumbe en la Mina," *Semana*, May 28, 1949, pp. 5-6.
28. *Ibid.*

Chapter Six

1. *El Catolicismo*, April 30, 1949, p. 1.
2. *Ibid.*
3. *Hispanic World Report*, May, 1949, p. 12.
4. "Testimonios de la Iglesia," *Semana*, May 7, 1949, pp. 5-6.
5. *Hispanic World Report*, July, 1949, p. 15.
6. "Liberal Victory," *Newsweek*, June 20, 1949, p. 44.
7. "On the Cliff," *Time*, June 20, 1949, p. 34.
8. *Ibid.*
9. "Balance Electoral," *Semana*, June 18, 1949, p. 6.
10. "Gómez: El Presidente," *Semana*, July 28, 1950, pp. 6-7.
11. Lucio Pabón Nuñez, *Quevedo: Político de la Oposición* (Bogotá, Editorial ARGRA, 1949), p. 101.
12. "Gómez: El Presidente," *Semana*, July 28, 1950, pp. 6-7.

13. Lucas Caballero Calderón, *Figuras Políticas de Colombia* (Bogotá: Editorial Kelly, 1945), p. 183.

14. Lilo Linke, *Andean Adventure: A Social and Political Study of Colombia, Ecuador and Bolivia* (London: Hutchinson & Co., Ltd., 1945), p. 269.

15. "God's Angry Man," *Time,* October 24, 1949, p. 43.

16. Caballero Calderón, *Figuras Políticas,* p. 183.

17. Antonio García, *Gaitán y el Problema de la Revolución Colombiana* (Bogotá: Cooperativa de Artes Gráficas, 1955), p. 303.

18. Vernon Lee Fluharty, *Dance of the Millions: Military Rule and the Social Revolution in Colombia, 1930-1956* (Pittsburgh: University of Pittsburgh Press, 1957), p. 51.

19. John Gunther, *Inside Latin America* (New York: Harper & Brothers, 1941), pp. 172-73.

20. Germán Arciniegas, *The State of Latin America,* trans. Harriet de Onis (New York: Alfred A. Knopf, Inc., 1952), p. 165.

21. "El Código de la Paz," *Semana,* July 16, 1949, pp. 6-7.

22. *Ibid.*

23. *Hispanic World Report,* October, 1949, p. 17.

24. "Trouble in the Offing," *Newsweek,* September 12, 1949, p. 42.

25. *Ibid.*

26. *Hispanic World Report,* October 1949, p. 16.

27. "Debate with Bullets," *Newsweek,* September 19, 1949, p. 42.

28. *Ibid.*

29. Arciniegas, *State of Latin America,* p. 167.

30. *Ibid.*

31. "Sinai Democrático," *Semana,* September 24, 1949, p. 7.

32. "Por Unanimidad," *Semana,* October 8, 1949, p. 5.

33. "God's Angry Man," *Time,* October 24, 1949, p. 43.

34. Arciniegas, *State of Latin America,* p. 164.

35. *Ibid.,* p. 167.

36. *Ibid.*

37. "Mensajes," *Semana,* November 5, 1949, pp. 12-13.

38. Abelardo Forero Benavides, *Un Testimonio contra la Barbarie Política; por la Conciliación Nacional* (Bogotá: Editorial Los Andes, 1953), pp. 16-17.

39. José Antonio Osorio Lizarazo, *Colombia donde los Andes se Disuelven* (Santiago de Chile: Editorial Universitaria, 1955), 123.

40. "Revolution of the Right," *Time,* November 21, 1949, p. 37.

41. "Estado de Sitio," *Semana,* November 19, 1949, pp. 5-6.

42. "Revolution of the Right," *Time,* November 21, 1949, p. 37.

43. *Ibid.*

44. Arciniegas, *State of Latin America,* pp. 171-72.

45. "Cloudy but Milder," *Newsweek,* November 21, 1949, p. 48.

46. "God's Angry Man," *Time,* October 24, 1949, p. 45.

47. *El Siglo,* November 28, 1949, p. 1.

48. *Life,* as cited in Arciniegas, *State of Latin America,* pp. 176-77.

49. *The Atlantic Monthly,* as cited in Arciniegas, *State of Latin America,* p. 178.

50. Olive Holmes, "Colombian Strife Epitomizes Latin American Crisis," *Foreign Policy Bulletin,* November 18, 1949, p. 4.

51. "No Peace in Sight," *Newsweek,* November 28, 1949, p. 38.

52. Arciniegas, *State of Latin America,* p. 176.

53. Germán Arciniegas from *Cuadernos Americanos,* Enero-Febrero, 1950, p. 33, as cited in Miguel Jorrín, *Governments of Latin America* (New York: D. Van Nostrand Co., Inc., 1953), p. 293.

CHAPTER SEVEN

1. *Hispanic American Report,* January, 1950, p. 20.
2. "Para la Historia," *Semana,* January 7, 1950, p. 6.
3. *The Political Situation in Colombia: The Opposition and the Government, April 9, 1948-April 9, 1950* (Bogotá: n.p., 1950), pp. 7-8.
4. *Ibid.,* p. 17.
5. *Hispanic American Report,* February, 1950, p. 22.
6. See the lengthy discussion in *El Liberal,* January, 30-31, February, 1-3, 1950.
7. "La Tésis del Gobierno," *Semana,* February 4, 1950, pp. 5-6.
8. "Profecía de la Semana," *Semana,* March 18, 1950, p. 5.
9. *Ibid.,* pp. 5-6.
10. *El Tiempo,* March 20, 1950, p. 1.
11. "El Reino de la Paz," *Semana,* April 1, 1950, p. 5.
12. "Political Peace—Perhaps," *Newsweek,* April 3, 1950, p. 40.
13. *Ibid.*
14. "Good and Bad Times," *Newsweek,* February 27, 1950, p. 40.
15. "Political Peace—Perhaps," *Newsweek,* April 3, 1950, p. 40.
16. "Blades of Grass," *Time,* August 14, 1950, p. 35.
17. *Hispanic American Report,* June, 1950, p. 22.
18. "Brindis y Votos," *Semana,* March 4, 1950, pp. 5-6.
19. "El Muro de Bronce," *Semana,* May 6, 1950, p. 10.
20. *Ibid.*
21. "Veneración y Acatamiento," *Semana,* December 10, 1949, pp. 7-8.
22. "Twilight of the Liberals," *Newsweek,* May 29, 1950, p. 36.
23. *Ibid.*
24. *Ibid.*
25. *Ibid.,* p. 38.
26. "Laureano Takes Over," *Newsweek,* August 21, 1950, p. 47.
27. "Transmisión del Mando," *Semana,* August 12, 1950, p. 5.
28. Germán Arciniegas, *The State of Latin America,* trans. Harriet de Onis (New York: Alfred A. Knopf, Inc., 1952), p. 178.
29. "Laureano Takes Over," *Newsweek,* August 21, 1950, p. 47.
30. W. O. Galbraith, *Colombia: A General Survey* (London: Royal Institute of International Affairs, 1953), p. 134.
31. "Blades of Grass," *Time,* August 14, 1950, p. 35.

CHAPTER EIGHT

1. Ignacio Escallón, *Itinerario de una Reconstrucción Nacional* (Bogotá: Dirección de Información y Propaganda de la Presidencia de la República, 1952), pp. 9-11.
2. "La Política Monetaria," *Semana,* March 3, 1951, p. 8.
3. *Hispanic American Report,* October, 1950, p. 26.
4. *Hispanic American Report,* April, 1950, p. 30.
5. Escallón, *Reconstrucción Nacional,* p. 15.
6. "Colombia Bids for Foreign Capital," *Business Week,* June 30, 1951, p. 114.
7. "La Política Monetaria," *Semana,* March 3, 1951, p. 8.
8. *Hispanic American Report,* January, 1951, p. 28.
9. *Ibid.,* May, 1951, p. 23.
10. Escallón, *Reconstrucción Nacional,* p. 16.
11. *Hispanic American Report,* August, 1951, p. 24.
12. "Colombia Bids for Foreign Capital," *Business Week,* June 30, 1951, p. 114.
13. Vernon Lee Fluharty, *Dance of the Millions: Military Rule and the Social Revolution in Colombia, 1930-1956* (Pittsburgh: University of Pittsburgh Press, 1957), p. 125.
14. "Biografías," *Semana,* June 25, 1949, p. 7.

15. Germán Arciniegas, *The State of Latin America*, trans. Harriet de Onis (New York: Alfred A. Knopf, Inc., 1952), p. 180.

16. *Ibid.*, pp. 180-81.

17. *Hispanic American Report*, January, 1951, p. 26.

18. "El Año Nuevo," *Semana*, December 30, 1950, pp. 6-7.

19. "Circulo Vicioso," *Semana*, May 26, 1951, pp. 6-7.

20. *Ibid.*

21. "Death in the Countryside," *Time*, August 6, 1951, pp. 30-31.

22. *Hispanic American Report*, October, 1950, p. 24.

23. "El Gran Adversario," *Semana*, January 20, 1951, p. 5.

24. "Convención de 600," *Semana*, May 26, 1951, pp. 6-7.

25. "Quinteto Combativo," *Semana*, June 23, 1951, p. 7.

26. *El Siglo*, June 25, 1951, p. 4.

27. "Peace Powwows," *Newsweek*, October 1, 1951, p. 40.

28. See complete constitutional section in William Marion Gibson, *The Constitutions of Colombia* (Durham: Duke University Press, 1948).

29. "Derecho de Sucesión," *Semana*, October 7, 1950, pp. 5-7.

30. "Historia de una Camisa," *Semana*, August 14, 1948, p. 14.

31. *Ibid.*

32. "El Gran Adversario," *Semana*, January 20, 1951, p. 5.

33. "Candidaturas," *Semana*, April 14, 1951, p. 14.

34. *Hispanic American Report*, June, 1951, p. 24.

35. *Ibid.*, September, 1951, p. 23.

36. "Las Elecciones," *Semana*, September 1, 1951, p. 6.

37. "Horas de Tensión," *Semana*, November 3, 1951, p. 8.

38. José Antonio Osorio Lizarazo, *Colombia donde los Andes se Disuelven* (Santiago de Chile: Editorial Universitaria, 1955), p. 124.

39. "La División," *Semana*, November 17, 1951, pp. 9-10.

40. *Ibid.*

CHAPTER NINE

1. *Hispanic American Report*, February, 1952, p. 24.

2. *Ibid.*, March, 1952, p. 23.

3. Roberto Urdaneta Arbeláez, *Declaraciones sobre importantes Temas de la Administración Pública* (Bogotá: Imprenta Nacional, 1952), p. 26.

4. *Hispanic American Report*, March, 1952, p. 23.

5. *El Tiempo*, January 5, 1952, p. 1.

6. *El Espectador*, August 22, 1952, p. 1.

7. *Hispanic American Report*, September, 1952, p. 22.

8. "Time of Crisis," *Newsweek*, September 29, 1952, p. 53.

9. "The Wheel of Hate," *Time*, September 22, 1952, p. 40.

10. "Noches de Colombia," *Semana*, September 13, 1952, p. 7.

11. *Ibid.*

12. *El Siglo*, September 7, 1952, p. 1.

13. "Noches de Colombia," *Semana*, September 13, 1952, p. 6.

14. "The Wheel of Hate," *Time*, September 22, 1952, p. 40.

15. *El Tiempo*, September 8, 1952, pp. 1-4.

16. Herbert Matthews, "Colombia: Political Volcano," *Nation*, November 8, 1952, p. 423.

17. *Hispanic American Report*, October, 1952, p. 20.

18. "Conferencia," *Semana*, September 20, 1952, p. 5.

19. *Ibid.*

20. "Time of Crisis," *Newsweek*, September 29, 1952, p. 54.

21. From *El Diario Colombiano,* September 15, 1952, p. 8, as cited in Vernon Lee Fluharty, *Dance of the Millions: Military Rule and the Social Revolution in Colombia, 1930-1956* (Pittsburgh: University of Pittsburgh Press, 1957), p. 129.

22. "Hechos," *Semana,* September 13, 1952, p. 5.

23. Urdaneta Arbeláez, *Administración Pública,* p. 28.

24. *Ibid.,* p. 24.

25. "Explicaciones Precisas," *Semana,* July 26, 1952, p. 8.

26. *Hispanic American Report,* March, 1951, p. 19.

27. John Caldwell Thiessen, *A Survey of World Missions* (Chicago: Inter-Varsity Press, 1955), pp. 357-58.

28. John Joseph Considine, *New Horizons in Latin America* (New York: Dodd, Mead & Company, 1958), p. 259.

29. Thiessen, *World Missions,* p. 359.

30. Considine, *New Horizons,* p. 258.

31. William C. Easton, *Colombian Conflict* (London: Christian Literature Crusade, 1954), p. 6.

32. Miner Searle Bates, *Religious Liberty: An Inquiry* (New York: International Missionary Council, 1945), p. 82.

33. Thiessen, *World Missions,* pp. 346-47.

34. Germán Arciniegas, *The State of Latin America,* trans. Harriet de Onis (New York: Alfred A. Knopf, Inc., 1952), p. 182.

35. "Colombia Mob Stones Presbyterian Church," *Christian Century,* April 9, 1952, p. 422.

36. "Priests Lead Children in Stoning Church," *Christian Century,* April 23, 1952, pp. 483-84.

37. David Bushnell, "What Has Happened to Democracy in Colombia?" *Current History,* January, 1953, p. 40.

38. "What is the Truth about Colombia?" *Christian Century,* October 1, 1952, pp. 1116-17.

39. Peter Schmid, "Sinners, Saints, and Civil War," *The American Mercury,* September, 1952, p. 29.

40. *Ibid.*

41. W. Stanley Rycroft, "Bitter Struggle in Colombia," *Christian Century,* February 1, 1950, p. 141.

42. Eduardo Ospina, *The Protestant Denominations in Colombia* (Bogotá: Imprenta Nacional, 1954), p. 202.

43. Bushnell, "What Has Happened to Democracy in Colombia?" *CH,* p. 41.

44. "War Without End," *Time,* August 18, 1952, p. 30.

45. "La Suficiente Ilustración," *Semana,* May 17, 1952, p. 9.

46. "War Without End," *Time,* August 18, 1952, p. 30.

47. Ospina, *Protestant Denominations,* p. 23.

48. *Hispanic American Report,* August, 1952, p. 25.

49. Edwin Lieuwen, *Arms and Politics in Latin America* (New York: Frederick A. Praeger, Inc., 1960), p. 87.

50. *Ibid.,* p. 88.

51. Tad Szulc, *Twilight of the Tyrants* (New York: Henry Holt Company, 1959), p. 223.

52. "Homenaje," *Semana,* October 11, 1952, p. 5.

53. "Vuelo al Orinoco," *Semana,* November 22, 1952, p. 6.

54. "Afirmación," *Semana,* December 27, 1952, pp. 7-8.

CHAPTER TEN

1. Silvio Villegas y Abel Naranjo, *Panegéricos de Mariano Ospina Pérez y Laureano Gómez* (Bogotá: Editorial Nuevo Muno, 1950), p. 55.

2. Harold Eugene Davis (ed.), *Government and Politics in Latin America* (New York: The Ronald Press Company, 1958), p. 96.

3. *Ibid.*, p. 200.

4. Germán Arciniegas, *The State of Latin America*, trans. Harriet de Onis (New York: Alfred A. Knopf, Inc., 1952), p. 163.

5. John Gunther, *Inside Latin America* (New York: Harper & Brothers, 1941), p. 166.

6. Vernon Lee Fluharty, *Dance of the Millions: Military Rule and the Social Revolution in Colombia, 1930-1956* (Pittsburgh: University of Pittsburgh Press, 1957, p. 62.

7. Samuel Guy Inman, *Latin America: Its Place in World Life* (rev. ed.: New York: Harcourt, Brace and Company, 1942), p. 346.

8. "Back to Bolivar," *Time*, February 25, 1952, pp. 40, 43.

9. *Ibid.*

10. Fluharty, *Dance of the Millions*, p. 63.

11. Antonio García, *Gaitán y el Problema de la Revolución Colombiana* (Bogotá: Cooperativa de Artes Gráficas, 1955), p. 299.

12. *Ibid.*, p. 300.

13. "CEDEC Report," *Christian Century*, July 1, 1953, p. 764.

14. Edward Tomlinson, *Look Southward, Uncle* (New York: The Devin-Adair Company, 1959), p. 102.

15. "Yerros Constitucionales," *El Siglo*, May 21, 1953, pp. 1-4.

16. "Biografía de una Idea," *Semana*, June 14, 1952, p. 5.

17. "La Segunda Vuelta," *Semana*, June 21, 1952, p. 7.

18. *Hispanic American Report*, September, 1952, pp. 23-24.

19. "Años de Historia," *Semana*, August 16, 1952, pp. 6, 8.

20. Roberto Urdaneta Arbeláez, *Mensaje al Congreso Nacional en sus Sesiones de 1952* (Bogotá: Imprenta Nacional, 1952), p. 17.

21. See special edition looking forward to next decade, *El Siglo*, December 30, 1952; also *Semana* report, January 10, 1953.

22. *Hispanic American Report*, July, 1952, p. 22.

23. "El Amado Recinto," *Semana*, October 25, 1952, p. 5.

24. "Carta," *Semana*, July 19, 1952, pp. 6-8.

25. David Bushnell, "What Has Happened to Democracy in Colombia?" *Current History*, January, 1953, pp. 40, 42.

26. See *Semana*, January 17, 1953, p. 6, as cited in Fluharty, *Dance of the Millions*, p. 133.

27. Bushnell, "What Has Happened to Democracy in Colombia?" *CH*, pp. 40, 42.

28. Fluharty, *Dance of the Millions*, p. 134.

29. *El Siglo*, see issues of April 3-6, 1953.

30. *El Siglo*, April 14, 1953, p. 1.

31. "El Discurso," *Semana*, April 25, 1953, p. 5.

32. Fluharty, *Dance of the Millions*, p. 135.

33. See *La Prensa* (New York), April 19, 1953, p. 1, as cited in *ibid.*, p. 135.

34. Tad Szulc, *Twilight of the Tyrants* (New York: Henry Holt Company, 1959), p. 216.

35. "Símbolos Patrios," *Semana*, May 16, 1953, pp. 13-14.

36. *Ibid.*, p. 12.

37. *New York Times*, May 15, 1953, p. 10.

38. *Ibid.*

39. Colombia, Dirección de Información y Propaganda, *Seis Meses de Gobierno* (Bogotá: Imprenta Nacional, 1953), pp. 5-6.

40. *New York Times*, May 15, 1953, p. 10.

41. Fluharty, *Dance of the Millions*, p. 137.

42. *El Diario*, July 28, 1953, p. 5.

43. "Yo Asumo el Mando!" *Semana*, June 20, 1953, pp. 5-6.
44. *Ibid.*, p. 7.
45. Szulc, *Twilight of the Tyrants*, p. 224.
46. "Yo Asumo el Mando!" *Semana*, June 20, 1953, p. 8.
47. *New York Times*, June 14, 1953, p. 1.
48. Colombia, *Seis Meses de Gobierno*, p. 10.
49. *New York Times*, June 14, 1953, p. 12.
50. Paul S. Lietz, "Colombia Gets Army Rule," *America*, July 4, 1953, p. 350.
51. "Opportunity for Colombia," *Nation*, July 11, 1953, p. 23.
52. José Antonio Osorio Lizarazo, *Colombia donde los Andes se Disuelven* (Santiago de Chile: Editorial Universitaria, 1955), p. 126.
53. García, *Gaitán*, p. 337.
54. Fluharty, *Dance of the Millions*, p. 139.

CHAPTER ELEVEN

1. Tad Szulc, *Twilight of the Tyrants* (New York: Henry Holt Company, 1959), p. 225.
2. Colombia, Dirección de Información y Propaganda, *Seis Meses de Gobierno* (Bogotá Imprenta Nacional, 1953), p. 12.
3. "General Satisfaction," *Time*, July 27, 1953, p. 24.
4. *New York Times*, June 15, 1953, p. 1.
5. Colombia, *Seis Meses de Gobierno*, p. 235.
6. "Fast Out of the Gate," *Newsweek*, June 29, 1953, p. 52.
7. Colombia, *Seis Meses de Gobierno*, p. 13.
8. *Ibid.*, p. 15.
9. *New York Times*, June 27, 1953, p. 11.
10. *New York Times*, June 18, 1953, p. 12.
11. *New York Times*, June 21, 1953, p. 23.
12. *El Tiempo*, August 24, 1953, p. 3.
13. Abelardo Forero Benavides, *Un Testimonio contra la Barbarie Política; por la Conciliación Nacional* (Bogotá: Editorial Los Andes, 1953), pp. 107, 109.
14. *New York Times*, May 17, 1953, p. 12.
15. "Opportunity for Colombia," *Nation*, July 11, 1953, p. 22.
16. *New York Times*, July 8, 1953, p. 5.
17. *New York Times*, August 22, 1953, p. 5.
18. *New York Times*, August 20, 1953, p. 13.
19. *New York Times*, August 28, 1953, p. 5.
20. *New York Times*, June 17, 1953, p. 18.
21. *El Tiempo*, June 24, 1953, p. 1.
22. Szulc, *Twilight of the Tyrants*, p. 226.
23. *New York Times*, August 20, 1953, p. 13.
24. *Diario Oficial*, August 22, 1953, p. 1.
25. *El Siglo*, August 22, 1953, p. 1.
26. *New York Times*, September 26, 1953, p. 3.
27. *New York Times*, October 2, 1953, p. 6.
28. *El Tiempo*, November 5, 1953, p. 1.
29. *El Tiempo*, November 29, 1953, p. 1.
30. Colombia, *Seis Meses de Gobierno*, p. 196.
31. *El Tiempo*, November 19, 1953, p. 1.
32. *New York Times*, April 4, 1954, p. 24.
33. *Ibid.*
34. *Ibid.*
35. *Economía Colombiana*, June, 1954, p. 257.

36. Ricardo Silva, *Los Trabajadores ante Los Partidos* (Bogotá: Editorial Antares, 1955), pp. 251-52.

37. *New York Times*, July 29, 1954, p. 7.

38. *New York Times*, August 8, 1954, p. 11.

39. Szulc, *Twilight of the Tyrants*, p. 228.

40. *New York Times*, August 26, 1954, p. 15.

41. *El Tiempo*, September 9, 1954, p. 1.

42. *New York Times*, September 4, 1954, p. 3.

43. Pedro Luis Belmonte, *Antecedentes Históricos de los Sucesos del 8 y 9 de Junio de 1954* (Bogotá: Imprenta Nacional, 1954), p. 135.

44. *New York Times*, June 10, 1954, p. 12.

45. *New York Times*, June 11, 1954, p. 8.

46. Belmonte, *Antecedentes Históricos*, pp. 131-32.

47. *Ibid.*, p. 136.

48. *Ibid.*, p. 169.

49. José Antonio Osorio Lizarazo, *Colombia donde los Andes se Disuelven* (Santiago de Chile: Editorial Universitaria, 1955), p. 127.

50. *New York Times*, December 16, 1954, p. 28.

51. *New York Times*, March 7, 1954, p. 43.

52. *New York Times*, March 17, 1954, p. 17.

CHAPTER TWELVE

1. *El Tiempo*, January 3, 1955, p. 1.

2. "Perspectiva," *Semana*, January 10, 1955, p. 7.

3. "La Guerra Fria y la Paz Económica?" *Visión*, January 7, 1955, p. 15.

4. Tad Szulc, *Twilight of the Tyrants* (New York: Henry Holt Company, 1959), pp. 225-26.

5. *New York Times*, February 26, 1955, p. 5.

6. Vernon Lee Fluharty, *Dance of the Millions: Military Rule and the Social Revolution in Colombia, 1930-1956* (Pittsburgh: University of Pittsburgh Press, 1957), p. 246.

7. *New York Times*, February 26, 1955, p. 5.

8. Fluharty, *Dance of the Millions*, p. 246.

9. *New York Times*, February 27, 1955, p. 23.

10. Szulc, p. 229.

11. *Ibid.*, p. 230.

12. The New York *Times*, April 2, 1954, p. 42.

13. The New York *Times*, May 14, 1954, p. 7.

14. The New York *Times*, January 5, 1955, p. 79.

15. *Hispanic American Report*, October, 1954, pp. 442-43.

16. *Diario Oficial*, October 23, 1954, pp. 2-3.

17. *New York Times*, January 5, 1955, p. 7.

18. *Hispanic American Report*, December, 1954, pp. 555-56.

19. *Semana*, January 18, 1954, p. 5, as cited in Fluharty, *Dance of the Millions*, p. 259.

20. "Batalla en Villarica," *La Prensa* (New York), April 8, 1955, p. 1, as cited in Fluharty, *Dance of the Millions*, p. 272.

21. *La Prensa* (New York), April 12, 1955, p. 3, as cited in *ibid.*

22. "Pruebas Evidentes," *Semana*, May 16, 1955, p. 8.

23. *Diario Oficial*, May 15, 1955, p. 1.

24. *El Tiempo*, June 11, 1955, p. 1.

25. *Diario Oficial*, June 14, 1955, p. 1.

26. Colombia, Ministerio de Gobierno, *Teoría y Práctica de una Política Colombianista* (Bogotá: Empresa Nacional de Publicaciones, 1956), p. 16.

27. Edwin Lieuwen, *Arms and Politics in Latin America* (New York: Frederick A. Praeger, Inc., 1960), p. 89.

28. William Sylvane Stokes, *Latin American Politics* (New York: Thomas Y. Crowell Company, 1959), p. 112.

29. *New York Times*, February 25, 1955, p. 2.

30. *New York Times*, March 3, 1955, p. 7.

31. *Ibid.*

32. *Hispanic American Report*, May, 1955, pp. 164-65.

33. *New York Times*, June 11, 1955, p. 3.

34. *Hispanic American Report*, August, 1955, p. 320.

35. *New York Times*, July 31, 1955, p. 31.

36. "Censorship as Usual," *Time*, August 15, 1955, p. 23.

37. Fluharty, *Dance of the Millions*, p. 286.

38. *New York Times*, August 5, 1955, p. 6.

39. *New York Times*, August 6, 1955, p. 6.

40. *El Espectador*, August 14, 1955, p. 1.

41. *Visión*, September 2, 1955, p. 13.

42. *New York Times*, August 27, 1955, p. 2.

43. "Trouble in Colombia," *Business Week*, August 20, 1955, p. 168.

44. *New York Times*, August 30, 1955, p. 3.

45. Fluharty, *Dance of the Millions*, p. 289.

46. *New York Times*, August 30, 1955, p. 3.

47. *Ibid.*, August 2, 1955, p. 21.

48. *Ibid.*, September 22, 1955, p. 30.

49. *Ibid.*, September 24, 1955, p. 3.

50. "Rojas Pinilla y la Libertad de Prensa," *Visión*, October 14, 1955, p. 14.

51. *Ibid.*

52. *New York Times*, September 17, 1955, p. 2.

53. *Hispanic American Report*, January, 1956, p. 34.

54. *New York Times*, January 25, 1956, p. 13.

55. *New York Times*, June 3, 1956, p. 14.

56. *New York Times*, June 10, 1956, p. 32.

57. *Ibid.*

58. *New York Times*, August 24, 1956, p. 4.

59. "Rojas Pinilla y la Liberated de Prensa," *Visión*, October 14, 1955, p. 14.

60. *El Intermedio*, May 7, 1956, p. 1.

61. *New York Times*, September 17, 1955, p. 2.

CHAPTER THIRTEEN

1. Colombia, Dirección de Información y Propaganda, *Seis Meses de Gobierno* (Bogotá: Imprenta Nacional, 1953), p. 86.

2. Colombia, Dirección de Información y Propaganda, *Colombia Trabaja: Conferencias Radiales de los Señores Ministros del Despacho Ejecutivo con Motivo del Primer Año de Gobierno* (Bogotá: Imprenta Nacional, 1954), p. 13.

3. Pedro Luis Belmonte, *Antecedentes Históricos de los Sucesos del 8 y 9 de Junio de 1954* (Bogotá: Imprenta Nacional, 1954), p. 122.

4. Eduardo Santos, "Latin American Realities," *Foreign Affairs*, January, 1956, p. 256.

5. Carlos Villaveces R., *Política Fiscal* (Bogotá: Imprenta Nacional, 1953), p. 7.

6. *Ibid.*, p. 17.

7. *Economía Colombiana*, June, 1954, pp. 245-47.

8. Colombia, *Seis Meses de Gobierno*, p. 78.

9. Colombia, *Colombia Trabaja*, p. 17.

10. Belmonte, *Antecedentes Históricos*, p. 42.

11. *Ibid.*, p. 142.

12. Colombia, Ministerio de Gobierno, *Teoría y Práctica de una Política Colombianista* (Bogotá: Empresa Nacional de Publicaciones, 1956), pp. 51-52.

13. *Ibid.*, p. 54.

14. "Reflejos," *Semana*, September 26, 1955, p. 8.

15. *La Prensa* (New York), June 12, 1956, p. 1, as cited in Vernon Lee Fluharty, *Dance of the Millions: Military Rule and the Social Revolution in Colombia, 1930-1956* (Pittsburgh: University of Pittsburgh Press, 1957), p. 306.

16. *Ibid.*, pp. 305-6.

17. "Third Force," *Time*, June 25, 1956, p. 33.

18. *New York Times*, August 23, 1956, p. 7.

19. Miguel Jorrín, *Governments of Latin American* (New York: D. Van Nostrand Co., Inc., 1953), p. 293.

20. Robert J. Alexander, *Communism in Latin America* (New Brunswick: Rutgers University Press, 1957), p. 251.

21. Jorrín, *Governments of Latin America*, p. 293.

22. "Nuevas Siglas," *Semana*, November 14, 1955, p. 11.

23. Aurelio Caicedo Ayerbe, *Lineamientos de una Política Social* (Bogotá: Imprenta Nacional, 1954), p. 17.

24. *Ibid.*, p. 19.

25. *New York Times*, August 23, 1956, p. 7.

26. *Ibid.*

27. *New York Times*, August 16, 1956, p. 4.

28. "Eterno Retorno," *Semana*, August 8, 1955, p. 17.

29. *New York Times*, August 20, 1953, p. 13.

30. *New York Times*, January 24, 1956, p. 9.

31. "Church Versus Schools," *Time*, December 26, 1955, p. 24.

32. *New York Times*, January 24, 1956, p. 9.

33. "Church Versus Schools," *Time*, December 26, 1955, p. 24.

34. "El Presidente," *Semana*, January 8, 1956, p. 9.

35. *Hispanic American Report*, November, 1955, p. 560.

36. *New York Times*, January 24, 1956, p. 9.

37. *Hispanic American Report*, November, 1955, p. 560.

38. "Bull-Ring Massacre," *Time*, February 20, 1956, p. 34.

39. Fluharty, *Dance of the Millions*, p. 296.

40. *El Catolicismo*, February 10, 1956, as cited in "Sangre en Bogotá," *Visión*, March 2, 1956, p. 16.

41. "Lucha sin Cuartel contra Políticos Resentidos, Anuncia," *La Prensa* (New York), February 6, 1956, p. 1, as cited in Fluharty, *Dance of the Millions*, pp. 295-96.

42. "Bull-Ring Massacre," *Time*, February 20, 1956, p. 34.

43. "Sangre en Bogotá," *Visión*, March 2, 1956, p. 16.

44. Rojas Pinilla Reprueba y Condena Sucesos," *La Prensa* (New York), February 20, 1956, p. 3, as cited in Fluharty, *Dance of the Millions*, p. 298.

45. "Sangre en Bogotá," *Visión*, March 2, 1956, p. 16.

46. "Bull-Ring Massacre," *Time*, February 20, 1956, p. 34.

47. *New York Times*, March 22, 1956, p. 14.

48. *Ibid.*

49. "Eduardo Santos: '15.770 ediciones,'" *Visión*, October 14, 1955, p. 17.

50. "El Retorno," *Semana*, October 3, 1955, p. 13.

51. *El Espectador*, November 14, 1955 and succeeding issues.

52. *New York Times*, January 25, 1956, p. 1.

53. Tad Szulc, *Twilight of the Tyrants* (New York: Henry Holt Company, 1959), p. 207.

54. *New York Times*, August 2, 1956, p. 15.

55. Szulc, *Twilight of the Tyrants*, p. 238.

56. "Laureano: '. . .para los dictadores, marea baja. . .,'" *Visión*, August 31, 1956, p. 10.

57. Szulc, *Twilight of the Tyrants*, p. 238.

58. "Prosperous President," *Time*, July 16, 1956, p. 30.
59. Szulc, *Twilight of the Tyrants*, p. 213.
60. *Ibid.*, p. 238.
61. *New York Times*, August 12, 1956, p. 16.
62. Szulc, *Twilight of the Tyrants*, p. 239.
63. *New York Times*, August 8, 1956, p. 1.
64. *New York Times*, August 9, 1956, p. 1.
65. *Ibid.*
66. *New York Times*, August 10, 1956, p. 4.
67. *New York Times*, August 14, 1956, p. 5
68. Szulc, *Twilight of the Tyrants*, p. 240.
69. *New York Times*, August 16, 1956, p. 4.
70. *New York Times*, August 19, 1956, p. 27.
71. *Ibid.*
72. "Dictator in Trouble," *US News & World Report*, August 31, 1956, p. 20.
73. *New York Times*, September 1, 1956, p. 14.

CHAPTER FOURTEEN

1. *New York Times*, October 12, 1956, p. 3.
2. Tad Szulc, *Twilight of the Tyrants* (New York: Henry Holt Company, 1959), p. 241.
3. *New York Times*, November 2, 1956, p. 21.
4. "La Tercera ANAC," *Visión*, November 9, 1956, p. 11.
5. *New York Times*, November 2, 1956, p. 21.
6. *New York Times*, October 25, 1956, p. 37.
7. Szulc, *Twilight of the Tyrants*, p. 241.
8. *New York Times*, November 4, 1956, p. 9.
9. "Auto-golpe de Estado," *Visión*, November 16, 1956, p. 20.
10. *Ibid.*
11. *New York Times*, December 4, 1956, p. 31.
12. "The Mess in Bogotá," *Time*, October 22, 1956, pp. 43-44.
13. *New York Times*, October 14, 1956, p. 13.
14. *New York Times*, November 18, 1956, p. 6.
15. *New York Times*, November 18, 1956, p. 88.
16. "Colombia Pays Off $62 Million in US But Fiscal Slate Still Shows Smudges," *Business Week*, February 16, 1957, p. 150.
17. *New York Times*, March 21, 1957, p. 16.
18. "Itinerario," *Semana*, March 29-April 5, 1957, pp. 11-12.
19. *New York Times*, March 24, 1957, p. 29.
20. "Composición," *Semana*, April 5-April 12, 1957, p. 8.
21. *New York Times*, April 14, 1957, p. 13.
22. "Hell-Bent for Election," *Time*, May 6, 1957, p. 38.
23. *New York Times*, April 24, 1957, p. 7.
24. Szulc, *Twilight of the Tyrants*, p. 245.
25. "Programa," *Semana*, May 3-May 10, 1957, p. 8.
26. William Marion Gibson, *The Constitutions of Colombia* (Durham: The Duke University Press, 1948), see Constitution of 1886, Article 129 on p. 336, Article 171 on p. 341.
27. *New York Times*, April 26, 1957, p. 8.
28. *New York Times*, May 2, 1957, p. 12.
29. *New York Times*, May 3, 1957, p. 1.
30. "The Strongman Falters," *Time*, May 13, 1957, p. 38.
31. "Now the Showdown," *Newsweek*, May 13, 1957, p. 62.
32. *New York Times*, May 4, 1957, p. 1.

33. Szulc, *Twilight of the Tyrants*, p. 246.
34. "Now the Showdown," *Newsweek*, May 13, 1957, p. 62.
35. *New York Times*, May 5, 1957, p. 1.
36. Szulc, *Twilight of the Tyrants*, p. 246.
37. *New York Times*, May 6, 1957, p. 14.
38. "The Strongman Falls," *Time*, May 20, 1957, p. 40.
39. *New York Times*, May 6, 1957, p. 14.
40. The Strongman Falls," *Time*, May 20, 1957, p. 40.
41. "Why a Ruler Toppled," *Newsweek*, May 20, 1957, p. 60.
42. *New York Times*, May 9, 1957, p. 1.
43. *New York Times*, May 8, 1957, p. 1.
44. "Why a Ruler Toppled," *Newsweek*, May 20, 1957, p. 60.
45. Szulc, *Twilight of the Tyrants*, pp. 243-44.
46. *Ibid.*, p. 248.
47. "La Batalla de la Madrugada del 10 de Mayo," *Semana*, May 17-May 24, 1957, p. 7.
48. "The Strongman Falls," *Time*, May 20, 1957, p. 40.
49. *New York Times*, May 11, 1957, p. 1.
50. *New York Times*, May 12, 1957, p. 1.
51. Szulc, *Twilight of the Tyrants*, p. 213.
52. *Ibid.*, 214.

CHAPTER FIFTEEN

1. Tad Szulc, *Twilight of the Tyrants* (New York: Henry Holt Company, 1959), p. 248.
2. *New York Times*, May 11, 1957, p. 1.
3. *New York Times*, May 13, 1957, p. 12.
4. Szulc, *Twilight of the Tyrants*, p. 243.
5. *New York Times*, May 12, 1957, p. 1.
6. *Ibid.*
7. "Optimistic Glow," *Time*, September 2, 1957, p. 27.
8. *New York Times*, May 13, 1957, p. 1.
9. "A Regime Changes," *The Economist*, May 18, 1957, p. 583.
10. *New York Times*, May 19, 1957, p. 26.
11. *Ibid.*, p. 6.
12. *Ibid.*, p. 26.
13. *Ibid.*, May 21, 1957, p. 3.
14. *Ibid.*, p. 18.
15. *Ibid.*
16. *Hispanic American Report*, August, 1957, p. 314.
17. "Fast Comeback in Colombia," *Business Week*, May 18, 1957, p. 142.
18. *New York Times*, June 1, 1957, p. 21.
19. *Ibid.*, January 8, 1958, p. 49.
20. "Fast Comeback in Colombia," *Business Week*, May 18, 1957, p. 142.
21. *New York Times*, June 23, 1957, p. 9.
22. "Colombia's New Regime Sweeps Up Fiscal Debris of Ousted Dictator," *Business Week*, June 29, 1957, p. 138.
23. *New York Times*, June 1, 1957, p. 21.
24. *Ibid.*, December 15, 1957, p. 25.
25. *Ibid.*, April 13, 1958, p. 18.
26. *Ibid.*, December 15, 1957, p. 25.
27. *Ibid.*, December 16, 1957, p. 14.
28. *Ibid.*, June 4, 1957, p. 13.
29. "Optimistic Glow," *Time*, September 2, 1957, p. 27.
30. "Declaración de Sitges," *Visión*, August 16, 1957, p. 13.

31. *New York Times*, August 22, 1957, p. 7.
32. "Contrast in Plebiscites," *The Economist*, November 30, 1957, p. 760.
33. "Convención Divisora," *Visión*, November 8, 1957, p. 14.
34. *New York Times*, November 18, 1957, p. 6.
35. *Ibid.*
36. "Una Falsa Alarma—Rojas: Sólo con Boleto de Ida," *Visión*, September 28, 1957, p. 12.
37. *New York Times*, November 19, 1957, p. 21.
38. *New York Times*, November 24, 1957, p. 25.
39. "Colombia Escoge su Destino," *Visión*, January 3, 1958, p. 21.
40. *New York Times*, November 24, 1957, p. 25.
41. *Ibid.*, December 1, 1957, p. 27.
42. *Ibid.*, December 2, 1957, p. 11.
43. *Ibid.*, December 3, 1957, p. 21.
44. "A 'Second Republic?'" *Newsweek*, December 16, 1957, p. 60.
45. "Sume y Compare," *Semana*, March 24-March 30, 1960, p. 9.
46. *El Tiempo*, December 2, 1957, p. 1.
47. *New York Times*, December 3, 1957, p. 34.
48. "Colombia Escoge su Destino," *Visión*, January 3, 1958, p. 21.
49. "Plan to End a Civil War: Government by Both Sides," *US News & World Report*, December 20, 1957, p. 75.
50. "The Restoration," *Time*, December 16, 1957, p. 28.
51. *New York Times*, December 12, 1957, p. 23.
52. *Ibid.*, March 4, 1958, p. 12.
53. "Los Conservadores Decidirán," *Visión*, March 14, 1958, p. 17.
54. "Sume y Compare," *Semana*, March 24-March 30, 1960, p. 9.
55. "Cuál de Todos 'incumplirá'?" *Visión*, April 11, 1958, p. 16.
56. "Colombia Escoge su Destino," *Visión*, January 3, 1958, p. 21.
57. *New York Times*, April 2, 1958, p. 3.
58. *Ibid.*, April 16, 1958, p. 2.
59. *Ibid.*, April 17, 1958, p. 3.
60. *Ibid.*, April 20, 1958, p. 9.
61. "Next President," *Time*, May 5, 1958, p. 30.
62. "The Half-Day Revolt," *Time*, May 12, 1958, p. 37.
63. Scott Seegers, "Most Influential Man in Latin America," *The Diplomat*, April, 1960, p. 17.
64. *New York Times*, May 3, 1958, p. 1.
65. "The Half-Day Revolt," *Time*, May 12, 1958, p. 37.
66. *New York Times*, May 4, 1958, p. 10.
67. "Why the Plot Failed," *Newsweek*, May 12, 1958, p. 58.
68. "Sume y Compare," *Semana*, March 24-March 30, 1960, p. 9.
69. *New York Times*, May 5, 1958, p. 1.
70. "Next President," *Time*, May 5, 1958, p. 30.

CHAPTER SIXTEEN

1. Scott Seegers, "Most Influential Man in Latin America," *The Diplomat*, April, 1960, p. 15.
2. *Ibid.*, p. 16.
3. *Ibid.*, p. 15.
4. Alberto Lleras Camargo, *The Inter-American Way of Life: Selections from the Recent Addresses and Writings of Alberto Lleras* (Washington: Pan American Union, 1951), p. 25.
5. *Ibid.*, p. 27.
6. *Ibid.*, p. 37.

7. "Renacimiento Colombiano," *Visión*, May 23, 1958, p. 10.
8. *Ibid.*, p. 12.
9. *Ibid.*, p. 10.
10. *New York Times*, May 6, 1958, p. 16.
11. *Ibid.*, August 8, 1958, p. 2.
12. "Renacimiento Colombiano," *Visión*, May 23, 1958, p. 11.
13. *New York Times*, August 8, 1958, p. 2.
14. *Ibid.*, August 29, 1958, p. 6.
15. "No Longer the Fear," *Newsweek*, September 8, 1958, p. 44.
16. *New York Times*, August 21, 1958, p. 3.
17. *Ibid.*, May 15, 1957, p. 18.
18. "One-Man Miracle," *Time*, May 11, 1959, p. 46.
19. "Lleras Frente a la Violencia," *Visión*, June 19, 1959, p. 18.
20. *Hispanic American Report*, August, 1959, p. 331.
21. *Ibid.*, October, 1959, p. 445.
22. Seegers, "Most Influential Man in Latin America," *Diplomat*, pp. 17, 42.
23. *Ibid.*, p. 42.
24. *Hispanic American Report*, April, 1959, p. 103.
25. "Renacimiento Colombiano," *Visión*, May 23, 1958, p. 10.
26. *New York Times*, September 27, 1958, p. 1.
27. "Rojas Pinilla Está Listo," *Visión*, October 10, 1958, p. 16.
28. *Ibid.*
29. "Atracción Estelar," *Visión*, October 24, 1958, p. 18.
30. *New York Times*, October 12, 1958, p. 24.
31. "End of a Strange Mission," *Newsweek*, December 15, 1958, p. 58.
32. *New York Times*, October 16, 1958, p. 12.
33. "Collared by the Cops," *Time*, November 3, 1958, p. 35.
34. *Ibid.*
35. *New York Times*, December 4, 1958, p. 1.
36. *Ibid.*, December 2, 1958, p. 39.
37. "Guilty Dictator," *Time*, March 30, 1959, p. 26.
38. "A Dictator's Bad Memory," *Time*, February 9, 1959, p. 27.
39. "Rojas Pinilla y el Senado," *Visión*, February 13, 1959, pp. 15-16.
40. *New York Times*, February 7, 1959, p. 6.
41. "Colombia: Democracia y Pan," *Visión*, April 10, 1959, p. 16.
42. *Ibid.*, p. 15.
43. *Ibid.*, p. 16.
44. "Guilty Dictator," *Time*, March 30, 1959, p. 26.
45. "Maniobra para Tapar Delitos," *Visión*, February 28, 1959, p. 16.
46. *New York Times*, March 19, 1959, p. 21.
47. *Ibid.*, January 13, 1960, p. 83.
48. *Ibid.*, September 5, 1958, p. 11.
49. *Ibid.*, January 14, 1959, p. 62.
50. "Colombia's Road to Recovery," *Latin American Report*, August, 1959, p. 8.
51. *New York Times*, January 14, 1959, p. 62.
52. "Colombia's Road to Recovery," LAR, p. 9.
53. "One-Man Miracle," *Time*, May 11, 1959, p. 46.
54. "La Crisis es Economica," *Visión*, January 2, 1959, p. 13.
55. *Hispanic American Report*, May, 1959, p. 156.
56. *Ibid.*, April, 1959, p. 103.
57. *Ibid.*, July, 1959, p. 277.
58. John Moors Cabot, "United States-Colombian Cooperation," *US Department of State Bulletin*, December 30, 1957, pp. 1038-39.

59. "Colombia's Road to Recovery," *LAR*, pp. 8-9.
60. *Hispanic American Report*, August, 1959, p. 333.
61. *New York Times*, January 14, 1959, p. 62.
62. "Renacimiento Colombiano," *Visión*, May 23, 1958, p. 11.
63. "Lleras Busca una Solución," *Visión*, July 3, 1959, p. 15.
64. *Hispanic American Report*, September, 1959, p. 390.
65. *Ibid.*, p. 391.
66. *Hispanic American Report*, October, 1959, p. 444.
67. "One-Man Miracle," *Time*, May 11, 1959, p. 46.
68. "Un Año de Gobierno," *Visión*, August 14, 1959, p. 20.
69. "Colombia's Road to Recovery," *LAR*, p. 9.

CHAPTER SEVENTEEN

1. *Hispanic American Report*, September, 1959, p. 389.
2. "Un Año de Gobierno," *Visión*, August 14, 1959, p. 20.
3. "Alternación o No," *Visión*, July 17, 1959, p. 15.
4. *Ibid.*, p. 14.
5. "Lastres Fuerzas," *ibid.*, September 11, 1959, p. 16.
6. " 'Viraje de 90 Grados,' " *ibid.*, October 9, 1959, p. 16.
7. "Elecciones Decisivas," *ibid.*, October 23, 1959, p. 18.
8. *Ibid.*
9. *Hispanic American Report*, December, 1959, p. 556.
10. *Ibid.*
11. *New York Times*, August 21, 1958, p. 5.
12. *Hispanic American Report*, January, 1960, p. 613.
13. "Mantener el Sistema Político," *Semana*, March 17-March 24, 1960, p. 10.
14. *Hispanic American Report*, February, 1960, p. 677.
15. "Ojos en Marzo," *Semana*, January 28-February 3, 1960, pp. 20-21.
16. "El Regreso de Ospina," *Semana*, February 11-February 17, 1960, pp. 10-11.
17. *Ibid.*, p. 11.
18. "Elección Colombiana," *Visión*, March 11, 1960, p. 14.
19. *Hispanic American Report*, April, 1960, p. 115.
20. "Elección Colombiana," *Visión*, March 11, 1960, p. 15.
21. *Ibid.*, p. 14.
22. *Hispanic American Report*, February, 1960, p. 677.
23. "Tiempo Incompleto," *Semana*, February 18-February 24, 1960, p. 9.
24. *Ibid.*, p. 10.
25. "Elección Colombiana," *Visión*, March 11, 1960, pp. 14-15.
26. *New York Times*, March 20, 1960, p. 12.
27. "Elección Colombiana," *Visión*, March 11, 1960, p. 15.
28. *Hispanic American Report*, March, 1960, p. 40.
29. *Ibid.*, April, 1960, p. 114.
30. "Eso Será," *Semana*, February 18-February 24, 1960, p. 42.
31. *New York Times*, March 20, 1960, p. 12.
32. *Ibid.*, March 21, 1960, p. 10.
33. "Reparto de la Abstención," *Semana*, March 24-March 30, 1960, p. 7.
34. "Por que no Votaron los Colombianos," *ibid.*, March 31-April 6, 1960, p. 26.
35. "Reparto de la Abstención," *ibid.*, March 24-March 30, 1960, p. 7.
36. "Por que no Votaron los Colombianos," *ibid.*, March 31-April 6, 1960, p. 25.
37. "Sume y Compare," *ibid.*, March 24-March 30, 1960, p. 15.
38. "Por que no Votaron los Colombianos," *ibid.*, March 31-April 6, 1960, p. 25.
39. *Ibid.*
40. *New York Times*, March 22, 1960, p. 13.
41. "Por que no Votaron los Colombianos," *Semana*, March 31-April 6, 1960, p. 25.

42. "Las Manos Limpios," *ibid.,* March 24-March 30, 1960, p. 8.
43. "Triqui-Traques," *ibid.,* March 31-April 6, 1960, p. 12.
44. *Ibid.*
45. *Ibid.*
46. "Cuadro Azul," *ibid.,* April 7-April 20, 1960, p. 8.
47. *Ibid.,* pp. 9-10.
48. "Se Agitó el Avispero," *Visión,* April 8, 1960, p. 16.
49. "Triqui-Traques," *Semana,* March 31-April 6, 1960, p. 14.

CHAPTER EIGHTEEN

1. "Colombia. . ." *Latin American Report,* October, 1959, p. 2.
2. *New York Times,* January 13, 1960, p. 82.
3. *Hispanic American Report,* November, 1960, p. 628.
4. *New York Times,* January 11, 1961, p. 67.
5. *Hispanic American Report,* January, 1961, p. 811.
6. *New York Times,* January 13, 1960, p. 82.
7. *Hispanic American Report,* December, 1960, p. 717.
8. *New York Times,* January 13, 1960, p. 82.
9. *Hispanic American Report,* March, 1960, p. 42.
10. *Ibid.,* August, 1960, p. 398.
11. *New York Times,* January 13, 1960, p. 69.
12. *Hispanic American Report,* February, 1961, p. 902.
13. *Ibid.,* December, 1960, p. 718.
14. *Ibid.,* March, 1960, p. 43.
15. Contents of the address were widely reported in the Bogotá papers as well as in *Semana.* *El Tiempo* carried the text in full. The *New York Times* reported the speech in its February 26, 1960, number.
16. *Hispanic American Report,* August, 1960, p. 398.
17. *New York Times,* January 11, 1961, p. 67.
18. *New York Times,* April 2, 1952, as cited in *America,* March 8, 1958, p. 654.
19. "Missionaries in Colombia," *America,* March 8, 1958, p. 654.
20. "Time and Events Will Tell," *Christian Century,* May 29, 1957, p. 675.
21. Richard M. Fagley, "Colombia: Major Issues," *Christian Century,* April 9, 1958, p. 436.
22. "Príncipe y Pastor," *Semana,* February 7, 1953, p. 20.
23. *Hispanic American Report,* July, 1959, p. 276.
24. *Ibid.,* February, 1961, p. 900.
25. Peter Schmid, *Beggars on Golden Stools,* trans. Merwyn Sevill (New York: Frederick A. Praeger, Inc., 1956), p. 151.
26. "Histórico Mensaje de Lleras Camargo a las . . . Fuerzas Armadas," *Visión,* June 20, 1958, pp. 16-17.
27. Scott Seegers, "Most Influential Man in Latin America," *The Diplomat,* April, 1960, p. 42.
28. " 'Viraje de 90 Grados,' " *Visión,* October 9, 1959, p. 16.
29. *Hispanic American Report,* February, 1960, p. 678.
30. *New York Times,* October 1, 1960, p. 5.
31. *Hispanic American Report,* March, 1960, p. 40.
32. *Ibid.,* September, 1960, p. 467.
33. *Ibid.,* November, 1960, pp. 627-28.
34. *Ibid.,* December, 1960, p. 717.
35. *El Tiempo,* August 18, 1960, p. 1.
36. *Hispanic American Report,* January, 1961, p. 809.
37. *Ibid.,* November, 1960, p. 627.
38. "Sigue El Contrabando," *Visión,* June 3, 1960.

39. The New York *Times,* January 14, 1960, p. 82.
40. *Ibid.*
41. *Hispanic American Report,* April, 1960, p. 115.

Chapter Nineteen

1. *New York Times,* July 4, 1960, p. 2.
2. *Ibid.,* November 11, 1960, p. 3.
3. *Ibid.,* July 21, 1960, p. 24.
4. Reproduced in *Hispanic American Report,* December, 1960, p. 666.
5. *New York Times,* November 7, 1960, p. 3.
6. *Ibid.,* January 13, 1960, p. 83.
7. Scott Seegers, "Most Influential Man in Latin America," *The Diplomat,* April, 1960, p. 42.
8. "La Bella Durmiente del Trópico," *Semana,* January 28-February 3, 1960, p. 19.
9. Rosendo Gómez, *Government and Politics in Latin America* (New York: Random House, 1960), p. 36.
10. *New York Times,* April 9, 1960, p. 5.

Bibliography

REMARKS

The annotated bibliography which follows is not considered exhaustive. At the same time, it is far more extensive than any the author has found for contemporary Colombia. Those interested in pursuing the subject personally should find adequate materials from these citations. Even so, many of the Spanish-language works are not widely available in the United States. This bibliography is based on materials found in the metropolitan area of Washington, D. C., probably the best single repository of Latin American materials in the country. Besides the Library of Congress and the library at the Pan American Union, there are several other sources in this region, including the appropriate embassies.

Organization of the books in Part I is somewhat arbitrary, and several works are pertinent to different topics. For the sake of convenience, the attempt has been made at classification under the various headings. Otherwise the results would have proved quite unwieldy. Comments on individual works have been kept as brief as possible. A particular attempt was made, in the case of Colombian works, to indicate the political affiliation or general orientation of the author.

The work of the late Professor Fluharty deserves individual comment. Fluharty's first thesis maintains that national problems have become critical in recent years, and until the mid-1950's went largely ignored by the traditional political parties. Furthermore, he praises the Rojas Pinilla regime for its attempts to meet these problems. My position agrees with the former, and severely disputes the latter. Even conceding that Fluharty completed his book before the overthrow of the military government, one must conclude that he saw in that regime what he wanted to see, not what should have been apparent. Unfortunately, his evaluation of Rojas Pinilla caused many to scorn his entire work, which received controversial comments upon publication. It should be emphasized that there are many valuable insights in this work, notwithstanding some of the unsound positions the author assumed. An opposite—and much more satisfactory—view of Rojas Pinilla is available in the recent journalistic work by the astute Tad Szulc of the *New York Times*.

Several Colombian writings should be mentioned. The Antonio García works are excellent, particularly the book discussing Jorge Gaitán at some length. Osorio Lizarazo is also worthwhile, if somewhat uneven. The Arciniegas work, treating all twenty American republics, has excellent if harsh evaluations of the Conservatives in the late 1940's. The various political viewpoints are all represented. It is interesting that several writers—including Silva, Londoño, and Restrepo Jaramillo—are intrigued by the corporative system.

Both the *bogotazo* and the church question are highly controversial, and widely deviating interpretations are available from the titles cited. The sections on the constitution, geography, and social matters are not extensive, as they are somewhat secondary to this study. The Law Division of the Library of Congress has a number of works on the Colombian legal section which have been omitted.

Part II is important in presenting the public statements of virtually all important political figures in the period under discussion. Each of the successive governments was reasonably active in propagandizing its policies. Less is available on the present experiment in divided government. Undoubtedly more will be forthcoming as that administration continues the pursuit of its objectives.

Several of the periodicals have been extensively quoted, particularly for the parts of the text dealing with events of recent years. The newsweekly *Semana* of Bogotá is invaluable; *Visión* is also good and contains a number of significant interviews. The *Hispanic American Report* edited by Ronald Hilton of Stanford is one of the best and most thorough sources of current developments. As always, the *New York Times* is important. Its analytical articles on Colombia are not universally sound, but its on-the-spot coverage of major events, reported in recent years by Sam Pope Brewer and Tad Szulc, are excellent. Most of the other periodicals only infrequently publish items dealing with Colombia. These are of variable quality, but some are deserving of attention. This is particulary true of the last two or three years, which are largely untouched insofar as books are concerned.

ANNOTATIONS

I. BOOKS

A. GENERAL WORKS

Alba, Victor. *Historia del Comunismo en América Latin.* Mexico: Ediciones Occidentales, 1954. A short general work containing scattered references to the Colombian situation.

Alexander, Robert J. *Communism in Latin America*. New Brunswick: Rutgers University Press, 1957. The standard work on the subject, it details Colombian communism and minimizes the extent of Red direction of the *bogotazo*.

Almond, Gabriel A., and James S. Coleman (eds.). *The Politics of the Developing Areas*. Princeton: Princeton University Press, 1960. The article by George I. Blanksten on Latin America is a notable contribution to the literature.

Arboleda Llorente, José María. *Historia de Colombia*. Popayán: Editorial Universidad del Cauca, 1952. A history which discusses the Ospina Pérez and Gómez regimes in the concluding pages.

Arciniegas, Germán. *The State of Latin America*. Translated by Harriet de Onis. New York: Alfred A. Knopf, Inc., 1952. A liberal educator of considerable stature writes with insight but bitterness of the Ospina Pérez and Gómez administrations.

Burnett, Ben G. *The Recent Colombia Party System: Its Organization and Procedure*. Unpublished Ph.D. dissertation, University of California at Los Angeles, 1955. I have lacked access to this, but Burnett's recent work suggests that this merits attention.

Bryson, Lyman (ed.). *Social Change in Latin America Today*. New York: Harper & Brothers, 1960. Note the chapter by John Gillin, which discusses the unconsolidated, emergent middle class in Latin American society.

Davis, Harold Eugene (ed.). *Government and Politics in Latin America*. New York: The Ronald Press Company, 1958. See Frank Brandenburg on political parties.

Duverger, Maurice. *Political Parties*. London: Methuen, 1951. An excellent work on comparative parties with European orientation but pertinence to Latin America.

Fluharty, Vernon Lee. *Dance of the Millions: Military Rule and the Social Revolution in Colombia, 1930-1956*. Pittsburgh: University of Pittsburgh Press, 1957. This controversial study is discussed in the bibliographical commentary.

Follick, Mont. *The Twelve Republics*. London: Williams & Norgate, Ltd., 1952. Follick is a British politician with utopian dreams of a Caribbean confederation. His comments are interesting, but there are many factual errors.

Galbraith, W. O. *Colombia: A General Survey*. London: Royal Institute of International Affairs, 1953. One of the several fine RIIA surveys on Latin America, this is a gold mine of information.

Gómez, Rosendo. *Government and Politics in Latin America*. New York: Random House, 1960. A brief but worthwhile look at contemporary Latin politics.

Gunther, John. *Inside Latin America*. New York: Harper & Brothers, 1941. This work is dated but contains interesting views of national leaders of the time.

Hansen, Harry (ed.). *The World Almanac, 1960.* New York: The New York World-Telegram and The Sun, 1960. A convenient source of current data.

Hanson, Simon G. *Economic Development in Latin America.* Washington: Inter-American Affairs Press, 1951. A general treatment by an astute observer who includes Colombia in his analysis.

Henao, Jesús María, and Gerardo Arrubla. *History of Colombia.* Translated by J. Fred Rippy. Chapel Hill: The University of North Carolina Press, 1938. The standard English history of Colombia, which leaves something to be desired.

Inman, Samuel Guy. *Latin America: Its Place in World Life,* rev. ed. New York: Harcourt, Brace and Company, 1942. An excellent general work by an experienced writer in the field.

James, Preston E. *Latin America,* 3rd. ed. New York: The Odyssey Press, 1959. The best such work for geographic and economic analysis.

Johnson, John J. *Political Change in Latin America: The Emergence of the Middle Sector.* Stanford: Stanford University Press, 1958. This admirable work is a pioneering effort in Latin American investigations and deserves thoughtful attention.

Jorrín, Miguel. *Governments of Latin America.* New York: D. Van Nostrand Co., Inc., 1953. A convenient work with excellent information on labor.

Lieuwen, Edwin. *Arms and Politics in Latin America.* New York: Frederick A. Praeger, Inc., 1960. This is not definitive but is nonetheless an excellent first treatment of the subject. There is worthwhile information on the Colombian military and Gustavo Rojas Pinilla.

Linke, Lilo. *Andean Adventure: A Social and Political Study of Colombia, Ecuador and Bolivia.* London: Hutchinson & Co., Ltd., 1945. This work by a German-born woman examines social questions, has interesting comments on Gómez.

Lippmann, Walter. *A Preface to Politics.* New York: The Macmillan Company, 1933. One of his many fine contributions. While not dealing with a Latin context, he makes a number of pertinent comments regarding the attitudes of ruling elites.

Macdonald, Austin F. *Latin American Politics and Government.* New York: Thomas Y. Crowell Company, 1949. This text has a thorough examination of constitutional organs in Colombia.

Michels, Robert. *Political Parties: A Sociological Study of the Oligarchical Tendencies of Modern Democracy.* Glencoe, Illinois: The Free Press, 1949. A reappearance of Michels' 1915 classic. The nature of oligarchical tendencies in Colombian political parties makes this work especially pertinent.

Molina, Gerardo. *Proceso y Destino de la Libertad.* Bogotá: Biblioteca de la Universidad Libre, 1955. This general treatment of liberty in a Latin American perspective discusses Colombia in the final chapter, where Conservatives are attacked.

Morales Benítez, Otto. *Testimonio de un Pueblo*. Bogotá: Editorial Antares, 1951. The author is a young native of Riosucio who writes of the city of Manizales. Despite a nineteenth-century emphasis, he closes with a treatment of contemporary Manizales.

Patiño B., Abelardo. *The Political Ideas of the Liberal and Conservative Parties in Colombia during the 1946-1953 Crisis*. Unpublished Ph.D. dissertation, The American University, 1954. A somewhat superficial narrative with a definite pro-Liberal bias.

Pierson, William Whatley, and Federico G. Gil. *Governments of Latin America*. New York: McGraw-Hill Book Company, Inc., 1957. A substantial text which treats its subject-matter topically rather than country-by-country.

Pike, Fredrick B. (ed.). *Freedom and Reform in Latin America*. South Bend: University of Notre Dame Press, 1959. Articles in this collective work include several discussions of freedom and the position of Catholicism.

Poblete Troncoso, Moisés, and Ben G. Burnett. *The Rise of the Latin American Labor Movement*. New York: Bookman Associates, 1960. One of the very few works devoted exclusively to the development of labor. Individual treatment of countries is necessarily a bit sketchy.

Romoli, Kathleen. *Colombia: Gateway to South America*. New York: Doubleday & Company, Inc., 1941. Miss Romoli looks at the people and society with perception. She is less good on political matters.

Russell, William Richard. *The Bolívar Countries: Colombia, Ecuador, Venezuela*. New York: Coward-McCann, 1949. Essentially a travel book, its accounts on the major Colombian cities are better than most. The writing is excellent.

Schmid, Peter. *Beggars on Golden Stools*. Translated from the German by Merwyn Sevill. New York: Frederick A. Praeger, Inc., 1956. The Swiss-born Schmid went through Latin America swiftly, and his comments are not always reliable.

Schurz, William Lytle. *Latin America*. New York: E. P. Dutton & Co., Inc., 1949. A general survey with less emphasis on politics than on geography and society.

Stokes, William Sylvane. *Latin American Politics*. New York: Thomas Y. Crowell Company, 1959. The most recent publication of a prominent Latin Americanist, the work is oddly organized at points but is full of valuable information. Bibliographic sections are detailed.

Szulc, Tad. *Twilight of the Tyrants*. New York: Henry Holt Company, 1959. A highly readable journalistic treatment of dictators, including an excellent chapter on Rojas Pinilla. *New York Times* correspondent Szulc is among the very best North American reporters in Latin America.

Tomlinson, Edward. *Look Southward, Uncle*. New York: The Devin-Adair Company, 1959. This diffuse work by the veteran NBC reporter for Latin America is disappointing. Individual passages stand out, however, including informal discussions of various 'isms' now or recently current in the hemisphere.

Whitaker, Arthur Preston. *The United States and South America*: *The Northern Republics*. Cambridge: Harvard University Press, 1948. One of Professor Whitaker's less recent works. The Colombian passages include an interesting look at Alberto Lleras in younger days.

B. POLITICS AND PUBLIC AFFAIRS

Andrade, Raúl. *La Internacional Negra en Colombia, y otros Ensayos*. Quito: Editora Quito, 1954. A critical look at contemporary political affairs in Colombia.

Azula Barrera, Rafael. *De la Revolución al Orden Nuevo*: *Proceso y Drama de un Pueblo*. Bogotá: Editorial Kelly, 1956. Written by a Boyacá Conservative who served in cabinet posts under Ospina Pérez and Gómez, this highly readable work looks particularly at the progressive breakdown of order in the late 1940's. The author was present with Ospina Pérez during much of the *bogotazo* and was first-hand observer of the involved political maneuvering. The book is written with moderation but is clearly the work of a Conservative.

Belmonte, Pedro Luis. *Antecedentes Históricos de los Sucesos del 8 y 9 de Junio de 1954*. Bogotá: Imprenta Nacional, 1954. The official account by the Rojas Pinilla regime of the student riots of 1954. Rojas Pinilla's speeches are included.

Bogotá, Concejo. *Colección Jorge Eliécer Gaitán; Documentos para una Biografía Compilados y Arreglados por Alberto Figueredo Salcedo*. Bogotá: Imprenta Municipal, 1949. Gaitán's career is reviewed in a prolific collection of testimonials worth the attention of those examining the career of this Liberal.

Caballero Calderón, Lucas. *Figuras Políticas de Colombia*. Bogotá: Editorial Kelly, 1945. A group of informal sketches of prominent politicians, written by "KLIM" in the columns of *El Tiempo* and *Sábado*.

Canal Ramírez, Gonzalo. *El Estado Cristiano y Bolivariano del 13 de Junio*. Bogotá: Editorial Antares, 1955. An unconvincing defense of the bases of the military revolution and its social and political goals.

Cano, Luis. *Periodismo*. Bogotá: Editorial Minerva, n. d. A general discussion of the national press and political affairs by the late famed journalist of *El Espectador*.

Colombia, Dirección de Información y Propaganda. *Colombia Trabaja*: *Conferencias Radiales de los Señores Ministros del Despacho Ejecutivo con Motivo del primer Año de Gobierno*. Bogotá: Imprenta Nacional, 1954. A collection of the addresses of Rojas Pinilla's cabinet ministers concluding his first year in power.

Forero Benavides, Abelardo. *Un Testimonio contra la Barbarie Política; por la Conciliación Nacional*. Bogotá: Editorial Los Andes, 1953. The author was a prominent young Liberal around 1950 who was for a time a member of his party directorate and a major publicist for party collaboration.

Forero Morales, Néstor. *Laureano Gómez; un Hombre, un Partido, una Nación.* Bogotá: Ediciones "Nuevo Mundo," 1950. The author, whose real name is Luis Gracían, is an ardent supporter of Gómez who wrote to praise that Conservative following his 1949 election as president.

Gaitán, Jorge Eliécer. *Las Ideas Socialistas en Colombia.* Bogotá: n. p., 1924. A basic work of the author written at an early age but outlining many of the beliefs he retained throughout his public career.

García, Antonio. *El Cristianismo en la Teoría y el la Práctica.* Bogotá: Fondo de Publicaciones "Vicente Azuero," 1952. Actually co-authored with Mario Revollo of *El Catolicismo,* this is an exchange of views in which the Socialist leader García argues his "third position" in some detail.

————. *Gaitán y el Problema de la Revolución Colombiana.* Bogotá Co-operativa de Artes Graficas, 1955. Here the esteemed García writes favorably of Gaitán and of the serious social problems of modern Colombia.

————. *La Rebelión de los Pueblos Débiles*: *Nacionalismo Popular y Anti-imperialismo,* 2nd. ed. La Paz: Editorial "Juventud," 1955. Outside his country during the Rojas Pinilla dictatorship, García writes political theory relating to the world's backward areas. He favors Latin American parties of the democratic left.

Gómez, Eugenio J. *Problema Colombianos.* Bogotá. Over a half-dozen separate works with the same heading, published by different houses, have appeared over the last twenty years. Most are politically oriented although, in ranging over other fields, somewhat disorganized.

Hilarión Sáchez, Alfonso. *Balas de la Ley.* Bogotá: Editorial Santafé, 1953. A semi-fictional work by a former lieutenant in the Policía Nacional, the presentation gives some flavor of the nature of public disturbances in the late 1940's.

Monsalve, Miguel. *Liberalismo.* Cali: Editorial Pacífico, 1953. A brief discussion of politics with, as the title suggests, a Liberal orientation.

Osorio Lizarazo, José Antonio. *Colombia donde los Andes de Disuelven.* Santiago de Chile: Editorial Universitaria, 1955. The prolific author, who in early 1960 suddenly turned up as editor of Generalissimo Trujillo's *El Caribe,* was a friend of Gaitán. He devotes one section of the book to Colombian politics, and unhesitatingly criticized Rojas Pinilla and his predecessors in power.

————. *El Bacilo de Marx.* Ciudad Trujillo, Editorial La Nación, 1959. This is characteristic of writings coming from the Dominican Republic, and the scourge of "marxian germs" has allegedly affected Colombia. The book is reportedly being published in English.

————. *Gaitán*: *Vida, Muerte y Permanente Presencia.* Buenos Aires: Ediciones López Negri, 1945. Here Osorio is of considerable value in discussing the career of Jorge Gaitán, including his own view of the *bogotazo* and aftermath.

Pabón Nuñez, Lucio. *La Tridivisión del Poder Público.* Bogotá: Editorial Librería Voluntad, 1943. For those interested in the early thought of Rojas Pinilla's most influential advisor, this is the thesis presented for Pabón Nuñez' doctorate.

———. *Quevedo: Político de la Oposición.* Bogotá: Editorial ARGRA, 1949. The author has gathered a number of articles he wrote for various journals during the 1940's, dealing with different subjects. A writer of erudition, he pays deep homage to Laureano Gómez.

Peña, Luis David. *Gaitán Intimo,* 2nd. ed. Bogotá: Editorial Iqueima, 1949. The author served for a time as editor of Gaitán's *Jornada.* He writes a one-sided polemic extolling the saintly virtues of the controversial Gaitán, concluding with a summary of the investigation of his hero's assassin.

Posada, Jaime. *La Revolución Democrática.* Bogotá: Editorial Iqueima, 1955. In a limited number of pages Posada argues for a revived Colombia while discussing the Rojas Pinilla government.

Puentes, Milton. *Historia del Partido Liberal Colombiano, 1810-1942.* Bogotá: Talleres Gráficas Mundo al Día, 1942. This tome of over 600 pages is a history of Colombia told with a Liberal slant. There are no formal discussions of platform programs that are current. Makes the debatable claim that Bolívar was a Liberal.

Quimbaya, Anteo. *Cuestiones Colombianas: Ensyos de Interpretación y Crítica.* Bogotá: Ediciones Sudamerica, 1958. This is of almost no value and is included only for those seeking a Marxian analysis of Colombian national development.

Ramírez Moreno, Augusto. *Una Política Triunfante.* Bogotá: Librería Voluntad, 1941. The author contributes an interesting discussion of politics at the close of the 1930's. Among his better passages are those treating the López-Santos split.

Restrepo Jaramillo, Gonzalo. *El Pensamiento Conservador: Ensayos Políticos.* Medellín: Tipografía Bedout, 1936. A prominent Conservative, one of Colombia's leading Catholic intellectuals, Restrepo Jaramillo explains what he considers the differences between the two parties. Liberals are attacked as anti-clerical.

Romero Aguirre, Alfonso. *Ayer, Hoy y Mañana del Liberalismo Colombiano,* 3rd. ed., 3 vols. in 1. Bogotá: Editorial Iqueima, 1949. Of particular interest is the third "volume," "Un Radical en el Congreso." Although oddly-organized, this includes a number of party proclamations, some of which relate to the period of the 1930's.

———. *El Partido Conservador ante la Historia.* Bogotá: Libreria Americana, 1944. Under a misleading title, the Liberal author examines what he calls consistent Conservative failure through the years.

Rueda Vargas, [General] Tomás. *El Ejército Nacional.* Bogotá: Librería

Colombiana Camacho Roldán & cia., Ltda., 1944. Discussion of Colombian military.

Ruiz Novoa, [Coronel] Alberto. *El Batallón Colombia en Korea, 1951-1954.* Bogotá: Empresa Nacional de Publicaciones, 1956. A lavishly-produced work of the Rojas regime that, through praise of the battalion in Korea, tried to bolster its own prestige.

Santos, Eduardo. *La Crisis de la Democracia en Colombia y "El Tiempo."* Mexico: Gráfica Panamericana, 1955. The former president and founder of *El Tiempo* describes the Rojas Pinilla closing of his newspaper in August, 1955. Much of the work includes protests from the international press. Insight into the Rojas Pinilla regime is good.

Silva, Ricardo. *Los Trabajadores ante Los Partidos.* Bogotá: Editorial Antares, 1955. The author, a distinguished jurist, writes favorably of the corporative system, putting social democracy ahead of political democracy. At the time of writing he favored the military regime as the instrument of national reform.

Vallejo, Alejandro. *Hombres de Colombia: Memorias de un Colombiano Exilado en Venezuela.* Caracas: Avila Gráfica, 1950. Vallejo was editor of *Jornada* in 1948 and a close friend of Gaitán. He was with the Liberal when Gaitán met his death. Chatty recollections of Liberal leaders are worth some attention.

Vallejo, Félix Angel. *Política: Misión y Destino.* Bogotá: Editorial Cosmos, 1954. In subjects as varied as administrative decentralization and the political rights of women, the author expresses highly personal opinions with forthrightness.

Villegas, Silvio and Abel Naranjo. *Panegéricos del Mariano Ospina Pérez y Laureano Gómez.* Bogotá: Editorial Nuevo Mundo, 1950. The co-authors, both rebels from the Conservative party in the 1930's, here write a pair of articles each in high praise of the two named Conservatives, with whom they had made their peace.

C. THE BOGOTAZO

Beaulac, Willard L. *Career Ambassador.* New York: Macmillan, 1951. Autobiographical recollections of the United States ambassador to Bogotá at the time of the riots. His account is favorable to President Ospina Pérez.

Dubois, Jules. *Freedom Is My Beat.* New York: Bobbs-Merrill Company, Inc., 1959. This veteran newsman, who was in Bogotá during the riots, gives a vivid description of the outburst. He is among those who blame the Communists almost entirely.

Estrada Monsalve, Joaquín. *El 9 de Abril en Palacio: Horario de un Golpe de Estado,* 3rd. ed. Bogotá: Editorial ABC, 1948. The author, a militant Conservative legislator and one-time director of *El Siglo,* witnessed many of the events. His account tallies with the official Conservative one.

Fandiño Silva, Francisco. *La Penetración Soviética en América y el 9 de*

Abril. Bogotá: Colección "Nuevos Tiempos," 1949. This is an intemperate and largely unsubstantiated version of the riots in which much blame is given Venezuela's *Acción Democrática,* which the author calls Moscow-trained.

Niño H., Alberto. *Antecedentes y Secretos del 9 de Abril.* Bogotá: Editorial Pax, 1949? Niño is former chief of the security forces and is convinced of Communist involvement, although less immoderate than Fandiño.

Orrego Duque, Gonzalo. *El 9 de Abril Fuera de Palacio.* Bogotá: Editorial Patria, 1949. Emphasis is given in describing the actions of rioters.

Palza S., Humberto. *La Noche Roja de Bogotá: Páginas de un Diario.* Buenos Aires: Imprenta López, 1949. The author is a former Bolivian delegate to the United Nations, and represented his country at the Bogotá Conference. His picture of violence presumably comes from a personal diary. Included is a text of official statements by various delegates to the Conference on the nature of the Communist threat to the Americas.

Pérez, Luis Carlos. *Los Delitos Políticos: Interpretación Jurídica del 9 de Abril.* Bogotá: Distribuidora Americana de Publicaciones, 1948. In a legalistic look at the subject, Pérez examines the Ospina Pérez view that a military *junta* would have disrupted the constitutional order to the detriment of Colombia.

Vallejo, Alejandro. *La Palabra Encadenada: Antes del 9 de Abril y Después.* Bogotá: Editorial Minerva, 1949. The analysis of a *gaitanista.*

D. THE CHURCH AND THE RELIGIOUS QUESTION

Arcila Robledo, Gregorio. *Las Misiones Franciscanas en Colombia: Estudio Documental.* Bogotá: Imprenta Nacional, 1950. In a scholarly history of the Colombian Franciscans, he mentions the Franciscan approach to the religious issue.

Bates, Miner Searle. *Religious Liberty: An Inquiry.* New York: International Missionary Council, 1945. A 600-page scholarly work on the general subject, by a Protestant. Passages on Colombia may be noted.

Botero Restrepo, Juan. *El Problema Misional.* Medellín: Ediciones Siglo XX, 1948. An extensive discussion of Catholic theory and practice in Colombia.

———. *Manuel del Trabajo.* Bogotá: Editorial "Prensa Católica," 1945. A short text setting down with little comment the social doctrine of the church.

Coleman, William Jackson. *Latin-American Catholicism: A Self-Evaluation.* Maryknoll, New York: Maryknoll Publications, 1958. Coleman offers a study of the Chimbote Report, which resulted from the 1953 Inter-American Catholic Action meeting in Lima, Peru. The Latin American view of Church problems is presented.

Considine, John Joseph. *New Horizons in Latin America.* New York: Dodd, Mead & Company, 1958. The respected Catholic writer includes information on the social activities of the Colombian church. He writes with moderation, although taking perhaps an overly-optimistic view in some instances.

Dain, Arthur John (ed.). *Mission Fields Today: A Brief World Survey.* London: Inter-Varsity Fellowship, 1956. The title indicates the nature of the work, and there is no individual treatment of the Latin republics.

Dunne, Peter Masten. *A Padre Views South America.* Milwaukee: The Bruce Publishing Company, 1945. For a Roman Catholic, Father Dunne is less optimistic than most. He argues at length for a more enlightened church approach.

Easton, William C. *Colombian Conflict.* London: Christian Literature Crusade, 1954. Easton, a worker in Colombia for the Worldwide Evangelical Crusade, illustrates the worst of the extreme Protestant position. His so-called interpretations are little short of outrageous. The most militant Protestant missionaries would agree with his analysis, however. His small book is filled with typographical errors as well.

Gibbons, William Joseph. *Basic Ecclesiastical Statistics for Latin America, 1958.* Maryknoll, New York: Maryknoll Publications, 1958. A compilation of Catholic data for Latin America, broken down into considerable detail.

Howard, George Parkinson. *Religious Liberty in Latin America?* Philadephia: The Westminster Press, 1944. Dr. Howard, an evangelical lecturer with wide experience in Latin America, examines the question posed in the title.

————. *We Americans: North and South.* New York: Friendship Press, 1951. Here the respected Howard urges tolerance and understanding on the part of both Protestants and Catholics.

Jaramillo Arango, Roberto. *El Clero en la Independencia.* Antioquia: Universidad de Antioquia, 1946. This deals almost entirely with the role of the clergy in earlier Colombian history, including long lists of active participants. The work is illustrative of the importance of the church in national development.

Lanao Loaiza, José Ramón. *La Cuestión Religiosa.* Manizales: Arturo H. Zapata, 1935. A philosophical discussion that looks at the Conservatives with particular favor, one should recall that it was published the year before the religious reforms of the 1936 constitutional codification.

Mecham, J. Lloyd. *Church and State in Latin America.* Chapel Hill: The University of North Carolina Press, 1934. The standard work on the subject.

Ospina, Eduardo. *The Protestant Denominations in Colombia.* Bogotá: Imprenta Nacional, 1954. Ospina, a professor at the Universidad Javeriana, presents an extreme Catholic view and criticizes harshly the "false" reports of Protestants under persecution.

Thiessen, John Caldwell. *A Survey of World Missions.* Chicago: Inter-Varsity Press, 1955. This is an extreme view by a Protestant who is completely unaware of the positive aspects of the church position.

E. THE CONSTITUTION AND JURIDICAL SYSTEM

Escobar Sierra, Hugo. *La Constituyente en nuestro Derecho Público y la Reforma Constitucional.* Bogotá: Pontificia Universidad Catholica Javeriana, 1953. A constitutional history with examinations of the various codifications.

Gibson, William Marion. *The Constitutions of Colombia.* Durham: The Duke University Press, 1948. A handy compilation which has introductory examinations of each of the documents, putting them into proper perspective.

Machado Góngora, Bernardo. *Monografía sobre Reforma Constitucional.* Bogotá: Pontificia Universidad Católica Javeriana, 1952. A thesis dealing with the matter indicated by the title.

Pineda, Néstor. *Constituciones de Colombia.* Bogotá: Editorial Cromos, 1950. A small compilation of constitutions with relatively little additional comment.

Riaño Pieschacon, Guillermo. *Hacia un Nuevo Estatuto del Estado Civil de las Personas.* Bogotá: Pontificia Universidad Católica Javeriana, 1953. A thesis which examines national laws with regard to voting and registration procedures.

Uribe Misas, Alfonso. *Entre Dos Polos: Ensayo sobre la Reforma Constitucional.* Medellín: Universidad de Antioquia, 1954. A lengthy discussion in which the two poles are communism and rightist dictatorship as exemplified by the 1936 condification and the 1953 *golpe,* respectively. The author attacks the Liberals, scoffs at the persecution of Protestants, and urges a return to the 1886 constitution and its "true" Catholic outlook.

F. ECONOMIC AFFAIRS

Banco de la República. *La Producción y las Economías Seccionales en Colombia.* Bogotá: Imprenta del Banco de la República, 1952. An expensive publication replete with maps, graphs, and tables, this analyzes the individual sectors of the national economy with particular emphasis on agriculture. Most figures are for either 1949 or 1950.

Currie, Lauchlin. *The Basis of a Development Program for Colombia.* Currie Mission Report. Baltimore: The Johns Hopkins Press, 1950. This is the famous 642-page economic report by the Currie group for the International Bank for Reconstruction and Development, basic for an understanding of economic problems.

―――. *The Basis of a Development Program for Colombia: Report of a Mission, The Summary.* Washington: International Bank for Reconstruction and Development, 1950. The summary of the entire report, first sent to the Colombian government, provides handy quick reference to the outlines of the complete report listed above.

Echavarría Olózaga, Hernán. *El Sentido Común en la Economía Colombiana,* 2nd. ed. Bogotá: Imprenta Nacional, 1958. A lengthy if disjointed examination of basic economic problems, with more emphasis on ideas and concepts that on concrete data.

Ellis, Cecil A. *Public Utilities in Colombia.* New York: United Nations, 1953. The subject was analyzed for the government by Mr. Ellis of the Technical Assistance Administration of the United Nations.

Federación Nacional de Comerciantes ("FENALCO"). *El Comercio Colombiano y la Economía Nacional.* Bogotá: Editorial Antares, 1951. An excellent if somewhat dated analysis of five economic studies undertaken under FENALCO direction.

Hirschman, Albert O., and George Kalmanoff. *Colombia: Highlights of a Developing Economy.* Bogotá: Banco de la República Press, 1955. This is a brief but detailed look at current economic conditions prepared by economic consultants for presentation at the Inter-American Investment Conference in New Orleans in early 1955. It emphasizes the strong points of the economy.

Londoño, Carlos Mario. *Economía Social Colombiana.* Bogotá: Imprenta Nacional, 1953. A fine examination of social and economic thought, the young author offers strong criticism of the capitalist system, which he calls a dehumanizing idea. He strongly favors state intervention. Many of his views are controversial, but they are deserving of attention.

Misión "Economía y Humanismo." *Estudio sobre las Condiciones del Desarrollo de Colombia.* Bogotá: Editorial Cromos, 1958. This study, directed by the Comité Nacional de Planeación, presents detailed analyses for the current government.

Pan American Union. *Selected Economic Data on the Latin American Republics.* Washington: Pan American Union. Periodic reports of the PAU on the Latin American economic conditions.

Rippy, J. Fred. *The Capitalists and Colombia.* New York: The Vanguard Press, 1931. One of the most prominent Latin Americanists examines largely the question of foreign oil interests in Colombia. Circumstances have changed, but his perceptive study remains worthy of attention.

Ruiz Luján, Samuel. *Para Construir un Nuevo Orden Económico.* St. Louis: University of St. Louis, 1949. A Catholic argument for the extension of the cooperatives in Colombia.

Scopes, L. A. *Colombia, Economic and Commercial Conditions.* London: British Board of Trade, 1950. An examination of circumstances when Laureano Gómez took office.

United States Department of Commerce, Bureau of Foreign Commerce. *Basic Data on the Economy of Colombia.* Washington: U.S. Department of Commerce, 1957. One of the periodic publications of the Commerce Department, this series is an excellent and generally reliable quick survey of Colombian economic situations.

———. *Investment in Colombia.* Washington: U.S. Department of Commerce, 1955. Another of the fine series of the Commerce Department.

G. GEOGRAPHY

Arango Cano, Jesús. *Geografía Física y Económica de Colombia.* Bogotá: Editorial Colombiana, 1955. Exactly what the title indicates.

Echeverri, Elío Fabio (ed.). *Colombia a la Mano.* Bogotá: n. p., 1955. This so-called historical-geographic text has much general information, handsomely presented but badly organized. There are a few scattered excerpts of speeches by Gustavo Rojas Pinilla.

Goez, Ramón Carlos. *Geografía de Colombia.* Mexico: Fondo de Cultura Económica, 1947. An orthodox geography of Colombia with excellent photographs and sketches.

Mejía Córdoba, Juvenal. *Geografía de Colombia.* Bogotá: n. p., 1945. Another acceptable treatment of the subject.

Platt, Raye Roberts. *Colombia.* Garden City, New York: Doubleday, 1959. A brief geographic sketch by a man long the head of the Department of Hispanic American Research at the American Geographical Society. The work verges on becoming a travel study.

Vila, Pablo. *Nueva Geografía de Colombia.* Bogotá: Librería Colombiana, 1945. This, one of the better works in the field, is a thorough study that is used as a text in the Colombian educational system.

H. SOCIAL MATTERS

Canal Ramírez, Gonzalo. *Función Social de la Propiedad.* Bogotá: Editorial Antares, 1953. A close look at property, ownership, and related social questions.

Fals-Borda, Orlando. *Peasant Society in the Colombian Andes: A Social Study of Saucio.* Gainesville: University of Florida Press, 1957. Originally a 1955 dissertation, this is a thorough study of institutionalized relationships in one area of the rugged Boyacá area.

Londoño, [General] Julio. *Nación en Crisis.* Bogotá: Ministerio de Educacion Nacional, División de Extensión Cultural, 1955. The general is concerned largely with questions of ethics and social culture in Colombia.

Montaña Cuéllar, Diego. *Sociología Americana.* Bogotá: Universidad Nacional de Colombia, Sección de Extensión Cultural, 1950. The author is a lawyer long prominent in the Colombian Communist party, particularly active in working with the petroleum workers. His approach to national social problems is interesting.

Parsons, James J. *Antioqueño Colonization in Western Colombia.* Berkeley: University of California Press, 1949. This examines matters of economy and the impact upon local society. Several fine plates are appended.

Piñeres Corpas, Joaquín. *Síntesis del Conflicto entre la Ciudad y la Provincia de Colombia.* Roma: Instituto Internacional de Sociología, 1951. The author writes of the social problems between city and province in the face of growing urbanization. He maintains that Colombia should remain essentially an agrarian country.

Pan American Union. *Problems of Housing of Social Interest.* Washington: Pan American Union, 1953. This PAU publication is precisely what the title suggests.

Restrepo, Ricardo. *Dicarquismo o Si la Razón Fuera Gobierno,* 3rd. ed. Bogotá: Editorial Cosmos, 1951. This is a rather cerebral discussion of political utopias and related social questions. In 1948 the author founded the short-lived *Partido Demócrata Colombiana.*

Smith, T. Lynn. *Tabio:* *A Study of Rural Organization.* Washington: U.S. Department of Agriculture, 1945. A social and economic study by an outstanding economist.

Ware, Caroline F. *Organización de la Comunidad para el Bienestar Social.* Washington: Pan American Union, 1954. An effective examination of Colombian social problems faced with the coming of urbanization and economic development.

West, Robert Cooper. *The Pacific Lowlands of Colombia.* Baton Rouge: Louisiana State University Press, 1957. This number of the LSU Social Science Series takes a thorough look at racial, cultural, social, and geographic matters in the Colombian lowlands.

II. PAMPHLETS, SPEECHES, PUBLIC DOCUMENTS

Andrade, Luis Ignacio. *Conferencia sobre Orden Público y otras Temas*: *Radiodifundida en la Noche de 15 de Agosto de 1952.* Bogotá: Dirección de Información y Propaganda de la Presidencia de la República, 1952. A speech by Urdaneta Arbeláez' Minister of Government in 1952, including discussion of forthcoming legal reforms.

Caicedo Ayerbe, Aurelio. *Lineamientos de una Política Social.* Bogotá: Imprenta Nacional, 1954. Text of a speech by General Rojas Pinilla's Minister of Labor on the closing of the congress of the Unión de Trabajadores Colombianos in 1954.

Colombia, Congreso. *Discursos Pronunciados con Motivo de la Transmisión del Mando Presidencial, Agosto de 1958.* Bogotá: Imprenta Nacional, 1958. Speeches delivered on the occasion of Lleras Camargo's 1958 inauguration.

————. Dirección de Información y Propaganda. *Seis Meses de Gobierno.* Bogotá: Imprenta Nacional, 1953. A lavish publication of almost 400 pages containing many speeches by Rojas Pinilla and his aides. Profusely illustrated, this is basic for any study of the Rojas Pinilla era.

————. Ministerio de Gobierno. *Asamblea Nacional Constituyente*: *Disposiciones Constitucionales y Legales, 1952-1955.* Bogotá: Imprenta Nacional, 1955. An expensive 800-page work including *rojista* speeches and some 150 pages of data, charts, and figures on 1955 voter registration, this is a major contribution of the Rojas Pinilla propaganda organ.

Colombia, Ministerio de Gobierno, *Teoría y Práctica de una Política Colombianista.* Bogotá: Empresa Nacional de Publicaciones, 1956. Another publication of the Rojas Pinilla regime including a variety of public statements by high-ranking members of that government.

Conservative National Directorate. *Los Programas Conservadores de 1849 a 1949*. Bogotá: Tip. Voto Nacional, 1952. A selective compilation of Conservative doctrine.

Escallón, Ignacio. *Itinerario de una Reconstrucción Nacional*. Bogotá: Dirección de Información y Propaganda de la Presidencia de la República, 1952. A brief work by a Conservative praising and listing alleged accomplishments of the Gómez and Ospina Pérez regimes. This *laureanista* pamphlet presents the Conservative view strongly.

Gómez, Laureano. *Comentarios a un Régimen*. Bogotá: Editorial Centro, 1935. A collection of articles written by Gómez for the press from late 1932 to mid-1934. Included are strong attacks on the Liberal administration of Olaya Herrera. A good sampling of Gómez' writing and his political personality.

————. *Interrogantes sobre el Progreso en Colombia*. Bogotá: Editorial Minerva, 1928. This old volume has several Gómez public statements delivered in 1928, before his control of the Conservatives was complete. Oratorical language gives little suggestion of the direction in which his beliefs later took him.

————. *Por la Cultura*: *Discursos del Presidente de la República, Laureano Gómez y del Director del Instituto Caro y Cuervo, José Manuel Rivas Sacconi*. Bogotá: n. p., 1952. Speeches by Gómez and Rivas Sacconi in October, 1951, shortly before Gómez stepped down from the active presidency.

La Oposición y el Gobierno del 9 de Abril de 1948 al 9 de Abril de 1950. Bogotá: Imprenta Nacional, 1950. A valuable document containing texts of the Liberal protest to President Ospina Pérez in 1950 and his reply to the party. This is also available in English, thanks to the Ospina Pérez government.

Liberal National Directorate. *El Liberalismo Colombiano Frente a la Dictadura*, Informe que rinde la Dirección Nacional del Liberalismo a la Convención del Partido. Bogotá: n. p., June, 1951. A statement of the Liberal position and its case against the administration in 1951.

Lleras Camargo, Alberto. *The Inter-American Way of Life*: *Selections from the Recent Addresses and Writings of Alberto Lleras*. Washington: Pan American Union, 1951. A short collection from Lleras Camargo's public declarations while serving as secretary-general of the Organization of American States.

————. *Un Año de Gobierno, 1945-1946*. Bogotá: Imprenta Nacional, 1946. A long collection of speeches and documents dealing with Lleras Camargo's year as chief executive following the resignation of López.

López, Alfonso. *La Integración Liberal*. Bogotá: Editorial Cromos, 1941. Statements preceding his ascension to the presidency for the second time.

Lozano y Lozano, Carlos. *Ideario del Liberalismo Actual*: *Conferencia Pro-*

nunciada por el doctor Carlos Lozano y Lozano el 14 Febrero 1939. Bogotá: Imprenta Nacional, 1939. Text of a statement of party beliefs by the temporary Liberal president, stating in highly literary style the reasons his party can bring Colombia, as he suggests, the best of all possible worlds.

Mosquera Garcé, Manuel. *Conferencia Pronunciada el 3 de Septiembre de 1952.* Bogotá: Dirección de Información y Propaganda de la Presidencia de la República, 1952. Text of a statement by Laureano Gómez' Minister of Labor. He later served for a time as Rojas Pinilla's Minister of Education.

Ospina Pérez, Mariano. *La Nueva Economía Colombiana.* Bogotá: Oficina de Información y Prensa de la Presidencia de la República, 1948. A statement by President Ospina Pérez discussing economic and social development.

———. *La Política de Unión Nacional: el Programa.* Bogotá: Imprenta Nacional, 1946. Speeches delivered by Ospina Pérez from March-August, 1946, from his acceptance at the Conservative convention to his presidential inaugural address.

Partido Liberal. *Programas y Estatutos del Partido Liberal Colombiano.* Bogotá: Departmento de Propaganda, 1944. Collection of Liberal platforms and programs in the late 1930's and the early 1940's.

Piedrahita Arango, Rubén. *Una Política en Obras Públicas.* Bogotá: Gobierno de las Fuerzas Armadas, 1955. Another expensive publication, with significant statements by Rojas Pinilla's Minister of Public Works, a navy admiral who later served as a member of the provisional *junta.*

Santos, Eduardo. *La Política Liberal en 1937.* Bogotá: Talleres Gráficos, Mundo al Día, 1937. *Santista* public statements upon his elevation to power.

Turbay Ayala, Gabriel. *Los Ideas Políticas de Gabriel Turbay.* Bogotá: Editorial Minerva, 1946. More than a dozen speeches and public discourses by Turbay Ayala during his unsuccessful bid for the presidency in 1945.

Urdaneta Arbeláez, Roberto. *Declaraciones sobre importantes Temas de la Administración Pública.* Bogotá: Imprenta Nacional, 1952. This is the text of an interview by the Acting President with Margarita Olano Cruz on the "Voz de Colombia" broadcast of February 15, 1952.

———. *Mensaje al Congreso Nacional en sus Sesiones de 1952.* Bogotá: Imprenta Nacional, 1952. The Acting President speaks of legislative matters and the problem of civil conflict.

Villaveces R., Carlos. *Economia y Fomento.* Bogotá: Imprenta Nacional, 1953. An extensive collection of public utterances by Urdaneta Arbeláez' Minister of Economy. Eighty pages are devoted to decrees of the Acting President.

———. *Política Fiscal.* Bogotá: Imprenta Nacional, 1953. A collection of Villaveces' speeches after joining the Rojas Pinilla government. Included is an examination of the July 15, 1953, projected tax reform, decree No. 1877.

III. SIGNED ARTICLES

Blanksten, George. "Political Groups in Latin America," *American Political Science Review,* LIII, No. 1 (March, 1959), 106-27.

Bushnell, David. "What Has Happened to Democracy in Colombia?" *Current History*, XXIV, No. 1 (January, 1953), 38-42.

Cabot, John Moors. "United States-Colombian Cooperation," *U.S. Department of State Bulletin*, XXXVII (December 30, 1957), 1038-42.

Dozer, Donald Marquand. "The Roots of Revolution in Latin America," *Foreign Affairs*, XXVII, No. 2 (January, 1949), 274-88.

Fagley, Richard M. "Colombia: Major Issues," *Christian Century*, LXXV (April 9, 1958), 434-36.

Fitzgibbon, Russell H. "The Party Potpourri in Latin America," *The Western Political Quarterly*, X, No. 1 (March, 1957), 3-22.

Gil, Federico G. "Responsible Parties in Latin America," *Journal of Politics*, XV, No. 3 (August, 1953), 333-48.

Gómez Grajales, Luis, "Financing a Small Nation," *UN World*, V (May, 1951), 54-55.

Holguera, J. León. "The Changing Role of the Military in Colombia," *Journal of Inter-American Studies*, III, No. 3 (July, 1961), 351-58.

Holmes, Olive. "Colombian Strife Epitomizes Latin American Crisis," *Foreign Policy Bulletin*, XXIX (November 18, 1949), 3-4.

Lietz, Paul S. "Colombia Gets Army Rule," *America*, LXXXIX (June 4, 1953), 350.

Ligutti, Luigi G. "Showdown in Colombia," *America*, XCIX (June 14, 1958), 330-33.

Matthews, Herbert L. "Colombia: Political Violence," *Nation*, CLXXV (November 8, 1952), 423-25.

Rycroft, W. Stanley. "Bitter Struggle in Colombia," *Christian Century*, LXVII (February 1, 1950), 140-42.

Santos, Eduardo. "Latin American Realities," *Foreign Affairs*, XXXIV, No. 2 (January, 1956), 245-57.

Schmid, Peter. "Sinners, Saints, and Civil War," *The American Mercury*, LXXV (September, 1952), 23-31.

Seegers, Scott. "Most Influential Man in Latin America," *The Diplomat* (April, 1960), 38-44.

Silvert, K. H. "Political Change in Latin America," from The American Assembly, *The United States and Latin America*. New York: Columbia University Press, December, 1959, 59-80.

Stokes, William Sylvane. "Parliamentary Government in Latin America," *American Political Science Review*, XXXIX, No. 3 (June, 1945), 522-36.

———. "Violence as a Power Factor in Latin-American Politics," *The Western Political Quarterly*, V, No. 3 (September, 1952), 445-68.

Tannenbaum, Frank. "A Note on Latin American Politics," *Political Science Quarterly*, LVIII, No. 3 (September, 1943), 415-21.

———. "The Political Dilemma in Latin America," *Foreign Affairs*, XXXVIII, No. 3 (April, 1960), 497-515.

Trujillo Gómez, Santiago. "Birth of a City," *UN World*, V (May, 1951), 57-60.

IV. PERIODICALS

America
American Mercury, The
Atlantic Monthly, The
Business Week
Christian Century
Commonweal
Cuadernos Americanos (Mexico City)
Current History
Diplomat, The
Economía Colombiana (Bogotá)
Economist, The
Foreign Affairs
Hispanic American Report (first

called Hispanic World Report)
Latin American Business Highlights
Latin American Report
Life
Nation
Newsweek
Semana (Bogotá)
Time
UN World
U.S. Department of State Bulletin
U.S. News & World Report
Visión (Mexico City)

V. NEWPAPERS

Diario Oficial — Official government bulletin; during Rojas Pinilla's regime became a daily journal for purposes of propagandizing him.

El Espectador — Bogotá; founded in 1887, pro-Liberal, often supporting the left wing of the party.

El Intermedio — Bogotá; the name under which El Tiempo appeared during latter period of Rojas Pinilla's regime.

El Liberal — Bogotá; represents left wing of Liberal party, was long the López organ during his rivalry with more moderate elements.

El Siglo — Bogotá; founded in 1935 by Laureano Gómez as an organ of the Conservative party.

El Tiempo — Bogotá; founded in 1911 by Eduardo Santos, generally represents view of the moderate Liberal wing, is widely considered one of finest dailies in the hemisphere.

New York Times

Index